MW01008416

Profits and Politics in Paradise

Profits and Politics in Paradise

The Development of Hilton Head Island

by
Michael N. Danielson
with the assistance of
Patricia R. F. Danielson

University of South Carolina Press

© 1995 by the University of South Carolina

Published in Columbia, South Carolina by the
University of South Carolina Press

Manufactured in the United States of America

99 98 97 96 95   5 4 3 2 1

Library of Congress Cataloging-in-Publication Data

Danielson, Michael N.
   Profits and politics in paradise : the development of Hilton Head
island / by Michael N. Danielson ; with the assistance of Patricia
R.F. Danielson.
      p. cm.
   Includes bibliographical references and index.
   ISBN 1–57003–039–1 (pbk)
   1. Planned communities—South Carolina—Sea Pines Plantation—
History. 2. Planned communities—South Carolina—Hilton Head
Island—History. 3. City planning—South Carolina—Sea Pines
Plantation—History.   4. Retirement communities—South Carolina—
Hilton Head Island—History. 5. Recreation areas—South Carolina—
Hilton Head Island—History. 6. Resorts—South Carolina—Hilton
Head Island—History. 7. Hilton Head Island (S.C.)—History.
8. Sea Pines Plantation (Hilton Head, S.C.)—History. I. Danielson,
Patricia R. F. II. Title.
HT169.57.U62S63 1995
333.7'15'0975799—dc20   95–4364

For Charles Elbert Fraser
whose genius made Hilton Head Island worth studying

Contents

Tables and Figures

Acknowledgments

Hilton Head Island is an irresistible place, both to enjoy and to study. Visits there beginning in 1979 led to the purchase of a vacation home in Sea Pines Plantation in 1983. An extended stay due to illness in 1985 provided an opportunity to think seriously about the remarkable development of Hilton Head. I devoted most of a leave of absence during the academic year 1986–87 to research on the island and spent the summer of 1990 in the same way. Patricia R. F. Danielson, my wife at the time, participated fully in the original design of the project, collected and analyzed research materials on Hilton Head, and conducted interviews. She read the manuscript and made valuable contributions to the pages that follow.

Charles E. Fraser, the creator of Sea Pines Plantation and modern Hilton Head, was extremely supportive from the start. He shared his thoughts freely on all aspects of the development of Hilton Head before, during, and after his quarter century of stewardship of the Sea Pines Company. Fraser also made available his extensive collection of documents of the Sea Pines Company and associated ventures and other materials on Hilton Head and resort development. Jackie Blackburn, Charles Fraser's assistant for many years, always offered a helping hand as the research progressed.

Michael L. M. Jordan shared his materials on the lengthy effort to secure political autonomy for Hilton Head Island as well as the manuscript of the study of incorporation that he prepared in collaboration with Harold Fleming. Thanks also are due Professor Fleming; his appraisals of Hilton Head's governmental alternatives provided the first comprehensive analysis of many of the issues treated in this study. Peter W. Bauman kindly made available materials dealing with the purchase of Sea Pines Plantation by residents, a move they accomplished under Bauman's leadership. Ben T. Banks graciously provided access to the library of the *Island Packet* and perspective on many of the issues examined in the pages that follow. Ben was also one of a number of Hilton Head residents whose hospitality and friendship made this project special. Among them are Bob Atkinson, Joni Banks, Peg and Jim Bowen, Madalyn and Ron Cerrudo, Jim DeTorre, Bob Donaldson, Diane and Marvin Hall, Frank Hart, Stu Jones, Ellie and Jack Kerkam, Ken Kunze, Jill and Ed McCullough, Anne and Ken Nyquist, Geneva and Don Patterson, Tom Reilley, Joe Sackett, and Henrietta Simmons.

A special note of thanks is owed to the many people who made time available for interviews in the course of the research. These discussions were typically extended and lively, and they provided a personal and human dimension that was invaluable to understanding the development of Hilton Head Island. Those interviewed include David Ames, David N. Axene, Thomas F. Baker, Todd Ballantine, Ben T. Banks, Thomas C. Barnwell Jr., Peter W. Bauman, Doris Bowers, Richard Clark, W. Douglas Corkern, Gordon Craighead, John F. Curry, Howard Davis, Richard Dey, Vance Fowler, Charles E. Fraser, Joseph B. Fraser Jr., J. Wilton Graves, Billie Hack, Frederick C. Hack Jr., Orion D. Hack, Arthur P. Hall, J. Prentiss Haworth, Michael L. M. Jordan, Robert Killingsworth, Philip Lader, James D. Littlejohn, Michael J. Malanick, William F. Marscher, Aileen McGinty, Richard A. McGinty, John M. McIntosh, Robert C. Onorato, Donald O'Quinn, Benjamin M. Racusin, Valborg Schaub, Fran Smith, John Gettys Smith, and Thomas F. Wamsley.

The study also benefited from the dedicated work of local journalists who chronicled the growth of Hilton Head Island, primarily in the pages of the *Island Packet*. Particularly noteworthy were the commentary and reporting of Todd Ballantine, Doris Bowers, Seward Bowers, Jonathan Daniels, Teresa Hill, Mary Kendall Hilton, Jim Littlejohn, Cabell Phillips, Gwen Richards, Nancy Rutter, Fran Smith, and Janet Smith.

Donald E. Stokes, dean of the Woodrow Wilson School at Princeton University from 1974 to 1992 and sometime visitor to Hilton Head, was supportive of the project in a variety of ways. Assistance was also provided by the Center of Domestic and Comparative Policy Studies at the Woodrow Wilson School. Helpful suggestions of one kind or another came from colleagues at Princeton, including Leigh Bienen, John J. DiIulio, Jameson W. Doig, Richard Roper, and Julian Wolpert. Robert Marks, Phillip Thune, and Clinton Uhlir provided excellent research assistance at Princeton. Ellen Kemp of the Woodrow Wilson School insured that the project profited from the latest in computer hardware and software as the work progressed. Monica Selinger and Patricia Trinity contributed both to the preparation of various incarnations of the manuscript and to helping me juggle the demands of teaching, research, and administrative responsibilities.

Linda Oppenheim and Laird Klingler, successively librarians at the Woodrow Wilson School, helped prepare bibliographies and locate materials. Susanne McNatt, interlibrary services librarian at the Princeton University Library, obtained microfilms of the *Island Packet* and other elusive materials.

ACKNOWLEDGMENTS

Jeff Danielson and Karl Fingerhood were partners in exploring the golf courses of Sea Pines, while Jessica Danielson and Louisa Fingerhood provided distinctive perspectives on the local social scene.

Linda K. Danielson took time from a much needed vacation to help collect research materials on Hilton Head during the summer of 1990 and has tolerated my periodic preoccupation with a project that took far more time than I ever planned.

To all, heartfelt thanks for your help. I, of course, am responsible for what appears on the pages that follow.

Chronology
Hilton Head since 1949

1949   Hilton Head Company is formed to acquire 8,000 acres of land at the southern end of Hilton Head Island.

1951   Partners in Hilton Head Company, organized as Honey Horn Plantation, acquire 12,000 additional acres; electric service is extended to Hilton Head.

1952   Harvesting of timber is completed on lands owned by Hilton Head Company and Honey Horn Plantation.

1953   Ferry service from mainland to Hilton Head begins; first vacation cottages are built on land acquired by Hilton Head Company.

1955   Legislation authorizing zoning on Hilton Head is enacted by the state legislature, then repealed following opposition from black landowners.

1956   Toll bridge to the mainland is opened; Fraser family withdraws from Hilton Head Company in return for 3,480 acres on the southern end of the island, which Charles Fraser begins to develop as Sea Pines Plantation.

1958   Sea Pines Plantation Company purchases 1,280 additional acres, on the southern tip of the island, from Hilton Head Company.

1959   Tolls on bridge to mainland are ended; Sea Pines opens William Hilton Inn, the island's first modern hotel.

1960   First golf course on the island is opened in Sea Pines Plantation.

1961   Island's first public service district is organized to handle sewage treatment in Forest Beach.

1962   Hilton Head Company begins development at Port Royal Plantation.

1964   Hilton Head's first condominiums are completed in Sea Pines Plantation.

1965   Medical clinic opens.

1966   Hilton Head Island Community Association is organized; Sea Pines Academy, the island's first private school, is established.

1967   Land for Palmetto Dunes is acquired from Hilton Head Agricultural Company; island's first security gates are installed at Sea Pines Plantation.

1969   Harbour Town and Harbour Town Links are completed in Sea Pines; first Heritage Classic is played at Harbour Town Links; BASF announces plans for a $100 million chemical plant three miles from Hilton Head Island.

1970   Hilton Head Company begins Shipyard Plantation; Phipps Land Company acquires Palmetto Dunes from original developers; *Island Packet* begins publication; BASF abandons its planned chemical plant; incorporation of Forest Beach as a municipality is proposed.

1971   Hilton Head Company is sold to Oxford First Corporation of Philadelphia; Sea Pines acquires land for the development of Hilton Head Plantation on the northern end of the island; resi dents of Port Royal Plantation create Hilton Head's first property owners' association in a planned community.

1972   Beaufort County's proposed zoning for Hilton Head is withdrawn in the face of opposition from black landowners, plantation residents, and other islanders; first movie theater opens.

1973   Development companies propose creation of a council based on the island's public service districts as an alternative to Hilton Head's incorporation as a municipality; Sea Pines residents organize Association of Sea Pines Plantation Property Owners; Family Circle tennis tournament is held at Sea Pines Racquet Club; development begins at Moss Creek Plantation, the area's first private planned community to be located off Hilton Head; *Island Packet* is acquired by the News and Observer Publishing Company of Raleigh.

1974   First phase of the modern development of Hilton Head ends as a result of rising interest rates, sharp increases in oil prices, and a troubled national economy; Beaufort County adopts weak land use controls; study of local government options for Hilton Head is undertaken; Beaufort County rejects proposal to create an elected island commission with taxing and planning authority. Heritage Classic golf tournament is televised.

1975   Sea Pines Company loses control of Hilton Head Plantation to Citibank of New York and First Chicago Bank; Sea Pines develops first time-sharing project on the island; Hilton Head Island Hospital opens.

1978   Beaufort County enacts development standards that fail to address density, building heights, and other concerns of island residents; second study of local government options is under taken.

1979   Phipps Land Company sells Palmetto Dunes to Greenwood Developement Company.

1980   Marathon Oil buys Hilton Head Company from Oxford First.

1982   Four-lane high bridge is opened to replace original two-lane drawbridge; first prefabricated modular housing development, dubbed the stack-a-shacks, is erected outside the planned communities; Beaufort County approves creation of appointed island commission with no taxing or planning powers.

1983   Island voters approve the incorporation of the Town of Hilton Head Island; first mayor and council are elected; Sea Pines is sold to Vacation Resorts.

1984   International Paper Realty Company acquires land on Daufuskie Island, near Hilton Head, for development of a planned residen tial community.

1985   Bobby Ginn buys Hilton Head Company from Marathon Oil and Sea Pines from Vacation Resorts; lot sales begin at Indigo Run Plantation; Melrose Company buys Hilton Head Plantation from Citibank and First Chicago; Hilton Head's town government approves the island's first comprehensive plan.

1986   Hilton Head Holdings takes over from Bobby Ginn; Hilton Head
            Holdings files for bankruptcy; John Curry is appointed trustee for
            Hilton Head Holdings by Judge Solomon Blatt Jr.; Grass
            Roots Amendment, designed to limit growth, is approved in a
            referendum.

1987   Town council approves land management ordinance; bankruptcy
            trustee sells Sea Pines to Sea Pines Associates and most of Hilton
            Head Company properties to Marathon Oil; South Carolina
            Supreme Court upholds real estate covenants of Sea Pines.

1989   Traffic Safety Amendment, proposed to halt growth, is defeated
            in referendum; Indigo Run Plantation goes to Federal Deposit
            Insurance Company and then to Resolution Trust Corporation;
            Marathon sells its properties at Port Royal, Shipyard, and
            Wexford Plantations; *Island Packet* is sold by the News and
            Observer Publishing Company to McClatchy Newspapers of
            Sacramento.

1990   Indigo Run is purchased by the Melrose Company; town council
            approves cross-island expressway; water utilities propose using
            Savannah River to meet Hilton Head's water needs.

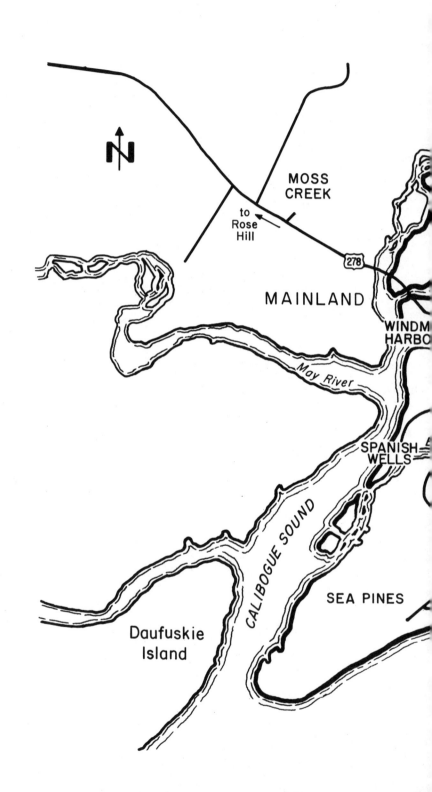

HILTON HEAD ISLAND
AND ENVIRONS

Profits and Politics in Paradise

Introduction

American communities come in a great variety of sizes, populations, economic bases, and governing arrangements. Cities are the largest and most complex, and they have attracted the most attention from social scientists. Suburbs are the fastest-growing communities, now encompassing more than half the population of the United State, and a rich literature has been produced by students of suburbia. Less attention has been paid to smaller towns. And very little work has been done on resort and retirement communities, an increasingly important segment of new urban growth in the United States. Most growing areas beyond the direct influence of metropolitan areas feature substantial resort, recreational, and retirement development—ski resorts in Colorado and Vermont, desert retirement communities in Arizona and California, and seaside resorts along the Atlantic, Gulf, and Pacific coasts.

This book examines the development of Hilton Head Island, South Carolina. The modern American resort and retirement community was invented on Hilton Head by Charles Fraser. His Sea Pines Plantation transformed an almost forgotten barrier island into one of the nation's premier resorts and provided a model for many other recreation-based communities that cater to affluent retirees, vacationers, second-home owners, and, increasingly, primary-home owners. Fraser's Sea Pines is a large planned community—seven square miles—in which the developer controlled every aspect of development from the location of streets and other infrastructure to the design of individual homes.

Planned communities have been part of the American scene for three centuries. William Penn laid out the plan for Philadelphia in 1682. Half a century later James Oglethorpe planned the development of Savannah. Pierre L'Enfant designed the new nation's capital in 1791. These plans and similar efforts elsewhere influenced to some degree the physical development of cities; much of Oglethorpe's design can still be seen in Savannah, and Washington's distinctive street pattern is a legacy of L'Enfant's plan. Plans in most cities, however, were overwhelmed by industrialization and rapid urban growth as the nineteenth century unfolded. Public controls on development were nonexistent in the industrial city. Private decisions—of industrialists, railroad magnates, merchants, home builders, and individuals—largely determined what would be built where, as Sam Warner shows in his study of the growth of Philadelphia.[1]

In a society in which the private sector has made most of the decisions about urban development, planned communities have more often been private

1

rather than public undertakings. Company towns were one manifestation of privately planned communities. The most ambitious effort of this kind was Pullman, built by the railroad car manufacturer. Suburbanization provided new opportunities for builders of privately planned communities.[2] One of the most successful planned suburbs was Radburn, New Jersey, where residences were clustered, open space was preserved, and curving streets substituted for the ubiquitous gridiron pattern. The Country Club district outside Kansas City was developed by Jessie Clyde Nichols, who pioneered in the use of private deed restrictions to regulate housing size, cost, design, and siting. Perhaps the most influential privately planned communities were the suburban developments built by William Levitt after World War II. Levitt's towns were far larger than most suburban subdivisions. The developer mass-produced housing, used deed restrictions to enforce rules for homeowners, and provided most of the infrastructure for the community. At the same time Fraser was building Sea Pines, the two most successful new towns in the United States were being privately developed at Reston, Virginia, and Columbia, Maryland.

Fraser built his community in the Sunbelt, where most resorts and retirement towns are located. Climate has been the principal appeal of this area for developers of such communities. In much of the Sunbelt, urban growth has been characterized by weak or nonexistent public controls.[3] On Hilton Head, private developers controlled everything at the outset, from planning and land use to almost all public services. Over time, the public sector expanded: county government provided some services and rudimentary land use controls; state and federal agencies underwrote water and sewer services and regulated development in wetlands and other environmentally sensitive areas; and the Town of Hilton Head Island, created in 1983, expanded public services and substantially strengthened public land use controls.

A central concern of this study is the interplay of private power and public authority. The role of private power, especially the influence of economic elites, has been the central theme of community research beginning with the seminal studies of the Lynds in Muncie, Indiana.[4] Following the Lynds, Floyd Hunter depicted Atlanta as controlled by a small economic circle, with political leaders playing secondary roles in making important local decisions.[5] Peter Bachrach and Morton S. Baratz underscore the ability of dominant economic figures to set the political agenda in communities and thus determine what issues are legitimate.[6] Especially relevant is the work of John R. Logan and Harvey Molotch on urban development; they argue that developers, bankers, and other economically influential citizens form "growth machines" that determine the fortunes of communities.[7]

2

The picture of community power that emerges from these studies has been criticized for underestimating the role of government and politics. In his classic study of New Haven, Robert Dahl portrayed a complex web of influence structured by the nature of issues and the stakes of various interests. In Dahl's New Haven, government was a central rather than subsidiary element, with political actors often prevailing over economic elites.[8] The importance of government in shaping urban development, and the conditions under which political power is effective, are the central themes of a study of the New York metropolitan area that I have made with Jameson W. Doig.[9] Stephen Elkin and Clarence Stone treat political factors more explicitly than the Lynds or Hunter in their studies of Dallas and Atlanta. They emphasize the importance of what they call regimes in shaping urban development decisions, and these regimes are usually dominated by business leaders, although the balance between economic and political influence varies from place to place.[10]

Most of the work on the influence of economic and political factors on urban development has dealt with larger cities and metropolitan areas. Much less attention has been paid to the interplay of private and public in the development of smaller communities. Hilton Head offers fertile ground for examining the influence of affluent private citizens and public officials. Private-community developers formed the initial growth machine; as Hilton Head flourished, they were joined by resort operators, real estate firms, bankers, and others whose fortunes were closely tied to growth. Private success in creating carefully planned and well-serviced communities with high-quality amenities, however, did not deflect increasingly insistent demands from residents for public institutions, public controls over development, and public services. Private power indelibly shaped Hilton Head, but it lacked the legitimacy to sustain private rule as the community grew and diversified.

The quest for local political autonomy has been examined largely in the context of suburbia.[11] Control over the vital parameters of community life—land use, schools, taxes—and political separation from the city have been the primary objectives of suburban residents. Developers and other economic interests also have sought to create politically independent suburbs in order to enhance their control over land, taxes, and public services. On Hilton Head, residents and business entities supported the creation of an independent local government. The primary objective of both groups was local control over development. Businesses wanted to protect their interest in Hilton Head's continued growth as a superior resort. Residents, particularly retirees who were the most politically active, desired to check growth to preserve what had attracted them to Hilton Head.

As it is in most developing areas, growth was the central political issue on Hilton Head, both before and after municipal incorporation. The island's natural attractions and fragile ecology were imperiled by all sorts of developers, ranging from the community builders who put Hilton Head on the map to large industrial operations lured to the area by abundant water, cheap labor, and eager public officials. Hilton Head illustrates many of the dilemmas inherent in public control of private development: the legacy of past land use decisions, the protection afforded private property by the U.S. Constitution and the courts, the lack of consensus on controlling growth, and the adoption of strict growth controls after much of the island was developed.[12] Growth politics tend to be particularly intense in communities that are built around the appeal of natural settings and amenities.

Places like Hilton Head are the result of the dispersion of urban growth in the United States. Urban life was once centered in cities, then in metropolitan areas composed of cities and suburbs. Today it is much more diffuse, spreading far beyond the boundaries of the metropolis and creating scores of freestanding new urban communities, many built around specialized functions, as was Hilton Head.[13] The suburban diaspora created new kinds of urban communities, which have been examined in great detail by social scientists, most notably in Herbert Gans's study of Levittown.[14] Resort and retirement communities share some features with suburbia, but they are also distinctive places. They are more self-contained than the typical suburbs, with fewer economic connections than suburbia, where most residents live and work in different communities. Resort and retirement communities like Hilton Head pose in particularly sharp terms the dilemma of growth: the reality that growth alters what attracted developers, residents, and vacationers to a particular place.

Growth continually changes the fortunes of places and their residents.[15] On Hilton Head it steadily reduced the power of the private-community builders who launched the island's modern development. With growth and intensification of the resort industry, economic power shifted from developers to resort operators. Expansion of the local economy also increased the number of residents with a stake in the resort and development industries, diluting over time the influence of retirees who dominated the local political system during the first years of local autonomy. Growth also radically altered the lives of Hilton Head's earlier long-time residents, descendants of slaves freed during the Union occupation of Hilton Head during the Civil War. The development of private communities, the influx of affluent retirees and vacationers, and the creation of a resort-based economy eroded the traditional culture of local African Americans and consigned them largely to marginal economic and political roles.

4

NOTES

1. Warner, *The Private City.*

2. See Eichler and Kaplan, *The Community Builders;* Weiss, *The Rise of the Community Builders;* and Feagin and Parker, *Building American Cities.*

3. For an excellent general treatment of the rise of the Sunbelt, see Abbott, *The New Urban America.* See also Bernard and Rice, *Sunbelt Cities,* and Perry and Watkins, *The Rise of the Sunbelt Cities.*

4. Lynd and Lynd, *Middletown* and *Middletown in Transition.*

5. Hunter, *Community Power Structure* and *Community Power Succession.*

6. Bachrach and Baratz, "Two Faces of Power" and *Power and Poverty.*

7. Logan and Molotch, *Urban Fortunes.*

8. Dahl, *Who Governs?* See also Polsby, *Community Power and Political Theory.*

9. Danielson and Doig, *New York.* For other perspectives on the development of the New York region, see Robert C. Wood, *1400 Governments,* and Caro, *The Power Broker.*

10. Elkin, *City and Regime in the American Republic,* and Stone, *Regime Politics.* See also Jennings, *Community Influentials.*

11. See Robert C. Wood, *Suburbia;* Oliver P. Williams, *Suburban Differences and Metropolitan Policies;* Wirt et al., *On the City's Rim;* Danielson, *The Politics of Exclusion;* Teaford, *City and Suburb;* Weiher, *The Fractured Metropolis;* and Schneider, *The Competitive City.*

12. See Logan and Zhou, "Do Suburban Growth Controls Control Growth?" Dowell, "An Examination of Population-Growth-Management Communities;" and Vogel and Swanson, "The Growth Machine versus the Antigrowth Coalition."

13. See Herbers, *The New Heartland,* and Garreau, *Edge City.*

14. Gans, *The Levittowners.* See also Jackson, *Crabgrass Frontier;* Dolce, *Suburbia;* and Donaldson, *The Suburban Myth.*

15. For analyses of growth and change in suburbia, see Baldassare, *Trouble in Paradise,* and Kling, Olin, and Poster, *Postsuburban California.*

Chapter One

Ripe for Development

When I first came here, the sellers were interested in showing me timber—but all the way back home, I couldn't forget . . . the most beautiful beach I had ever seen.

—Fred C. Hack, quoted in the *Islander,* March 1970

Just north of where the Savannah River flows into the Atlantic lies one of the largest and most beautiful islands that punctuate the east coast of the United States. Twelve miles of magnificent beaches flank the ocean, wide and sparkling white with gentle surf and clear, balmy waters. Beyond the gleaming strand fringed by pine and palm trees, the foot-shaped island is 5 miles across at its widest point and encompasses 42 square miles. Like the other sea isles that stretch along the southern Atlantic coast, Hilton Head Island is flat and sandy, reaching only 25 feet above sea level at its highest point. Its climate is glorious in spring and fall and moderate, with brilliant blue skies, in winter. Its summer heat and humidity are tempered by cooling trade winds.

As the twentieth century reached its midpoint, Hilton Head Island was a sparsely settled tropical paradise of seashore and forests and marshes, abundant wildlife, and brilliant wild flowers. Cruising the Carolina coast in 1953, Samuel Hopkins Adams marveled at the forest-lined beach: "Hilton Head is perhaps the wildest and most beautiful island of the archipelago. On its ocean side stretch . . . miles of flawless beach."[1] By 1953 this lush tropical treasure was ripe for development. The island was 30 miles from Savannah; Charleston was only 110 miles away; and Atlanta and Charlotte were within 250 miles. Major north-south highways were nearby, and Hilton Head was at the edge of a growing region with an increasingly strong economic base and large military facilities. The natural beauty of the sea islands and the wonderful spring and fall weather had already attracted wealthy Americans to St. Simons and Sea Island in Georgia and to hunting preserves scattered along the coast. The major obstacle to development on Hilton Head was inaccessibility, the lack of regular ferry service or a bridge to the mainland.

HILTON HEAD BEFORE 1950

The island poised on the brink of development in the early 1950s had a long history. Native American settlements on the island date to the second millennium B.C.[2] When Europeans reached Port Royal Sound early in the sixteenth century, they met Indians who hunted, farmed and fished the area of the coastal islands. For the next two hundred years, Indians were its most numerous occupants. Eventually the encounter with white explorers and settlers proved fatal for the various tribes that inhabited the sea islands. The last tribe in the area was the Yemassee, which was decimated in the struggle between colonists early in the eighteenth century.

Seeking treasure and glory, land and slaves, a succession of European adventurers followed trade winds out of the Caribbean to the southeastern coast of the North American mainland. First to explore the coastal islands were the Spanish. Whether expeditions in 1521 and 1526 actually set foot on Hilton Head is unknown, although Pedro de Quexo sighted the distinctive headlands on the island's north shore in August 1521. The French came next—a band of Huguenots seeking refuge from religious persecution in their native land. In 1562 they sailed along the coast to a "mightie river" that they named Port Royall, sighted Hilton Head with its high bluffs, and founded a settlement on the river that did not survive through the following year.[3] Four years later the Spanish returned, this time to stay on nearby Parris Island, where the Broad and Beaufort rivers form what we know today as Port Royal Sound. No Spaniards settled on Hilton Head, but the island supplied fresh water for ships' casks from the spring that became known as Spanish Wells. Three decades after its founding, the Spanish abandoned Port Royal in the face of Indian attacks and growing English sea power.[4] Almost a century would pass before the English attempted to colonize the area. In 1662 King Charles II granted Carolina to eight lords proprietors, who promptly sought settlers for their possessions.[5] Among those interested in the new lands were a group of sugar and indigo planters in Barbados who commissioned Captain William Hilton in 1663 to explore the Carolina coast. Sailing into Port Royal Sound, Hilton spied the headland and named for himself the land he described as "laden with large tall Oaks, Walnut and Bayes, except facing on the Sea it is most Pines tall and good. . . . The Ayr is clear and sweet, the Countrey very pleasant and delightful." Prophetically, he noted that "we could wish that all they that want a happy settlement . . . were well transported thither."[6]

Initial efforts to follow Hilton's advice and settle the island were unsuccessful. Hostile Indians and a fearsome hurricane persuaded the English in 1670 to concentrate their colonial energies some 100 miles north at Charles Town. Thirty years later Hilton Head was part of a large land grant, or barony, from the lords proprietors to John Bayley. The first white settler on Hilton Head was Colonel John Barnwell, who arrived in 1717 to lay claim to a 1,000-acre grant on the northwestern tip of the island. Over the next decade, more settlers came as the threat of hostile Indians was finally eliminated. Growing rice and indigo, they established a plantation economy based on slavery that dominated Hilton Head for more than a century. Ten years before the colonies declared their independence, twenty-five families were operating plantations on Hilton Head, most on land leased from the Bayleys. During the Revolutionary War, as well in the War of 1812, Hilton Head's planters suffered because of the island's strategic location for naval forces blockading Charleston and Savannah and from the near impossibility of defending the seaward island. The British captured Savannah in 1778 and Charleston in 1780 and occupied much of the area, including Beaufort, located at the head of Port Royal Sound. Hilton Head was periodically attacked by British warships as well as by Tories who controlled neighboring Daufuskie Island. In the War of 1812, Britain struck again, burning most of the plantation homes that were easily accessible from the sea.

After the Revolution, Hilton Head faced potential catastrophe from loss of the British market for indigo. Fortunately for the landed interests, indigo was replaced by a new variety of prized cotton, ushering in the island's most successful period of plantation agriculture. Long-staple cotton from Barbados was introduced by William Elliott II on his Myrtle Bank Plantation in 1790, and the island's climate and soil proved ideal for this new variety. Sea island cotton sold for three to four times the price of inland cotton; it made "the sea islands famous all over the world . . . and the wealth that went with it. . . opened a new era, a new way of living for the whole coastal area."[7]

After the Revolution, the Bayleys sold off their land on Hilton Head to wealthy planters from Edisto and other islands to the north. A few families, connected through intermarriage, controlled the island's 25,000 acres and reaped the benefits of Sea island cotton grown with slave labor for the insatiable English spinning mills.[8] Planters divided their time between plantations on Hilton Head and mansions in Charleston, Savannah, and nearby Beaufort. By 1860 Beaufort had 7,000 residents, and the Port Royal area was one of the richest agricultural regions in the South, producing $3 million worth of cotton annually. Underpinning this flourishing economy were slaves, who accounted for more than 80 percent of the area's 40,000 inhabitants.

Plantation life on Hilton Head came to an end early in the Civil War. Less than seven months after the first shots were fired on Fort Sumter, more than 12,000 Union soldiers and marines landed on Hilton Head in the largest naval engagement ever fought in American waters. The assault was mounted to blockade Confederate coastal ports and to provide a desperately needed triumph following the disaster at Bull Run. Control of the deep waters of Port Royal Sound was a crucial element in the Union's naval strategy, providing a means of fueling and supplying the ships blockading Savannah, Charleston, and other Confederate ports. The Port Royal area also offered a base from which troops could cut the railroad that linked Charleston and Savannah. Recognizing the strategic importance of Port Royal Sound, the Confederacy hastened to construct fortifications on Hilton Head and across the sound. On the morning of November 7, 1861, fifteen Union warships sailed into Port Royal Sound, bombarding the forts until all Confederate guns were silenced. As Union troopers splashed ashore, the defenders retreated to the mainland. The Battle of Port Royal lasted less than five hours, and not a single shot was fired by the invading troops.

Hilton Head was in Union hands. The planters were gone and their homes, slaves, and cotton abandoned. The island was occupied from November 7, 1861, until the surrender at Appomattox on April 9, 1865. Fortifications were built, as were facilities to service the blockade fleet. Hilton Head became the base for a large garrison force that supplied the ships, cared for the sick and wounded, and guarded prisoners of war. By the end of the war, Port Royal, as Hilton Head was officially called until 1872, contained almost 50,000 people. It boasted two weekly newspapers, three hotels, a theater, a hospital, a prison, a bakery, and a string of bars and shops along Robbers Row. Crowded into the hastily constructed "city" were soldiers, sailors, politicians, merchants, camp followers, and an assortment of operators looking for a fast dollar. Corruption was rampant as goods poured onto the island from the steady stream of ships that arrived from the North. Smugglers thrived, serving the flourishing black market in Savannah for "drugs, liquors, fine tobacco, silk goods, corsets, dresses made from the latest Parisian fashions in New York, ribbons, gloves, and other luxury items all specially ordered."[9]

Bolstering the new city's population were thousands of blacks. For the island's slaves, "the day of victory for the Union was a day of freedom."[10] In the weeks and months after the battle, former slaves poured onto Hilton Head and other occupied sea islands. They were in limbo, liberated from slavery but not yet legally free; they were declared "contrabands of war" by the conquering Northerners. Blacks were dependent on Union forces for food and shelter and were depended on to provide labor, food, and information to the strangers in blue. They harvested and planted cotton; moved into a new black town, which had a mayor and elected council; and went to schools operated by the Freedman's Association.

Most important for the future of Hilton Head was what happened to the island's land during the Union occupation. A few months after the invasion, Congress enacted a law that taxed occupied land in the Confederacy and provided for forfeiture of lands and property to the national government if the tax were not paid. For plantation owners loyal to the Southern cause, the practical effect was confiscation. On Hilton Head, federal authorities seized and sold land for as little as 5 percent of prewar values. Officially, land sales were supposed to be limited to 20 acres—40 if the owner was married and double for military personnel; but the rules were poorly enforced, and there were no restrictions on resale. One company organized by speculators was able to acquire four of Hilton Head's plantations, comprising 5,000 acres. Freeman Dodd, an enterprising carpetbagger, bought Honey Horn Plantation for $200 in 1863 and later resold the 1,000-acre property for $10,000.

After the war, a few plantation owners reclaimed their land under federal law by paying back taxes, but those whose land had been sold had no legal claim and were eligible only for nominal reimbursement.[11] Because of the long occupation and extensive sales, far less land was reclaimed on Hilton Head and the surrounding area than in the rest of the South. Those who returned were unable to restore their fortunes. Houses, barns, tools, livestock, seed, field hands—all were gone. To make matters worse, the market for sea island cotton never revived: from its high of around a dollar a pound, prices fell steadily, descending to four cents in 1890. Before the end of the century, most of the reclaimed land was sold for a pittance by hard-pressed former planters and their heirs.

With money they had earned during the occupation, freed slaves were able to purchase some of the land sold by the federal tax commissioners. Their chances to acquire land improved after the establishment of new federal rules in 1865 that provided for the sale of sea island land only to blacks. After the occupation, they bought land from former owners and speculators at rock-bottom prices. Typical black holdings on Hilton Head were small, the proverbial 40 acres and a mule, and most of their plots were on the northern end of the island.

With the departure of the soldiers and speculators began eighty years of isolation as the island settled into a cycle of subsistence farming and oystering by a largely black population. Within a decade there was barely a trace of Port Royal or the horde of bluecoats and their entourage. Also vanished were almost all the plantation houses and cotton fields. Most of Hilton Head returned to nature, covered with pine and oak forests. Eventually only a few traces remained of plantations and wartime structures—crumbling foundations and overgrown fortifications—and more than a few ghost stories were told about these eerie places.

As the nineteenth century drew to a close, Hilton Head was a forgotten island with a dwindling black population and few visitors from the outside world. Then it was discovered again, this time by local hunters attracted by the abundance of game. A hunting club from nearby Beaufort bought 1,000 acres of the former Leamington Plantation along the Atlantic. This land was later sold to a group of sportsmen from North Carolina, who added another 1,000 acres to their hunting preserve. Word spread north of fabulous hunting on Hilton Head and surrounding islands. A New England shipping magnate, W. P. Clyde, accumulated 9,000 acres in bits and pieces for a dollar or two an acre, including Honey Horn, the only surviving plantation house on the island.[12] Clyde eventually sold out to Roy Rainey, a wealthy New Yorker who acquired half the island during the 1920s before being forced to sell after the stock market crash. Rainey's holdings were purchased for six dollars an acre by a pair of New York financiers, Alfred L. Loomis and Landon K. Thorne, who were buying all the land they could get on the island. Within a few years, Loomis and Thorne owned over two-thirds of Hilton Head, everything except the North Carolinians' hunting preserve and the farm plots of the descendants of the freedmen. Whatever happened next on the island would be shaped by this consolidation of most of its land into a single holding, far larger than anything since the Bayleys had sold off their barony.

Other than hunters, few outsiders visited Hilton Head during the first half of the twentieth century. Small detachments were assigned to the island in both world wars—on the site of Fort Walker in 1917–18 and on the ocean at the midpoint of the island during World War II. At midcentury, Hilton Head counted 1,100 black and only 25 white residents, all concentrated on the northern end of the island. No one lived on the southern two-thirds, which was covered with dense forests. Farming was the principal occupation, and most blacks lived on small farms that comprised 20 percent of the island. Unlike most blacks in the rural south in 1950, Hilton Head's blacks were owners rather than tenants; nevertheless, almost all were poor, living in a near-subsistence economy based on farming and fishing. They grew corn and vegetables, the boll weevil having finally finished off sea island cotton in the 1920s. Many black farmers added to their meager incomes by harvesting the shellfish that flourished in the local waters. Oysters were steamed and canned at small processing plants owned by a pair of white families who had arrived early in the century.

The only paved road ran 9 miles from the boat landing on Skull Creek to the site of the World War II shore patrol camp. The island was so remote that drivers' licenses were not required, and the few cars and trucks there were not registered and had no license plates. Blacks traveled around the island's paths in wagons pulled by marsh tackys, ponies descended from the horses brought by the Spanish. Hilton Head had no electricity, no telephones, and only ten houses with indoor plumbing. Neither bridge nor ferry service connected the island to the rest of the world, so all supplies came by boat, including the mail, which arrived three times a week from Savannah.

Hilton Head was part of the rural South, a segregated and stratified society. Island blacks lived in close-knit communities organized around churches.[13] Excluded by law from regular politics, they created their own isolated and largely self-governed little world. Education was limited to four months a year for blacks in rural Beaufort County, and schooling ended early for most children since there was no high school for blacks in southern Beaufort County.[14] Even the islanders' language was different. Hilton Head's blacks spoke Gullah, a blend of West African languages and English that came to the new world with slavery. Gullah was the language of the plantations along the Carolina coast, the means of communications between masters and slaves, and it survived primarily among rural blacks on the isolated sea islands. Indicative of this isolation was a visit to Hilton Head in the fall of 1949 by state health officials, which was covered in the Beaufort newspaper in terms reminiscent of those used to describe an exploration of the Amazon or Borneo. The reporter talked about meeting "the easy-going natives" with their "alien island curiosity" while traversing the "island's jungle-like terrain."[15] In short, it was another world, even to a reporter based in a town only 15 miles away as the crow flies.

THE HILTON HEAD COMPANY

Most of the island was covered with virgin timber, and after World War II the majestic pines attracted people in the lumbering business whose activities set in motion forces that led to the modern development of Hilton Head. Talk of the island's fine stands of trees reached Fred C. Hack, who scouted properties for lumber companies. Hack was from Hinesville, Georgia, a small town 40 miles southwest of Savannah, and one of his neighbors was Joseph B. Fraser, who controlled substantial timber holdings and operated the Fraser Lumber Company. Hack told Fraser that he planned to go to Hilton Head Island and evaluate the timber prospects there. Fraser replied that "he might be interested,"

Hack later related, "and we agreed to take no action without the other being informed. We shook hands, and that's how it started."[16]

Hack journeyed to the island and found that, indeed, some 8,000 acres of fine timber on the southern third of the island was available. Hack had hoped to lease the land from Loomis and Thorne, paying royalties on timber that would be cut. But the owners wanted to sell. Lacking resources to buy the land by himself, Hack went back to Hinesville and asked Fraser to join him in acquiring the Loomis-Thorne holdings. Fraser visited Hilton Head and was as impressed as Hack by the island's potential: "I never expected to see such timber, and the appeal of the island's riotous natural charm had a great impact. We would not leave that day until we had signed an option."[17]

To acquire the Loomis-Thorne properties, Fraser and Hack organized the Hilton Head Company in 1949. Fraser was president and major investor, holding 51 percent of the stock, while Hack had a 10 percent share. Among the other investors were Hack's father-in-law, C. C. Stebbins, who brought in Olin T. McIntosh of Savannah, a long-time business friend of Fraser and Stebbins.[18] The Hilton Head Company paid $60 an acre for 8,000 acres on the south end of the island, where the best timber was located. Old hands in Beaufort were convinced that the Georgians had been taken by Loomis and Thorne. They regarded the price as much too high in light of the fact that Kiawah Island, up the coast, had recently sold for $50 an acre and was connected to the mainland by a bridge.

A few months after the purchase, Fraser was forced to put his business affairs aside. A general in the National Guard and a veteran of both world wars, he was recalled to active duty after the invasion of South Korea in June 1950. With Fraser away, Fred Hack took over direction of the Hilton Head Company. Early the following year, Hack and McIntosh negotiated the purchase of the 12,000-acre balance of the Loomis-Thorne holdings on the island for $600,000. A new company was formed for the second acquisition and called Honey Horn Plantation. Fraser had an 18 percent share of the second purchase. Now two interlocked enterprises (the Hilton Head Company and Honey Horn Plantation) and three families (the Frasers, Hacks, and McIntoshes) owned most of the island.

Three lumber mills were set up to harvest the wood on the southern end of the island. The Fraser Lumber Company's crews were directed by the general's son, Joseph B. Fraser Jr., and numbered sixty workers. Workers, supplies, equipment, and everything else used in cutting, processing, and shipping timber had to be ferried across to the island by private boat. Fred Hack moved to the island with his family, living on Honey Horn Plantation. His children attended the one-room school for whites with a handful of other youngsters. For the Hacks, Hilton Head was a step back in time. Hack's son, Frederick, recounts that he was brought up in much the same way the grandparents of his generation were reared. "I grew up in another era." There was "no electricity, no phone, a wood stove . . . we worried about snakes, and fires in the woods."[19]

The timbering operations were highly successful. Within six months the Hilton Head Company had cut enough pine to make the business profitable. Millions of board feet were loaded by crane for shipment on Broad Creek, which divides the northern and southern parts of the island. Cutting the marketable trees did not take long, and in 1952 timber operations ended. With the timber cut, the Hilton Head Company under Fred Hack and his partners turned to exploring the broader potential for profit on the island. The idea of developing Hilton Head as a seaside resort had intrigued the Georgia businessmen from the start. According to Hack, "there was never any doubt in our minds but that it was going to be a real estate bonanza."[20] Trees had been cut selectively with an eye toward the island's future development potential, saving the hardwood forests and preserving much of Hilton Head's wild beauty. After the timber was gone, Hack, who had dabbled in development in Hinesville, decided to change careers. He would remain on Hilton Head and develop the island with his partners. Their prospects seemed promising: they owned a big piece of land and had no debt. What they needed was a development plan and a means of getting customers to the island.

The first obstacle to developing Hilton Head was the island's isolation. The Hilton Head Company brought electricity to the island in 1951. The partners persuaded the South Carolina Highway Department to open ferry service to Hilton Head in 1953, an essential step in making the island accessible to visitors. Central to the provision of ferry service was the support of Wilton Graves, who represented Beaufort County in the state legislature. Graves first came to Hilton Head in 1950 during his initial political campaign, seeking support from the island's handful of voters, and was impressed by the broad, tree-lined beach and its potential to stimulate growth in this forgotten corner of the state. As Fred Hack later explained, Graves "promised to work to make the island more accessible and to promote its development. He was elected and he set about keeping the promise."[21]

Graves brought a necessary ingredient to the development of Hilton Head—the ability to get things done in Columbia, the state capital. He convinced highway officials that a ferry was needed and, with their support, secured passage of legislation authorizing the highway department to operate a ferry. Hack was impressed by his "unique political finesse and confidence in his community."[22]

Graves also had his own fish to fry on Hilton Head, with business interests that were closely intertwined with his efforts for the Hilton Head Company. He founded the first real estate agency on the island in the early 1950s and in 1955 built the Sea Crest Motel, the initial lodging for visitors on Hilton Head.

Establishment of the ferry only underlined the need for a bridge, at least in the minds of the most interested parties on Hilton Head. The first ferry, *Gay Times,* was a barge that carried five cars; its replacement, the *Pocahontas,* was power driven but held only nine autos. State officials, however, opposed a bridge, claiming that the ferry was underutilized and that potential traffic did not justify the expense of a bridge from the mainland. Graves worked in Columbia to persuade state officials that a bridge was needed, while one of the Hilton Head Company partners, Olin T. McIntosh, built 20 cottages at the Folly Field Beach to generate ferry traffic and thus convince the state to erect a bridge. Priced at $4,400 each, the cottages sold quickly, and soon enough people were going to the island to overload the ferry. Only six trips each way were made daily, and no more than seventy cars a day could be ferried to the island even after the larger boat went into service. "Things got pretty complicated around the docks," recalls the captain of the ferry. "People became indignant when told they couldn't be taken over on that particular trip and, on the island side, people were having to sleep in their cars to wait for the first trip next morning."[23] Despite growing traffic to the island and frayed tempers at the ferry, South Carolina officials continued to resist the Hilton Head Company's pleas for a bridge. With all the other road needs in the state, they were not inclined to build a bridge for the benefit of a group of Georgians. As would happen often in the future, the developers of Hilton Head then proposed to do privately what could not be accomplished in the public sector. Olin T. McIntosh, suggested a privately financed toll bridge, with the island companies guaranteeing payments to bondholders should revenues be insufficient. Graves played his part, sponsoring legislation enacted in 1954 to establish the Hilton Head Toll Bridge Authority; and Hack was appointed as one of three members of the new authority. Completed in May 1956, the $1.5 million bridge was an immediate success, with traffic exceeding the expectations of its backers.[24] Despite the $2.50 toll, approximately 200,000 people came to the island in the year after the span's completion. Tolls were halved in mid-1957, which doubled the number of visitors a month, with about 15,000 coming on peak summer days. The bridge was freed from tolls in 1959, thanks in part to the efforts of the ubiquitous J. Wilton Graves, no longer in the legislature but retaining substantial clout in the state capital as a lobbyist for the island's developers.

The bridge presented the developers with a golden opportunity. Now Hilton

Head was accessible, and more and more people were visiting the island. But there were substantial barriers to realizing the new era anticipated by the Hilton Head Company, Graves, and other interested parties. The island may have been a gem, but in 1956 it was at best a diamond in the rough. For many who came over the new bridge to have a look, "the obstacles seemed to outweigh the overwhelming beauty of the beaches. Mostly dirt roads followed the same paths as plantation roads."[25] The only way to the most desirable beach was a narrow Jeep trail. Nonetheless, as access improved, the Hilton Head Company turned to the task of making Hilton Head a pleasant place to visit and buy property. Roads were located and land subdivided, with streets paved to the beach property the Hilton Head Company was trying to sell. With roads as with the bridge and most of the infrastructure that would follow, the underlying motivation was to sell land. By the end of the summer of 1956, the Hilton Head Company had sold more than 300 lots, with beachfront parcels priced as low as $1,100. Most of the company's customers were from nearby areas—nine out of ten were from Georgia and South Carolina, and 26 percent were only an hour away in Savannah.[26]

A year after the bridge was completed, approximately 100 vacation cottages had been finished. The typical dwelling was a simple beach house on stilts with no air conditioning. The island had a supermarket, a couple of small motels, two restaurants for whites and two for blacks, a nursery school, and a pair of churches. And housing was being developed for year-round residents, for the first settlers of the new resort town. Typical of the pioneers who came to stay as development began were Norris and Lois Richardson, who built the Forest Beach Supermarket in 1956. Like so many others who would follow in their footsteps and begin businesses on the island, the Richardsons came on a vacation to visit relatives who had a cottage at Forest Beach. Richardson, who had been in the grocery business in Georgia for thirty years, decided that Hilton Head needed a modern market. So the Richardsons took the big step and invested $50,000 in what was viewed as a very problematic venture—their arrival was delayed when their bank loan was held up for a year because "no one thought Hilton Head would take off."[27]

DILEMMAS OF GROWTH

But Hilton Head did take off—slowly and hesitantly, yet it was airborne a year after the opening of the bridge. The building of the bridge was the key to the beginning of major development efforts on Hilton Head Island. The skeptics were wrong, as they would be often over the coming years as the island grew and changed. More and more people were visiting the now accessible island, and many liked what they saw. Though Hilton Head was rough-hewn and the company's initial efforts had not capitalized on its natural attractions, the island's economy was growing steadily. Lots were being sold, cottages built, and new businesses opened.

No longer was the question whether or not Hilton Head would be developed; the question was how this island paradise was going to grow. What would growth do to this beautiful place, its wide beaches protected by rolling dunes, its lush foliage, its rich habitat for creatures of land and sea? Fred Hack and his associates "wanted to give full sway to the island's natural beauty, emphasize its historic past, bring in all the modern conveniences that would aid its future happiness and make Hilton Head easy of access so that many others could come and share its fascination."[28] But even with the best intentions, natural beauty and historic pasts tend to be overwhelmed by modern conveniences and easy access.

Hilton Head Island was poised on the cusp of growth at a time when few Americans questioned growth. Growth was good; growth was the American creed. Capitalism depended on profits generated by development. Growth would mean profits, as lots were sold, land values increased, and businesses developed. Growth would bring jobs and prosperity, certainly welcome in Beaufort County, South Carolina, one of the poorest areas in the United States. With growth would come increased tax revenues and better public services. Surely growth on Hilton Head would bring "improvements"—more paved roads, telephones, stores, new business opportunities, and higher property values.

Just as certain was that growth would bring change. Roads would be built, lots cleared, water and sewer lines dug, houses and businesses built, parking lots paved. And growth would involve costs as well as benefits. Growth destroys as well as creates. Growth permanently alters natural settings and uproots existing communities. Growth can be particularly devastating to fragile environments such as those of the barrier islands that stretch along the Atlantic and Gulf coasts. All along the seashore, growth had leveled sand dunes, polluted waters, destroyed marshlands, and ignored the natural forces of waves, tides, winds, and storms that constantly alter barrier islands. If Hilton Head were to follow the pattern common along the coast, growth would bulldoze the dunes and clear the forests that lined the beaches. Development would be brought to water's edge to maximize the profit that could be squeezed from the most desirable land. In the process, much of the natural beauty that had attracted development to the seaside would be irrevocably lost. Fragile environments like Hilton Head Island's pose in particularly sharp terms the underlying dilemma of growth: what draws people to them is inevitably altered by development, and the greater the growth, the more the enticing natural setting is destroyed.

Development would bring more than tourists and their dollars. Residents would be attracted to the island as local businesses multiplied, and with better services others would come to live because the place was so attractive. Residents would have their own perspectives on growth. Some would press for development to increase their business; others would want to maintain the natural amenities that drew them to Hilton Head. These different perspectives and interests would produce conflicts between residents and developers and among residents themselves, and the outcomes of these conflicts would help shape the nature, pace, direction, and impact of change.

Growth would also affect those who lived on the island before the ferry and the bridge brought outsiders to Hilton Head. Almost all were black and poor. Development promised jobs, perhaps higher property values for their small holdings, perhaps a better life. But growth would bring change, pressures on their land, higher taxes, and a challenge to a traditional way of life organized around families and churches. Blacks would also have to struggle to get anyone to pay attention to their concerns. Disenfranchised and segregated, they lacked political as well as economic resources and could easily be ignored by the Georgia businessmen and local politicians.

Developers, newcomers, and natives were a familiar triangle in nascent communities, but the triangle's dimensions were beginning to change for many remote places at the time Hilton Head became accessible. Changing lifestyles and rising incomes would generate demand for new kinds of resorts and retirement communities, and these developments would spur growth in unlikely places like Hilton Head Island. With prosperity, more middle- and upper-income families could afford extended vacations and could own vacation homes at the shore or in the mountains or on the lake. With more money and leisure time, more Americans could engage in active recreational activities such as golf, tennis, skiing, and boating and would seek out places that offered the facilities for these pastimes. The affluent among an aging population would seek to combine retirement and recreation at pleasant places in warmer climates. As a result, leisure and retirement would spur new forms of urban development in attractive locales across the nation.

Resort and retirement communities pose distinctive issues as they develop. Their economic base is highly sensitive to the attractions of the particular place, the caliber of its environment, and the quality of life in the community. Attractiveness, after all, is their reason for being. The value of land, the prospects for growth, and the profits to be made are closely linked to these attractions. Of course, there are class-mass tradeoffs. Quality and large numbers are an unlikely mix in a resort because the well-off will go elsewhere for vacations, second homes, recreation, and retirement if a place becomes too popular. At the time Hilton Head Island was starting to blossom, most seaside resorts along the Atlantic catered to mass rather than class clienteles, with cheap lodgings, food stands, honky-tonk amusements, and crowded beaches. But the balance in seaside resorts would shift toward upscale development in more attractive locations as the postwar boom gathered steam, rapidly increasing the ranks of affluent customers for resort and retirement communities.

Another distinctive element in many new resorts would be affluent retirees, who are a special kind of resident. They are knowledgeable and experienced people, familiar with business and government, and often have been active in community affairs. Retirees have different interests from those of other residents of resort communities, and their interests have become increasingly important as more Americans are older and as more communities cater to senior citizens. Typically they have more focused concerns about community and residential amenities than other residents have. Retired people live in resort communities by choice. They are substantially less dependent on the fortunes of the local economy than are people who rely on a place for their livelihood. And retirees have more time to get involved in planning and environmental issues than most other residents, even if they prefer to spend their time on the golf course or the water.

As these trends strengthened, more places would grow because they were attractive for active vacations and retirements—from the sunny climes of Arizona and California to the warm beaches that stretch from the Carolinas to the Gulf of Mexico. Along the coast, rising prices for land as demand outpaced supply would push growth into more and more previously undeveloped areas. New highways would improve accessibility of remote areas as the interstate system was begun in the mid-1950s, as would the rapidly growing network of air connections. Hilton Head would be strongly influenced by all of these developments and by the ability of the private entrepreneurs who controlled the island's future to anticipate these changes and compete effectively with all the other undeveloped places that might grow and prosper.

On Hilton Head, what development would bring was almost entirely in private hands during the crucial formative years. While governmental intervention in the form of planning and zoning might shape the forces of growth, in the mid-1950s there were few models of successful public control of private development along the seashore. Concern for the environment would not capture public and political attention for more than a decade. And Hilton Head, like most resort sites, was an isolated locale with a minimal public sector. Beaufort County's formal role in the development process was limited to issuing building permits—for a dollar, with few questions asked. Informally, local politicians looked for a piece of the action for themselves, their associates, and their constituency. Beaufort County was not interested in managing growth or worrying about its costs. Instead, the county's business and political elite wanted the benefits of growth in the form of jobs, business, and profits.

Thus how Hilton Head would grow was almost completely in private hands. That private decisions would determine Hilton Head's future, however, did not make the island unique. In a society built on private enterprise, private real estate development and quest for profit have always been the basic forces shaping American communities. What is striking in the case of Hilton Head is how few private hands would fashion the future. Two-thirds of the island, more than 30 square miles, belonged to Fraser, Hack, and their associates in the Hilton Head Company and Honey Horn Plantation. Their decisions—shaped by their visions of the future, their concern for the natural setting, and their desire for profits—would determine what kind of place Hilton Head Island would become.

NOTES

1. Adams, "Carolina Cruise," 80.
2. See Trinkley, "Archaeological Survey of Hilton Head Island" and "Indian and Freedman Occupation at the Fish Haul Site."
3. Quoted in Greer, *The Sands of Time,* 8.
4. See Judge, "Exploring Our Forgotten Century."
5. Carolina stretched from 29 degrees north to 36 degrees 30 minutes north and was divided into two territories, North and South Carolina, early in the eighteenth century. Charles I had granted Carolina to Sir Robert Heath in 1629, but Heath was unable to establish any settlements before his monarch was overthrown by Oliver Cromwell.
6. William Hilton, *A Relation of a Discovery Lately Made on the Coast of Florida,* 8; reprinted in Force, *Tracts and Other Papers.*
7. Holmgren, *Hilton Head,* 65.
8. See Peeples, *Tales of Ante Bellum Hilton Head Island Families.* The best account of plantation life during the era of sea island cotton is Rosengarten, *Tombee,* which examines in detail the life and times of a planter on St. Helena

Island across Port Royal Sound from Hilton Head.

9. Carse, *Department of the South,* 98.

10. Greer, *The Sands of Time,* 42.

11. Planters whose land had been sold by the federal government received $5 per cultivated acre and $1 an acre for the rest.

12. Honey Horn Plantation was originally the property of John Hanahan of Edisto Island, who bought the land in 1789 and 1792. The name Hanahan, "probably as a result of the local Gullah dialect, got corrupted to Honey Horn," according to Inglesby, "Low Country Sketches—Honey Horn Plantation," 12.

13. See Moses Alexander Grant, *Looking Back,* and Jones-Jackson, *When Roots Die.*

14. Some Hilton Head blacks were able to complete their secondary education as boarding students at the Penn School on St. Helena Island, which was founded during the Civil War by Laura M. Towne, a teacher from Pennsylvania.

15. Coleman, "'Operation Hilton Head' Is Fight against Venereal Disease."

16. Quoted in "Milestone Reached by Island Developer," 6.

17. Quoted in Mary Kendall Hilton, "Islander: Joseph B. Fraser, Sr.," 12.

18. Fraser put up $80,000 in equity, with $50,000 coming from McIntosh, Stebbins, Fraser Rambo, and T. H. McDowell, the latter of whom was president of the Hinesville Bank. The rest was financed through a loan from the Citizens and Southern National Bank in Atlanta.

19. Frederick C. Hack, interview.

20. Quoted in "Milestone Reached by Island Developer," 7.

21. Mary Kendall Hilton, "Islander: Wilton Graves," 4.

22. Quoted in Hilton, "Islander: Fred C. Hack," 4.

23. Donald O'Quinn, quoted in "Memories of Hilton Head Island."

24. The crossing was named for James F. Byrnes, former South Carolina governor and U.S. secretary of state. Its total length was 15,000 feet, spanning Mackay Creek between the mainland and Pinckney Island, then crossing Skull Creek and the Intercoastal waterway with a draw bridge to Hilton Head.

25. Greer, *The Sands of Time,* 63.

26. Of the total of 305 purchasers, 78 were residents of Savannah, 69 from elsewhere in Georgia, 125 from South Carolina, 5 from North Carolina, and the rest from thirteen other states. See Coverdale and Colpitts, "Hilton Head Toll Bridge," 13.

27. Lois Richardson, quoted in McNeill, "Faith in Island 30 Years Ago Key to Richardson's Success."

28. Holmgren, *Hilton Head,* 136.

Chapter Two

Uncommon Vision

As much as anyone in the United States or the world at large, Charles Fraser invented the modern concept of resort/retirement living—and Hilton Head became the Mecca for all who worshipped at that shrine.

—Jim Littlejohn, *Island Events,* March 25, 1978

A dozen years after completion of the James F. Byrnes Crossing opened Hilton Head to rapid development, the island was widely recognized as one of the most desirable resort and retirement communities in the United States. In large part, the transformation of Hilton Head Island resulted from the vision and skill of one individual, Charles Elbert Fraser. Fraser saw what no one else perceived during the island's formative years: an opportunity to build a unique community. Blessed with enormous energy and restless intelligence, he created Sea Pines Plantation along Hilton Head's beautiful southern shore. The planning of Sea Pines, its architecture, concern for the natural surroundings, and the mix of recreational and residential amenities set the standard for the development of the rest of Hilton Head. Fraser's Sea Pines soon became a model nationally for what a superior resort and retirement community could be. "If it weren't for Charles Fraser, none of us would be here," emphasizes a developer who directed one of Sea Pines' major rivals; "nobody did it like Fraser."[1]

Fraser turned to resort development in the mid-1950s with an enormous advantage—he was the second son of Joseph B. Fraser Sr., the principal owner of the Hilton Head Company. His family had a substantial interest in the island he would seek to develop and also had the financial means to help him pursue his ideas. Fraser became familiar with the isolated and little-known island because of his father's business interests. After graduating from college in 1950, he spent the summer working in his father's lumber camp, exploring the island's woods and water after work. The more the young man saw that summer of Hilton Head's wide beaches and striking natural beauty, the more intrigued he became with its potential to become a special place, and he convinced his father that the tall stands of pine along the ocean should be preserved to enhance that potential.

Fraser grew up in Hinesville, Georgia, the precocious son of well-educated parents whose world reached beyond the confines of a rural Southern town of 1,500 people. His father was a successful businessman who founded the Fraser Lumber Company in 1920 and prospered. Charles was different from the other children in Hinesville, a reader and a thinker drawn to his mother, Pearl, a former schoolteacher. While Fraser the man would have an impact on how Americans played, Fraser the boy preferred books to sports; he was the one who "didn't know which end of a baseball bat to hold."[2] Fraser was intrigued by design. His mother emphasized his "sense of beauty and balance" and thought "he would have been a painter if he hadn't chosen to do something else."[3] He maintained an interest in architecture and planning while attending Presbyterian College and the University of Georgia. After his summer on Hilton Head, Fraser went north to attend Yale Law School. While he was in New Haven, his thoughts kept returning to Hilton Head, and his choice of studies was shaped by his growing sense of the potential of the holdings of his father's company on the island. Pursuing this interest, Fraser studied design and planning as well as law; and he persistently asked "law school colleagues, law and architecture professors what could be done with four miles of virgin South Carolina beachfront and adjacent forests."[4]

Fraser found few satisfactory answers to the questions he posed. In the early 1950s, little thought had been given to the kind of seaside development he envisaged for Hilton Head. A few places, notably California's Pebble Beach and Georgia's Sea Island, indicated the possibilities of careful planning. Fraser was also impressed by the handful of existing planned communities, particularly Radburn in New Jersey, Kansas City's Country Club district, and the greenbelt towns built during the New Deal. He was also strongly influenced by a course at Yale called "Land Use Planning and Allocation by Private Agreement" and taught by Myres McDougal, a specialist in the use of private covenants to implement comprehensive land use planning. The more Fraser thought about covenants, the more he became convinced that private restrictions could be used on Hilton Head to determine what the place would look like in the future.

A DIFFERENT APPROACH

Fraser returned to Hilton Head in 1956; he was twenty-six and eager to put into practice the ideas that had been evolving in his thoughts about the island.[5] He was encouraged by his father, who made him vice-president of the Hilton

Head Company. Although General Fraser was president of the company, he had devoted little time and thought to Hilton Head. Returning to the military in 1950 during the Korean War had been very disruptive to his business life. He was away when the initial development decisions were made as the company looked past the timber operations on Hilton Head, and after the war he was obliged to spend most of his time tending his interests in Hinesville. The elder Fraser welcomed his son's interest in the emerging enterprise on Hilton Head Island. But the general's partners were far from eager to have young Fraser playing a central role on what they had come to view as their island. As a consequence, Charles Fraser's involvement precipitated conflict within the Hilton Head Company, a split among the investors, and the subsequent separate development of the southern end of the island by the Frasers.

Underlying the conflict that erupted were different perspectives about how Hilton Head should be developed. General Fraser's partners wanted to manage their property in a traditional beachfront manner. Their model was Tybee Island, Savannah's beach community, with its simple gridiron subdivision along the beach. Fred Hack and Olin McIntosh were not interested in untested alternatives to traditional beachfront development. Before Charles Fraser's return, they had rejected suggestions for less conventional development from both the company's planner and a young designer at Yale whose work was financed by the Frasers.[6]

From the start, Charles Fraser was unimpressed by the company's plans. The young lawyer "was certain that eventual development of the island would follow what had been the natural course of lousy development with massive visual pollution on the Atlantic coastline unless something contrary was done."[7] For Fraser, "the place was just too attractive to let it go the way of all typical United States beach developments, which have a way of becoming a hodge-podge of conflicting uses, a joy and delight to all maniac builders and hot dog stand operators, but a nightmare to anyone with reasonable aesthetic standards."[8] As an alternative to the company's conventional ideas about developing the island, Fraser prepared a plan that sought to attract affluent families by providing abundant parks and open spaces, attractive accommodations and recreational facilities, and strict controls to exclude undesirable activities. Company efforts, he argued, should be focused on "the magnificent beach strand on the southern end," which was Hilton Head's "chief asset."[9] The southern tip of Hilton Head was also the part of the island Fraser knew best from his explorations five summers before; this area, which he designated Sea Pines in his report, was the object of his dreams.

His proposals reflected five years of thinking, studying, talking with pro-

24

fessors and fellow students, and interviewing hundreds of landowners and planners along the east coast. From this endeavor Fraser learned more about what not to do than about what worked well. Still, he collected scores of good ideas, which he culled and synthesized and elaborated as he prepared his recommendations. He was particularly impressed with the efforts of the Sea Island Company on the Georgia coast, whose concern for natural beauty and general aesthetics he considered essential in selling resort property to affluent customers and whose private development controls had helped maintain high standards.

At the heart of Fraser's proposals was the notion that Hilton Head could do even better. By attracting more affluent visitors, a developer could bring in more potential buyers with higher incomes, who would pay more for property, which would increase land values and thus make the venture more profitable. Tapping this market required provision of public services and recreational facilities and assurances that areas designed for higher income groups would be protected from cheap housing and tawdry commercial establishments. High-quality development in a place as attractive as Hilton Head Island was both the right thing to do and the most attractive financially. The owners could do well by doing good, so to speak, because "enlightened behavior" offered "the most promising avenue to the production of the greatest profit."[10]

The more Fraser worked on the economics and financing of the plan, the more convinced he became that his ideas were viable and profitable. Affluent customers were plentiful in the surrounding area; and the demand for seaside property, he concluded, would continue to increase sharply as incomes rose, leisure time lengthened, and more people retired with the means to resettle in attractive environments. Incomes in the Southeast, he emphasized, were rising more rapidly than anywhere else in the United States in the early 1950s. Federal money was pouring into the Marine camp at Parris Island and the new atomic weapons plant on the Savannah River, which would have thousands of well-paid employees. Not too far away were the vibrant Atlanta metropolitan area and the thriving industrial cities of the Carolina Piedmont. Also fueling the potential demand for coastal resort property was rising interest in water-related recreation—Fraser was particularly impressed by the explosion in small-boat ownership in the first postwar decade. Another critical factor enhancing the island's prospects was the improved accessibility that would result from the impending federal interstate highway program, which would bring more affluent people in the Southeast closer to Hilton Head.

Charles Fraser's proposals were more than an alternative to the plans developed by the Hilton Head Company; they were a vote of no confidence in

Fred Hack and his associates. Fraser did not think anything imaginative could emerge from an enterprise run by Fred Hack. The company's failure to provide adequate public services, nice restaurants, boating facilities, and other essential amenities, Fraser bluntly told his elders, had led to "the current public conception of Hilton Head as being primarily a place for cheap week-end cottages."[11] He was also critical of the Hilton Head Company's financial performance. In its first three years in the development business, it had sold only $296,000 worth of property while it had incurred $266,000 in expenses, producing a return of less than 7 percent for the shareholders after taxes.[12] Because the company was not very profitable, most of the partners were reluctant to invest more in the island. Some were not even interested in development, wanting either to sell the land or divide the property so that they could dispose of their shares. What resulted was a minimalist approach that Fraser argued was self-defeating: "This method of 'development,'" he said, "can . . . be expected to generate the minimum amount of public enthusiasm over the project; result in the slowest rise of lot prices with little or no prospect that any could be marketed at premium levels; produce the lowest net profits; and result in rapid downgrading of the completed development."[13]

Personal differences between Charles Fraser and Fred Hack and between the Frasers and the other partners complicated the conflict over the future direction of the Hilton Head Company. To Fred Hack, Charles Fraser was a brash interloper, an outsider who was, unfortunately, the son of the controlling partner in the Hilton Head Company. Hack saw Charles Fraser as a disruptive influence on his father. Young Fraser, in the view of Hack and his associates, did not know anything about Hilton Head; he had not been involved in the company's early efforts to develop the island or the long fight to improve its accessibility. Without paying his dues and earning their respect, Fraser materialized with a grand plan that ignored what had been done by the Hilton Head Company. For Fraser, on the other hand, the interloper was Fred Hack, running a company in which the Fraser family held a majority interest and running it badly, with no appreciation of the opportunity presented by their holdings on Hilton Head.

Hack and McIntosh were particularly offended by the notion that the Frasers were trying to tell them how to develop Hilton Head. They had made a commitment to the island—Fred Hack and his family lived at Honey Horn Plantation, and McIntosh owned one of the cottages built by the company, as did McIntosh's son and Hack's mother and brother. The Frasers, they believed, were the outsiders from Hinesville, not real "islanders" like the rest. This question of who was an islander, of whether one lived on Hilton Head before the ferry or before the bridge and what sort of moral authority was bestowed by the relative time of one's arrival would be a recurrent theme as Hilton Head wrestled with its destiny.

Charles Fraser and Fred Hack were also very different people, and their personal incompatibility would have an important influence on Hilton Head's development for almost two decades. Hack, like Fraser, was a native of Hinesville, and the two men's families "had known each other for lifetimes."[14] But the Fraser family was more cosmopolitan and better connected to the larger world. Charles was a Yale-trained lawyer who had worked in Washington while he was in the Air Force and had traveled widely. Hack was the son of a country doctor. He was trained as a surveyor and had been a sawmill operator and timber scout before he went to work on Hilton Head. He was a provincial, his experience limited largely to the Georgia and South Carolina coasts. The two men's personalities and interests were almost diametrical opposites. Fraser was an intellectual, a reader, and a dreamer, intoxicated with ideas. Hack was the practical engineer, solid and responsible but neither imaginative nor innovative. Hack was open and friendly; Charles Fraser was aloof and impatient. Brash and egotistical, he had little time for people who did not share his intellectual interests. In addition to these contrasts, there was a fifteen-year difference in the men's ages. For Hack, young Fraser was the "snotty-nosed kid next door" back in Hinesville, not an equal to be taken seriously in business matters.[15] At every turn, on important questions and minor matters, Fraser and Hack rubbed each other the wrong way, and the friction would worsen as the island developed under their control.

These conflicts were reinforced by other tensions between the Frasers and the rest of the Hilton Head Company. The second purchase from Loomis and Thorne was engineered by Hack and McIntosh while General Fraser was in Korea, and it significantly reduced Fraser's share of the group's overall holdings at very little cost to the others since timber sales covered the purchase price. For their part, Hack and McIntosh saw Charles Fraser's proposal for the original 8,000 acres as a means of shifting development away from the land they controlled in the north toward the southern parcel, in which the Frasers had the dominant interest. Hack and the others opposed such a move, arguing that development should be focused in the center of the island. This territorial dispute between the two groups would echo over the years, affecting the location of almost every major facility on Hilton Head.

In the end, Charles Fraser's ideas tore the Hilton Head Company apart. General Fraser steadfastly supported his son, even though he found his proposals "somewhat startling."[16] His business partners would not budge in their opposition to young Fraser's ideas for the island. The plan "was hooted at in derision by many of the directors of the company," Charles Fraser later wrote. "They thought my proposals that the island could eventually support at least two golf courses were the 'wild visions' of an immature 25-year-old youth."[17] Relations between the Frasers and the others soured as the dispute continued. Not long after what should have been a triumphal moment for the Hilton Head Company, the inauguration of the James F. Byrnes Crossing in 1956, General Fraser set in motion the division of the company's assets.

Under the agreement that effected the division, the Fraser family exchanged its 51 percent interest for 3,480 acres of beachfront, forests, and sea marshes in the southern part of the island, a little less than half of the original purchase from Loomis and Thorne. The Frasers then sold the land to the newly formed Sea Pines Plantation Company. Charles Fraser was the president of the new company; Sea Pines was his baby, and whether it would sink or swim was his responsibility. Thus Fraser's family provided him not only the opportunity but the means to realize his dreams of a new kind of American community. As Fraser emphasizes, "I was remarkably fortunate in that my family entrusted half of the family property to me at the age of twenty-six with no strings and no controls."[18] Fraser also had the benefit of a low interest rate, and the $1 million purchase price was to be repaid to his father, mother, and brother when he could afford to make payments.

For the Frasers, the Sea Pines Plantation Company was a leap of faith. Their family's major asset, their holdings on Hilton Head Island, was committed to an unproven idea to be carried out by a young man with no experience in real estate or community development. Fraser's family agreed to back Charles for a number of reasons. He had developed a logical and persuasive case that dealt with specifics. They were convinced that the project could be successful—especially his mother, who had been sympathetic to her son's views on the development of the island from the beginning. Although she worried that Charles was wasting his time and frittering away his legal talent, she had faith in his ideas and provided critical support. Last but hardly least, Pearl and Joseph Fraser were loving parents, willing to risk a sizable portion of their wealth on their son's future.

A RISKY BUSINESS

Opportunity and means are extremely important, but these advantages do not guarantee success in business or any other endeavor. Obviously, being fortunate in one's parents is an enormous advantage in most walks of life. Real estate, however, is an inherently risky business; witness the succession of booms and busts that punctuate physical growth in market societies, as well as the littering of the landscape with failed real estate projects. The land business was particularly risky in a place that, for all its beauty, was not an obvious choice for implementing innovative ideas about resort communities. Formidable obstacles existed to developing a little-known island well off the beaten track of vacationers. Moreover, Fraser's venture was located in South Carolina, which was not widely considered a preferable place to visit or live. It was "near the bottom of the list when it came to desirable vacation spots in the United States. Fewer than two percent of people in America wanted to visit anything in South Carolina, despite its wonders, charms and glories."[19] As Fraser would later confess, "It was an almost foolhardy effort to build a national resort here, but the land was magnificent."[20]

Other uncertainties abounded as Fraser turned to the daunting task of transforming his dreams and plans into something tangible, a community that would attract visitors and purchasers. There was no way to know whether his ambitious plans could be brought to fruition or whether customers would be attracted to this new kind of resort community. Could natural features be preserved and large amounts of land be set aside for open space without undermining the profitability of the venture? There was also the question of where the money would come from to develop Fraser's 3,480 acres. To be sure, no pressing financial obligations were associated with the land itself; but roads had to be built, utilities provided, recreational facilities developed, planners and engineers hired, and the new resort marketed to potential customers. Large-scale planned development poses particular heavy burdens and risks because of the necessity for sizable investments at the outset to develop the infrastructure and amenities that enhance land values and thus, developers hope, make the whole venture profitable.

Charles Fraser succeeded because he brought ability to the advantages and opportunity his family provided. He had imagination and a strong sense of what could be done with his family's holdings, and he was able to translate vision into reality because of his skill, creativity, leadership, and hard work. The young man who launched Sea Pines in 1956 was creative, energetic and daring, a visionary who longed to build something lasting. John McPhee captures his underlying motivation: "Fraser's drive seems to have been directed toward accomplishment for its own sake, toward aesthetics for the sake of aesthetic criterion. Sea Pines has evolved, perhaps, as a kind of monument."[21]

Fraser was always willing to consider the possibility of doing something different, of exploring an exciting possibility. Underpinning this quest for new ideas were insatiable curiosity and restless intelligence. An omnivorous reader with knowledge of a wide range of topics, Fraser had a remarkable grasp of detail, as well as self-confidence about his intellectual gifts: "I'm richly endowed with a rare treasure of mental images. The process is: read and travel, stock my brain, talk to experienced people, stock my brain, scan thousands of architectural photographs, stock my brain."[22] Dipping into the storehouse of information he had accumulated in this way, Fraser was an eclectic borrower of ideas, ready to "accept a new idea, no matter how radical, almost instantly. . . . If it fits into my knowledge of sociology and demographics and vacationers' habits, I will accept it even if it's never been done before."[23]

Unlike most intellectuals, Fraser was prepared to back his ideas with action. Throughout his career, according to an associate, he "had unyielding courage to bet on his ideas."[24] His sizable ego was an important part of his success; his enormous faith in himself kept him going when the going was tough, as often was the case at Sea Pines. In pursuing his ideas, Fraser was tenacious and often combative, a formidable adversary who loved controversy. He also understood that risk taking involves uncertainty, that innovation requires the willingness to take chances, to be unconventional. "In any pioneering endeavor it is injurious to the success of the venture to know too much. If you know all the hazards that might befall the venture you might elect not to undertake it. It takes a certain lack of experience to charge into some new areas. Improvement comes from assuming someone else is wrong and making a change."[25]

A NEW KIND OF COMMUNITY

At Sea Pines, Charles Fraser broke through the conventional wisdom about beachfront communities. He invented an approach to private real estate development that created a new kind of resort in purpose, architecture and design, and environmental sensitivity. "We didn't want to just sell land, we wanted to implement the master plan, to develop homesites, to walk that tightwire between the desire for a hideaway and the desire for community which are the opposites everyone is looking for in a resort residence."[26] To do this Fraser was largely on his own. He had control over a large parcel of land, a variety of ideas, and a commitment to quality; but there were no prototypes for the kind of resort he wanted to build. His studies and travels taught him many lessons but supplied few models for his acres of beachfront and forests. So, as one of his early associates emphasizes, Fraser "literally created out of nothing (but an island and a dream) something that had never been done before and . . . had never really been thought of before."[27]

30

Sea Pines would combine a beautiful natural setting with attractive housing and golf courses, boat slips, tennis courts, and other recreational facilities to complement the beach. In effect, a resort community and its amenities were woven into a striking environment of beaches, marshes, and forests. The scenery and the amenities, especially the golf courses, were used to enhance the attractions of land away from the ocean, making the whole community desirable rather than focusing on the beach, as had been done in most existing seaside resorts. From the start, Fraser realized that the real development challenge on Hilton Head was to enhance the value of interior land. In his spurned report to the Hilton Head Company, he emphasized the need for bold measures to increase the appeal of the company's extensive inland holdings. Among the suggestions that fell on deaf ears were the basic ideas that turned forests into valuable real estate—mixing nature and development, golf courses with homes along the fairways, and other attractions for "retired individuals moving to Hilton Head Island who do not necessarily want a lot on the beach."[28]

Fraser's Sea Pines offered a new way of life with enormous appeal in a society that increasingly valued recreation and had growing numbers of affluent people retiring sooner and living longer. By developing an attractive resort with golf, tennis, swimming, boating, biking, and other adult activities, Fraser tied community development to the rapidly growing market for high-quality leisure. Like almost everything he did, the marriage of community and market he shaped in Sea Pines was a mix of systematic inquiry, creative thinking, and a dash of good fortune. During Sea Pines' gestation period, Fraser examined leisure and sports participation as well as other resorts. He studied demographics and leisure preferences among the income group he was aiming at and built Sea Pines around golf and other activities that would appeal to that group.

Fraser was convinced that his market would be best served by development that was sensitive to the environment. Affluent people would not build a vacation or retirement home "except where the continued maintenance of the natural beauty of the surrounding areas is assured."[29] The basic goal was to introduce the built environment with minimal disruption of the natural environment. In Sea Pines "every man-made addition was blended into its surroundings. Architects worked in a style best described as contemporary camouflage . . . to create a harmonious relationship between the artificial structures and their lush natural environments."[30] The harmonious blend of the natural setting and the man-made environment, the "Sea Pines look," was highly innovative and widely copied. "People almost take it for granted now," notes Edward Pinckney, a landscape architect who worked with Fraser from the beginning; "but believe me, in the early days of Sea Pines it was not done anywhere else."[31]

Concern for the natural setting was not fashionable when Sea Pines was developed. When Fraser began, public regulation even of environmentally sensitive areas like Hilton Head Island was minimal, and there were few pressures on private developers to behave in an ecologically responsible manner. Fraser cared about the environment, but he was a developer rather than a preservationist. His dream was always to develop Hilton Head Island; he never saw it as a place preserved in its natural state and free from people. Nature was an essential part of what he was selling, and he sought to use Hilton Head's striking beauty as a backdrop for his Sea Pines. He considered himself an old-fashioned conservationist, "an advocate of the mixture of man and nature. I get angry at people who would destroy one or exclude the other. The idea that 'this is a beautiful place, let's not let anybody else come here,' is repulsive to me."[32]

Cynics would argue that Fraser merely did what maximized his profits—that environmentally sensitive development produced a higher return on his investment. Caring about the environment, they could say, was a "rational" strategy. It attracted wealthier customers, increased demand, and produced higher land prices—and selling land was the bottom line for Sea Pines. This line of argument leaves open the question of why so few entrepreneurs, presumably also rational profit maximizers, pursued Fraser's approach to the natural setting. In reality, environmental sensitivity was not the obvious choice in 1957, and most developers would have opted for profits over the environment then as they would now. In Fraser's case, the concern for nature resulted from personal as well as economic considerations, the conviction that profit must be balanced against respect for the land. Fraser believed that ownership of land brought a stewardship obligation that "requires that you act in accordance with your best intelligence and knowledge, and the more intelligent you are, the more advanced is the stewardship."[33] Certainly Fraser wanted to make money, but he also was interested in "people, history, architecture, trees and birds."[34]

Environmentally sensitive development was both a product of careful planning and a pervasive influence on the design of Sea Pines. Blending man's work into nature necessitated fitting individual buildings into the grand scheme in an architectural style that complemented the natural environment. Architects were encouraged to design modern homes and to emphasize natural materials and finishes—cedar and cypress and redwood in earth tones. Lots were "consciously laid out to provide occupants of Sea Pines homes with spectacular views of ocean, rivers, marshes, and golf fairways."[35] Homes were dramatically opened up to nature with large windows, balconies, skylights, and patios. Roads were winding and well landscaped, emphasizing the dramatic foliage and vistas and masking the high residential densities. The result emphasized the whole rather than the parts, with houses that "blend into the landscape with a certain amount of continuity among them so that all fit together as part of a composition creating a continuous picture of related materials."[36] Fraser took special delight in the physical shape of his plantation. He was a designer at heart, much happier planning than selling real estate. He was involved in every aspect of the work, poring over individual house plans, worrying about the shape of Sea Pines' signs, deciding what color the fireplugs should be painted. From this pervasive concern with the shape of things came a distinctive architectural style that was influential on the rest of Hilton Head, on resort and retirement communities elsewhere, and on housing and commercial building design more generally. Design proved to be the most transferable of Charles Fraser's innovations at Sea Pines, far more exportable than the singular natural setting. The Sea Pines or Hilton Head style became a generic term among architects and landscape designers. As one explains, "Charles Fraser and his people at Sea Pines have influenced our entire industry with their architectural form of using natural colors, building into wooded areas, cutting patches of light and grass, and many other similar things that have become the vogue all across our country."[37]

Sea Pines' design standards were enforced through innovative deed covenants devised by Charles Fraser. Drawing on his work with McDougal at Yale, experience with covenants elsewhere, and his own ideas, the young attorney provided the means for exercising tight private control over the development process. One lesson he learned during his travels from Cape Cod to Key West was the need for absolute control. At Sea Pines, Fraser expanded the concept of private real estate covenants, using them for everything from architectural criteria to the preservative of open space. Covenants were his preferred solution to most development issues; they could, he argued, insure that master plans were followed, dedicate environmentally sensitive areas, and promote aesthetic design while providing "permanent protection against blighted neighborhoods, encroaching commercial establishments, overcrowding, intermixing of public and residential areas, unsightly buildings and other conditions which plague most older beach areas."[38] His covenants regulated both the developer and individual property owners, promising security about future development and certainty about externalities.

More than anything else at Sea Pines, the covenants were created by Charles Fraser. He trained as a lawyer, not as an architect or planner. Others ultimately did the designs; Fraser wrote the covenants. They were his way of locking his vision into the future. His pioneering covenants were widely emulated. All the other major real estate developments on Hilton Head followed Sea Pines' lead in providing private land use and building controls, and their combined effect contributed significantly to the distinctiveness of the island and its communities. Beyond the island, both on projects initiated by Fraser and on those developed by others, Sea Pines' land-use covenants provided a much-used model that was often imitated word for word.

No one builds communities alone. At Sea Pines, Charles Fraser brought together a variety of creative people. Most came because of the opportunity to work with Fraser. Although he was strong-willed and demanding, he proved to be a gifted orchestrator of talented individuals. Planners, architects, developers, builders, and golf course designers found him receptive to unconventional ideas. Sea Pines became a training ground for developers, architects, landscape designers, and others who later took their lessons to resorts and new communities across the nation.

NEW COMMUNITIES AND FAMILIAR CONFLICTS

Charles Fraser set in motion the process that shaped Hilton Head and thus framed the politics of growth on the island. Other things helped to bring Fraser's dream into the realm of possibility—for example, insecticides to control the voracious mosquitoes that thrived in Hilton Head's marshes and lagoons, and the increasing availability and affordability of modern air conditioning. But Fraser was the driving force in creating a distinctive resort community catering to well-off vacationers and retirees. His Sea Pines triggered a remarkable and rapid transformation of Hilton Head into a world-class resort. Three decades after Fraser began, the island was attracting over a million visitors a year and had more than 20,000 residents, many of them affluent retirees. For the prospective property owner, homes were selling from $1 million or more to as little as $500 for an off-season week in a time-sharing condominium. Thousands of hotel rooms and condominiums were available to vacationers, and to help fill these accommodations, Hilton Head was host to scores of meetings and conventions. Twenty-odd golf courses dotted the island, along with tennis complexes, marinas, cycling paths, horseback trails, and nature preserves. Restaurant offerings ranged from fine French cuisine to the fast-food staples of the American diet in the late twentieth century. Malls, convenience stores, and elegant shops catered to affluent residents and visitors, offering fine wines, imported cheeses, fresh croissants, and quiche—all progeny of the growth stimulated by Charles Fraser's improbable dream.

Sea Pines was a privately designed and controlled community of substantially greater size than most private developments. Eventually it would encompass almost 5,000 acres—nearly 8 square miles. All the land was controlled by Fraser, and its use was privately regulated by covenants. Sea Pines was privately financed. Almost all services were provided privately. There were no public zoning or planning controls. There were few public services, and there was minimal environmental regulation by government. The absence of public controls provided Fraser with carte blanche, effectively freeing him from the necessity of obtaining public approval for his plans and projects. And the lack of public services necessitated private provision of almost everything that local governments normally provided. The other large planned communities on Hilton Head followed the Sea Pines model, so developers dominated the local political economy. As a result, Hilton Head presents a classic instance of large-scale development dominated by private enterprise, which is of particular interest, given increased reliance on the private sector in almost every aspect of American life.

Control of development on Hilton Head by a handful of private companies has been highly successful in many respects. Hilton Head is widely and appropriately seen as a model of well-planned upscale resort development. Fraser and his competitors paid far more attention to planning, environment, and amenity than private developers usually do in the United States. Hilton Head looks good; much of its natural beauty has been retained. For those who can afford homes and accommodations in Sea Pines and the other major developments, the island is a highly desirable place to live or visit. Private control of land use and design has enhanced Hilton Head's appeal, as has private provision of first-rate services and amenities. But private development has its limits—even in paradise. Growth has taken its toll on Hilton Head's fragile environment, and the public sector has steadily expanded in response to the demands of a diversifying population for both public services and public control of development.

Private development, no matter how successful in establishing attractive communities, inevitably creates the need for political legitimacy and public involvement in decisions that affect peoples' lives. As Hilton Head grew, those who settled in Sea Pines and the other planned communities had interests distinct from those of Fraser and his fellow developers and were increasingly unwilling to rely wholly on the private sector. Residents have stakes in their homes and their communities that are bound to clash with the interests of those who build homes and communities; settlers will want less development than the community builder has planned and more control over future growth. Inherent tensions exist between what has built American communities—the desire for profit—and what happens after they are built—people arrive and seek a voice in shaping their community through the political process.[39] These tensions are intensified in places that grow because of their natural attractions, especially those like Hilton Head that attract large numbers of retirees and second-home owners with strong residential and weak economic interests in their adopted communities.

Among the many lessons to be learned from Hilton Head is that even the most careful planning of conscientious developers and their best efforts to preserve the natural beauty of a place cannot guarantee that everyone will live happily there ever after. A study of the interplay of private and public interests—of profits and politics—in the development of Hilton Head Island in the third of a century following the creation of the Sea Pines Plantation Company can provide a broader understanding of the benefits and costs to a community of relying so heavily on the private sector. Hilton Head's experience sheds light on a wide range of important and difficult issues that bedevil more and more Americans: environmental protection, property rights, growth management, conflict between developers and residents, strife between more responsible developers and less responsible ones, impact of growth on indigenous population, and provision of private or public services—all in the context of a rapidly growing community located on a fragile barrier island.

NOTES

1. Axene, interview. David N. Axene managed the Hilton Head Company between 1980 and 1985.

2. McGrath, "Sea Pines Plantation Alumni," 24.

3. Pearl Fraser, quoted in McPhee, *Encounters with the Archdruid,* 91.

4. Charles E. Fraser, interview, August 15, 1987.

5. After Yale Law School, Fraser served in the Air Force, working in the office of the general counsel in Washington, and practiced law briefly with Hull, Willingham, Towill and Norman in Augusta, Georgia.

6. The company's planner was Richard A. McGinty, later a leading architect on the island. The designer was Bernard Berg, a graduate student at the Yale School of Design. See Charles E. Fraser, "A Program of Development Activities," 33–34.

7. Quoted in "The Little Emperor of Hilton Head," 50.

8. Quoted in Mary Kendall Hilton, "Islander: Charles E. Fraser," 4.

9. Charles E. Fraser, "A Program of Development Activities," 4.

10. Ibid., 1.

11. Ibid., 26.

12. Charles E. Fraser, "Financial Aspects of Development Activities," 1.

13. Charles E. Fraser, "A Program of Development Activities," 6.

14. Billie Hack, interview.

15. Fowler, interview.

16. Quoted in Mary Kendall Hilton, "Islander: Joseph B. Fraser, Sr.," 12.

17. Charles E. Fraser, *The Art of Community Building,* 6.

18. Quoted in Olson, "BT Interview: Charles Fraser," 15.

19. Charles E. Fraser, quoted in Martin, "Hilton Head: Once-Isolated Island Now a Tourist's Utopia."

20. Quoted in Otis, "Sea Pines," 6.

21. McPhee, *Encounters with the Archdruid,* 95.

22. Quoted in Patrick, "Fraser's Edge," 23.

23. Quoted in Drake, "Developer Charles Fraser Learns Secret of Turning Beaches into Gold," 57.

24. Lader, "A Shared Responsibility," 88.

25. Quoted in Cornelison, "One Man's Island in the Sun."

26. Charles E. Fraser, quoted in Horton, "The Hideaway and Community Tightwire," 55.

27. McGrath, "Sea Pines Plantation Alumni," 26. McGrath went to Yale Law School with Fraser and joined the Sea Pines Company in 1956.

28. Charles E. Fraser, "A Program of Development Activities," 29. Less prescient was Fraser's emphasis in 1955 on what he called "Project Scarlet O'Hara," using Hilton Head Island's history as a means of attracting buyers to inland properties. As it turned out, affluent northerners were more interested in golf than in Dixie history.

29. Ibid., 10.

30. Schlecter, "The Blossoming of the Barrier Islands," 22.

31. Quoted in Cathy Wood, "The Sea Pines Architectural Influence," 34.

32. Quoted in "Palmas Del Mar: The Doomed Gem of Puerto Rico," 66.

33. Quoted in "Hilton Head: Something Beautiful Being Created."

34. Quoted in Mary Kendall Hilton, "Islander: Charles E. Fraser," 4.

35. Fraser, *The Art of Community Building,* 9.

36. Richard A. McGinty, quoted in Mary Kendall Hilton, "Islander: Richard A. McGinty," 4. McGinty was one of the architects who helped developed Sea Pines' distinctive approach to design.

37. Robert Marvin, quoted in "Sea Pines: Bench Mark for Scores of New Resorts," 14.

38. Charles E. Fraser, "Basic Data on the Sea Pines Development," 1.

39. Logan and Molotch underscore the conflict between developers and their allies interested in the exchange value of land and residential and community interests concerned with its use value. See *Urban Fortunes,* 17–29.

Chapter Three

Developing Sea Pines Plantation

Each American has his individual dream. Mine involves the process by which good human settlements are built. . . . I derive a great deal of pleasure in the process itself—planning, directing the effort, the sheer activity of doing it.

—Charles E. Fraser, quoted by James A. Martin
in the *Charleston News and Courier,* August 8, 1982

The Sea Pines Plantation Company was incorporated on June 20, 1957, "to develop, over a period of several years, a coordinated series of residential communities, a beach club and yacht club, a golf course, and related recreational facilities on a seven square mile forest preserve."[1] Charles E. Fraser was president, his brother was senior vice-president, and his father was chairman of the board. But the Sea Pines Company was Charles Fraser's show.[2] His brother was engaged in the family business in Hinesville during the formative years at Sea Pines, and his father was not actively involved in the development of Sea Pines. General Fraser and his wife vacationed on the island but continued to live in Hinesville. The elder Frasers' place in Sea Pines was symbolic of the new styles of living that their son would develop; they owned a condominium on a lagoon astride a fairway of the island's first golf course. From his glass-walled living room, General Fraser could see what his son had created from the wilderness and take great satisfaction in a development that "exceeded my most extravagant dreams."[3]

Charles Fraser was twenty-eight years old when the Sea Pines Company was formed and, as he puts it, had "absolute control over a beautiful piece of land."[4] He was liberated from the constraints imposed by trying to work within the Hilton Head Company, from having to please a diverse group of investors reluctant to spend money or entertain novel ideas. Fraser was free to elaborate his vision, assuming that he could find the money to turn his dreams into a viable resort community. Corporate titles, bold objectives, and absolute control, however, suggest a grander organization than the reality of Fraser's small, personal, and primitive operation. Sea Pines' initial office was in a trailer, and there were no telephones. Fraser showed visitors around his "plantation" in a jeep, dodging wild pigs, deer, and an occasional alligator. What was to become

39

Sea Pines' first golf course was "comparable to the wilderness jungle along the Amazon in South America."[5] The island lacked a skilled labor force to build or operate a resort community. Secretarial work was done by Lois Richardson in the back office of the Forest Beach Supermarket during lulls in the Richardsons' grocery business, which were frequent—"If you'd hear a car going down the road, you'd run out and look! Yes sir, that was a big thing."[6]

Hilton Head in 1957 offered visitors lush scenery and Spartan accommodations; it was the kind of undiscovered place that travel writers typically extol from a distance. Wilton Graves began the Sea Crest Motel in 1953 with two rooms. By the time Sea Pines was beginning, the motel had ten rooms. Dining out was strong on local color: at the Roadside Restaurant, customers could feast on "fresh vegetables, meat, corn bread and very, very sweet iced tea while observing a painting of the Last Supper on velvet."[7] Mosquitoes were abundant in the numerous shallow ponds that dotted the island; tiny but vicious, they were, in Fraser's words, "a terrible plague" capable of delivering "forty to seventy bites a minute if one stood still in a breezeless area."[8] Early on, Fraser realized that the mosquitoes had to go before people would flock to Sea Pines. He enlisted the state's entomologist, Frank Arnold, and financed the development of a mosquito control program that made Sea Pines and Hilton Head livable.

Among the many obstacles to developing Sea Pines was the curious way the original Hilton Head Company holdings had been divided between the Frasers and the other partners. Instead of splitting the property into two parcels, Fred Hack had insisted on a more complex arrangement to insure a fair division of the land. The middle of the tract went to the Frasers, and the land on either side was retained by the Hilton Head Company. The partition left Hack's beach and waterfront properties at the southern tip cut off from the rest of the Hilton Head Company's holdings, while Fraser did not have control over an area of 1,280 acres that was essential to his plans. In a bold move, considering the shaky finances of Sea Pines in 1958, Fraser offered Hack $1.1 million for the southernmost parcel. The offer was hard for Hack to refuse since the Hilton Head Company's financial problems were even more severe than those of Sea Pines. At almost $800 an acre, Hack and McIntosh thought they had gotten the best of the deal, which supplied them with $50,000 in desperately needed cash and $120,000 in annual income for ten years.[9] Now Sea Pines Plantation was complete, encompassing 4,500 acres—all of the southern end of Hilton Head. Fraser's property was the most beautiful part of the island, with 4 miles of magnificent forested beach on one side and striking vistas of Calibogue Sound on the other.

PLANNING SEA PINES

Fraser's land and ideas came together in the initial development plans for Sea Pines. The first master plan was prepared by Hideo Sasaki, a landscape architect on the Harvard faculty. Sasaki and Fraser were kindred spirits in their interest in melding people and the environment, and the newly minted developer turned to Sasaki to translate his ideas into an overall design for Sea Pines. Underlying the plan was sensitivity to the lush setting. As one of Sasaki's associates explains, at Sea Pines, "a master plan concept was created in which the natural environment deliberately dominates the man-made environment. . . . Land uses were assigned in direct relationship to the ability of the landscape to absorb the character and density of the proposed program."[10] Overall housing densities were planned at a unit per acre, clustered on about half of the Sea Pines land, with the rest for beaches, golf courses, parks, wildlife preserves, tidal marshes, and other open space. Approximately 1,400 acres were protected against development through open space covenants, including the 600-odd acres that became the Sea Pines Forest Preserve.

Planning, conservation, and stringent land use controls were the means used to attract affluent buyers of vacation, weekend, and retirement residences. Planning and control were the way to preserve paradise and thus enhance profits. "The protected environment within Sea Pines Plantation," Fraser explained in 1963, "adds a subtle but very important ingredient to the well-educated vacationer's delight," providing "first a sense of relief and contentment, and then appreciation of the planning effort that has been embodied in the Sea Pines Plantation development. Thus the excellence of land planning plays an important role in helping to generate vacationer enthusiasm, tending to high revenues."[11]

The plans for Sea Pines were flexible rather than fixed; they evolved as the plantation developed. "They are guides," Fraser explained, "not unchangeable designs, and will be implemented, within the overall pattern originally established, in a way responsive to the developing needs of the community."[12] The initial plan was the starting point, a way of thinking about developing Sea Pines. Plans were adjusted to take natural features into account, to respond to changing market conditions, and to reflect experience as development unfolded. What worked was elaborated; what did not was discarded. New planning techniques, financial requirements, and changes in government regulations affected Sea Pines plans. As residents arrived, the plans were adapted to their needs and interests, particularly the demand for recreational facilities, which were "vastly underestimated" in Fraser's original design.[13] Altogether, nine plans were prepared between 1957 and 1974. The number of golf courses increased from one to four, an airstrip disappeared, more condominiums were included, and the village of Harbour Town was added as the plantation's main activity focus.

Development in Sea Pines began along the beach. The broad white strand along the Atlantic was Sea Pines' principal selling point, and oceanside property was the most attractive to prospective buyers. This land was also relatively accessible from the roads built by the Hilton Head Company. Houses on the ocean were located behind the dunes, preserving both the sandy knolls and the great trees lining the beach. Fraser departed from the common seaside pattern of beachfront homes on a linear road that cut everyone else off from the beach. Sea Pines' planners located the main thoroughfare a distance back from the beach and serviced rows of houses with short dead-end streets providing access to beachfront property and the lots behind those on the ocean. Pathways between these T-shaped streets provided homesites near the beach with safe passage to the beach without crossing roads.

This innovative arrangement was a product of Fraser's research and thinking about seaside development. In his travels, he was repeatedly told that traditional building along the beach was a mistake; the road paralleling the shore was a safety hazard and reduced the value of the lots on the other side away from the beach. "There's less drop in prestige than there'd be if you had to cross the main road to get to the beach," Fraser emphasized; "there's a psychological lift in being on the ocean side."[14] (Obviously this arrangement also allowed for more lots that could be sold at a premium because they were not cut off from the beach by a main road.) Initially oceanfront lots sold for $5,350, second row lots for $3,400, and the remaining sites for $2,400 or $2,100, depending on their distance from the beach.[15]

More challenging than beachfront property was development of the interior portions of Sea Pines Plantation. Enhancing the value of land away from the beach by providing amenities might seem simple in theory: provide a view, build attractive recreational facilities such as golf and boating, develop high-quality community settings. In practice, luring customers inland was difficult and expensive. To make the interior attractive, Fraser would dig lagoons, develop boating facilities, and lay out streets in such a way as to provide dramatic views of marshland, forests, and Calibogue Sound.

Golf courses proved to be the most dramatic and successful means of enhancing interior property values. They created a lot of green space and water around which building lots could be wrapped, and they could be threaded through less attractive land to enhance its value. Fraser had been aware from the start of golf's potential for increasing the island's attractions, but at that point he did not fully grasp its potential for bolstering property values, and he experimented unsuccessfully with hunting as a means of attracting people to Sea Pines. "During the fall and winter months we thought hunting would be the thing, so we established a quail and dove-raising operation, until we finally determined that we were spending $3 on that operation for every $1 that we took in. Next we started working on golf."[16]

The problem with golf was money. Golf courses were expensive to develop, especially when golf was going to be used to attract people. Normally, private golf clubs were organized by affluent people who pooled their resources to build a course. But there were no golfers on Hilton Head as Sea Pines began, and there was little prospect of selling memberships for a planned golf course in a new resort with an uncertain future. Nor was South Carolina a hotbed of golf in the mid-1950s; only one course had been built in the Palmetto State in three decades. Fortunately for Fraser, one of his early supporters was James C. Self, a wealthy textile manufacturer and avid golfer.[17] Self was enthusiastic about Sea Pines' future, and he was convinced that golf would attract the kind of customers Fraser sought and would raise land values. So certain was Self that golf would work at Sea Pines that he formed a partnership in 1958 to finance the island's first golf course and provide the equipment and manpower to build it.[18]

Fraser's first thoughts about golf were instrumental: "We had in mind just something we could build houses around that would give us a year-round attraction and would give the duffers something to do."[19] But he changed his mind after talking with Self and George Cobb, a noted golf course designer from Greenville, South Carolina. Self convinced Fraser that a first-rate resort needed an eighteen-hole course rather than the nine-hole layout Fraser initially planned. Cobb also urged Fraser to go first class. "Right off the bat I told Charlie that a second-class golf course was the best way I could think of to create a second-class community," relates Cobb. "But a first-class course! Now that's what would bring the first-class golfers, the people with first-class taste."[20] Cobb designed an excellent course that took advantage of the natural beauty and rich foliage of the site. It was the first of four eventually built on Sea Pines. The fifteenth hole, with its dramatic vista overlooking the Atlantic, was quickly ranked as one of the nation's great golf holes and provided a photogenic subject for Sea Pines' marketing efforts.

For an investment of $750,000, Fraser had a golf course in 1960 to attract visitors and more than 300 lots spread along its fairways and lagoons. The Sea Pines Golf Course and the new properties were intrinsically intertwined. The golf course, as Fraser explained in 1962, "would have been a financial folly except for the fact that we created about $2 million worth of fairway lots at the same time. On the other side of the coin, the same land would have been virtually unsalable without the golf course in front of it. It has turned out to be a rather pleasant mutual accommodation."[21] Golf also broadened the appeal of Sea Pines to prospective visitors and buyers and lengthened the season, in the process transforming Hilton Head from a beach-oriented place for summer holidays to a year-round resort. "Golf," emphasizes Joseph B. Fraser Jr., "made Sea Pines what it became, changing the nature of the place from the original conception of summer cottages."[22]

Along with golf, other investments were essential to lure potential purchasers to Sea Pines. Fraser built the $1 million William Hilton Inn in 1959 to draw prospective customers to his plantation. The inn was aggressively promoted to attract people to Sea Pines and was operated to provide visitors with a pleasant experience and extensive exposure to Fraser's marketing efforts.[23] Visitors were immersed in the beauty of Sea Pines in the hope that this would lead them to purchase a lot. "We were selling real estate at the inn," emphasizes a former Sea Pines executive; the idea was "stay for a week, buy for life."[24] Another critical investment was the Plantation Club, an $800,000 complex completed in 1966, with a fine restaurant and meeting rooms along with a clubhouse and pro shop for the golf course, tennis courts, swimming pool, health club, and other facilities for residents and guests.

Fraser also offered his customers an elaborate set of private land use and building restrictions. Fraser's covenants provided for absolute control over everything within the plantation: "No building, fence or other structure shall be erected, placed or altered on any lot in . . . Residence Areas until the proposed building plans, specifications, exterior color or finish, plot plans (showing the proposed location of such building or structure, drives and parking areas), and construction schedule shall have been approved in writing by Sea Pines Plantation Company." Sea Pines could deny approval "upon any ground, including purely aesthetic considerations, which in the sole and uncontrolled discretion of the Company shall seem sufficient."[25] Once plans were approved, no alterations were permitted without consent. The covenants gave Sea Pines the right to match the highest bid for property, and it set forth sanctions for violations including the suspension of golf privileges—for many residents of Sea Pines, perhaps the severest punishment imaginable.

Design standards were enforced by a review board composed of local architects with Fraser as chairman and ultimate arbiter of what his plantation would look like. Minimum house size and side setbacks were specified, and look-a-likes were restricted "to sites out-of-sight of the next closest comparable homes."[26] Bleached cypress and redwood were the preferred exteriors, and red brick, that old Southern favorite, was normally not approved. While Fraser assured prospective buyers that covenants "will be administered in a manner designed to reasonably accommodate differing individual desires and tastes," he emphasized that "they are sufficiently complete to provide legal authority on the part of the Company and the property owners in the community to stop any activities which represent abuses by an individual of the rights of the neighborhood."[27] Fraser routinely nixed plans for "English Tudor, Spanish Adobe, mountain log cabins, French Provincial . . . Gothic Revival, geodesic-domed houses, Georgian, Williamsburg Colonial . . . Southern Greek temples, Victorian Egyptian Revival, Western ranch houses," and "just plain tacky designs."[28]

Fraser aggressively and successfully promoted his covenants in marketing Sea Pines to the affluent customers he was seeking. Restrictions embedded in deeds protected property owners against blight, incompatible land uses, overcrowding, and unattractive buildings. They insured that open space and recreational areas would be preserved by Sea Pines. The design review process allowed Sea Pines to blend large, expensive homes with smaller, more modest ones, thus broadening the range of options to customers. In this way the covenants benefited both the developers and Sea Pines property owners, serving their common interest in creating and maintaining a high-quality community, preserving the environment, and enhancing land values and resale prices. Most of those who purchased property in Sea Pines were very positive about the restrictive covenants and the protections they afforded plantation residents. As a Sea Pines sales executive emphasized in 1969, "The stringent restrictions are . . . one of the strongest sales points we have."[29] Attracted to Sea Pines in part by Fraser's legal protections, purchasers became fervent defenders of covenants and would seek to extend restrictions on the company in defense of their own interests, often to the dismay of the master of the covenants.

In practice, applying the design policies was difficult, particularly at the beginning, when everything was new and a cohesive set of standards had not yet evolved, and when customers were not so plentiful that they could be easily turned away because their tastes in home design were at odds with Fraser's. Sea Pines' high standards raised the expectations of buyers, and nonconforming homes were "considered highly undesirable by the remainder of the residents of the Plantation."[30] Fraser lived and learned. Standards for individual homes were tightened after 1965, primarily by promoting custom-built homes. Stock plans were no longer made available to lot purchasers—most were not up to Fraser's standards, and the best designs were too popular and therefore excessively duplicated. Well-designed custom homes were essential to the appeal of Sea Pines and the enhancement of land values.

Architects flourished under Fraser's controls. His standards provided a buffer between good design and the preferences of the customer, protecting architects from clients' desires for colonial and other traditional homes. Architects used the review process to advance the style they were evolving with Fraser's encouragement. Clients bought the approach because they liked the overall effect if not the individual house designs; they wanted to live in Sea Pines, to fit in. Designers forged a critical connection for Fraser, helping "our new residents bridge the gap between their personal desires and our plan. They convince the people of the maintenance assets of cypress, of the appeal of big windows to catch the view, and of the immeasurable value of our trees."[31] And their skill in siting individual houses created the illusion that Sea Pines was much less intensively settled. "An aerial view of Sea Pines Plantation," John McPhee noted in 1970, "reveals the great number of houses there, and how close to one another they really are, whereas an observer on the ground—even in the most densely built areas—feels that he is in a partly cleared woodland with some houses blended into it, nothing more."[32]

Within Fraser's design framework, a few young architects created the distinctive Hilton Head style with its emphasis on natural materials, muted finishes, outdoor vistas, and sites that blended with the setting. The initial steps were taken by John Wade, who designed the first model homes at Sea Pines. Most influential were Richard McGinty and Douglas Corkern. McGinty was a true island pioneer, recruited in 1954 by Fred Hack to work on the initial plans of the Hilton Head Company. He laid out roads and lots, suggested alternatives to traditional beachfront development that were rejected by Hack and McIntosh, and drew the lines for the division of the Hilton Head Company land when the Frasers split with their partners. Corkern arrived a few years later, working first at Sea Pines with one of Sasaki's associates. Corkern and McGinty would design much of what was built during the early years, including the William Hilton Inn, the Plantation Center, and numerous homes in Sea Pines. From their work and contributions of other designers, "the style just sort of evolved," as Corkern explains—"the wide overhangs, and the expanses of glass: a little Wrightian, a little bit of Japanese."[33] Their innovative style became a key part of Sea Pines; Fraser's controls and the designers' creativity combined to make attractive and distinctive homes the standard in Sea Pines and to create a strong sense of place, thus increasing the appeal of the plantation and the value of the land Fraser was trying to sell.

STRUGGLING TO STAY AFLOAT

Imaginative plans, creative designs, and strong controls, and Fraser's other accomplishments were shadowed by Sea Pines' financial weakness. Sea Pines was a small, undercapitalized operation, and the early years were an ongoing struggle to survive. Land costs were not a heavy burden for Fraser, thanks to the generous arrangement with his family for the bulk of the Sea Pines land, but working capital was another story. Capital is particularly critical for the developer of new communities that involve heavy front-end costs. Substantial investments have to be made before much land can be sold. At Sea Pines, roads had to be paved, maintenance facilities built, and public utilities and services developed—all privately. Concern for the environment further increased capital needs because preserving nature cost more than bulldozing large tracts for development. Adding to Fraser's financial problems was his practice of underpricing amenities to attract buyers, as a result of which Sea Pines lost money on its ancillary operations.

Most bankers were not interested in the confident young man with the grand plans. This was the conservative 1950s, and go-go banking was some years down the road. Fraser scrambled, borrowing sums from several sources, swapping land for money, and tirelessly seeking more secure financing, using his father's connections and new ones he nurtured. He learned the hard way that "most investors care nothing about planning."[34] Unable to convince investors to take a chance on large-scale planned development, Fraser survived the early years with short-term loans, which could not provide a stable basis for building a community over two or more decades. Initial financing from Travelers Insurance Company, which was to prove Sea Pines' most reliable source of funds, was a timber loan: Travelers "would only advance the funds equal to the value of the standing pine trees because they had so little to go by in terms of records of starting large scale new coastal resorts."[35]

Critical help came from a few bankers and businessmen with resources who thought Fraser's ideas were sound. Most important was James Self, the textile magnate who played a critical financial role in the development of the first golf course. Self and some wealthy friends bought enough beach lots at the outset to provide Fraser with financial breathing space. Self also advanced funds for the acquisition of the southern tip from the Hilton Head Company. He was an enthusiast but not an altruist. His group's $300,000 equity in the golf course was swapped for half the lots bordering the course—land that was later sold for $725,000. Self's $100,000 loan for the purchase of the southern tip of Sea Pines in 1958 was an even better investment: it was exchanged for land that was worth over $1.7 million in 1980.

Sea Pines' financial problems were complicated by Fraser's need to undertake costly investments in amenities, especially the William Hilton Inn and the golf course. Only $275,000 of the million needed for the hotel could be raised through a conventional mortgage; the rest came from creative financing in the form of trust certificates convertible into developed lots. Substantial cost overruns on the golf course led Fraser to the Bessemer Securities Corporation, which provided $1.1 million in exchange for a first mortgage on all raw land and the golf course, a second mortgage on the inn, and $100,000 worth of interior land, which was later sold for a substantial profit. These deals kept Sea Pines going, but they involved trading land for time and thus trading future profits for the chance to survive.

Underfinanced and unknown to most prospective customers, Sea Pines struggled to turn its good ideas into good business. Four years after Fraser began, his development had fewer than 20 homes, and most were essentially beach cottages on unpaved sand lanes. Fraser's house, the first built in the plantation, had no air conditioning, which Sea Pines' early advertising optimistically claimed was unnecessary. Air conditioning soon became standard, making the summer's heat and humidity bearable, and residential streets began to be paved. But in 1962 there was still no fire department or pharmacy. There were no doctors or medical facilities and few telephones. Only one tennis court had been built; the new golf course was sparsely used. A newcomer who came to this "backwater" to run the fledgling chamber of commerce "could not imagine Sea Pines building more golf courses."[36]

Table 3.1
Homes Built and Lots Sold in Sea Pines, 1958–1964

Year	Homes Built	Lots Sold
1958	3	45
1959	6	54
1960	10	78
1961	17	93
1962	31	92
1963	25	131
1964	57	132

Source: Sea Pines Company.

Keeping Sea Pines afloat was extremely difficult during these years. Fraser's life was "a constant struggle for money. We had to sell a lot each week in order to meet our payroll, to keep the tractors going and to pay for the roofs going on places."[37] During a low point in 1960, Fraser told his staff that "if we don't sell two lots by Friday, we're out of business."[38] A year later, he was distraught, his cash was depleted, lots were not selling, and he could not meet the next payroll. What should he do? he asked his father back in Hinesville. Get out of the kitchen if you can't take the heat, General Fraser advised. "My Dad said that if I couldn't stand the strain of figuring out a way to meet the payroll, I should sell the company and go to work for somebody else . . . so, I immediately went back to Hilton Head and sold the lot for that week's payroll."[39]

Through the lean years, Charles Fraser stuck by his principles, refusing to compromise his standards. Reinforcing his commitment to his dream were the bright spots, the indications that Sea Pines had a future. Land values and sales were rising. By the beginning of 1962 beachfront lots that had initially sold for $5,350 were bringing as much as $9,600. Land along the ocean opened for development by construction of the golf course was selling for up to $17,000, while choice fairway land brought $7,000.[40] By the end of 1964 Sea Pines had sold more than 600 homesites, and almost 150 homes had been built. Costs, however, were rising as the company expanded, undertaking more construction, providing more amenities, and hiring more employees. From 5 employees in 1957 Sea Pines expanded to 160 in 1963. Paying the bills, meeting payrolls, and making payments on notes remained a struggle, and selling land continued to be the key to survival.

During the early years, Charles Fraser was better at attracting attention than securing customers or financing. He worked tirelessly to promote his ideas and his enterprise by cultivating the media. Fraser was good copy—articulate, voluble, argumentative, controversial, accessible, and never reluctant to expound his views at length. By attracting attention, he magnified his successes and enhanced Sea Pines' prospects. Fraser's gift for publicity and the attractiveness of his venture, however, did not alone secure widespread notice for Sea Pines. A lot of hard work was required to build a national image, especially since most editors "had not only never heard of Sea Pines, they had never heard of Hilton Head and were not real sure about South Carolina."[41]

Sea Pines first attracted attention for its plans, which Fraser zealously promoted among the design and planning fraternity. In 1957 his plantation was the only residential and recreational community to be exhibited at the International Urban Design Conference. Two years later the plans for Sea Pines were cited for excellence by the American Society of Landscape Architects, and in 1960 they were praised in an article in *Progressive Architecture.*[42] Not many prospective customers, however, were aware of design awards or articles in architectural journals. But they did read *Sports Illustrated,* which provided Fraser's big breakthrough on the national scene in 1962 with an article that lavishly praised the fledgling project as "second to none" among leisure-oriented communities being developed in the United States, with "one of the finest courses on the Atlantic seaboard."[43] This put Sea Pines on the map, along with Hilton Head, and stories followed in magazines and newspapers across the nation. *Fortune,* another publication that reached many of Fraser's potential customers, extolled Sea Pines Plantation in 1967 as a "rare holdout against tasteless commercialism" in an article entitled "Charlie Fraser's Island Paradise."[44]

Everything undertaken at Sea Pines was part of Fraser's marketing effort. Grand plans, good design, environmental sensitivity, golf and other amenities—all contributed to attracting customers and selling them land.[45] Fraser's skill at public relations was an enormous asset because his basic advertising strategy was to extol the beautiful mix of nature and people that was being created at Sea Pines. His efforts were so successful in attracting attention that they changed the Sea Pines market from potential buyers interested in vacation cottages to year-round residents, from middle-class families to affluent retired couples, and from the immediate region to the nation and beyond. Drawn by the publicity Fraser generated in national publications and by word of mouth among people who had visited the lush island, those who came to Sea Pines redefined its market. Many were from the Northeast and Midwest, and they tended to be older and more affluent than the original target population, which was the expanding market for vacation homes in Georgia and South Carolina.

These changes were not a result of Fraser's marketing strategy but rather fortuitous, and they created opportunities far beyond his original plans. While he had not anticipated the kind of clients who became his primary customers, Fraser adapted quickly to the exciting possibilities offered by this more extensive market. As he admits, his "marketing strategy was dictated by who got attracted to Sea Pines. It shifted from resort to retirement, and to higher-income purchasers."[46] These new market segments, along with the broader geographical base, promised higher rewards: "When we shifted to a national market, it at least tripled the number of high-income families moving here, and added a very stimulating diversity of people."[47]

NEW MONEY AND OPPORTUNITIES

National publicity, a widening market, an increasing volume of visitors, and rising sales opened the door to more stable financing. With more golfers coming to Sea Pines, lenders were willing to underwrite another golf course in 1964. The new layout, Sea Marsh, was financed by a land development investment firm and a Savannah savings and loan bank.[48] Sea Marsh opened hundreds of acres of interior forest land for additional development of fairway lots. The following year, Fraser raised $1.5 million from Allstate Insurance in exchange for preferred stock, but this arrangement proved very constraining, requiring the retirement of existing debt and providing an effective veto for Allstate over Sea Pines' projects.

Figure 3.1 - Sea Pines Land Sales, 1960–1968

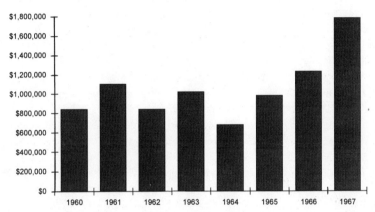

Far more productive was Sea Pines' financial relationship with Travelers Insurance Company, which provided $3 million in sorely needed long-term financing in 1965, the first installment in what became an investment of more than $15 million by Travelers.[49] Funds from Travelers also permitted Fraser to buy back Allstate's preferred shares. Now Fraser was able to develop the plantation and market his product more aggressively. During the next few years, Sea Pines came of age, realizing much of Charles Fraser's dream and filling Sea Pines' coffers as business boomed. Sales of land, homes, and condominiums increased rapidly in the years after 1965; resort revenues were rising; and property values were escalating. By 1968 an oceanfront lot purchased in 1957 for $5,350 was resold for $34,000—more than a sixfold increase in a bit more than a decade—and choice property on the beach was selling for $50,000 a year later.

The centerpiece of the surge of activity after 1965 was Harbour Town, an intimate circular boat basin ringed by shops and housing, with a red and white lighthouse that became Sea Pines' photogenic trademark. Completed in 1969,

Harbour Town was the most dramatic, most expensive, and most successful amenity built to enhance interior real estate values at Sea Pines. Stores and restaurants and boats, along with another golf course and tennis club, drew people deep into the plantation, where Fraser offered potential customers a variety of housing and lots, ranging from town houses on the harbor to homesites on fairways, sea marshes, and the sparkling waters of Calibogue Sound.

Planning for Harbour Town began in 1965, and Charles Fraser was determined to build something unique, an activity center that would be as singular as his melding of nature, homesites, and recreation elsewhere in the plantation. Harbour Town was influenced by the Italian Riviera but built in coastal Carolina style with town houses patterned after those of Charleston, with their walled gardens, and shops painted in a variety of muted pastel hues reminiscent of Charleston's Rainbow Row. In Harbour Town, Fraser and his associates took a marina and created a work of art, "easily the most beautiful" of the hundreds of boat basins along the east coast with its "apartments, homes, villas and tiny shops, all painted in subtle shades of white, pink, blue and salmon, giving the town a neo-Portofino look."[50] Of Harbour Town's many visual delights, the 90-foot working lighthouse was Charles Fraser's favorite. "It doesn't need to be there," he explains, "but it's essential for appropriate romance. Little harbors ought to have lighthouses."[51]

This little harbor was costly—$7.5 million just to dredge and line the boat basin that berthed eighty pleasure craft. Densities were high; by design Harbour Town was a concentrating place with 450 housing units on 120 acres. The village was oriented toward pedestrians rather than automobiles, which were relegated to the background. Walkways, grassy areas, gardens, benches, and food stands enticed the visitor to stroll around Harbour Town's shops and boats. Despite the relatively high densities, the area felt spacious rather than concentrated. This too was by design. As in the development of homes elsewhere in Sea Pines, Fraser and his planners located Harbour Town's town houses to reduce crowding and enhance views. By staggering individual buildings and using landscape courts "radiating from the harbor edge around which town houses and condominium apartments were sited," the designers provided each unit with "a direct view and physical access to the harbor through a landscaped court."[52] In the process, they almost tripled valuable frontage real estate around the harbor, providing 5,600 feet of building fronting the 2,000-foot marina.

Completing the picture at Harbour Town was the finishing hole of a new golf course, framed on the left by magnificent vistas of Calibogue Sound with Fraser's lighthouse rising behind the green. For Harbour Town Links, Fraser wanted something special, ideally a course designed by one of the biggest names in professional golf. "What an attraction," he mused, "the first Jack Nicklaus-designed golf course might be."[53] Nicklaus, interested but not yet ready to embark on a second career in golf course design, suggested Pete Dye, an unconventional designer who would make his reputation on Hilton Head.[54] Dye brought a new perspective to designing golf courses, laying them out so that they rewarded precision and skill rather than power alone. Drawing his inspiration from the links courses in Scotland, he made the greens small, the fairways narrow, and the hazards innovative with railroad ties and waste bunkers. What resulted has been described by one golf writer as "moody, scenic, mossy, watery, creaturish, inventive, demanding . . . a course to strike the old golfer with new fantasies."[55] And Fraser had something special: the signature course of the most successful golf designer of his time, a lovely layout consistently ranked among the top courses in the United States.

While Harbour Town and Dye's course were under construction, Fraser sought to attract additional attention to Sea Pines by staging a professional golf tournament. Nicklaus agreed to play on the course he had helped design, as did Arnold Palmer, then the reigning monarch of professional golf. Fraser grandly dubbed his tournament the Heritage Classic, offered a purse of $100,000, and prayed that Harbour Town Links would be finished in time. In a fitting metaphor for an enterprise in which ideas often outdistanced reality, Sea Pines had a golf tournament firmly set before having the golf course it was to be played on. After a mad scramble to get the course ready, the Heritage Classic was played over Thanksgiving in 1969. Along with Palmer and Nicklaus and the rest of the touring pros came scores of sportswriters to report on the tournament, be wined and dined, and see the glories of Sea Pines. In addition to golf, Fraser provided a bit of pageantry and instant tradition: an opening parade of officials complete with bagpipers clad in tartan kilts, followed by the firing of a cannon before golfers tackled Dye's untested course. Fraser's luck held—the winner was Arnold Palmer, earning his first victory in eighteen months, and the sentimental favorite of the golf-crazed senior citizens who lived in Sea Pines. Palmer's victory brought a great deal of free publicity to the Heritage, Harbour Town Links, Sea Pines, and Hilton Head. As one Sea Pines official exulted, "We got the big press down to cover it and then Palmer wins it. What else could you ask?"[56]

The Heritage was both the perfect means for getting Fraser the publicity he wanted and the kind of attraction that was right for Sea Pines residents, present and potential. With only 2,500 residents on the island, the first Heritage drew a gallery of 5,000, and succeeding tournaments lured steadily larger crowds and more publicity for Sea Pines and Hilton Head. In 1974 the Heritage was rescheduled out of the football season and into the early spring, a strategic move designed to get the tournament on national television. Now millions were exposed to the lush woods, understated elegance, dramatic vistas, and red and white lighthouse behind the grandstand at the eighteenth hole. Sea Pines lost money on the first few Heritage tournaments but gained reams of favorable publicity, hordes of visitors, and many customers. At the second Heritage, narrow town house lots along the eighteenth fairway were sold out at $22,000, while advertisements for property in the wooded areas opened for development by the construction of Harbour Town Links emphasized that "lots fronting on the fairways have been set back sufficiently to allow for spectator viewing of the Heritage Classic played annually on this course."[57]

FROM COMMUNITY TO RESORT

Harbour Town and the Heritage marked the emergence of Sea Pines as a complete resort offering a wide range of accommodations and recreation. More visitors were attracted to the plantation; there was more to do, and there were more places to stay. Whereas privacy and the splendor of the natural surroundings had been the hallmarks of the initial development of Sea Pines, now the emphasis was on activity and man-made facilities. A growing proportion of the housing being built was condominiums, many of which were available to vacationers for short-term rental. Condos were clustered in three locations, which increasingly catered more to tourists than residents. The units around the Plantation Club were convenient to golf at the original courses and to the beach. Another set of condominiums was located at South Beach, which was also developed jointly with Travelers. At the southern tip of the island, South Beach offered water sports, a lovely stretch of beach, ocean views, and magnificent sunsets. Here Fraser's inspiration was the quaint New England fishing village with a few shops and restaurants crowded around a small harbor, along with some very Hilton Head–like touches—a tennis club, a swimming pool, and 455 condominiums on 145 acres. By design, Sea Pines' hub of tourist activity was Harbour Town, where shops, restaurants, golf, boats, tennis, bike rentals, and real estate sales were in close proximity. Lodgings were available over the shops and in elegant apartments and town houses ringing the harbor and flanking the eighteenth fairway of Harbour Town Golf Links.

With the proliferation of condominiums, the nature of development in Sea Pines changed. To sell condos, Sea Pines had to attract renters, since most condominiums were not occupied by their owners, and the decision to buy was heavily conditioned by a property's ability to generate rental income. Luring renters meant more emphasis on a resort economy for Sea Pines and Hilton Head—developing more things for tourists to do. The signs that proclaimed "Sea Pines, a Private Residential Community" disappeared, replaced by a reception center for rental guests at the main entrance. Along with the golf and tennis, the beach club, riding stables, cycling, sightseeing boats at Harbour Town, tabby ruins, fishing, bird watching, and the forest preserve were aggressively promoted to assure tourists that no one need be bored in paradise.

To showcase Sea Pines and draw more visitors, tennis was developed along the same lines as golf with the Heritage. A year after the opening of the Sea Pines Racquet Club in Harbour Town, the four top-ranking players in the world competed in the Sea Pines Tournament of Champions. The tournament was aired on national television and was the first major televised tennis event played at a resort location. In 1973 Fraser snared the Family Circle tennis tournament, the richest event on the women's professional tour and another opportunity for an annual airing of Sea Pines' attractions on national television. By then, Sea Pines had seventy tennis courts, making it the largest tennis resort in the world. And with two major televised sporting events, Sea Pines orchestrated broadcasts that were "a loving commercial, with cameras playing over Harbour Town and Calibogue Sound and other features of the plantation."[58]

By the time Harbour Town was built, Sea Pines was largely completed. More would be added, including a fourth golf course in whose design Arnold Palmer would have a hand and which would be for the exclusive use of Sea Pines residents. Hundreds of interior lots would be opened for development along the fairways of Harbour Town Links, Sea Marsh, and the residents' Club Course. Just how far Sea Pines had come was indicated by the success of the Club Course area. Although they were located on Sea Pines' least attractive and last-developed land, the 750 new homesites sold quickly in the early 1970s. A shopping and office center and many individual projects were still to be developed, but the basic shape of the plantation was fixed, as was its residential and developmental capacity, unless significant changes were made in the plans and covenants.

Quality worked; Sea Pines was a success. Fraser's vision had taken shape and met the test of the market. Instances of professional recognition of Sea Pines multiplied, measures of success that Charles Fraser valued as much as customers and investors. Among other notices, Sea Pines was cited for excellence in private-community planning in 1968 by the American Institute of Architects "in recognition of private entrepreneurs who create an orderly environment and sense of place through design of cohesive and meaningful communities."[59]

In succeeding beyond anyone's expectations, including Fraser's, Sea Pines set the standard for the rest of Hilton Head. Sea Pines *was* Hilton Head. The identification between the island itself and the development was so strong that Fraser marketed them interchangeably: "Come home to Hilton Head. It's a great place to visit—but to live here is to love it."[60] Sea Pines was the pioneering and flagship community; as it would go, so would Hilton Head go, at least for the first quarter century of the island's development. Sea Pines not only set the pace but established a set of expectations for Hilton Head that would frame all sorts of development issues as the island prospered and grew.

Charles Fraser shaped Hilton Head not only physically and aesthetically but socially and politically because of the kind of people he attracted to the island. He was always forthright about his desire to attract a higher class of clientele than frequented most beach resorts. At Sea Pines, he would succeed beyond his wildest dreams, luring wealthy people from the upper ranks of the corporate world, the military, and the professions. Because Fraser had succeeded so dramatically, creating a luxuriant paradise for the privileged, some would see him as "an elitist of the worst type—catering to fanciful whims of the well-to-do at the expense of many others less fortunate."[61] Critics would dismiss Sea Pines as trivial at best and socially irresponsible at worst. To condemn Fraser for doing well what private developers do, which is to build homes and communities for those who can afford to buy them, is to expect more of the private sector than can be delivered at a profit. Fraser, in fact, was more socially responsible than most real estate developers, but he understood that the quality of a private community was closely related to the resources of its residents.

Other developers on Hilton Head, particularly the other development companies with their large holdings, followed Fraser's lead, seeking well-off vacationers and affluent retirees. Their efforts combined with Fraser's success at Sea Pines to skew development toward the upper end of the income scale, setting the direction in which the community would grow and the kind of place Hilton Head would become. Because a handful of development companies controlled almost all of the land, private determinations had more effect than in most communities on the kind of people who could and could not live on Hilton Head and the adjacent areas and what kinds of services were available. Private decisions molded the set of interests that would be articulated and the demands that would be generated in the developing area.

Beyond the inherent interest of Sea Pines's evolution and the continuing development it paved the way and set the standards for, the development process deserves study because the private sector is now more important than ever in determining what kind of places are built in America and who can live in them. Private controls, private provision of infrastructure, and private rather than public services—the hallmarks of the development of Sea Pines and Hilton Head Island—are increasingly the norm in the United States, especially in large-scale development. The experience of Sea Pines and Hilton Head are instructive about what the private sector can and cannot accomplish. Attractive environments for those who can afford them are far easier to develop than places with housing and services for everyone who is part of a functioning community. Fraser set in motion a complex process that generated demand for housing that Sea Pines and other plantations could not supply, needs for public services that private companies could not provide, and a desire for public authority in the form of responsive local government that the private sector could not satisfy.

NOTES

1. Charles E. Fraser, "Basic Data on the Sea Pines Development," 1.
2. Charles Fraser owned 79 percent of the company's stock, and the remaining 21 percent was held by his brother, Joseph B. Fraser Jr.
3. Quoted in Mary Kendall Hilton, "Islander: Joseph B. Fraser, Sr.," 12.
4. Charles E. Fraser, interview, August 15, 1987.
5. Donald O'Quinn, quoted in "Memories of Hilton Head Island."
6. Quoted in McNeill, "Faith in Island 30 Years Ago Key to Richardson's Success."
7. Greer, *The Sands of Time: A History of Hilton Head Island,* 63.
8. Charles E. Fraser, "A Thoroughly Incomplete Chronology of Hilton Head Island."
9. The final price was $1,011,000 for 1,281 acres, with a $50,000 down payment and the rest financed at 4 percent for ten years with a two-year deferral of payment of the loan. The Sea Pines Land Company was organized for this purchase. Half of its stock was held by James C. Self, president of Greenwood Mills, who provided $100,000 for the down payment and operating capital.
10. Galehouse, "Land Planning for Large-Scale Residential Development," 13.
11. Sea Pines Plantation Company, "Jobs for the Future," 20.
12. Charles E. Fraser, "Basic Data on the Sea Pines Development," 1.
13. Charles E. Fraser, quoted in "Second-Home Communities," 144.
14. Quoted in Horn, "Nothing to Do—but Enjoy Yourself," 62.
15. Beachfront lots measured between 15,000 and 20,000 square feet; the rest were 10,000 to 12,000 square feet. Prices covered the costs of paving the

streets and creating walkways to the beach. See Sea Pines Plantation Company, "Introductory Price Lists."

16. Quoted in Grafton, "Exclusively Charles Fraser," 13.

17. Self was president of Greenwood Mills in Greenwood, S.C.

18. Self and his partners were organized as Ferris Service Corporation of Greenwood, S.C.

19. Quoted in Horn, "Nothing to Do—but Enjoy Yourself," 64.

20. Quoted in ibid.

21. Quoted in ibid.

22. Joseph B. Fraser Jr., interview.

23. A room on the ocean for two with breakfast and dinner cost $30 during the inn's first season; the price fell to $22 during the winter.

24. Craighead, interview. Gordon Craighead was recruited by Fraser in 1966 to run resort operations at Sea Pines.

25. Sea Pines Plantation Company, "Land Use Restrictions," 1.

26. Sea Pines Plantation Company, "Sea Pines Plantation: Community Basic Data," 29.

27. Charles E. Fraser, "Basic Data on the Sea Pines Development," 7.

28. Charles E. Fraser, *The Art of Community Building,* 12.

29. Harold Depkin, vice-president for sales, Sea Pines Plantation Company, quoted in Liston, "The Fraser/Sea Pines Concept," 71.

30. Charles E. Fraser, "Confidential Policy Statement on Architecture, Design and Construction," 2.

31. Quoted in Bisher, "The Island World of Charles Fraser," 72.

32. McPhee, *Encounters with the Archdruid,* 92.

33. Corkern, interview.

34. Quoted in Reichley, "Charlie Fraser's Island Paradise," 173.

35. Charles E. Fraser, quoted in Olson, "BT Interview: Charles Fraser," 15.

36. Littlejohn, interview.

37. Quoted in Grafton, "Exclusively Charles Fraser," 13.

38. Quoted in McGrath, "Sea Pines Plantation Alumni," 26.

39. Quoted in Grafton, "Exclusively Charles Fraser," 13.

40. Sea Pines Plantation Company, "Sea Pines Plantation Price List," 1–2.

41. John Gettys Smith, "Sea Pines Plantation Alumni," 28.

42. See Rowan, "Design of Exterior Spaces," 108–126.

43. Horn, "Nothing to Do—but Enjoy Yourself," 58, 64.

44. Reichley, "Charlie Fraser's Island Paradise," 171.

45. For a general discussion of the marketing of Sea Pines during the company's first dozen years, see James Playsted Wood, *This Little Pig,* 132–144.

46. Charles E. Fraser, interview, August 15, 1987.

47. Quoted in "Charles Fraser Looks to the Future He'll Help," 29.

48. The lenders were Continental Mortgage Investors and First Federal Savings and Loan Association of Savannah.

49. Sea Pines and Travelers created the Lighthouse Beach Company, of which 49.5 percent was owned by Sea Pines and 50.5 percent by Travelers, to develop what became Harbour Town and South Beach. Under the terms of the joint venture, Travelers provided the investment capital in return for land, while Sea Pines supplied planning, development, and management expertise.

50. Price, "Slightly South of Heaven, S.C.," 26.

51. Quoted in Drake, "Developer Charles Fraser Learns Secret of Turning Beaches into Gold," 56.

52. Galehouse, "Land Planning for Large-Scale Residential Development," 14.

53. Quoted in Bisher, "The Island World of Charles Fraser," 72.

54. Before Harbour Town, Dye and his wife, Alice, had designed a few courses in the Midwest, including the well-regarded Crooked Stick in Carmel, Indiana. Nicklaus assisted Dye at Harbour Town and is sometimes listed as codesigner despite Dye's preeminent role in creating the course.

55. Jenkins, "A Course with Rare Bite," 35.

56. Charles Price, quoted in Littlejohn, "Islander of the Month: Charles Price," 15. Price, a noted golf writer, played a central role in organizing the Heritage Classic. Among the flood of publicity resulting from Palmer's dramatic victory was a glowing article by Jenkins, "Jack's Course Is Arnie's Too," 24–27. For an account of the evolution of the tournament, see Bunton, *The History of the Heritage.*

57. Sea Pines Plantation Company, Advertisement. 26–27.

58. John Gettys Smith, interview.

59. American Institute of Architects, "Citation for Excellence in Private Community Planning to Sea Pines Plantation." A similar award for excellence in private community planning came from the American Society of Landscape Architects in 1974.

60. Charles E. Fraser, *This Other Eden.*

61. Gardo, "Sea Pines Plantation Alumni," 23. Gardo was writing about his first impression of Charles Fraser. He later worked for Sea Pines—between 1973 and 1979.

Chapter Four

Beyond the Sea Pines Gates

Fraser made Sea Pines, Sea Pines made the plantations, the plantations made Hilton Head—thus, Charles Fraser made Hilton Head.

—Vance Fowler, Interview, July 22, 1987

Charles Fraser provided the model for other large landowners on Hilton Head. By the time Sea Pines was an established success, much of the rest of the island was covered with plantations either under construction or marked for future development. All followed Fraser's basic formula with variations depending on location and size. They were private communities catering to affluent homeowners and vacationers, with a mix of residential and recreational development, along with commercial facilities in some plantations. Planning concepts, design practices, and deed covenants borrowed heavily from Sea Pines. Homes were blended into settings and sited to enhance views; muted colors and natural materials were used; dunes and trees were preserved; and man-made amenities were employed to enhance property values. Golf courses, an afterthought at Sea Pines, became centerpieces in the other plantations.

Not only did the other plantations follow in Fraser's footsteps on basic concepts; they depended heavily on Sea Pines to bring them customers. Well into the 1960s, the action on Hilton Head was largely at Sea Pines. Fraser got national attention and Sea Pines advertised widely, attracting vacationers and potential purchasers. As Sea Pines flourished, benefits spread to other plantation companies and entrepreneurs. Sea Pines' blossoming as a resort with sizable clusters of condominiums strongly influenced the other development companies. Condos proliferated, which necessitated attracting more visitors to Hilton Head to provide the rental income that purchasers had been promised. This in turn led developers to join Fraser in the resort business.

The other plantations were also competition for Sea Pines. As they developed, visitors and customers had more choices in places to stay, homesites and condos to purchase, golf courses to play, and other recreational facilities to enjoy. Competition put pressure on Sea Pines to maintain its standards and facilities, especially since the other plantations accepted Sea Pines as the benchmark and sought to surpass the pacesetter. Each offered its package of goodies to entice vacationers and the prime target— purchasers. The flavor of plantation marketing in the heady days of the early 1970s is captured by an advertisement for Palmetto Dunes, which was developed along the ocean north of Sea Pines. After presenting the menu at the plantation's restaurant under the heading "body food," the other half of the full-page ad has a "living" menu for "soul food." "Appetizers" were the golf course and 3 miles of beach; "salads" were tennis courts, swimming pool, fishing, and boating; for "dessert" there was abundant wildlife. At the heart of the menu were what Hilton Head's plantations were all about—the "entrées" of homesites, condominiums, villa rentals, and hotel rooms.[1]

FOLLOWING THE LEADER

Most important among the other major developers was the Hilton Head Company.[2] Two decades after the original purchases from Loomis and Thorne, the Hilton Head Company held 11,000 acres, which accounted for 75 percent of the undeveloped land on the island.[3] The company was owned by the Hack and McIntosh families. Olin T. McIntosh Sr. had served as president after the split with the Frasers until 1962 and was chairman of the board until his death in 1966 at the age of eighty-five. As McIntosh's role diminished, Fred Hack became the dominant figure in the Hilton Head Company. As much as Sea Pines reflected Charles Fraser, the Hilton Head Company was a projection of Fred Hack.

In striking contrast to Fraser, Hack was, as one observer noted, "a quiet and deliberate man who seeks always to avoid the limelight."[4] He was personable and forthright. But he was not imaginative. Hilton Head's potential for a special and highly profitable kind of development had eluded him from the start. His company's slowness to seize opportunities was a reflection of Hack's methodical style. He was not a promoter, and he did not understand public relations or marketing. While Fraser's growing corps of publicists was spreading the word about the wonders of Sea Pines near and far, the Hilton Head Company plodded along with a part-timer handling publicity. Equally anemic were Hack's efforts to market his land in competition with the sophisticated research and selling operation that Fraser developed. As one of his associates points out, "Hack backed into development and never learned the business as Fraser did."[5] Hack saw what Fraser was doing and followed as best he could, pulled along by the momentum generated by Sea Pines.

Hack, unlike Fraser, was ambivalent about developing Hilton Head. "We were happy here," he told an interviewer, "long before this era of building began."[6] Fraser saw nature as the canvas on which to paint his creations, and Hilton Head provided him the superb raw materials to shape to his design. For Hack, nature was more intrinsically valuable and best appreciated with minimal intrusion by man. Hack cherished the island and its history; he spoke wistfully of Hilton Head before the changes brought by development, recalling "the most beautiful wilderness you ever saw" and how "my family hated to see it opened to the public because we were enjoying the island by ourselves."[7] Fraser's success left Hack with little choice but to follow the leader, but Hack made no secret of the fact that he "personally would have been happy with far less development than the economics of the day require."[8]

Ambivalent, limited, but gamely determined to demonstrate that he too could play the plantation game, Hack changed course after Fraser paved the way with Sea Pines. He abandoned the Hilton Head Company's piecemeal approach to land development in favor of large planned communities on the Sea Pines model. Even more than Fraser, Hack was handicapped by inadequate financing. The Hilton Head Company was land-poor; Hack was hard-pressed to raise money for the heavy front-end costs of large-scale community development. Lenders who were chary of Fraser, with his grand plans, were far less interested in Hack, who had trouble even developing a strategy for his business, so the Hilton Head Company survived by securing small amounts of capital from a variety of sources and by selling land. Choice properties were sold off to make ends meet—including the gorgeous southern end of the island, which went to Fraser; the golf and inn operation at Hack's Port Royal Plantation; and the golf course at what would become Shipyard Plantation.

Hack's initial venture in large-scale development was Port Royal Plantation, begun in 1962 on 1,000 acres on the northeast corner of the island. The location was attractive, with 3 miles of beachfront on the Atlantic and Port Royal Sound, lush woods, serene marshes, and historic ruins in abundance. Port Royal was built on the site of Civil War forts, whose earthworks were still visible. Golf came before the plantation and, like so much of what happened at the Hilton Head Company, in response to developments at Sea Pines. After James Self invested in golf at Sea Pines, another businessman from Greenwood, C. Y. Thomason, acquired land from Hack for a golf course and built an inn on the ocean for vacationing golfers.

Port Royal was Hack's showcase, the place he planned "every millimeter and inch of the way," the result of his "painstaking care and nurtured development plus his idealism and unfaltering attention."[9] Whatever the intentions, the initial results at Port Royal suffered in comparison with Sea Pines. Hack was seriously handicapped by his chronic funding problems as well as his lack of appreciation for the importance of details and appearance in marketing. In 1964 "Port Royal had no gate; utility lines were just going in and were jarring to the eye. No one knew Port Royal was there, and there was no shrubbery or eye appeal."[10] Hack was persuaded to dress up the plantation, but his marketing remained primitive, and he was unable to draw much attention to Port Royal despite its beautiful setting and historic sites. The journalists Fraser enticed to Hilton Head went to Sea Pines, wrote about Sea Pines, and thought Hilton Head *was* Sea Pines; most never knew Port Royal existed.

Sea Pines might have gotten most of the attention, but Port Royal inevitably got some of the business that Fraser was luring to Hilton Head. As more visitors came to the island, they discovered that there was more there than Sea Pines. Port Royal also had wide beaches, challenging golf, majestic forests, peaceful marshes, and shimmering lagoons. Hack's ability to capitalize on these opportunities was enhanced in 1967 when he acquired Thomason's franchise for the golf course and inn for $1 million. Resort facilities were expanded, and work was begun on another golf course. In promoting Port Royal, Hack emphasized that the plantation was different from Sea Pines with its multiplying condos and growing hordes of tourists. Port Royal was presented as a quiet uncrowded resort. Sea Pines might be the spot to visit, but Port Royal was the place to live. Property owners came first; recreational facilities were not overrun with transients; and golf was less affected by the elements since Port Royal's location on relatively high land kept its golf courses dry when Sea Pines' low-lying fairways were soggy from heavy rains. Hack's ads also claimed that Port Royal's covenants and design standards protected property owners while providing them with more freedom than Sea Pines.

With Sea Pines drawing more and more people to Hilton Head, Port Royal prospered. By 1971 the Hilton Head Company had sold more than 400 of Port Royal's planned 700 lots and had two golf courses in operation along with the Port Royal Inn and a few beachfront condos. But Port Royal was not another of Sea Pines. Fred Hack's plantation was far less distinctive, both in general design and in its individual components. Architectural controls in Port Royal were looser than in Sea Pines in provisions and implementation. No counterpart to Charles Fraser existed in the Hilton Head Company with respect to concern for design and aesthetics, and Fred Hack was less willing than Fraser to lose a sale on architectural grounds. As a result, despite the general emphasis on wood and earth tones, Port Royal does not impart the distinctive visual sense of Sea Pines. It looks more like an affluent suburb than Charles Fraser's work of art.

In sharp contrast with Port Royal and its emphasis on single-family homes and shielding residents from tourists was the Hilton Head Company's second major development, located on 800 hundred acres north of Sea Pines. Begun in 1970, Shipyard Plantation was designed to compete directly with Sea Pines as a golf and tennis resort attracting short-term visitors. Along with twenty-seven holes of golf, Shipyard would have a tennis club with twenty courts and super-star Billie Jean King. "Shipyard Surf and Racquet Club," proclaimed one ad, "isn't just being built for a King. King is helping build it. . . . Soon to become the King of Clubs."[11] More than 1,200 condominiums were included in plans announced in 1970, along with a 300-room hotel. Although it was planned for substantially higher densities than Sea Pines or Port Royal, Shipyard neverthe-less sought to sell lush tranquility: "In the green heart of this quiet island," ran another ad, "lies a new residential plantation called Shipyard. . . . Within its stillness you can build a home, buy a condominium, enjoy the beach, thwack a tennis ball and curse a water hazard. . . . This is where the action isn't."[12]

Development of Shipyard was complicated because choice properties had already been developed piecemeal by the Hilton Head Company. Most unfortu-nate for a resort that was supposed to compete with Sea Pines was lack of ac-cess to the beach. The Hilton Head Company had sold all of the oceanfront lots before developing Shipyard Plantation. To remedy this lack of foresight, Hack sought to repurchase the two northernmost beachfront lots, which had been bought by a local merchant, Wilbert Roller. A shrewd dealer, Roller drove a hard bargain, trading his lots for a large tract of land that was later developed to the substantial benefit of the Roller family fortunes. As a result, Shipyard had only 500 feet of seashore compared to Sea Pines' 3 miles.

A third part of the Hilton Head Company's holdings was developed by the McIntosh family as Spanish Wells Plantation. The McIntoshes were sailors and wanted to live near deep water. In 1961 they took title to 360 acres of company land on a scenic peninsula on the west side of the island bounded by Calibogue Sound and Broad Creek, an area where Spaniards had reputedly filled their casks with fresh water three centuries earlier.[13] Spanish Wells was planned as a residential community built around boating and a nine-hole golf course. The site was too small for Spanish Wells to be a major development, compared with the other large plantations on Hilton Head, and the family was not interested in resort or commercial development; Spanish Wells had no condominiums, and its golf course was private. Nor was the project the principal business interest of the McIntosh family, as the Hilton Head Company was to Hack and Sea Pines was to Fraser.[14] Lots were large for Hilton Head, a minimum of one acre, so that each property on the water had ample frontage for a dock.[15] Spaciousness was the most distinctive aspect of Spanish Wells, a private and secluded place of magnificent trees and sweeping views of water and sky. Its size and location kept Spanish Wells off center stage as Hilton Head Island grew, which was one of its attractions to residents. The development's beauty underscored that Hilton Head's natural delights did not need the artistry of Charles Fraser to be enjoyed by those wealthy enough to afford a choice piece of paradise.

In the mid-1960s only one large tract of property was not owned by companies controlled by Fraser, Hack, and McIntosh—the 1,900-acre hunting preserve acquired half a century earlier by a group of Southern sportsmen. Strategically located between Broad Creek and the Atlantic in the middle of the island, the parcel ran along the ocean for almost 3 miles. Little had disturbed the land since the Leamington Plantation had returned to nature after the Civil War, except for the periodic forays of hunters stalking deer and quail. Ownership was diffused. The original combine of hunters had created the Hilton Head Agricultural Company to acquire the land, and their holdings in the company were widely distributed among family members and others who had purchased shares.

Early in 1966 the directors of the Hilton Head Agricultural Company decided to sell their land. Because of growth on the island, the club's hunting days were numbered, and the loosely organized combine was in no position to participate directly in the development of the property. They decided to take advantage of the substantial increase in their land's value in the wake of Sea Pines' blossoming. One prospective buyer was Charles Fraser, but his interest was tempered by the steady erosion of the property's beachfront. Fraser was outbid in 1967 by a group of businessmen and doctors from Greenwood who offered $1,000 an acre. The new owners formed Palmetto Dunes Corporation and began planning the development of property under the leadership of William T. Gregory. In what was to become the standard arrival message of new developers on Hilton Head, Gregory announced that Palmetto Dunes would be "equal to, or better than anything previously carried out elsewhere on the island."[16]

Palmetto Dunes was conceived as a more intensive vacation community than Sea Pines. The plans called for large resort hotels and three times as many condominiums as single-family homes. In combining a resort with a residential community, Lewis Clarke, the landscape designer who prepared the overall plan for Palmetto Dunes, learned from Sea Pines where resort and residential functions were mixed together. At Palmetto Dunes, hotels, villas, golf clubhouses, and tennis courts were located in a resort corridor that ran from the ocean to a marina on Broad Creek. The corridor was open to the public, while access to single-family housing was controlled by gates, thus reducing friction between resort activities and residential areas. This innovative arrangement permitted Palmetto Dunes to market its residential areas as more private than those in Sea Pines, even though its 2,000 acres would be planned to accommodate more visitors in less than half the area of Sea Pines.

Gregory and his associates also reached out boldly to outdo Sea Pines in other respects. They hired Robert Trent Jones, the dean of American golf course architects, to design the first of three projected golf courses. Palmetto Dunes also challenged Sea Pines with a lavish tennis facility that would eventually be directed by Rod Laver, the Australian tennis great whose fame eclipsed that of Stan Smith, Fraser's resident tennis guru. And Palmetto Dunes' planners rearranged nature to meet the needs of people on a far larger scale than anything undertaken at Sea Pines, including Harbour Town. Palmetto Dunes was shaped around a 10-mile network of saltwater canals, lagoons, and lakes designed to drain the extensive soggy bottom lands on the tract.[17] More important for the developers, the waterways enhanced the value of interior property by providing attractive vistas; and dredging canals and lagoons produced 1.6 million cubic yards of sand, which was pumped along the ocean to bolster Palmetto Dunes' badly eroded stretch of beach.

Construction of the inland water system and building up the beach made Palmetto Dunes' front-end costs particularly punishing. Gregory and his associates soon came to grips with the sobering financial realities of large-scale real estate development, as they were unable to generate sufficient income to service their debts to the Florida financing company that underwrote the initial development of the plantation. Palmetto Dunes' notes were acquired in 1969 by Phipps Land Company, a subsidiary of Bessemer Securities Corporation, which was already involved on Hilton Head with loans to Fraser and substantial landholdings in Sea Pines.[18] Even with additional financing from Phipps, the Greenwood group barely survived completion of the golf course and the major building projects. They were neophytes in the development business, a Phipps consultant concluded, and their venture was "under-financed, poorly . . . and shabbily managed."[19] At the end of 1970, Phipps bought out the original developers. Success, the Greenwood group learned, was not assured by innovative ideas and an attractive hunk of real estate. Besting Sea Pines was easier said than done, and they lacked the requisite skills, especially the ability to command financing commensurate with their plans.

Phipps Land installed an experienced resort developer and manager as president early in 1972.[20] Robert C. Onorato was aggressive, articulate, and self-confident; he loved what he was doing and was eager to have a whack at Charles Fraser and Sea Pines. Onorato's marketing approach was simple and effective.

Instead of competing with Fraser on all fronts, Palmetto Dunes would attempt to take advantage of Sea Pines' national image and marketing. Let Fraser attract visitors to the island, then Onorato would lure them to Palmetto Dunes, where things were done better. Under Onorato's leadership, Palmetto Dunes hit its stride. Another golf course was built, villa and lot sales generated increasing income, and the island's first resort hotel was completed. Palmetto Dunes would not rival Sea Pines, especially as a place to live; but the attractive community, with its heavy emphasis on vacationers and energetic leadership, played an important part in accelerating resort development on Hilton Head.

At the same time that Sea Pines was drawing customers to Hilton Head for Palmetto Dunes, Port Royal, and Shipyard Plantation, Fraser's success was rapidly reducing the amount of land he had available for sale. Intensive development at Harbour Town and South Beach had increased the total number of housing units, but the supply of residential parcels was finite, and they were selling fast in the early 1970s. Land sales were the profitable aspect of community development, and Fraser was eager to acquire more property on the island. One of his efforts was checked when he was outbid for Palmetto Dunes, and another failed when he was unable to acquire part of the Hilton Head Company following the death of Olin McIntosh Sr.[21] Fraser finally succeeded in expanding his holdings late in 1971, purchasing almost 4,000 acres on the northeast corner of the island for over $8 million from a group of investors that had acquired the property from the Hilton Head Company. On land rich in history—the site contained Myrtle Bank Plantation, where William Elliott had first cultivated sea island cotton, and Civil War forts and earthworks—Sea Pines would develop a new community, Hilton Head Plantation.

The acquisition provided Fraser with more land on Hilton Head to sell. But the new plantation would not be a clone of Sea Pines. This site was different, primarily an inland mixture of towering woods and open fields. It was not in the same class as Sea Pines as a resort location. Moreover, the success of the interior Club Course area at Sea Pines underscored the interest of retirees and working islanders in attractive housing and recreational facilities in a nonresort setting. Hilton Head Plantation was thus planned primarily for permanent residents rather than resort guests; it was marketed as a "private residential community . . . devoid of high-activity commercial and resort areas," which were be located outside the plantation gates to shield residents from traffic and transients.[22] Land and housing would be less expensive here than at Sea Pines, thus broadening Fraser's market.

Fraser's new venture was a smash hit when it opened in the spring of 1973, with the initial 125 lots selling immediately. "It was like a carnival," recalls one executive; "we literally had people putting their names in a hat—and we drew them out one at a time in order to discuss property. We sold everything we had released that first day and there were about 30 to 50 people who were on hand but who couldn't be served because of the demand."[23] But the carnival proved to have a short season. Just as Fraser's new plantation was moving into full gear, the national economy took a sharp turn downward, severely constraining all development activities on Hilton Head. With hard times came high interest rates and a sharp drop in sales at Hilton Head Plantation. Overextended by real estate ventures undertaken off the island and under severe financial pressure, Fraser lost Hilton Head Plantation to his bankers in 1975. The community did not blossom until the 1980s.[24]

SPREADING THE BENEFITS

Outside the plantations, development was strongly influenced by the major companies, especially Sea Pines, which was the magnet drawing people and businesses to the island. Most land developed in the two decades following the establishment of Sea Pines was either inside plantations or owned by the major companies. Sea Pines and the Hilton Head Company had substantial holdings outside the plantations, and they controlled the land adjacent to Sea Pines, the location of almost all the early external development. Some of this land was used directly by the companies, as in the case of Sea Pines and the William Hilton Inn. The rest was sold and developed under conditions imposed through covenants by Sea Pines and the Hilton Head Company. Many of the developers who bought land from the two companies had been associated with Fraser or Hack and shared their concerns for producing a high-quality product and protecting the environment.

Outside developers and other businessmen were also heavily dependent on the plantations to provide customers. As the plantations went, so went the fortunes of the architects, builders, suppliers, real estate agents, bankers, lawyers, insurance brokers, merchants, restaurateurs, and smaller developers seeking to grab a piece of the basic action with condos and hotels outside the plantations. The relationships were symbiotic. Growth at Sea Pines and the other plantations drove the island's economy, fueling demand for complementary goods and services and also providing the posh settings and recreational facilities that were Hilton Head's basic attractions. Access to plantation golf courses was particularly critical for hotel and resort developers outside the plantation gates, since none had enough land to develop golf on their own property. By the same token, the plantations needed the entrepreneurs they attracted to the island. The companies lacked resources to develop everything themselves; they depended on businesses and professionals to provide essential services and thus make Hilton Head a more attractive place for potential residents and vacationers.

Well into the 1960s, growth outside the plantations was development adjacent to Sea Pines, and the bulk of this activity was in Forest Beach, immediately to the north of Sea Pines. Before the boom, Forest Beach was a checkerboard of vacant lots, beach cottages, and more substantial homes subdivided by sandy lanes off North and South Forest Beach Drive, a narrow and often flooded road that was far from the promenade suggested by the term *beach drive.* About the only elegant features of Forest Beach were the streets that the developers named for French and Spanish explorers and their patrons: Coligny Circle, honoring Admiral Gaspard de Coligny, who sponsored Ribaut's voyage in 1562; Cordillo Parkway, which derived its name from the captain of one of the Spanish ships that reached Port Royal Sound in 1521; and De Ayllon Avenue, named for Lucas Vásquez de Ayllón, who sponsored the initial Spanish expedition along the Carolina coast.

Undeveloped land in Forest Beach had been divided equally when the Frasers separated from the Hilton Head Company. Except for parcels sold before the 1956 division, Fraser wound up with all of the land to the south of Pope Avenue, the road that connected Forest Beach to the main highway, U.S. 278. As Sea Pines developed, much of this land became extremely attractive for commercial and resort development, particularly property along the ocean on South Forest Beach Drive and flanking Pope Avenue. Hack's holdings in Forest Beach offered fewer initial opportunities for profit than Fraser's land. Located north of Pope Avenue, the Hilton Head Company acreage was more distant from Sea Pines, and its land along the ocean in North Forest Beach had already been subdivided and sold for residential development.

Hotels and condominiums transformed Forest Beach from a sleepy string of beach cottages into a booming oceanside resort area. First came the Seacrest on the beach at Coligny Circle, which predated Sea Pines. Wilton Graves built the motel on land acquired from the Hilton Head Company and rebuilt with 30 units in 1962 after a fire, then expanded again to 90 rooms. Next was Fraser's William Hilton Inn, opened in 1959 with 80 rooms on the ocean on South Forest Beach Drive, a half mile from the entrance to Sea Pines. Now Forest Beach was the place to be, and the pace of development quickened over the next decade. The 60-room Adventure Inn was constructed next to the William Hilton Inn in 1963 by Atlantis Development, along with 30 villas next to the hotel on the ocean. Atlantis also built a lighted par-three golf course across South Forest

Beach Drive. Rising land prices and increased opportunities for profit, however, soon doomed the pitch-and-putt course, which made way for an $11 million complex of condominiums and shops. Four buildings with 180 units would be surrounded by lagoons and designed to "rise symbolically from a watery base just as the mythical city of Atlantis once did."[25] Presumably, for their next project Atlantis Development could build the Venus villas rising symbolically from clam shells or the Phoenix condos rising symbolically from the ashes.

Between 1966 and 1972 land prices in South Forest Beach increased sharply. Oceanfront property sold for $275 a foot in 1966; six years later beachside parcels were bringing from $1,200 to $1,800 a front foot. On one of these tracts, 3 acres purchased for $500,000 from Sea Pines, construction began in mid-1972 on a $4 million Holiday Inn with 200 rooms. The developers of the Holiday Inn acquired additional beachfront land from Sea Pines for a $7.5 million condo complex next to their hotel. Along with selling the land for these projects, Fraser contracted with the Holiday Inn to provide golf privileges for its guests at Sea Pines and on the courses to be built at Hilton Head Plantation.

By the time Sea Pines had embarked on the major expansion of resort operations at Harbour Town and South Beach, independent developers had accelerated their land purchases for condominium projects in Forest Beach. Sea Pines was the principal beneficiary of the condo boom, supplying most of the land that was developed south of Pope Avenue and Coligny Circle. As beachfront property disappeared, a second and third row of condos were developed across South Forest Beach Drive. The Hilton Head Beach Club was more than a quarter of mile from the beach, across South Forest Beach Drive and behind the Surf Court Villas. The developer bragged about "the natural beauty of the lush forest"—or what was left of it after constructing eight buildings on less than 3 acres.[26]

As resort facilities multiplied along South Forest Beach, retail development centered on the intersection of Pope Avenue and Forest Beach Drive, the busiest crossroads on Hilton Head and the location of the main public access to the beach. What began as the Richardsons' 2,500-square-foot grocery store slowly evolved into Forest Beach Shopping Center. By 1961 Norris and Lois Richardson had doubled the size of the grocery store and added a laundromat, beauty parlor, and barbershop. Six years later the shopping center had expanded to 100,000 square feet. Along the way, the name was changed to Coligny Plaza to add a dash of history and class. By 1972 Coligny Plaza was a meandering $5 million complex of 40 shops, offices, and a theater; and Richardson could afford to pay $300,000 for 5 acres across the street, on which he planned to build $5 million worth of condominiums and shops.

The Hilton Head Company also benefited from the rapid development of Coligny Plaza, which was on the north side of Pope Avenue and was flanked by land controlled by Fred Hack. In 1972 the Hilton Head Company sold 32 acres next to Coligny Plaza for almost $1 million to a partnership headed by Wilbert Roller, which planned a complex of condominiums and shops. Roller was another homegrown entrepreneur who throve on the business brought to Forest Beach by Sea Pines and the strip of hotels and condos; he parlayed a liquor store and a shrewd business sense into a string of deals, in one of which he had acquired choice property in the heart of Forest Beach in exchange for the strategic parcel that Fred Hack needed to provide beach access for Shipyard Plantation. Across from Roller's land, between Coligny Plaza and Shipyard Plantation, another parcel acquired from the Hilton Head Company became Cordillo Villitas, 50 town houses complete with lagoons. Here the developers were a local architect, lawyer, and builder. By the early 1970s everyone was getting into the development game—grocers and architects, liquor merchants and lawyers—as the growth triggered by Sea Pines promised ever larger profits as more and more land became ripe for conversion into resort and commercial properties.

As plantations and other resort facilities generated more demand for goods and services, commercial development spread from Forest Beach along the main roads. The most strategic location was the traffic circle at the junction of Pope Avenue and U.S. 278, a few hundred yards from the new main gate into Sea Pines, which opened in 1969. Sea Pines built its reception center at the intersection, began a $2.5 million shopping center on 13 acres of adjacent company land in 1973, and sold additional parcels for commercial development along Pope Avenue. The Hilton Head Company also reaped benefits from spillover growth at Sea Pines Circle from its holdings on the north side of Pope Avenue and along U.S. 278. The first of many commercial projects on Hilton Head Company land adjacent to Shipyard Plantation was an executive office park on Pope Avenue that housed the local newspaper and other businesses.

Commerce began to creep along U.S. 278 in the initial phase of what would become almost continuous strip development. In 1973 a trailer park next to Palmetto Dunes gave way to 100,000 square feet of offices; and a shopping center was begun at mid-island on 22 acres acquired from the Hilton Head Company. Off the highway at the northern tip of Hilton Head, Benny Hudson opened a restaurant adjacent to his family's seafood processing plant that would become an island landmark. As tourists and residents flocked to Hudson's dining room overlooking fishing docks and the inland waterway, Wilbert Roller and other high rollers were acquiring property along the highway in anticipation of what "some real estate observers" saw as "the near future's hottest real estate market."[27]

Real estate was the name of the game during the booming early 1970s, and many players wanted a piece of the resort action that was proving so profitable outside Sea Pines. New "resorts" began to sprout around the island following the Forest Beach model—condos built at substantially higher overall densities than prevailed in the plantations, with a swimming pool and a few tennis courts, all done in a vaguely Hilton Head "style" without much grace or space on relatively small plots. Some were little more than housing projects with fancy names. Others, such as the Island Club, actively sought their share of the growing resort business with aggressive marketing aimed at nonresident buyers. The Island Club squeezed 115 condos, tennis courts, and a health club on 25 acres with 1,000 feet of beach next to Port Royal Plantation.[28]

All the new resort developers paid homage to the standards set by the plantation builders. The Island Club's developer lauded the "intelligent concern for preservation of Hilton Head Island's magnificent environment" by its original developers and promised that his project would be "a harmonious marriage of man and nature."[29] Similar thoughts had been repeatedly expressed along Forest Beach. In developing Surf Court Villas, for example, Wilbert Roller had promised that "we are not going to do anything that isn't nice and in keeping with the island's natural setting."[30] The architects often were Corkern or McGinty, who were sometimes partners in resort and commercial projects they designed. Few of these efforts, however, matched the quality and sensitivity that were the hallmarks of Sea Pines and were emulated if not always matched by the other plantations. Sites were too small, settings often pedestrian, development too extensive, and the desire for profits too great to reproduce Sea Pines beyond the plantation gates.

To be sure, a fair amount of the outside development was better designed than what is usually strung along America's highways and beaches. For that, credit was due Fraser and Hack, who exercised some control through covenants on the land they sold outside their planned communities, as well as to the concerned involvement of plantation alumni in many of these projects and to the skill of island architects who did what they could with difficult sites and financial constraints. Nonetheless, too many of the new developments were badly designed and poorly sited, testaments to greed and bad taste; and more would come as growth spread to land beyond the control of Sea Pines and the Hilton Head Company. In turn, ugly development outside the plantations would fuel concerns about growth as the ranks of Hilton Head's residents steadily increased.

Growth inevitably generated more jobs on the island. Normally, a growing economy with a rising labor force fuels demand for housing, and this happened on Hilton Head. But the island did not resemble most self-contained communities with respect to housing. The lion's share of its land was located in plantations whose primary business was selling land for expensive homes and building condos for affluent purchasers. Housing developers outside plantations were far more interested in the resort trade than local workers. This tilt in the housing market served the needs of the well-paid top of the island labor force, professionals and successful business people attracted to Hilton Head by the prospects of living in Sea Pines or one of the other plantations. The bottom of the labor pool was filled in the early years by local blacks, who already had homes on the island or nearby. The gap was in the middle, and the shortage of moderately-priced housing worsened as the island grew. Exacerbating the problem were construction costs 20 percent higher than those in the surrounding area. With mushrooming growth in the early 1970s, demand for a limited supply of inexpensive housing pushed up prices, forcing the island's growing labor force to commute from an ever widening area on the mainland. In 1972 workers building the Island Club were commuting an average of 150 miles daily, leading the project manager to lament that the "largest industry on the island—construction—has little or no housing for its workers."[31]

As their labor needs expanded, the major companies became increasingly concerned about the housing shortage. Sea Pines was the most active, reflecting its role as the largest employer on the island. Some less expensive housing was developed outside the plantation for Sea Pines employees. At Palmetto Dunes, 52 modular units were erected in 1972 for the resort's workers. The Hilton Head Company joined forces with a Savannah home builder in 1973 to build 450 rental apartments off Highway 278 on company land in the middle of the island. While these projects helped ease the housing shortage, modestly priced shelter remained a sideshow on Hilton Head, with little appeal to developers, investors, or the growing ranks of affluent homeowners in the plantations.

THE OTHER HILTON HEAD

Another sideshow for most of those drawn to the island by the promise of profits or paradise was the other Hilton Head, the native blacks whose insular little world was being transformed by plantations, resorts, and hordes of white outsiders. Development brought changes that few blacks on the isolated island had anticipated, but all were affected by the newcomers and the new enterprises. Change would erode their way of life and traditional sea island culture.

The blacks were poor, while most of the newcomers were well-off; they lived off the land on an island whose emerging economy was based on selling off land. As Hilton Head changed, blacks shifted from farming and fishing to jobs brought by development, mostly low-wage service positions as unskilled laborers, maids, yardmen, waiters, and kitchen help. A few black entrepreneurs prospered by operating small businesses, and the jobs that came to Hilton Head brought better housing and a higher standard of living for a number of black islanders. The majority of African Americans, however, made the transition from subsistence farm labor to the bottom rungs of the service industries without significant change in their economic status. Wages were low, and advancement to better jobs was slow. There were few openings for blacks in the island's leading industry, the development business. As a result, most of them remained poor despite the money that poured over the bridge as white Hilton Head prospered.

Two decades after the organization of the Hilton Head Company, substantial numbers of black families earned less than the federal poverty threshold. Private development of the plantations and adjacent areas brought neither water nor sewer lines to black Hilton Head, and at least a third of the island's blacks lived in dwellings that lacked running water or safe heating or kitchens. Many others depended on shallow wells that were contaminated by outhouses. Abysmal sanitary conditions left many children afflicted with intestinal parasites.

Some newcomers were troubled by the existence of two Hilton Heads, "the depressing contrast between the stagnation of much of the black community and the glittering elegance of the all-white 'plantations.'"[32] More troubling to many white islanders than the reality of black life was bad publicity about conditions in the native community. Hilton Head, like most places whose economic fortunes depend on the perceptions of the larger world, tolerated internal criticism more easily than the barbs of "uninformed" outsiders. Islanders were annoyed by a 1972 report in South Carolina's largest newspaper entitled "Plush Living Contrasts Poverty at Hilton Head," which pictured the island as increasingly populated by white snobs indifferent to the plight of oppressed blacks and dominated by developers who would love to get rid of the remaining African Americans.[33] One leading citizen complained of the "absurdity" of this effort to stir racial animosity on "an island where blacks and whites in so many things depend upon each other for their welfare and happiness."[34] A few months later, the local newspaper wished "for a happier island" in an editorial emphasizing that "poor people here have been blessed by the employment resulting from development."[35]

The editorial, however, stressed what white islanders usually ignored: that "development here would have been impossible without the labor which the poorer people have provided."[36] Blacks were taken for granted by most whites; they were the polite women who cleaned houses and condos and hotel rooms, the young men with bandannas who picked up the trash and palmetto fronds, the courteous older men who opened doors at the hotels and took orders in restaurants. Each morning they arrived at the plantations and resorts, and they disappeared in the evening, most nameless to those they served in the hotels and rental units. White and black Hilton Head saw little of each other outside the working day; African Americans lived apart, worshiped apart, and patronized the few black-owned restaurants and small businesses. The newspaper that began publishing in 1970 paid little attention to native islanders. And the elaborate pageantry of Fraser's Heritage golf tournament, a black leader complained, "never included any of the original islanders in the ceremonies as meaningful participants."[37]

For their part, most native islanders adapted to change realistically, welcoming the benefits and bearing the costs stoically. For one lifelong inhabitant, the most important thing that happened was "the day they turned on the electricity."[38] Development also brought the bridge and accessibility to the mainland, doctors and eventually a hospital, some public services, and increased private opportunities. One local leader, Thomas Barnwell, spoke for many island blacks in a 1973 interview: "Change was needed, and we must adjust, even though it is painful at times. The island's growth has lifted the economic status of the people, and that is good. It has brought people who left the area back home, and that is good."[39] Growth, however, was seen as a mixed blessing by blacks. Barnwell, who had worked for fifty cents an hour at the William Hilton Inn, where his father was doorman and his uncle headwaiter, was troubled by the failure of development to create more than menial jobs. Few managerial posts at the development companies were available to blacks, regardless of their qualifications; and almost all the attractive jobs in real estate, development, commerce, and services were filled by white newcomers to Hilton Head.

The sweeping changes brought by Fraser and the other developers also drastically altered the patterns of black life on Hilton Head. Farmers and fishermen became wage earners; the use of Gullah faded as native islanders were assimilated into an economy that had little patience with an obscure local language. Lost was the freedom of movement that had characterized the island before the arrival of the Hilton Head Company. Although blacks owned less than 20 percent of Hilton Head, they had roamed freely, gathering wood, fishing, and hunting on the land that belonged to the absentee landlords. With the developers came fences and plantation gates, limiting access to old haunts and special places, including old cemeteries such as the one surrounded by town houses and a parking lot in Harbour Town. The newcomers were largely oblivious to black Hilton Head's distinctive culture and heritage as they came in ever larger numbers to the island that had been "discovered" by Fraser and Hack.

Last but hardly least, African Americans worried about the implications of growth for the land they owned, the legacy from slavery that most families had tenaciously retained during many bad times. During the initial years of the island's development and the boom that followed in the early 1970s, native holdings were ignored by developers, since the most desirable land was owned by the plantation companies. The attractions of the black holdings, however, were bound to increase as other land was consumed, and blacks were fearful that growth would imperil their birthright.

CLOSING THE CIRCLE

Concerns about growth—of blacks and other islanders—were fueled by the sustained boom that pushed Hilton Head's economy to new heights each year during the early 1970s. More than $30 million worth of building permits were issued in 1971, more than three times the average of the preceding two years; 1971 alone accounted for 38 percent of the total of $83 million in permitted development between 1952 and 1971. In 1972, construction almost doubled, to $57 million, and it reached $69 million in 1974. Developers glowingly forecast more growth. Bold projections were made that the island's population would exceed 50,000 in 1980. Options were taken on more land, financing arranged, and future profits anticipated. Atlantis Development confidently predicted in 1973 that the Adventure Inn would be torn down in three or four years so that something bigger and better could be built.

Two decades later, the Adventure Inn still stood in Forest Beach, having neither sunk into the sea (although the beach had steadily eroded) nor been replaced by a more imposing real estate development. The grandiose plans of Atlantis and those of almost every developer on Hilton Head Island were shelved as the island economy was hard hit by rising interest rates in 1973–1974 and a resulting severe shortage of home buyers. The nation's economic difficulties in the mid-1970s were particularly difficult for the development industry generally, and development was Hilton Head's principal industry. Steep increases in fuel prices and gasoline shortages further battered the island's resort-based economy. Construction volume on the island collapsed; real estate sales plummeted; plantations cut back their work forces; and architects, builders, laborers,

Figure 4.1 - New Construction, 1960–1975 (1975 Dollars)

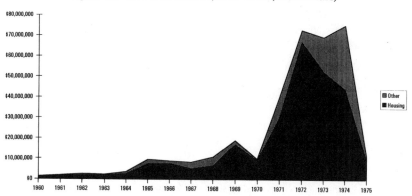

and many others dependent on the development business changed jobs or left the island.

Hilton Head's first boom ended with the 1974 economic downturn, a period of rapid growth that began in Sea Pines and was spreading across the island by 1974. By this time a critical mass had been achieved. Hilton Head was a community with approximately 3,000 year-round residents, a full range of public and private services, cable television, a newspaper, and a dizzying array of communal activities. The recession also marked the end of the dominant role of the plantation companies on Hilton Head Island, which is the subject of the next chapter, and the concomitant beginning of the quest for more public control over what private development had wrought.

NOTES

1. Palmetto Dunes, advertisement.

2. The Hilton Head Company was a set of companies, including Honey Horn Plantation, which throughout are referred to as the Hilton Head Company.

3. This includes the land purchased by the Hilton Head Company in 1950 and by Honey Horn Plantation in 1951, excluding the two tracts that became Sea Pines, lots sold in Forest Beach and Folly Field, and land used by the MacIntoshes for Spanish Wells Plantation.

4. Mary Kendall Hilton, "Islander: Fred C. Hack," 4.

5. Wamsley, interview.

6. Quoted in Bowers and Bowers, "What Does the Future Hold for Hilton Head Island?"

7. Quoted in "Milestone Reached by Island Developer," 7.

8. Bowers and Bowers, "What Does the Future Hold for Hilton Head Island?"

9. "'Lifestyle' Set by Hilton Head Co." The article was a promotional piece prepared by the Hilton Head Company for a special travel edition of the *Island Packet*.

10. Wamsley, interview. Tom Wamsley joined the Hilton Head Company in 1964 to sell real estate.

11. Shipyard Plantation, advertisement, March 1, 1973.

12. Shipyard Plantation, advertisement, March 30, 1972.

13. In exchange for the land for Spanish Wells, the Hacks acquired Honey Horn Plantation from the company.

14. In 1973 John McIntosh assumed the management of Spanish Wells from his brother Olin McIntosh Jr. after acquiring his interest and the interests of his brother William and his sister Jane McIntosh Dearnley.

15. In all, 186 lots were platted on 230 of the plantation's acres.

16. Quoted in "Multi-Million Dollar Development Program Begins for Gun Club Lands," 3.

17. The waterway system was designed by Dr. Per Bruun, a Danish engineer with worldwide experience.

18. Bessemer Securities was the investment arm of the Bessemer Trust Company, the trust of the heirs of Henry Phipps, a partner of Andrew Carnegie.

19. Robert C. Onorato, quoted in Callahan, "The Godfather of Palmetto Dunes," 24. Onorato evaluated Palmetto Dunes for Phipps in 1971 before being hired to run the plantation.

20. Phipps initially owned Palmetto Dunes jointly with Trans International Properties, a New York investment firm, but soon secured a controlling interest.

21. Fraser's efforts and the sale of the Hilton Head Company are discussed in the next chapter.

22. Hilton Head Plantation, advertisement.

23. Chip Dolan, Hilton Head Plantation, quoted in Littlejohn, "Neighborhoods Form Plantation's Backbone."

24. The expansion of Sea Pines and the difficulties the company experienced are discussed in chapter 5. The development of Hilton Head Plantation

under new ownership is treated in chapter 12.

25. "Atlantis Announces $11 Million Project."

26. Hilton Head Beach Club, advertisement, 6.

27. "100 Apartments, Shops, Small Plants for Buckingham."

28. The site, purchased for $1.2 million, was land that originally belonged to the Hilton Head Company but was traded in the mid-1950s in exchange for the liquidation of timber leases after the company ceased lumbering operations.

29. George B. Jamme, president, Andrick Development Corporation, quoted in "Island Club's $15 Million Project Is Announced."

30. Quoted in "First Phase Started on $35 Million Island Project."

31. C. H. Ussery, quoted in "$10 Million Island Club Rises above Shoreline."

32. Phillips, "Let's Not Blow Up the Bridge—Yet," 12.

33. Hamrick, "Plush Living Contrasts with Poverty at Hilton Head."

34. Daniels, "Sojourner's Scrapbook," March 2, 1972. Daniels, author and former editor of the *News and Observer* in Raleigh, N.C., was an early settler at Sea Pines and one of the founders of the *Island Packet.*

35. "For a Happier Island."

36. Ibid.

37. Campbell, letter to the editor.

38. Quoted in Greer, *The Sands of Time,* 62.

39. Quoted in Ramsey, "Islander of the Month: Thomas C. Barnwell, Jr.," 8.

Chapter Five

Benevolent Dictators

Development was fun when the three major companies did what they thought was right with a sense of stewardship. And it worked; the benevolent dictators produced lovely places on a beautiful island.

—Robert C. Onorato, Interview, August 7, 1987

Their realms were separated by Pope Avenue and its extension to Broad Creek, Palmetto Bay Road. South of the dividing line was Charles Fraser's territory; to the north lay Fred Hack's land. Together Fraser and Hack ruled the island during the first two decades of development on Hilton Head. They owned most of the land and determined its development through their plans and covenants. Private development fueled private control over community life. The plantation companies provided essential services, public infrastructure, and community facilities. From private power came substantial political influence: Fraser and Hack dominated the county government's limited activities on Hilton Head. In effect, they *were* government; as Fraser explained, "our corporate contracts and deed covenants are the constitution and bylaws of the community."[1]

Their influence was also based on the economic success and the aesthetic quality of the plantation developments. Land itself would have meant little if the companies had not developed their holdings, attracted customers, enhanced property values, and provided the stimulus for other businesses. People who moved to Hilton Head would have been far less willing to accept the developers' dominant role if Fraser and Hack had not been committed to quality. Because they clearly cared about Hilton Head and its environment, their rule was legitimated. Speaking of "the only island governors we possess," one of the founders of the local newspaper emphasized that "even when critical a first faith of islanders is that such men as Charles Fraser and Fred Hack have done about the best job in the world of turning a sleeping beauty into a living queen among islands."[2]

Fraser and Hack were the dominant figures during the era of the benevolent dictators. The third major plantation company, Palmetto Dunes, arrived on the scene more than a decade after the founding of the Sea Pines Company and played a minor role in island affairs before Robert Onorato took charge in 1972. Fraser and Hack reigned in very different fashion. Charles Fraser's style was imperial; he spoke of himself in the third person, preferred to act unilaterally, and used Sea Pines and Hilton Head as his base for a far-flung set of business and political activities. An elitist who firmly believed he knew what was best for his subjects, Fraser thoroughly enjoyed his role as benevolent dictator. "There is democracy of communication here but autocracy of decision-making," Fraser told John McPhee in 1970.[3] Islanders called him Prince Charles and King Charles only partially in jest. Hack was paternal rather than regal, a local in contrast to Fraser the cosmopolitan, and on closer personal terms with islanders than Fraser.

Of the two, Fraser was far more influential. He was the innovator; his company was the leader. Fraser determined the course of plantation development and devised the legal instruments of control. Sea Pines brought customers to Hilton Head and was the largest purchaser of goods and services from other businesses. Fraser was more active politically and better equipped to deal with political and administrative intricacies. As a result, Fraser cast a wider political web and was more effective than Hack in using his influence in governmental arenas. Both Fraser and Hack served on the county governing body, with Fraser taking a turn as chairman. Better than Hack, Fraser understood that state and federal connections paid dividends in terms of access and influence, and he served on many commissions and advisory bodies.[4]

PRIVATE RULE

Land was the base of the power exercised by Fraser and Hack and their companies. Their holdings were extensive, encompassing three-quarters of Hilton Head when modern development began. Almost half the island belonged to the Hilton Head Company alone in 1972. Ownership of most of Hilton Head provided far-reaching control since all this property was developed under private rather than public restrictions, with Fraser and Hack regulating the use of land they sold both within the plantations and beyond their gates. Land provided additional control because almost all of Hilton Head's communal facilities—streets, utilities, schools, churches, hospital, library, and airport—were on land provided by the development companies.

Fraser saw private control over land as the key to achieving his goals for Sea Pines and Hilton Head. He called this "responsible private entrepreneurial management" through "private land use planning, enforced by private land use covenants."[5] The other companies eagerly embraced a system in which private firms rather than public bodies decided what would be more intensively developed and what would not. Private planning and controls were preferable to public land use regulation, Fraser argued, because they were insulated from political pressure and less likely to be threatened by judicial worries about property rights. Fraser was also convinced that private control by someone like him was essential in matters of design and aesthetics, since people who served on planning and zoning boards rarely had the capacity to make sound decisions. "The only way you can have aesthetic control is through the power of ownership," Fraser explained in 1970, emphasizing that "we have more power than a zoning board."[6] In exercising control over land, the major companies were more successful inside than outside the plantations. To be sure, restrictions imposed by Sea Pines and the Hilton Head Company had a beneficial impact on much of the development beyond plantation gates. Buildings were limited by covenant to five stories in height along Forest Beach, a regulation that prevented the wall of tall hotels typical of many Florida seaside resorts. Nonetheless, private control and planning were much more effective in Sea Pines than in Forest Beach. Inside their plantations, Fraser and Hack were endeavoring to enhance property values and future profits by creating amenities and controlling externalities on land they were trying to sell. Beyond the gates, the companies' primary interest was in selling land to raise money. While they wanted to protect their plantations and the island generally from bad development, the two men had a strong interest in maximizing short-run profits. Because their motivation was different outside the gates of their plantations, controls were less stringent; private control and benevolent dictatorship produced the most satisfactory results when public and private objectives were consonant.

Land plans on Hilton Head were also private rather than public, prepared by the major companies for their plantations. These plans looked like those prepared by local governments, specifying land uses and the location of roads and other public facilities, but they reflected private rather than public determinations about the island's development. In addition to plantation master plans, the Hilton Head Company commissioned in 1970 a comprehensive plan for its 11,000 acres that dealt more generally with development of the island and surrounding areas.[7] The plan emphasized the potential of tourism, recreation, and convention business, recommending construction of more hotels and larger convention facilities and reduced reliance on cars and highways. Nothing came of this visionary study, with its images of ferries cruising the islands and people enjoying a resort free of automobiles. Hack did no more than have the study prepared, hoping the other plantation companies would be guided by the plan, but they were not interested. Private plans, like private land use controls, worked best when private interests were directly involved.

Along with controlling land, the major companies provided most public services on Hilton Head. The plantations developed public services out of necessity—real estate could not be sold without water and sewers, police and fire protection, roads and other facilities; and few services and little infrastructure were supplied by Beaufort County. So the development companies undertook directly and indirectly many of the tasks of local government, supplying services that were eventually paid for by residents. These services were under private rather than public control; the guiding hands were those of Charles Fraser and Fred Hack instead of an elected local government.

Private provision of basic services divided Hilton Head into two worlds—the plantations and other areas served by the developers, with substantial services, and the rest of the island, with primitive utilities and residents who could not afford private services. The first of these worlds was almost all white, the second largely black, adding an important racial dimension to the private provision of public services. These differences, in both the quality of services and the groups served, would structure debate over private control, public services, and the role of government as Hilton Head developed.

Sea Pines established the basic pattern for public services on the plantations. The company built and maintained a private road system. Plantation security guards deputized by the county sheriff substituted for local police. Fraser also took care of erosion problems, community landscaping, and mosquito control. All of these services were partially underwritten by assessments on property owners. Water in Sea Pines was originally supplied from company wells, and sewage was handled through septic tanks on individual lots. Septic tanks, however, worked poorly on a low-lying island with sandy soil. Similar problems with septic tanks outside Sea Pines led to the organization in 1961 of a public service district for Forest Beach to develop conventional sewage treatment. Fraser followed the same path, securing state approval in 1964 for creation of the Sea Pines Public Service District.[8] The agency was empowered to provide water and sewage systems, fire protection, a medical clinic, bike trails, and other public services to Sea Pines residents. Other plantations followed Sea Pines' lead, organizing new public service districts or tapping into existing agencies. The Hilton Head Company organized a public service district in 1969 to provide water, sewers, and other services to Port Royal and adjacent areas. In Shipyard Plantation, water and sewer lines were connected to the Forest Beach district's utility system. After an unsuccessful effort to treat sewage by using oxidation ponds and aeration, Palmetto Dunes formed its district in 1971.[9]

Hilton Head's public service districts were creatures of the development companies, which set their boundaries, determined their powers, and secured the support of local members of the state legislature, thus insuring that enabling legislation would be approved.[10] Plantation officials organized and managed the Broad Creek Public Service District, which Onorato called "a slave to Palmetto Dunes."[11] Like many local utility authorities in the United States, the districts were public agencies designed primarily to serve private ends. Public service districts permitted plantations to secure essential water, sewer, and fire service while reducing front-end costs for the private companies. Providing services through a public instrumentality allowed developers to raise capital in the municipal bond market and have property owners finance debt through user fees, assessments, and property taxes. These arrangements were designed for and by plantations, and the companies' primary concerns were developing their properties, selling real estate, and shifting financial burdens to residents.

Private considerations were also critical in the development of major public works on Hilton Head. The basic pattern was established with the James F. Byrnes Crossing—a project designed primarily to benefit the Hilton Head Company rather than the traveling public, few of whom journeyed to the isolated island. The bridge was conceived and underwritten by the island's developers, and the resulting public agency was controlled by private companies. The same general model was used in building an airport; the site was donated to the county government, construction was underwritten largely by federal and state funds, and the airport was operated by a private company controlled by Fraser and Hack.[12]

The logic that led the plantation companies to provide public services and develop public works also involved them in the development of health, education and other community facilities. Hilton Head's remote location was an essential part of its appeal, but because of its isolation, the island lacked almost everything that communities normally offered. Fraser had conceived of his community in terms of residences and recreation and natural surroundings, giving little thought to many elements that are taken for granted, such as doctors and churches. To attract prospective purchasers of homesites and persuade them to live on Hilton Head, Sea Pines had to get far more involved in community services than Fraser had anticipated. So did the other major developers, and this necessity extended the scope of the companies, entwining them in all sorts of activities and furthering their influence on everyday life.

Perhaps the most pressing community need as Sea Pines began to attract residents was medical facilities on the island, a problem intensified by the substantial percentage of retired people among the early plantation settlers. The nearest doctor was in Beaufort, and specialized medical care required trips to Savannah or Charleston. This situation troubled people who relocated to Hilton

Head and deterred others from making the move. Property owners surveyed by Sea Pines in 1964 indicated that most would not build homes on their lots unless medical treatment was available on the island. In health care, as would be the case later with development of most community facilities and services, change was produced by the interplay between dedicated individuals and one of the development companies. The moving force in bringing medicine to Hilton Head was Dr. Chester R. Goddard, an internist from Iowa who, like so many other islanders, came to play golf and decided to stay. Goddard built a home in Sea Pines and joined forces with Charles Fraser to create Hilton Head's first medical center. Fraser donated the land on Pope Avenue, and the Sea Pines Public Service District built and equipped the clinic in 1965 and leased the facility to Goddard. Although the clinic was initially underwritten by taxes on Sea Pines property owners, Goddard insisted that the medical center serve the entire island rather than just Sea Pines, setting a pattern that was followed for other community facilities and services developed under the aegis of the plantation companies.[13] Together Goddard and Fraser filled a critical community need and, in the process of doing so, enhanced the appeal of Sea Pines and Hilton Head for prospective residents. Goddard's clinic attracted other doctors to the island and paved the way for the development of the Hilton Head Island Hospital a decade later, thus adding good medical care to the island's selling points.

Schools were another serious deficiency that caused anyone with children to think twice about moving to Hilton Head. Whites on Hilton Head went to public school over the bridge in Bluffton or to private school more than an hour away in Savannah. Complicating the problem was the poor quality of local public schools and the clouded future of public education in South Carolina, given the state's resistance to desegregation. Spurred by company executives with children, Fraser established the Sea Pines Academy in 1966.[14] The private school began in temporary quarters Fraser provided, built a permanent campus on land donated in Sea Pines, and was heavily subsidized for seven years by the company. Fraser's wife, Mary, set up the island's first preschool, and Sea Pines, with Palmetto Dunes, donated the land for a new public elementary school.

Over the years, congregations, cultural interests, and all sorts of good causes would look to the development companies for support and more often than not would find help from businessmen who were both good citizens and convinced that their success depended on making Hilton Head a vibrant community. Sea Pines supplied sites for a string of churches along Pope Avenue, while the Hilton Head Company donated land for the First Presbyterian Church on U.S. 278. Sea Pines played a key role in creating the Hilton Head Island Health Project, a black-led effort to eliminate parasites and other health hazards and secure safe water supplies, and both companies helped finance the project. Land and funds for Hilton Head's hospital, opened in 1975, came from all three development companies, while the site for the island's public library was provided by the Hilton Head Company.

Recreational facilities and open space were almost entirely in the hands of the plantation companies. In addition to golf and tennis, Fraser and Hack operated the island's first marinas, provided bike paths on their developments, and jointly owned access land to the main public beach. Over 600 acres of Sea Pines Plantation were deeded by Fraser to a forest preserve open to the public. Fraser also donated 50 acres next to Sea Pines for a wildlife preserve and arboretum. Sea Pines' plans for Hilton Head Plantation included preservation of an active rookery for whooping cranes. In all of these endeavors, concern for public welfare, open space, and wildlife was combined with economic self-interest, a fact of life well understood on Hilton Head. In welcoming Fraser's plans for the rookery, the local Audubon Society noted that "not only from the ecological standpoint is it important to save these sites but from a cold economic viewpoint they are also important. The beautiful large birds add to the beauty of this island, and natural beauty is one of the things this island has to sell."[15]

To point out economic motivations behind these myriad actions by the major companies is not to belittle their substantial contributions to the development of Hilton Head as a multifaceted community with a rich range of facilities and activities. Doctors, schools, churches, forest trails, and wildlife preserves were essential and effective marketing devices; they were also expressions of commitment and concern for Hilton Head, its residents, and its natural setting. Fraser did not have to devote almost 15 percent of Sea Pines to a forest preserve; much less would have served for marketing nature. No government forced him to set aside this valuable property, and he neither sought nor received a tax benefit for it. Both Fraser and Hack cared about the island and its land.

COOPERATION AND CONFLICT

Joint ventures and cooperative activities reflected the major companies' shared interests in the island and its people. Sea Pines, the Hilton Head Company, and Palmetto Dunes were competitors, each seeking a piece of essentially the same market, but they had a common stake in controlling growth and maintaining high development standards. As Fraser had understood from the start, private resort communities catering to affluent customers required an attractive setting; they could not coexist with banal development. To protect their investments, the companies had a mutual stake in maintaining private control over development and preserving their preeminent role in determining what was built. With more rapid growth came a greater imperative for cooperation and joint action.

After Onorato took the helm at Palmetto Dunes in 1972, informal consultation among the three companies evolved into monthly meetings to discuss mutual concerns under the banner of the Community Developers Association. Fraser, Hack, and Onorato pondered traffic, housing, police and fire protection, land use controls, and other issues and attempted to settle on common courses of action. These sessions marked the height of benevolent dictatorship and the peak of developer influence. Neither the island's residents nor the county government was represented; other interests were considered, but the companies made the important decisions about planning, public services, roads, other infrastructure, and community facilities and activities. The developers filled a vacuum left by weak local government—one they had helped create. They were in the best position to deal with the challenge of growth, which they had largely stimulated. Development was the island's business; the three companies essentially controlled the development business and thus the island. In Onorato's unequivocal words, "the three companies ran everything."[16]

One of the most pressing issues confronting the developers was building heights. Nothing taller than three stories had been built before Harbour Town, where the tallest buildings had five floors. Then in 1971, with accelerating growth causing growing concern among island residents, Hilton Head was suddenly awash in plans for taller buildings. Seven- and eight-floor condominiums were to be built at South Beach in Sea Pines; a ten-story hotel was unveiled for Palmetto Dunes; and the Hilton Head Company's plans for Shipyard Plantation included condos of ten to fifteen stories. Residents, particularly in the plantations, were incensed; tall buildings represented everything most of them had come to Hilton Head to escape. For one, high-rises were "invitations to invasion, plans for people pollution."[17] Palmetto Dunes' hotel was opposed by almost everyone who attended a crowded gathering in mid-1971, and community leaders emphasized that the beachfront hotel was "clearly repugnant to most island residents," who "do not want another Miami Beach."[18]

Fraser responded positively to these concerns, announcing a permanent ban in Sea Pines on buildings taller than five stories. He called on the other companies to endorse a similar limit and proposed that height restrictions be included in deed covenants covering the 15,000 acres still held by major developers. Under pressure from Fraser and residents, Hack agreed to the five-floor limit; he also called for cooperative efforts among developers to limit population density to 2 or 3 units per acre. Among themselves, the big three agreed to limit future development to five stories, with Fraser and Hack endorsing Palmetto Dunes' hotel as an exception to the five-story limit.

For the developers, limiting building heights was both responsive to local concerns and good business. Their market was people who wanted something different from Miami Beach, and whatever each developer lost by foregoing an occasional taller building was more than repaid by the mutual protection the agreement provided against high-rise developments on land owned by the other plantations. Moreover, the restriction could be extended to other developers who acquired their land from one of the companies. Some architects would complain that the five-story limit produced monotonous roof lines along Forest Beach and led to more extensive coverage of small plots than would have been the case with taller buildings. What these criticisms underscore is the effectiveness of the agreement on building heights, which embodied the essence of rule by benevolent dictators. No government ratified this private accord; nor did residents participate in making the decision. Yet the agreement proved as binding as any public land regulation, perhaps more so considering the malleability of much local zoning in the face of development pressures. Two decades after the agreement was struck, Hilton Head's only building taller than five floors was the ten-story Hyatt Hotel in Palmetto Dunes.

Cooperation among major developers was complicated by frosty relations between Charles Fraser and Fred Hack. Their animosity began with the conflict over Fraser's original proposals for the island, led to the split in 1956, and structured relations between the island's major landowners for almost two decades. From the start, Hack saw Fraser as a master of words who made the rules and then tried to change them to his benefit. Fraser continued to view Hack as lacking vision and plans, a man with an abundance of land but no ideas, unwilling to shoulder his responsibilities as the island's largest landowner. The fact that Sea Pines was far more successful than the Hilton Head Company heightened the antagonism. Hack resented his rival's claiming all the credit for everything good that happened on Hilton Head and receiving so much publicity for the island's development.

Old conflicts and new resentments combined to produce constant friction between Fraser and Hack. Feeding the conflict was the continuing struggle between the companies for the advantage in providing services and facilities. Land was the principal weapon in most of these battles, with the two combatants using gifts of property to secure a locational edge. Fraser wanted medical facilities, schools, and churches near Sea Pines; Hack wanted the center of gravity to be located farther north, near his company's holdings. One nasty conflict was over the placement of the Presbyterian church that was going to be built on

Sea Pines land on Pope Avenue until Hack persuaded the congregation to locate near Port Royal Plantation on property donated by his company. Fraser also lost out on the library, which went next to Port Royal rather than outside Sea Pines. But Fraser had more customers and more clout, and he wound up winning many of these contests. The medical center and most other churches were on Pope Avenue. The school was built on Fraser's plantation and named the Sea Pines Academy despite Hack's objections. While the private academy was eventually open to all islanders, Sea Pines residents had priority in admissions and paid less tuition, which gave Fraser one more edge in selling property.

Perhaps the most bizarre struggle over location concerned the airport. Both Fraser and Hack originally saw an airport as essential in attracting conventions and corporate meetings to Hilton Head. Both shortsightedly wanted the airport on their property, thinking about the convenience of having it next to a resort and forgetting about the nuisance it could be to a residential community. Fraser moved first, clearing a mile-long grass strip within Sea Pines. Hack saw Fraser's airport as one more economic and promotional advantage for Sea Pines. The Hilton Head Company countered successfully with political pressure, persuading public officials to kill state funding for the airport in Sea Pines, then donating land near Port Royal Plantation for an airport to be developed by Beaufort County. Hack had won—or had he? The airport was not in Sea Pines; instead it was adjacent to Port Royal, where Hack wanted everything. But so were the noise and the possible dangers associated with a busy airport. As business expanded at the airport, Port Royal residents grew increasingly unhappy with the intruders on their piece of paradise. Instead of helping business, the airport was hurting the Hilton Head Company. By "winning" the contest with Fraser, Hack wound up giving Sea Pines another advantage.

Like most conflicts between Fraser and Hack, the airport dispute was over means rather than ends. Both men were developers. Their business was growth, and they wanted more air transportation capacity to bring more customers. In their push for growth they were no different from developers in other communities. What was singular on Hilton Head was the degree of control the principal developers exercised over the major parameters of community life. They were benevolent, to be sure, but dictators nonetheless, in control of private investment, public services, and community facilities. Certainly their private and public actions enriched lives and fostered a vibrant community. Without question, they loved their island and its natural treasures; and generally they developed with sensitivity and a commitment to quality. They were part of the community they controlled, and they cared deeply about its future. Making money was important to them, but not at all costs—so densities and building heights were limited, trees saved, open space preserved, and wildlife protected.

Private control fostered innovative architecture and discouraged schlock, making Hilton Head a nicer place for everyone to enjoy. "We have demonstrated," said Fred Hack, "that 'the good life' can be compatible with a quality of environment and wise growth."[19]

Developing the "good life" was, as has been noted, good business. The developers' rewards were substantial as the island grew and prospered. For all their genuine concerns about their island and its well-being, the first and foremost use of their power was to advance their companies' interests in a growing island that remained attractive for vacationers, second-home purchasers, and retirees. Control was essential; natural beauty and attractive development had to be preserved or the companies would not be able to continue serving their up-scale market. Writing of the concerns expressed by Fraser and Hack about excessive growth, a local commentator wryly observed that "it is easy to think of them as men crying all the way to the bank."[20]

WINDS OF CHANGE

While growth benefited the development companies enormously, it also eroded their control of both private and public realms on Hilton Head. Growth brought more developers, more businesses, and more private interests that inevitably chafed under the rule of the major companies. Moreover, growth swelled the island's population, and an increasing number of the new arrivals would question the terms imposed by benevolent dictators who paid scant attention to residents and their mounting concerns. Together these developments were bound to erode the arrangements by which Hilton Head was ruled. The process of erosion was accelerated by turmoil within the development companies. Beginning in 1970, financial pressures triggered changes in control of the plantations and reduced the influence of the companies. New hands took the helm of the Hilton Head Company and Palmetto Dunes, while Charles Fraser embarked on a set of risky ventures far from the island.

The winds of change whistled first through the Hilton Head Company as Fred Hack lost control of the company five years after the death of Olin McIntosh Sr. in 1966. The Hilton Head Company was more than Hack's business; the company and its land were his life. And not only his: Hack's brother Orion was a vice-president, and his son Frederick joined the company after graduating from Duke University in 1969. Hack's goal was to retain all the company's extensive holdings. His enemies were time, money, and Charles Fraser as the island's three founding families played out their last act together in a drama that underscored the fragility of family-owned businesses and the role of inheritance taxes in determining the fate of closely held firms.

After McIntosh's death, half of the Hilton Head Company was owned by his seven children. The McIntoshes gave Fred Hack first option to purchase; their asking price of $5 million was fair but far beyond Hack's resources. Hack might raise funds through a public stock issue, but the McIntoshes were pressured by inheritance tax deadlines that precluded this time-consuming option. Hack's other alternatives involved finding outside investors, but this option jeopardized his desire to retain command of the Hilton Head Company and its extensive land holdings. Putting additional pressure on the beleaguered Hack was the looming presence of Charles Fraser. The McIntosh sale offered Fraser an opportunity for expansion on the island. Fraser pursued his interests on two fronts, seeking deals with both Hack and the McIntoshes. He offered to buy much of what would become Hilton Head Plantation at a price that would have provided Hack with money to settle with the McIntosh family. But Hack did not want to lose any more land, especially to his rival. Fraser also dealt directly with the McIntoshes, who agreed to give Sea Pines an opportunity to buy their share for $5 million if Hack could not find funding.

Framing all these efforts was the deadline by which the McIntoshes had to sell to raise money for heavy estate taxes. As time ran out in 1971, Fraser was working on the final details with the McIntoshes' lawyers. At the last moment, the McIntoshes informed a startled Fraser that they were joining Fred Hack in selling two-thirds of the Hilton Head Company's land for $9 million to a group of wealthy Georgians headed by Jack P. Ashmore Jr. of Atlanta.[21] Hack won the McIntosh battle with Fraser, but the price of victory was high: the Ashmore group took Port Royal Plantation and the land that would become Hilton Head Plantation, while Hack retained Shipyard Plantation and other acreage along U.S. 278.

Less land did not solve Hack's problems, since he still lacked the resources to develop his holdings. Having run out of alternatives, Hack reluctantly sold the Hilton Head Company to Oxford First Corporation, a financial services company from Philadelphia seeking to get into development on the island.[22] While Hack and Fraser both wound up losing as a result of the sale of the McIntosh interest, the Ashmore group did very well. Soon after Oxford First bought out Hack, they sold Port Royal Plantation back to the Hilton Head Company. They also disposed of another 1,200 acres near the airport to the Phipps Land Company, which owned Palmetto Dunes. The Ashmore group finished their wheeling and dealing before the end of 1971, when they sold their remaining property to Sea Pines. Fraser paid $8 million for the land that became Hilton Head Plantation—more than twice its cost a year earlier in the year. The deal left the Ashmore group with a hefty profit for their short sojourn on the island,

and they disappeared as quietly as they had materialized.

With Hack out of the picture, two of the three major companies were controlled by outsiders. Palmetto Dunes had never been owned by islanders and had already changed hands by the time Oxford First had taken over the Hilton Head Company. Only Sea Pines had a familiar face at the top, but that face was seen less and less on Hilton Head. Fraser was riding high on the success of Sea Pines, and as the plantation moved into the final stages of development in the late 1960s, he looked for new worlds to conquer. No longer content to be the ruler of Sea Pines and the biggest fish in Hilton Head's pond, he was "restless. . . . I knew there was the rest of the world out there. Frankly, I preferred to lead a more exciting development life than a very cautious and very safe development life."[23] Hilton Head would now be Fraser's base rather his obsession. Sea Pines became only one of his many operations—still the biggest and the best, but not the object of his personal attention.[24]

What Fraser had learned at Sea Pines about development, planning controls, and financing he would apply to building new communities throughout the United States and beyond. Expansion appealed to his desire for accomplishment and recognition, and it was possible for him to enlarge his reach because the success of Sea Pines had brought him national visibility. Money and land were offered to Fraser for all kinds of developments. "Charles," he was told, "you've done such a nice job at Sea Pines Plantation, we want you to buy our land, and develop our land in the same way Sea Pines has been developed— with care and attention to the environment."[25] Funds that were so hard to raise at the beginning were now easily acquired from a new breed of go-go bankers and their new real estate investment trusts; $64 million in financing was available for Hilton Head Plantation and $74 million for Sea Pines' Puerto Rican venture—dizzying sums compared to what Fraser borrowed to build Sea Pines Plantation.

For his initial venture beyond Hilton Head, Fraser chose familiar terrain: Cumberland Island, the southernmost of Georgia's string of sea islands. In 1968 he bought 3,000 of Cumberland's 18,000 acres for $1.5 million from heirs of the Carnegies who had owned most of the island. Fraser planned to develop on the Sea Pines model; Cumberland Oaks would have forested beaches, lakes and lagoons, golf and tennis, and homesites and resort facilities carefully fitted into the wild natural terrain of the almost uninhabited island. What came of Fraser's initiative was not another Sea Pines, however, but a new national park. Fraser was opposed by conservationists, many of the Carnegies, and property owners on the rest of the island. The struggle echoed the arguments that were increasingly being heard on Hilton Head. Some saw Fraser as a visionary, a developer who did things right; more contended that he was an unprincipled profit seeker who talked about the people and built for the rich, whose game was greed rather than conservation. The opposition was too powerful, and Fraser threw in the trowel, selling his land to the National Park Service. Similar pressures blocked Fraser's plans to develop Bald Head Island in North Carolina. On Cumberland and Bald Head, Fraser escaped with a bruised ego; he would be less fortunate elsewhere.

Fraser's desire to develop a winter resort took him to the Caribbean. After examining property on Barbados, Jamaica, and Nassau, he settled on 2,400 acres with 6 miles of beach on the southeastern coast of Puerto Rico. Fraser's Sea Pines Company paid $8.5 million for the land in 1970 and began planning Palmas Del Mar. While the ideas were exciting, the realities of doing business in Puerto Rico were daunting. Sea Pines was saddled with inflated labor costs and forced to bear the burden of providing utilities, roads, and other facilities for Palmas Del Mar. In venturing into unfamiliar terrain, as Fraser ruefully acknowledged, "we slowly discovered" that Puerto Rico was "a bottomless pit of intractable problems for the community builder."[26] Inflated costs and weak revenues combined with high interest rates to doom Palmas Del Mar at an eventual cost of $13 million to Sea Pines.

While Palmas Del Mar was slipping away, Sea Pines pursued a number of other ventures. Most promising was 2,400 seaside acres on Amelia Island in Florida, 30 miles north of Jacksonville. With 4 miles of beach and distinctive high dunes, Amelia Island provided a striking locale for the development of a Sea Pines clone in which the lessons from Hilton Head were applied imaginatively. Sea Pines was also involved in developing resort communities on the South Carolina coast and in the mountains of northern Georgia as well as large residential developments in North Carolina and Virginia. At the same time, the company was moving ahead locally with Hilton Head Plantation and a projected development on neighboring Daufuskie Island.

With enlarged operations came rapid expansion of the Sea Pines Company; employment increased tenfold between 1968 and 1974, and revenues jumped from $11.6 million to $130.4 million. Growth magnified the idiosyncrasies of Charles Fraser's approach to management. As he always had, Fraser surrounded himself with bright young people and created an atmosphere that prospered on new ideas, unconventional approaches, and interchangeable roles. Fraser had a weakness for graduates of the best business schools, hiring eleven from Harvard alone in 1973 and a number from Wharton and other top schools. What all these bright, ambitious, and inexperienced people would do in what was still a relatively small company was not always clear to anyone, including Fraser. "I should have had a better age mixture, and better experience," he would later concede.[27] The newcomers complicated decision making and diluted the authority of the company's top executives, one of whom regarded them as "an army of young warriors who had never fought a battle."[28]

Fraser loved ideas and research, so his burgeoning staff brainstormed and produced reams of studies. Out of this approach had come much of what made Sea Pines innovative and daring, but time and money were increasingly wasted on grand efforts that were not well focused on business objectives. Moreover, Fraser never paid much attention to management and detailed business operations. Ideas were always more interesting to him than results; creating was more challenging than completing. Sea Pines was haphazardly managed. The plantation was plagued by pilferage, kickbacks, and high prices from suppliers. Expansion magnified these shortcomings, increasing the scope of Sea Pines far more rapidly than the company was able to improve its managerial controls. Complicating the situation was Fraser's ambivalence about profits, his desire to build what he wanted regardless of cost. Sea Pines often seemed to be an extension of his personality as much as his business.

Business, however, is ultimately about bottom lines, a lesson brought home to Fraser in stark terms as the national economy plunged in 1974. Large-scale developers were particularly hard hit by recession: interest rates shot up, and demand for housing plummeted. Resort communities were additionally burdened by gasoline shortages and sharply increased motor fuel prices following the oil embargo in 1973. The Sea Pines Company was especially vulnerable, having grown too fast and undertaken too many risky ventures. Fraser expanded into areas that he knew less well and had far less control over than the friendly confines of Hilton Head. Land costs for these ventures were much higher than they had been at Sea Pines, while easy money and rapid development required substantially greater front-end costs than had been the case there. Fraser had to borrow large amounts of capital at floating interest rates that jumped from 7.5 percent to 13.5 percent in 1974. He had built Sea Pines during an era of stable interest rates, but now the cost of money was both higher and less predictable. When Washington's tight money policies pushed the prime rate to 12 percent, Sea Pines was faced with interest rates of 13.5 percent to 17 percent. Sea Pines Plantation, the only significant source of revenue in Fraser's $300-million empire, could not generate enough cash flow to service the company's mounting debt from its new ventures. By early 1975, Sea Pines owed $283 million to a host of banks including Chase Manhattan, First National City, and First National Bank of Chicago.

Rumors of Sea Pines' financial difficulties further depressed real estate sales. Sea Pines hit bottom in the fall of 1974, strapped by acute cash flow problems and the reluctance of its creditors to provide desperately needed financing. Fraser circled the wagons to save his company, scrambling to keep the lenders at bay and fend off bankruptcy. To calm those distressed by Sea Pines' management problems, operating responsibilities were turned over to the company's thirty-one-year-old president, James W. Light.[29] Most of the other bright young men from the business schools departed as the professional staff was cut by 80 percent. One by one, the new ventures fell by the wayside: Palmas Del Mar; Amelia Island, forced into reorganization under the federal bankruptcy laws; Hilton Head Plantation, which went to its creditors.

Table 5.1
Liabilities of the Sea Pines Company, 1969–1975

Date		Amount ($)
August	1969	12,603,000
August	1972	84,501,000
February	1973	120,720,000
February	1974	238,335,000
February	1975	282,968,000

Source: Fraser, "The Sea Pines Company: An Overview of Current Prospects and Summary of the Successful Recession Era Debt Elimination," 13.

Sea Pines pulled through, surviving lawsuits, absorbing substantial financial losses, restructuring debt through complicated negotiations with banks and insurance companies, and disposing of properties for as little as twenty cents on the dollar. Fraser fended off internal revolts and bankers who wanted him out, retreating back to Sea Pines Plantation, where he had begun. The company was battered, as were Fraser's finances. He came home to Hilton Head a good deal poorer. Fraser's substantial ego also took a beating. The boy wonder of resort development had been humbled; now he paid for his brashness and the attention he had lavished on his accomplishments. Critics, reported the *Island Packet,* "relished the deflation of Charles Fraser in Sea Pines"; his arrogance made him "seem fairer game in distress."[30]

TRANSITION

Fraser's misadventures and Hack's displacement signaled the end of the era of benevolent dictators on Hilton Head. Plantation companies would remain the most powerful players in the island's economy and politics. But two of the three major companies were in outside hands, with the ultimate decisions made by Oxford First in Philadelphia and Phipps Land in Atlanta; and beleaguered Sea Pines was tightly constrained by creditors in New York, Chicago, and other distant financial centers. Now the companies' role would be less personal, and their share of economic and political power would decline as the island continued to grow and diversify. Change within the development companies also undermined paternalistic rule by the plantations. The influence wielded by Charles Fraser and Fred Hack was legitimized by their commitment to the island, its people, its unique character, and its fragile environment. Fraser and Hack, for all their quirks and conflicts, were known quantities. They lived and worked on Hilton Head, raised their children on the island, and went to the churches they had helped to build. The two developers cared about Hilton Head in strong personal terms; they imposed on themselves the development controls that shaped the texture of the island.

With newcomers at the helm, plantation companies were bound to lose influence. Hilton Head was no longer in familiar hands. Islanders worried about whether new owners would share the original developers' values; they were outsiders and corporations, not local individuals with deep roots on Hilton Head. Local anxieties were compounded by the quickening pace of growth in the early 1970s. The new faces at the Hilton Head Company and Palmetto Dunes were sensitive to these worries, and they hastened to assure islanders that they would continue the caring tradition. Hack's successor pledged to respect "the sound environmental and conservation standards which have been established on the island" and maintain "the quality and dignity which the Hack family and others have created, and even to exceed these standards, if that is possible."[31] The new management at Palmetto Dunes indicated that its efforts would be guided by the example set by Sea Pines and the Hilton Head Company. "We are pleased to follow these leaders," enthused Phipps' president, "and expect to replan the property to create a development environment which will be unique even to Hilton Head."[32] For Phipps, however, part of Palmetto Dunes' unique environment was the high-rise hotel opposed by most residents. And the man at the helm at Palmetto Dunes embodied what many islanders distrusted in the outsiders. Robert Onorato was a tough New Yorker, street-smart and aggressive; he was eager to expand Palmetto Dunes and increase its profitability by featuring resort development.

Hotels and condominiums, resorts instead of residential communities, more development and tourists—all were what islanders feared as control passed to outsiders, corporate executives from New York and Philadelphia who, in the words of one local leader, "did not know anything about Hilton Head, or care much about the island."[33] Their paramount concern was the bottom line, and to increase profits they would press for more of everything. Onorato expansively talked of 50,000 people on the island by 1980, an alarming prospect to most of the 5,000 or so residents. After Oxford First took over, the Hilton Head Company emphasized that its 5,500 acres provided "a unique opportunity to offer something for everybody."[34] But something for everybody was what increasingly bothered those already on Hilton Head, as they worried about too much growth, too many people, and destruction of the beautiful and fragile environment that were their island's prime attractions.

Regardless of their intentions, the new leaders of the development companies would have far less influence than Charles Fraser and Fred Hack. Benevolent dictatorship could not be passed from the founders to their corporate heirs. Investment combines, land companies, banks, and finance companies had no real claims on the community or its residents of the kind that legitimized the rule of Fraser and Hack. Whatever regime came after benevolent dictators would have to respond to the desire of their former subjects for more control over the community and its future, which inevitably meant a larger role for public institutions and a lesser part for private ones. Certainly the island's economic interests would remain potent participants in the community, since development and the resort business would remain Hilton Head's only industries. Business, however, like other interests on the growing island, would become more diverse. The new public order on Hilton Head would have to deal with disagreements over growth, differences among developers and other businesses, and disputes within the residential community. New divisions and conflicts would emerge as Hilton Head grappled with complex questions of community character, environmental impact, and development control. The most basic cleavage on Hilton Head, however, was between those who came to make money and those who came to live, the fundamental fault line in conflict over growth in American communities.

NOTES

1. Quoted in McPhee, *Encounters with the Archdruid,* 93.

2. Jonathan Daniels, quoted in "Executives Discuss Ad Topics; Daniels Is Banquet Speaker."

3. Quoted in McPhee, *Encounters with the Archdruid,* 93.

4. Fraser was a member of the South Carolina Commission on Parks, Recreation, and Tourism and chaired the state's Low Country Resource Conservation and Development Commission. His federal assignments included membership on the Commission on Outdoor Recreation, the Advisory Commission

on Environmental Quality, and the Coastal Zone Advisory Committee. He also served as chairman of the board of the National Recreation and Park Association.

5. Charles E. Fraser, *The Art of Community Building,* 20.

6. Quoted in McPhee, *Encounters with the Archdruid,* 93.

7. The plan was prepared by a noted design firm, Skidmore, Owings and Merrill; see Skidmore, Owings, and Merrill, *Master Plan for Hilton Head Island.* The planning effort was motivated in part by the desire of the Hilton Head Company to bolster the case against proposals for large-scale industrial development in the immediate vicinity of Hilton Head. The resulting conflicts are discussed in chapter 8.

8. The district encompassed all of Sea Pines plus the land outside the plantation acquired by the Frasers from the Hilton Head Company in 1956.

9. The district created in 1972 was called the Palmetto Dunes Public Service District. New enabling legislation was secured the following year for a successor agency, the Broad Creek Public Service District, which was authorized to serve both Palmetto Dunes and the Hilton Head Company's planned Long Cove Plantation on the other side of U.S. 278.

10. See Fleming, *Hilton Head Island Government,* 132.

11. Onorato, interview.

12. The Airport Company of Hilton Head Island was set up by the Sea Pines Company and later expanded to include Hilton Head Company and other developers, with Sea Pines and the Hilton Head Company each owning 30 percent of the stock.

13. Reflecting the island-wide scope of services provided by the clinic, responsibility for the facility was transferred to a new public service district created in 1970, the Hilton Head Public Medical Clinic District.

14. The leading role was played by John Gettys Smith, who directed public relations at Sea Pines. Smith successfully sought a place on the county school board in a futile effort to secure a public school on the island.

15. Bowers, letter to the editor.

16. Onorato, interview.

17. Daniels, "Sojourner's Scrapbook," March 25, 1971.

18. Letter from Hilton Head Island Community Association to the Palmetto Dunes Resort, quoted in "Dunes Asked to Change 'High Rise' Project."

19. Quoted in "Hack Leaving Hilton Head Presidency."

20. Daniels, "Sojourner's Scrapbook," January 25, 1973.

21. Ashton's partners were Ben J. Tarbutton and Hugh Tarbutton of Sandersville and Herbert C. Skinner Jr. of Savannah.

22. Hack received $8 million in Oxford First stock in the transaction.

23. Quoted in Grafton, "Exclusively Charles Fraser," 14.

24. Sea Pines Plantation was set up as a subsidiary of the Sea Pines Company to operate the plantation, and most of the new ventures were managed by subsidiaries such as the Hilton Head Plantation Company. Throughout, the name Sea Pines is used to refer to the Sea Pines Company, Sea Pines Plantation, Sea Pines Plantation Company, and the other subsidiaries, since distinctions between these entities are not important for the purposes of this study.

25. Charles E. Fraser, quoted in Olson, "BT Interview: Charles Fraser," 16.

26. Fraser, "Charting the Directions of New Communities and Growth Area Land Use Management in the Era of President Carter and Chairman Burns," 11–12.

27. Quoted in Olson, "BT Interview: Charles Fraser," 17.

28. Curry, interview. John F. Curry joined Sea Pines as executive vice-president for resort operations in 1973.

29. James W. Light was president of the Sea Pines Company from early 1975 through the end of 1977, when he departed to develop a ski resort in Colorado and Fraser reassumed the presidency.

30. "Alive and Well and Dream Intact."

31. T. Richard Butera, president, Hilton Head Company, quoted in "Butera New Hilton Head President."

32. Joel H. Cowan, quoted in "Palmetto Dunes Now under Phipps Control."

33. Dey, interview. Richard Dey became executive director of the Hilton Head Island Chamber of Commerce in 1974.

34. Fred C. Hack, quoted in "H.H. Co., Oxford 1st Biggest Developer."

Chapter Six

Plantations and People

No island on earth has more loving residents than this one.
Their critical comments about it are actually expressions of their
adoration. That love grows stronger as it grows older.

—Jonathan Daniels, quoted in the *Island Packet,* August 31, 1972

Hilton Head was a state of mind as well as a geographic location. The good life on the island involved more than natural beauty, beaches and golf, mild climate and warm ocean, and amenities provided by plantation builders. People as well as plantations made Hilton Head a special place; those attracted to the island created a distinctive community that increased its appeal and forged strong bonds of loyalty. "Some mysterious island ingredient makes pleasant people even more pleasant," said a Philadelphia banker who bought one of the first lots in Sea Pines and moved to the island when he retired in 1961.[1] Many visitors were drawn back by the dual attractions of plantations and people, often to drive more permanent stakes.

Those who settled on plantations were mostly retirees, but Hilton Head was not a retirement community in any organized sense. Fraser and the other developers did not offer packaged lifestyles along the lines of some Sunbelt havens for the elderly. Nor were plantations exclusive developments for those over fifty-five or some other magic age; mature and more youthful residents were interspersed from the start in Sea Pines. Both retirees and working residents migrated to Hilton Head by choice, drawn by the attractions of the place and its people. Architects and entrepreneurs, doctors and lawyers—most came to Hilton Head because they were captivated by the island and its way of life. Some were ready to change their lives radically so they could spend their days in paradise.

One was Charles W. Doughtie, bitten by the Hilton Head bug in 1961. The forty-year-old advertising executive abandoned Madison Avenue and suburban Connecticut. He moved his family to a house on the ocean in Sea Pines, and, with his wife, opened the island's first upscale shop. Another was Dr. William H. Fries, who stopped on Hilton Head in 1963 on a trip to Florida, bought a lot in Sea Pines, and soon built a house. Fries had planned to spend to spend ten more years practicing medicine in Dayton, but the lure of the island was too strong. When the medical center grew to more than Dr. Chester Goodard could handle alone, Fries decided to change his life. "Why not go now?" he asked himself. "Why wait and perhaps not be alive to come to the island at all? Why not begin now to live longer and better."[2]

Places where people live largely by choice tend to have strongly articulated residential interests. Resort and retirement development amplifies these interests, producing a substantial population whose stakes are almost entirely residential, devoted to maintaining a high-quality environment and rising property values. On Hilton Head, as in many carefully developed communities that attract the affluent, residential interests were further structured by high standards and lofty expectations. Most who came were drawn by the environment produced by the plantation companies and the protections afforded by private controls; they were dedicated to preserving the attractions of the environment and community they had chosen. These feelings were strongest among retirees, who had selected Hilton Head from many other places where they could spend the rest of their lives. From the start, retired residents worried about development and sought to limit growth. Working islanders were more ambivalent; they too were drawn by Hilton Head's natural and human charms, but most depended on growth for their livelihood since development and tourism were the only industries in town.

Politics on Hilton Head would be structured by tension between residents and the development industry, a politics that emerged slowly because of predominant developer influence during the era of benevolent dictators. As the island grew and became more diverse, and with change at the major companies, residents articulated their interests more effectively. Developers, they insisted, were "not the only parties of interest" on Hilton Head; "possibly the first in interest are those who have already settled on this serene and hopefully never-to-be overrun shore."[3] Institutions evolved outside the control of the companies, including property owners' associations in the plantations and a community-wide residents' organization. Residents would emerge from the 1970s as the most influential group on Hilton Head, filling in part the power vacuum left by contraction of the plantation companies. Despite divisions among retirees and working residents and local blacks, residents would dominate the search for new governmental arrangements and public policies for a growing Hilton Head.

Development of residential interests on Hilton Head was rooted in the pattern of settlement, in the interplay of plantations and people. Most of those who settled on the island lived in plantations. Because the companies dominated so many phases of life, plantations loomed large for most residents during the first two decades of the island's modern development. Plantations were the primary focus of residents' initial efforts to secure more influence over community life. These efforts were affected by the kind of people who settled on Hilton Head and the sort of community they created from the raw materials provided by nature and the development companies. At the same time, who was able to live on the island was largely determined by plantation developers, whose successful efforts to attract an affluent clientele strongly structured the socioeconomic composition of those who migrated to Hilton Head in search of paradise.

AFFLUENT INFLUENTIALS

Charles Fraser called Sea Pines "a high quality destination resort."[4] His plantation was a vacation and retirement destination primarily for affluent and successful people. Among those who came were businessmen and bankers, captains of industry and military officers, doctors and lawyers, along with a sprinkling of writers, artists, and musicians. In 1972 half of Sea Pines' residents were retired; the average age was fifty-two.[5] Initially they came from the Southeast—half of the first five hundred property owners were from south Atlantic states. But the proportions from the Northeast and Midwest steadily increased as Fraser attracted attention and expanded his marketing activities.[6]

People who could afford Sea Pines were relatively well-off; seven out of ten property owners in 1973 were in business or the professions, and their average income was $47,000—57 percent higher than the median national family income.[7] Wealth was a sensitive subject on Hilton Head. Fraser and other island leaders did not want the island to be known as a rich man's community; such a reputation might scare off customers who were affluent but would steer clear of a development perceived as a playground for the leisure class. Marketing for Sea Pines emphasized the plantation's range of ages, income levels, and backgrounds as well as underscoring its casual lifestyles. Hilton Head attracted a variety of people, and the community reflected their diversity. Nonetheless, the island was definitely not an average slice of America in socioeconomic terms. More than thirty of those who settled in Sea Pines during the first decade were millionaires, and most of the rest were very comfortable financially.[8] The typical resident was well-off, educated, and accomplished, and these attributes strongly influenced the sort of place Hilton Head would become.

What was on Hilton Head influenced the kind of affluent middle-aged people who moved to plantations. Those in search of glitzy nightlife found little to do, and those whose idea of a resort included fine restaurants and fashionable shops were unimpressed by the island's meager offerings during the early years. The well-off who migrated to Hilton Head were content to enjoy the island's natural beauty, beaches, and active recreation. They preferred informality, creating an island style that rarely required anyone to wear a jacket or tie, or socks for that matter. Many were devoted to sport, and of the games they played, the most important was golf. Because golf courses quickly became one of Hilton Head's prime attractions, the residential population in the plantations was skewed toward the kind of people who play golf—successful men who belonged to country clubs, typically solid corporate types, and establishment professionals.

As a result, the first wave of settlers was heavily populated by couples in which the men had recently retired from large corporations and the military. Accustomed to large organizations, hierarchy, and conservative managerial practices, these men's distinctive style shaped their relations with the plantation companies and influenced development of community institutions on Hilton Head. Having held substantial positions of authority, they expected things to get done and were impatient with the often slow progress of the struggling plantation companies in the years before the boom. They also had time on their hands, which some used to scrutinize the development of Sea Pines and the other plantations. From the start, Fraser in particular performed in front of a critical audience of elders that was often very vocal about its differences with the young master of Sea Pines.

The early settlers cared deeply for the place they had chosen to live, and they came together to make a community in their image. They were fairly closely knit in the beginning; their numbers were relatively small in the early years, and most lived in Sea Pines. Moreover, they were sharing an experience as pioneers, coming together to build a community and celebrating a series of firsts, as Hilton Head secured a doctor, pharmacy, upscale restaurant, library, school, dress shop, then a newspaper and hospital. New residents as well as new businesses were written up in the local papers; they were welcome additions in a growing small town in which most people knew each other. Retirees and working islanders shared many interests in these formative years. The developers and their supporting casts lived on the island, scattered among the retirees. They had similar needs for services, activities, and facilities. All were pioneers, working together to make Hilton Head home, and their collective efforts increased their stake in the community.

Adding to the connections that marked the early residents was the tendency of people to migrate to Hilton Head to be close to friends who had already made the move. Migrants the world over often follow in the footsteps of people they know who have blazed the trail to new lands, so the affluent who followed friends to the plantations were treading a familiar path. On Hilton Head, this pattern was most common among retirees, but it also bolstered the ranks of the island's professionals and entrepreneurs. This process reinforced the socioeconomic cast of the island, as business and military heavyweights followed their friends, neighbors, and associates.

As residents arrived, Hilton Head was soon amply supplied with capable and energetic people with time to devote to community activities. Many retirees were looking for things to do, and a substantial number were experienced in civic affairs. They were eager to get involved and, in the process, to make friends with kindred spirits in their new surroundings. There was no shortage of tasks, since the plantation builders had provided only partial communities. Residents became an essential dynamic in the development of Hilton Head, organizing a variety of activities, working with the companies in getting facilities built, and creating a strong tradition of voluntarism that sustained civic life on the island. While critical help in creating community institutions often came from Fraser and Hack, residents provided the know-how and enthusiasm that nurtured the library, hospital, emergency squad, youth center, churches, schools, animal shelter, chamber orchestra, community theater, and arts institute.

Paralleling these developments were changes brought by growth that enlarged the scale and diversity of the residential community. Growth brought more people and a more varied set of residential interests. With expanding housing options came retirees from a wider range of backgrounds, many with less experience in community affairs than the earlier group of successful executives and their wives. As the local economy expanded, more residents were working islanders with less time for community activities and a larger stake in the development business than retirees. Growth and diversity eroded the sense of community established by the pioneers. Recent arrivals had not shared the adventure of the early years together. They were less intimately connected with plantation companies, which were no longer the personal instruments of Charles Fraser and Fred Hack. Inevitably, long-time residents pined for the good old days when Hilton Head was more intimate, the people were friendlier, and the developers were more accessible. New arrivals, on the other hand, developed their own agendas, often focused on their plantations, which provided a haven of comparative stability as growth soared. What had been a cohesive community was increasingly subdivided: the plantations were one frame of reference; length of time on Hilton Head was another. In a growing community, "the good old days" is a moving point of reference, changing for each cohort of residents.

Growth also sharply increased the ranks of absentee owners, many of whose stakes were different from those of permanent residents. The shift in emphasis from residential to resort development and construction of large numbers of condominiums brought more nonresident property owners who depended on developers to attract vacationers to rent their homes. By 1973 absentee owners outnumbered residents by three to two, and the ratio was almost two to one in Sea Pines (see table 6.1). A good deal of housing was acquired for rental income or tax shelters by owners who spent little or no time on the island. For these owners, property on Hilton Head was an investment to be protected rather than a place to live or a community in which to devote time and energy.

Table 6.1
Resident and Absentee Property Ownership, 1973

	Resident	**Absentee**	**Percent Absentee**
Sea Pines	1,078	1,951	64.4
Forest Beach	490	675	57.9
Port Royal area	263	485	64.8
Rest of Hilton Head	933	1,050	53.0
Total	2,764	4,161	60.1

Source: Fleming, *Hilton Head Island Government: Analysis and Alternatives,* 108.

RESIDENTIAL INTERESTS

Within the plantations, resident homeowners defined residential interests. They dealt with plantation companies, organized property owners' associations, and represented owners as relations with the companies were formalized. Residents had higher stakes than absentee owners. They lived on Hilton Head and had invested personally in the community and a particular plantation; their lives were far more intimately affected by local developments than were those of nonresident owners, whose concerns were often limited to their properties' rental receipts and resale value and their own periodic vacations on Hilton Head. Residents were on the scene, more or less aware of what was happening on their plantation and on the island generally. Retirees, who were the dominant group both numerically and in terms of influence as residential interests crystallized, also had time, financial acumen, technical skills, and leadership experience to bring to the tasks of defining, organizing, and representing property owners.

Residential interests in plantations overlapped with those of the companies. Rising property values, attractive amenities, and a high-quality environment were the principal concerns of property owners as well as basic objectives of the major developers. Perspectives would never be identical: residents sought more amenities at little or no cost than the companies could economically provide, while plantations wanted to develop more than residents preferred. Nonetheless, underlying the relationship was a base of mutual interests reinforced by reciprocal respect between residents and plantation companies. Most of those who moved to Hilton Head were positively attracted by what had been provided by developers, especially at Sea Pines, which was the destination of almost all early settlers. The companies were sensitive to property owners' concerns because they needed the enthusiastic approval of their customers. Residents were Hilton Head's best salespeople, particularly during the early years. Property owners influenced others to visit and provided names of friends and associates who might be interested in the plantation. Property was much easier to sell if those who had already bought a piece of paradise were happy with their choice.

Mutual interests, however, did not give residents the same agenda as Fraser and Hack's. As residents moved into plantations, they brought distinctive concerns about their individual homes and surroundings. They worried about property values and externalities and were troubled by inadequate services and nuisances. In short, they were resident homeowners, with the same kinds of interests that most resident owners have anywhere. What was different about Hilton Head compared to most American communities was that residents had so little influence in a system completely dominated by plantation developers. For all the thought and planning that went into Sea Pines, Fraser acknowledges that "no attention was given to the people that would live there, and how they would relate to the plantation and its future development."[9] So residents almost from the start sought means for having their interests recognized as relevant and legitimate in the decision-making process.

Relations between residents and plantations were most important in Sea Pines. Until well into the 1970s, the great majority of people who came to the island settled in Sea Pines, so developments there affected the largest number of people. At the heart of the evolving relationship between the plantation and its residents was Fraser, who personally controlled everything at Sea Pines in the early days. Fraser and his customers were a strange match. He was young, brash, and not very respectful of his elders and their often conventional ideas about architecture and community development. Sea Pines residents were important people, used to being in charge. By their standards, Fraser was an unconventional businessman, a lawyer with little experience who mismanaged a poorly organized company. The fact that most of them came from large companies or the military complicated their relationship with Fraser; few understood real estate development, marketing, or small businesses.

Settlers in Sea Pines both admired the daring young man whose handiwork had brought them to Hilton Head and chafed under his rule. "My feelings about Charles are mixed," notes an influential resident who frequently differed with Fraser, "but if it hadn't been for him, I wouldn't be here."[10] The heralded community builder was also, in the words of one, "a little dictator with a stranglehold on the plantation."[11] Many could speak, but only one decided. Fraser made the plans and decided whether they would be changed, such as including resort and condominium development at Harbour Town and South Beach. He determined what would be built when, what the levels of maintenance would be, and who could use his golf courses under what terms. All of these matters affected residents, but in none of them did they have an authoritative voice. Most had lived in affluent suburbs where local officials were responsive to the interests of affluent residents. Now they found themselves in a company town ruled by a imperious young man who was convinced that he knew what was best for everyone.

These tensions were muted in the early days by Fraser's accessibility. Most residents knew him personally and could see him easily. For a number of years, Fraser hosted a weekly cocktail party for residents, listening to their concerns about plantation security, fetid lagoons, rogue alligators, maintenance problems, and inconveniences caused by construction. Residents also were surveyed periodically, and their priorities helped shape Fraser's agenda. Of course, the decisions that followed conversations, cocktail party encounters, and company surveys were made by Fraser. Such decisions primarily reflected the interests of the Sea Pines Company in its property owners, present and prospective, which were not identical to the interests of its current residents.

Dissatisfaction among residents over their lack of power was mitigated also by the attractive arrangements they enjoyed at Sea Pines. Because Fraser desperately needed customers at the outset, Sea Pines practically gave away amenities and services. Initially, property owners were charged only $15 annually for roads, mosquito control, and other services provided by the plantation. Having gotten a good deal for very little, they continually asked for more. Fraser, wanting to keep his present customers happy and attract new ones, usually responded positively. Services grew much faster than revenues from fees, which by 1973 had risen to only $75 for new sales.[12] With land in Sea Pines selling rapidly in the booming early 1970s, Fraser's pricing policies became more burdensome to the company and more difficult to justify in terms of attracting customers. Fraser wanted fees raised sufficiently to bring operating revenues into line with costs. But past practices had created expectations that Sea Pines would underwrite much of the cost of services, and property owners resisted paying more for the good life.

Fraser's problems with residents were further complicated by his expansion of the Sea Pines Company and his growing detachment from operations at the plantation. Preoccupied with new ventures and frequently away from Hilton Head, Fraser was less and less involved with Sea Pines and its residents. He was no longer easily accessible, but he retained control, making all important decisions that affected property owners. For most residents, he was an increasingly absent figure with little interest in their welfare rather than a neighbor and senior partner in the exciting venture of building a community. His style became more imperial; the mayor of Sea Pines had become ruler of a vast empire of resorts. He had never been an easy man for many residents to like. Now his increasing detachment broke the personal bond that led property owners to accept benevolent dictatorship and hastened their organization to further their interests.

On the other plantations, similar patterns developed. Residents felt a strong kinship with the development company at the outset, and their positive feelings were reinforced by underpriced amenities and services. The need to compete with Sea Pines and its inexpensive fees kept charges low at the other plantations. At Palmetto Dunes, for example, annual assessments were initially pegged at $25, and membership in the golf club cost less than at Sea Pines because Palmetto Dunes was seeking a competitive advantage over Fraser's resort. As long as plantations were primarily in the land business, prices remained low. When land sales tapered off and operating costs became increasingly larger, the other development companies also would press for higher charges, and residents would resist.

Within these common patterns were variations rooted in the different personalities at the helm of the other companies. Fred Hack was less commanding and more responsive than Charles Fraser. Customer preferences had more impact on architectural styles at Hack's plantation. Formation of the Port Royal Property Owners Association was encouraged by the Hilton Head Company, which "felt that it had to work closely with residents if its efforts were to be successful."[13] After people began to settle at Palmetto Dunes, Robert Onorato met monthly with residents to hear their concerns and defend company policies. Onorato, like Fraser, was autocratic, running what he calls "a democratic dictatorship" in which he "stood up for the property owners when they had a good case" and insisted on his "own way when necessary."[14] What was a good case and what was necessary, of course, was determined by Onorato on the basis of what made sense for his company.

At the heart of the relationship between residents and plantations was the question of growth. Settlers and plantation companies were bound to differ over development. Conflict was inherent because residents inevitably desired less development than the companies. Settlers wanted to enjoy what they had purchased without the disruption of constant change and construction. Plantations, on the other hand, had to develop in order to survive. As the pace of building in Sea Pines quickened in the late 1960s, residential concerns mounted about the large amount of construction and the perils posed by excessive development. Fraser acknowledged in 1971 that the boom was disruptive to those who had chosen to live in Sea Pines. "In my own personal preference and taste, there has been too much building at one time within Sea Pines Plantation, and we hope that we can bring the pace of construction and the volume of construction to a more orderly level."[15]

Fraser, of course, was talking about moderating the pace of development, not modifying Sea Pines' intention to build out to its planned capacity. Residents, on the other hand, increasingly questioned the plans themselves. Plantation master plans had been prepared by the companies before any homesites had been sold; they reflected developers' objectives rather than the interests of residents, who had not been consulted when plans were created or amended. The plans were not guarantees but general outlines that usually included everything the company might develop. The fact that condos and an oceanfront inn were included in the original Sea Pines plans did not make settlers less unhappy about condominiums and resort development. The prospect of more construction, more condos, and more tourists only reinforced the conviction of residents that they had rights and interests that had to be taken into account by Sea Pines and the other companies.

As plantations grew, conflict between residential and company interests affected more and more activities. Illustrative is the dispute that festered over the size of the company-financed Sea Pines Golf Club. Residents wanted membership limited to insure that golf facilities would not be overwhelmed. For the company, the opportunity to join the golf club was an important element in selling lots and condos. Resident golfers bitterly opposed enlarging the club, arguing that "the objectives, needs and interests of the members should have priority where there is a conflict of interests."[16] But giving priority to residential interests would restrict developers' ability to complete their planned communities and retire their debts. Their biggest returns came as development progressed, since unit costs were lower and land values higher in these later stages. What was considered financially essential by the development companies was seen by most residents as detrimental to their interests.

Conflict over development was intensified because Hilton Head was a resort whose business interests were dedicated to increasing the number of visitors. Most settlers wanted to live in a residential rather than resort atmosphere. They resented the growing numbers of tourists that descended on Sea Pines with the development of Harbour Town and South Beach and the mounting emphasis on resort activities by Fraser and other island developers and business leaders. Living in a booming resort meant crowded golf courses and tennis courts, and, outside the plantation gates, traffic jams and littered beaches, noisy youths and boisterous drunks, increased crime and security problems, and—as the 1960s unfolded—drugs and unconventional sexual behavior.

To be sure, plantation residents benefited from resort development. Superlative recreational facilities and inexpensive golf and tennis were possible because plantations were resorts as well as residential communities. Without tourists and their dollars, residents of Sea Pines could not have supported four golf courses and two racquet clubs. Residents, plantation companies insisted, were getting more for less, to say nothing of enhanced property values, because Hilton Head was a successful resort. While most residents recognized the positive side of the resort equation, many were bothered by the realities of living in a busy playground rather than the anticipated tranquil island paradise. Arguments emphasizing property values were not persuasive to many retired residents, who valued quality of life more than resale value of their homes.

With some justification, residents felt that plantations cared more about the resort business and tourists than about those who had chosen to live permanently on Hilton Head. Residents pointed to developers' strenuous efforts to extend the tourist season by enlarging the airport, adding tourist attractions, and marketing the island aggressively as a resort. For many settlers, particularly retired plantation residents, resort development was a zero-sum game in which the companies' gain was their loss. The plantation companies were not indifferent to these growing concerns. After all, present and prospective residents were their most important customers. Separation of resort and residential activities at Palmetto Dunes reduced conflicts, despite the plantation's intensive resort development. Port Royal and Hilton Head Plantation were marketed as residential communities. Sea Pines built its fourth golf course for the exclusive use of residents in response to complaints that they were being squeezed off the plantation's three public courses by the growing numbers of visitors.

Despite these responses, differences over development and resort activity widened the estrangement between residents and plantations. For many settlers, the underlying problem on Hilton Head was greed, and from this perception emerged a "greedy developer" syndrome that increasingly poisoned relationships on the island. Self-serving motives were seen in everything undertaken by plantations, especially by Charles Fraser, whom some saw as the greediest, always trying to milk money out of Sea Pines. Fraser was an easy target; among developers he was the most visible, most powerful, most successful, and most outspoken.

ORGANIZING PROPERTY OWNERS

Inevitably, as issues and conflicts multiplied in the wake of population growth and resort development, plantation residents organized to advance their common interests. Recognition of the divergent objectives of residents and development companies, however, came slowly. More than fifteen years elapsed between the arrival of the first settlers in Sea Pines and the creation of a formal property owners' association. To some degree, the delay reflected Charles Fraser's skill in leading Sea Pines in directions that were generally consonant with the interests of those who settled on his plantation. But accelerating resort development, changes in the company, and Fraser's involvement elsewhere combined to alter fundamentally the relationship between Sea Pines and its residents. In addition, the number of residents and absentee owners rapidly increased during the boom years, and this larger population was more diverse and less easily represented through informal arrangements.

Regularized relations between residents and company officials began with the operation of plantation facilities, particularly the Sea Pines golf club and courses. Members belonged to the club, and club officers dealt with the company. Those drawn through golf and club activity into more systematic relations with the Sea Pines Company were almost all retirees, and most had belonged to country clubs before coming to Hilton Head. They quickly discovered that Sea Pines was different from a regular golf club because members did not own the facilities. Here they had to deal with the company to get anything done. In the process, residents developed close relationships with Sea Pines personnel, learned a good deal about company finances and management, and influenced operations in their area of special interest and expertise. Out of these activities emerged a cadre of active residents with experience in working with the company who would provide leadership when property owners formally organized.

Sea Pines residents finally created an owners' association in 1973. The immediate cause was a dispute between Sea Pines and condo owners over the company's decision to increase rental commissions and raise housekeeping rates for properties managed by the plantation. A distressed landlord proposed creation of an association so that "property owners could develop a composite view to present to Sea Pines on matters that are of concern to them."[17] This approach, however, had little appeal to people who lived in Sea Pines, since absentee owners' concerns were emphasized rather than issues that troubled residents. Their alternative was a property owners' association created and controlled by settlers. An organizing committee formed by permanent residents framed the agenda largely in terms of its members' worries—"maintenance, security and traffic, parking, villas, construction approval, trail system, erosion, marine life protection, protection of forests, marshes and wildlife and cultural events."[18] The committee called for a single organization encompassing all property owners, noting that while "owners of various types of property have varied and special interests . . . the decision has been made that one incorporated Association can be most effective." The decision was made unilaterally by permanent residents.[19]

Thus was born the Association of Sea Pines Plantation Property Owners, an organization that would be dominated by settlers and their interests, particularly retired male residents. They had the time to give the association, staff its committees, and meet with plantation officials. They tended to run the organization along corporate and military lines; the association was long on structure and procedures and short on responsiveness to the plantation's growing diversity. Its paramount concerns were those of retired residents with single-family homes. Less attention was given to the interests of nonresidents, condominium owners, and working islanders, whose numbers in the plantation steadily increased.

Elsewhere property owners organized along similar lines with permanent residents firmly in control. Port Royal owners formed their association two years before residents in Sea Pines. At Spanish Wells, common property and architectural review was controlled by the owners' association, and the golf course by club members. Property owners were most influential on plantations with substantial numbers of permanent residents. Spanish Wells was entirely residential, and its homeowners financed and managed all common facilities. Port Royal was settled primarily by people who made Hilton Head their home; and Sea Pines, despite substantial condo development and many absentee owners, had a large and restive residential population. Palmetto Dunes, on the other hand, was primarily a resort with absentee property owners. Residents there did not organize until 1977, a delay that reflected the lack of a critical mass of settlers as well as the insulation from resort activities provided by the community's physical design. Once formed, the Palmetto Dunes association was much less influential than its counterparts on more settler-oriented plantations, collecting minimal dues and playing no formal role in architectural review or community services. Shipyard Plantation was even more resort-oriented than Palmetto Dunes, with resident owners a small minority in a sea of absentee owners of condos. Property owners at Shipyard organized late and played no significant role in plantation affairs.

At the plantations with substantial numbers of settlers, residential influence over company policies and operations was boosted by the developers' desire to shift operating costs to residents. In return for larger assessments, property owners secured roles in developing policies, allocating funds, overseeing administration, and enforcing design standards. The most sweeping changes were made at Sea Pines, where negotiations in 1973–1974 between company and residents produced restrictions on future development of the plantation, better protection of property owners' interests, and direct involvement of residents in operations in return for higher assessments for services and facilities. These negotiations were framed by the covenants devised by Charles Fraser, sets of binding obligations that would structure many conflicts as Hilton Head developed. Assessments could not be changed without approval of property owners, nor could anything else covered by covenants. The need for owner consent provided essential leverage for residents to open a wide range of issues in negotiations with the company over the impasse on financing services.

In the deal that emerged from these discussions, Sea Pines obtained higher assessments. Owners would pay $180 per dwelling unit and $110 for unimproved lots. In return, residents exacted concessions that limited future development of the plantation. Total planned dwelling units in Sea Pines were reduced from 7,000 to 5,890; condominiums were cut back from 3,000 to 2,100; commercial development in the plantation was restricted to 105 acres; and the limit of building heights to five stories was formalized. Other residential concerns were addressed in the agreements, which provided liberalized golf privileges and raised barriers to outsiders by increasing gate fees. Relationships between plantation and property owners also were institutionalized, with formation of a Property Owners Advisory Board.[20] For most property owners, the proposed agreements were a good deal, and 85 percent agreed in 1974 to the new arrangements and higher assessments.[21]

The agreement forged a partnership between the plantation and its people that one company official called the Sea Pines Magna Carta.[22] Implementation secured residents a steadily enlarging role in the management of Sea Pines Plantation. They sat on the architectural review board and became custodians of open space in Sea Pines. Assessments on property owners and the company's contributions for community services went into a trust fund, from which expenditures required approval by the company and the advisory board. This arrangement provided residents with an opportunity to influence the setting of priorities for the plantation. Committees established under the advisory board worked closely with company officials on budgets, maintenance, and capital plans, providing an outlet for the experience and energy of retired executives and producing protracted negotiations. The expanding influence of residents opened the processes by which private decisions were made at Sea Pines and the other planned communities. More parties were involved, debate was more public, and information and financial data were more readily available. These developments varied from plantation to plantation, but the overall effect was similar, eroding company control and replacing benevolent dictatorship with a form of corporatism in which company officials and residents' representatives shared decision-making authority.

Residents drawn into operations of plantations had to wrestle with their fellow property owners as well as company officials. Property owners were a diverse and often contentious constituency, disagreeing among themselves over priorities, policies, and fees. At Sea Pines, money was a constant problem since the new assessment schedule did not generate sufficient revenues to maintain the plantation adequately. Property owners, however, resisted increased fees even when they were arduously promoted by their representatives. Complicating the issue of higher charges was the policy of uniform assessments, according to which the owner of the smallest condo paid the same fee for community services as the owner of the most expensive house. Not fair, argued those with less valuable property—many of whom were absentee owners of condominiums—pointing to property taxes based on home values as the proper model for community service fees. Nonsense, replied the well-off retirees who controlled the association; uniform rates were fair because everyone had equal access to the services funded by assessments—an argument that conveniently ignored the fact that residents derived substantially more benefit from most services than absentee owners.

In carving themselves an authoritative role at Sea Pines, residents not only insured attention to their interests and growing influence over the plantation but also insulated property owners from the fortunes of Fraser and his company. By the time the agreements were concluded in mid-1974, Fraser was overextended financially, and the first years of the new arrangements coincided with the company's greatest time of troubles. After Fraser's fall, they congratulated themselves on having had the foresight to enhance owners' rights and protections. Sea Pines was theirs. They, rather than the company, owned most of the land and financed the lion's share of plantation services; they were the real protectors and preservers of where they lived. Writing of the durability of Sea Pines during the perilous mid-1970s, a settler underscored the transition from benevolent dictators to residents: "The dream remains intact and, which is more, largely in the possession of residents with the power and purpose to resist the collapse or destruction of a place for which they have not only ownership but devotion."[23]

PLANTATION MENTALITY

Devotion to one's plantation was a fundamental reality of life on Hilton Head. Plantations were the central institutional and communal concern of most inhabitants of the island. They provided public services and recreational facilities as well as residents' primary identification. Islanders usually thought of themselves and other residents in terms of their plantation (or lack thereof). More than most small places, Hilton Head developed as a series of private communities instead of a single public community, with residents more concerned with their plantation than with the island as a whole. Island developers, in the words of one, "created a set of tribes, the Sea Pines tribe, the Port Royal tribe, with each thinking their tribe was best. . . . And those outside the plantations were also divided into tribes, which felt they were being walked on by the plantation tribes."[24]

Each tribe viewed itself and the other tribes in a distinctive frame of reference. Sea Pines residents saw themselves as the elite, the real islanders living in the place that was Hilton Head. Sea Pines provided almost all of the island's leaders before 1980 because most settlers lived there and many of them were able and energetic. Those who settled on other plantations resented the snobbery of Sea Pines residents, who assumed that theirs was better. As the island grew, the dominance of people from Sea Pines would fade, especially with the rapid development of Hilton Head Plantation during the 1980s. Hilton Head Plantation was almost as extensive as Sea Pines, and its homeowners were largely permanent residents. Settlers in Hilton Head Plantation were the new kids on the block, more interested in the future than the past. In the struggles over growth that would preoccupy Hilton Head in the 1980s, Hilton Head Plantation would provide the best organized and most vehement advocates of stringent building controls, moratoriums on development, and public referendums on growth issues.

Reinforcing these divisions was the seclusion of plantations as private communities with security gates. Access to most plantations was limited, and outsiders needed a pass or special permission to gain access. Gates were first installed at Sea Pines in 1967 in response to the residents' desire for more privacy, better security, less traffic on narrow, winding roads, and fewer people using the plantation's facilities. Open to everyone during the first decade, Sea Pines became increasingly crowded by outsiders who flocked to the plantation's beaches, golf courses, tennis courts, and restaurants. Sea Pines residents constantly pressed the company to tighten access controls, improve security, and increase the tolls and permit fees. Gatehouses were added at Port Royal and Shipyard Plantations in 1972 and would be a regular feature at Hilton Head Plantation, the residential portions of Palmetto Dunes, and other planned communities on Hilton Head and its environs.

For some islanders, plantation gates were a nuisance that interfered with business and social intercourse. Among business owners, those within Sea Pines were particularly unhappy because gate fees and limited access to the plantation discouraged potential customers. For others, plantation gates were a metaphor for the snobbery and exclusivity of the private worlds created by Fraser and other developers. Gates may well have improved security, kept out suspicious types, reduced fear of crime, relieved crowding of plantation facilities, enhanced property values, and helped developers sell lots and condos; but they were also elitist and exclusionary by design. Suggestions that gates be torn down or that access be eased for residents of other plantations or islanders in general were not welcomed by most property owners. Plantation gates, owners argued, insured security, privacy, and property values, not exclusivity. Speaking of gates and private communities, an official of a property owners' association declared flatly, "That's the whole basis for the island."[25]

Private plantations and the mentality they fostered among some residents posed challenges to those seeking to bring islanders together on matters of common concern. Broader community issues were difficult to articulate for water and sewers, parks and recreation, security, local roads, and other needs met by the plantation companies. Awareness of local interdependence and the island as a distinctive entity was further obscured by the absence of a local political system to define the community. Like so many newly settled areas, particularly in the Sunbelt, Hilton Head lacked the focus provided by a local government whose jurisdiction was coincident with the community.

Growing concern about the island's civic health and welfare spurred the creation of the Hilton Head Island Community Association in 1966. The prime mover was Charles Fraser, who thought Hilton Head needed a civic organization. The follow-up came from a group of settlers, most of them living in Sea Pines. One of the organizers and the first president of the Community Association was Arthur Hall, a quintessential early migrant: he had risen to the top ranks of a major corporation, was retired, lived in Sea Pines, and wanted to stay involved in community issues. The organization created by Hall and his fellow settlers was open to all island residents and actively sought a diverse membership, but its primary appeal was to retirees on plantations. The association's basic objective was to preserve paradise, "to retain the natural beauty of the appealing environment which has attracted many newcomers."[26] For more than a decade, the association was the primary forum for discussion of community concerns. One leader viewed the organization as an essential substitute for the local government that Hilton Head lacked, a "government in exile."[27]

The association, however, was far from a local government, lacking public authority or revenues; and its political activity was limited by its status as a nonprofit corporation. Within these constraints, the civic group grappled primarily with problems that affected the entire island or at least troubled its constituency in more than one plantation, including the library and hospital. Widespread settler unhappiness drew the organization into the controversies over the airport and the high-rise hotel in Palmetto Dunes. It advocated road and bridge improvements, county action to provide planning and development controls, an effective building code, and adequate fire prevention standards; and it took the lead in the early explorations of creating local government on Hilton Head.[28] On most issues, however, the civic association was better at talk than at action, a safety valve rather than an institution able to build durable bridges across the divisions that separated islanders.

One bridge not built by the Hilton Head Island Community Association was between the growing white majority and local blacks. Efforts were made by the group to enlist blacks, and some association activities were of particular interest to the black community, including day care and water supply. Nonetheless, few blacks were active in the organization. They did not feel part of the "community" represented by the association, the community of affluent plantation residents. More generally, blacks were troubled by the rising tide of well-off whites on Hilton Head. Their own share of the island's population was steadily declining, from over 90 percent in 1950 to less than 15 percent twenty-five years later. Ironically, at the same time that the civil rights revolution was giving African Americans a political voice throughout the South, development on Hilton Head was diluting the political influence of local blacks, bringing in more and more people who saw the island as theirs and shared no interests with these earlier islanders.

Local blacks were particularly troubled because the newcomers were different from the whites that they had dealt with in the past. Hilton Head's blacks trusted Sheriff Ed McTeer of Beaufort County, a white man who spoke Gullah and knew everyone. McTeer settled disputes informally, kept track of black landholdings, and helped them in dealings with government agencies. Fraser and Hack were also Southerners and sensitive to the concerns of local blacks. With growth came corporate types from wealthy Northern suburbs who had little experience with African Americans either at work or in their communities. Their views were often shaped by negative stereotypes of urban blacks rather than the reality of Hilton Head's black community. Settlers on plantations largely ignored native islanders and their concerns; few knew anything about local blacks, their community, and their culture. Most newcomers drawn into community affairs saw blacks as insular and uncooperative, obstacles to the changes that settlers insisted were needed for "their" Hilton Head.

Black islanders reciprocated, distrusting white residents, worrying about their land as growth spread, and resenting the elaborate private facilities in plantations while black areas lacked rudimentary public services. "I realized that whites had taken over the island" by 1974, relates an influential black resident. "At first it was a shock just watching the occupation. . . . Now we live with it every day."[29] For African Americans, plantation gates were "a symbol of white primacy," physical barriers with armed guards meant to keep them out of the exclusive preserves of white Hilton Head.[30] Black resentment was compounded by the unfortunate term *plantation;* whatever the attractions it had for marketing luxury and gentility, plantations were places where blacks had been slaves, and the term was offensive to those whose forebears had been exploited on Hilton Head's original plantations.

Black fears, resentment over gates, concern about exclusivity and tribalism—all were rooted in tensions inherent in the kind of community created by the combination of private plantations and affluent people. Hilton Head was based on conflicting notions of community. The dominant theme was paradise, the marriage of people and nature on an idyllic island insulated from the troubles of less perfect places. Paradise was best approximated in private and exclusive communities, the plantations that attracted people to Hilton Head. Barriers were an inherent part of the appeal of plantations; their pricing policies and development controls protected residents from unwanted neighbors. Most who settled on plantations were conservative socially; they had lived in exclusionary neighborhoods and towns, belonged to country clubs that excluded Jews and blacks, and spent their careers in organizations that had few if any Jews in top positions and no African Americans in command of anything. Some wanted Sea Pines to exclude Jews and opposed Fraser's policy of accommodating blacks at plantation facilities. Though they cared deeply about "their" adopted island and built an impressive array of community institutions, these settlers defined paradise in terms of their interests, with institutions to serve their needs and preserve their notion of the good life.

As the island grew, preserving paradise became the rallying point of people in plantations. The threats posed by uncontrolled and inappropriate development brought settlers together. They battled with developers and other local business people, native blacks, county and state officials, and eventually the local government created by island voters primarily as a means of controlling growth. The shape of these struggles was determined largely by the forces that produced modern Hilton Head: private plantations, benevolent dictators, an economy based on development and tourists, well-off settlers with increasing influence, and apprehensive blacks squeezed by change. Inevitably, the issue of growth was entangled with the question of exclusivity, with the kind of place the plantations and their residents had made. Caught in the paradox of growth—the fact that what attracts is changed by what is attracted—Hilton Head, like other desirable places, harbored many residents who wanted to pull up the gangplank now that they were in paradise.

NOTES

1. Frank Royce, quoted in Mary Kendall Hilton, "Islander: Frank Royce," 4. Royce, like many others, came out of retirement—in his case, to become the manager of the Hilton Head branch of the Bank of Beaufort.

2. Quoted in Mary Kendall Hilton, "Islander: William H. Fries, M.D.," 8.

3. Daniels, "Sojourner's Scrapbook," February 17, 1972.

4. Quoted in McPhee, *Encounters with the Archdruid,* 94.

5. "Sea Pines Property Owners Respond to Questionnaire."

6. The 500 property owners in 1963 came from thirty-five states and seven foreign countries. Of those from the United States, 256 were from the south Atlantic states, 41 from the middle Atlantic, 23 from the north central area, and 21 from New England.

7. See Simpson, "Analysis and Profile of the Sea Pines Market," and Sea Pines Company, "1973 Sea Pines Plantation Owners Survey."

8. In 1964 Sea Pines counted 32 millionaires among its property owners; Sea Pines Company, "Ownership of Property within Sea Pines Plantation."

9. Charles E. Fraser, interview, June 30, 1990.

10. Hall, interview.

11. Wamsley, interview.

12. The increases were not retroactive since the lower charges were locked into the original contract between the plantation and the purchaser.

13. Orion D. Hack, interview.

14. Onorato, interview.

15. Quoted in Bowers and Bowers, "What Does the Future Hold for Hilton Head Island?"

16. "Sea Pines Golf Club, Inc. Enlargement Is Opposed."

17. T. C. Keeling Jr., quoted in "Sea Pines Resident Advocates Property Owners Association." More than 150 unhappy owners responded and persuaded Sea Pines to drop the housekeeping increase and modify the higher commission rates.

18. "Sea Pines Property Owners Organizing Association."

19. The first quotation is from the draft constitution. The second is from a letter sent by the organizing committee to all property owners; see ibid. The committee members were Roy Davis, Arthur P. Hall, Hunter Hicks, and Lt. Gen. E. J. Timberlake, all retired and substantial citizens. Rental property owners in Sea Pines also organized, but their group was far less important than the general property owners' association.

20. The Property Owners Advisory Board had nine members, chosen by an annual election of three members to serve three-year terms. The board was initially separate from the property owners' association until 1984, when it merged with the association.

21. Approval by 75 percent was required to modify the covenants. Those who rejected the new arrangements continued to pay the fees provided under their original contracts and covenants.

22. Fowler, interview. Fowler was one of Sea Pines' representatives in the negotiations.

23. Daniels, "Sojourner's Scrapbook," May 27, 1976.

24. Orion D. Hack, interview.

25. Bob Bergin, Hilton Head Plantation Property Owners, quoted in "Plantation Leaders Debate Call to Open the Gates."

26. Emerson Mulford, president, Hilton Head Island Community Association, quoted in Mary Kendall Hilton, "Islander: Emerson Mulford," 4. Mulford succeeded Hall as president of the Community Association.

27. Racusin, interview. Benjamin Racusin was elected president of the Community Association in 1972.

28. The activities of the Community Association during the twelve-year

search for responsive local political institutions for the island are examined in chapter 9.

29. Emory Campbell, quoted in Harris, "Plantations Again."

30. The quotation is from Jordan and Fleming, "Organizing Local Government," chapter 5, 21.

Chapter Seven

Growing Pains

*The chief threat to this Island, most residents now agree, is
"people pollution" and the inevitable defacement of landscape
and life-style that go along inexorably with unregulated growth.*

—Cabell Phillips, *Islander,* May 1973

Hilton Head was opened to development by completion of the James F.
Byrnes Crossing in 1956. Fifteen years later some settlers were ready to blow
up the bridge to save the island from developers. Talk of blowing up the bridge
was a state of mind rather than a realistic alternative; it reflected islanders' fears
and frustrations as Hilton Head grew and changed. Concern began to mount as
the pace of development quickened in the 1960s. Population more than doubled
during the decade, from 1,100 to over 2,500.[1] Housing construction increased
sharply as development accelerated in Sea Pines, rising from 36 houses a year
between 1956 and 1963 to an annual average of 187 for the rest of the decade.
In 1969 alone, 351 homes were built. An increasing share of housing was condominiums. The first condos were built in 1964; in 1969 condos accounted for
45 percent of new housing on Hilton Head. Population and housing continued
to surge through the booming early 1970s. Resort development attracted ever
larger numbers of people to the island, with more than 72,000 tourists in 1972.
The genie was out of the bottle—growth was changing Hilton Head, bringing
more settlers, more vacationers, more business, and more development. Despite the recession of the mid-1970s, the island's population topped 6,500 in
1975.[2] Five years later Hilton Head had more than 11,000 residents and was
accommodating almost 650,000 visitors.[3] Between 1972 and 1980, the local
economy grew from 120 businesses with almost 3,000 employees to more than
850 enterprises with 9,500 workers.[4]

Worries about growth mounted as rapidly as the pace of development. At
cocktail parties, on the golf course, and in articles and letters in local publications, islanders decried new construction, condos, tourists, litter, noise, traffic,
ugliness, and all the people like them who wanted to share in paradise. Doris
and Seward Bowers captured the feeling of many of their neighbors during the
peak of the boom when they said, "Perhaps no one expected such run-away
growth as the island is experiencing. Many old-time residents would like to

stop it. Not-quite-so-old-timers would like at least to apply the brakes. And even newcomers quickly learn to say, 'Now that I'm here let's blow up the bridge.'"[5] Uncontrolled growth threatened what had made Hilton Head so attractive; what had happened along most of the Atlantic and Gulf coasts could overwhelm their island. The recurring nightmare was that Hilton Head would become like Myrtle Beach, at the other end of the South Carolina coast, with its amusement parks, garish signs and blaring music, tall hotels and mobbed beaches—the epitome of everything that Charles Fraser wanted to prevent from occurring at Hilton Head.

Table 7.1
Visitors to Hilton Head Island, 1972–1980

Year	Visitors	Index (1972 = 100)
1972	72,000	100
1973	112,000	156
1974	194,000	269
1975	266,000	369
1976	392,000	544
1977	429,000	596
1978	550,000	764
1979	600,000	833
1980	648,000	900

Source: Data are from the South Carolina Division of Tourism.

Underlying growth was the attraction of Hilton Head to residents and visitors. Those who came drew others to provide services, to build more houses and hotels and golf courses. The process was circular—more people brought more business that sought more customers. From one perspective, this was progress—the American way, with the magic of the marketplace turning a forgotten island into a cornucopia of profit and jobs. From another angle, growth was increasingly troublesome. Having too many people would cause a variety of problems that had not been anticipated when Fraser and other entrepreneurs planned their private communities. Hilton Head's beauty and climate, its plantations and charm, were both a blessing and a curse for those who chose to live on the island.

Some people blamed those who told their friends about the wonders of Hilton Head; others resented Fraser's successful efforts to publicize Sea Pines and its island setting. Of course, those who complained had once been tourists; they too had originally learned of Hilton Head from an acquaintance, an article or advertisement, or a travel agent. The desire to keep Hilton Head a secret was unrealistic. As one community leader noted in 1973, "We had each found our paradise here and we couldn't expect that someone else wouldn't find it too."[6]

That people were troubled by development that made their presence possible was only part of the dilemma of growth. Another aspect was that development brought benefits as well as costs. A larger population supported more services and facilities. Nicer shops and better restaurants, a newspaper and movie theater, more doctors and a hospital—all were consequences of growth, as were more construction, crowds, traffic, and changes in scale. So were enhanced property values for owners and more customers and profits for local businesses. On Hilton Head as elsewhere, people wanted the benefits that came with growth. As a result, they were ambivalent about growth, embracing expanding opportunities while suffering from growing pains. Should newcomers be welcomed for confirming the choices of their predecessors or deterred as latecomers for whom there was not enough room? Should new businesses be greeted for the additional choices they offered islanders or discouraged for making Hilton Head more attractive? Answers were usually equivocal and at times inconsistent, producing a "combination of hostility and hospitality. Please don't crowd us but 'Y'all come.'"[7]

Sensitivity about growth's costs was intensified by the nature of the place and its inhabitants. Hilton Head was a beautiful island with a fragile ecology that had been developed with care. Sea Pines in particular created high expectations about high-quality design and environmental concern, with its subdued structures blended into natural settings. Those attracted to Hilton Head appreciated how the island had been developed; for most, lush greenery and lovely vistas had been critical factors in the decision to retire to Sea Pines or one of the other plantations. Their expectations, however, were often unrealistic, shaped by memories of idyllic vacations that prompted them to buy property and eventually move to Hilton Head; and many felt let down by the sobering facts of life in a rapidly growing community. Fantasies about an island paradise were encouraged by developers who were happy to sell illusions as well as property. Plantation master plans and binding covenants provided a false sense of security to those tucked behind their gates, since the plans called for more development than most settlers realized, and the standards set by the plantations were bound to be downgraded as less committed developers sought their piece of the action.

As Hilton Head developed, islanders would be told over and over that growth was inevitable and continuous, that they could neither turn back the clock nor blow up the bridge. Acknowledging these realities, however, largely failed to satisfy their concerns about the changes that growth would bring. The struggle would be over what kind of change. The contestants would be primarily permanent residents versus those whose economic interests depended on growth. The issues would be the quality, intensity, and pace of development as well as the impact of growth on the fragile ecology of a barrier island. The arenas would multiply as the island moved beyond benevolent dictators. And outcomes would increasingly be determined by public rather than private decisions.

THE ONLY GAME IN TOWN

Conflict over growth on Hilton Head, as in most places, was structured by the community's nature and economy. Most settlers located on Hilton Head by choice, drawn largely by the island's attractions rather than its proximity to employment or related considerations that normally determine where people live. The settlers' overriding concern was to preserve and protect their community. In this respect Hilton Head resembled many affluent suburbs that house the same kind of people with similar interests in community and environmental quality. The intensity of residential concern was greater on Hilton Head, however, than in upscale suburbs because of the character of the community and its population. Retired people tend to organize their lives around amenities and the quality of community life to a greater degree than individuals with jobs and careers and young children. They are also less mobile than working individuals; having already made the physical and emotional investment in relocating after retiring, they prefer to stay put.

Resorts also differ economically from most suburbs. On Hilton Head, development and tourism were the only games in town; the fortunes of almost every business were tied to growth, either directly in selling, renting, designing, building, decorating, lending, insuring, and lawyering or indirectly in servicing the needs of people who lived on the island, owned property, or visited. To be sure, real estate and construction are extremely important throughout the vast realm of suburbia. In most areas, however, growth either produces primarily residential communities dominated by homeowners' concerns or generates diversified local economies that serve a variety of markets and become progressively less dependent on real estate and development. Places like Hilton Head do not diversify easily. Except for developers, resort operators, and associated enterprises, Hilton Head was not an attractive location for most businesses—land and housing were expensive, labor scarce, markets distant, and transportation inadequate. Development was Hilton Head's game; growth was essential to practically every business on the island. Businesses are people; in a local economy dominated by development, nearly everyone who worked on Hilton Head depended heavily on growth for his or her livelihood. Growth, in turn, steadily increased the island's work force. By 1972 nearly 1,000 people were involved annually in construction on Hilton Head. Resort operations were also labor-intensive, and retail and service employment expanded as more retirees settled on the island and more visitors came to plantations, hotels, and condo developments. This economic base combined with Hilton Head's relatively isolated location to produce a resident working population whose fortunes were closely tied to growth. Very few islanders worked elsewhere. Hilton Head was not a bedroom community—just the opposite, as more and more of its work force commuted to service and construction jobs from ever more distant locations across the bridge. When the development business slumped during the mid-1970s, everyone who worked for a living on Hilton Head was adversely affected.

As a result of these dynamics, conflict over development on Hilton Head tended to be polarized between residents with especially strong attachments to their community and business people highly dependent on growth. Those who lived on Hilton Head were divided between retired households with intensely residential interests and everyone else, whose livelihood depended on development and the resort economy. Neither of these clusters was monolithic or cohesive on all issues. Retired residents differed over many specifics yet generally came down on the side of less growth, more controls, and fewer tourist attractions. Working islanders also disagreed among themselves over particulars. An architect who designed many of the buildings that fueled the island's growth rued the pace of development in the early 1970s, feeling that "growth is healthier if it is slower."[8] But slower growth still involved more development, and businesses and working islanders almost always favored more, even if reluctantly. "I feel the island is over-commercialized," one merchant indicated as the island's economy surged in the 1980s, "but we have to grow and move forward in order to survive. I just hope we don't move forward too fast."[9]

Business leaders sought to paper over their differences with settlers, insisting that "we're all islanders" with shared interests in maintaining Hilton Head's quality. Everyone, they argued, had a stake in Hilton Head's basic industries, development and tourism. These industries, however, presumed a shared interest in growth that glossed over settlers' concerns. More visitors were the key to selling everything from real estate to beer, so island businesses were dedicated to attracting more visitors and extending the tourist season. Developers sought to increase their business by expanding the market with accommodations that appealed to a wider range of patrons. These interests were not shared by most retired residents. They trusted neither developers nor the magic of the market-place to preserve paradise. Quite the opposite, as evidence mounted during the first boom that developers could not resist the temptation to overbuild: condos marched along Forest Beach, and plantation developers talked about high-rise buildings. Moreover, if residents trusted developers, they would have to live with their errors of judgment. As a former Sea Pines executive conceded, "Mistakes . . . in this business get poured into concrete and greet you every morning for the next thirty years."[10]

Because growth drove the local economy, almost all of Hilton Head's influential residents were connected with the island's dominant industry. Fraser and Hack, their family members and associates, architects and developers who designed and built the plantations, and pioneering businessmen, bankers, and lawyers were the local elite. Some could claim membership in Hilton Head's equivalent of the *Mayflower,* having come over on the ferry *Pocahontas.* As the island developed, this group flourished. Like Fraser and Hack, they both cared about the island and depended on growth for their livelihood. Most had worked with the founding fathers of modern Hilton Head, and those who struck out on their own developed land that had been acquired from Sea Pines or the Hilton Head Company. By and large, they were committed to high-quality development, good stewardship, and the island where they lived.

The lure of becoming a developer proved irresistible to many who came to pursue other occupations. Pete McGinty and Doug Corkern, the young architects who were largely responsible for creating the island's distinctive building style, soon expanded into developing as well as designing. Plantation executives also joined the rush to become independent developers. One who "felt the entrepreneurial urge to form my own development company" was Dennie McCrary, who spent six years as an executive at Sea Pines.[11] McCrary formed Hilton Head Beach Properties and developed condominiums. Settlers were also bitten by the development bug. Gerald McBride moved to Sea Pines in 1960, formed Atlantis Development, and built the Adventure Inn. Over the years, many would follow McBride's path, developing local businesses so that they could enjoy the attractions of living on Hilton Head. Some would become developers like McBride; more would open an ever-widening range of commercial and professional enterprises. Living on Hilton Head was worth a career change for many in this group who decided to try their luck in local business. The growing ranks of resident entrepreneurs blurred the distinctions between residential and development interests while sharpening differences between settlers who worked and those who were retired. Resident entrepreneurs, no matter how enamored of their adopted island, would be heavily dependent on the growth machine that drove Hilton Head's economy.

A local economy almost totally dependent on development and a cluster of founding families that loved the island they had to develop strongly influenced the emergence of growth as an issue on Hilton Head. Retired residents were intensely concerned with the adverse consequences of growth, but so were many of the developers, business owners, and other working islanders who were their friends and neighbors. Residential distrust of developers was muted by Fraser's high standards and their emulation by other plantations and many lesser developers. Reinforcing these factors in easing tensions between residential and development interests was the scale of Hilton Head. The community was small and relatively closely knit during the early years, with good connections between residents and the pioneers who controlled the development industry and its satellite endeavors. All of these circumstances, however, would be altered as the island grew and changed. Plantation companies lost power; connections were broken as the community became larger and more diverse; and pioneers played a declining role as the local economy successively surged, collapsed, and then expanded rapidly once again. In the process, the nature of the development business changed, and so did tensions between residential interests and the growth machine.

With boom times came a new breed of developer eager to cash in on what plantation companies had created. They were less connected and less committed than Fraser, Hack, and other pioneers. Many newcomers were drawn to Hilton Head by the opportunity to make money rather than by the island's charms. They had not come over on the *Pocahontas* or worked for Sea Pines. Lacking ties to the island except as a place to make money, they had no claim on the loyalties and affection of island residents. Often they developed properties that lay outside the domain of the plantation companies, parcels that were essentially unregulated, given the absence of public land use controls. Some of this land belonged to local blacks; other properties were acquired during the financial difficulties of Sea Pines and the Hilton Head Company by banks that "were not as choosy" as the companies "about who they sold to or what was built."[12] On this land, developers could build high-density clusters of inexpensive condominiums that could tap markets priced out of plantations.

Typical of the new breed was the Carolina Bay Company, which sought in 1982 to cram almost 350 condos on a few acres on the north end of the island. "This is not Hilton Head anymore—it's not a pristine place where you are going to see sea gulls flying, said Carolina Bay's president; "it's essentially cast to be a high-rise condominium place."[13] These were fighting words for residents who much preferred sea gulls to high-rise condos, words that made settlers realize they could no longer rely on developers' good intentions. Hilton Head's

128

economic establishment also railed against newcomers whose activities not only violated the island's self-imposed standards but jeopardized their dominant position. The problem was neither growth nor development, pioneers insisted, but a few bad apples, unscrupulous people who did not care about an island treasured by local businesses. Few would disagree that the fast-buck artists were a far cry from Fraser and Hack. Yet some features of development that most disturbed settlers—condos and time-sharing in particular—were introduced by the establishment, proving to more and more islanders that no developers were to be trusted.

Figure 7.1 - New Housing, 1960–1974

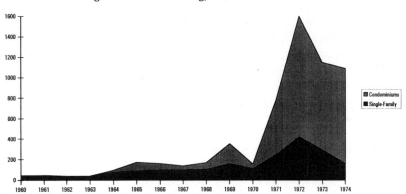

Condominiums were brought to Hilton Head by Charles Fraser in 1964 and dubbed "villas" in the same hyperbolic spirit that had turned subdivisions into plantations. Soon condo construction was substantially outpacing single-family residences; 1,090 condos were built in 1972, compared with only 400 detached houses. For developers, condominiums spelled higher land values and larger profits. The market for condos was also larger, since units were usually priced lower than single-family houses and were more attractive as rental properties. What appealed to developers troubled most settlers. Condos increased densities, traffic, and crowding of facilities. They also changed the nature of the community visually and socially. Most condominium developments were not as attractive as individual homes; they blended less well into surroundings and required substantial parking areas. Perhaps most distressing for retired residents, condos were inhabited by transients. Their absentee owners had at best a limited stake in the community; short-time renters had none. Intensively used by strangers, condominiums were an unwelcome intrusion in paradise for those whose interests were primarily residential.

All condominiums, of course, were not the same, although disgruntled residents often disparaged them collectively. On the whole, condos in Sea Pines were attractively designed and sited, as were similar projects in other plantations. Elsewhere, condominiums generally were not done as well. Forest Beach was inundated with large projects on small plots; densities were high and designs unimpressive. Here too insiders rather than outsiders took the lead. Forest Beach was developed on land acquired from and controlled by Sea Pines and the Hilton Head Company, and the developers were pioneers and plantation alumni, islanders one and all. To be sure, later developments by outsiders on land not owned by plantations would be less attractive and more crowded than anything built along Forest Beach. Nonetheless, what the development establishment produced in Forest Beach marked a substantial lowering of the standards that Fraser had established. Lower-quality development by those who cared helped pave the way for schlock by those who did not, and it helped convince settlers that there was really not much difference among developers.

Even more distressing to residents was time-sharing. Of all the methods devised to squeeze more golden eggs from the Hilton Head goose, none was more attractive to developers than time-sharing. By selling a condo to fifty different buyers, each of whom would "own" a week, they could make much larger profits than with an individual sale.[14] For example, a town house priced at $75,000 if sold normally could bring $200,000 or more if successfully marketed as time-shares. Some of this increased revenue covered higher marketing costs; most was profit. Many developers found the idea irresistible. The first time-shares were offered during the recession, and by 1983 more than 800 units were under way for 40,000 "interval owners."[15] Time-shares were marketed aggressively, with relentless shills pursuing potential buyers from parking lots to beach with offers of free meals and other inducements. Local merchants liked time-shares because they increased the tourist season; people who bought weeks during off-season (when time-shares were least expensive) were a welcome boost to restaurants and shops from November to February.[16]

A bonanza for developers and a benefit for business, time-shares were a bane for residents. Time-shares increased the volume of transients, who tended during their brief stay to use golf courses, tennis courts, and other facilities intensively. While individually owned condos might be used fifteen or twenty weeks annually, many time-share units were occupied all year, further increasing inconvenience to full-time residents. Foes also argued, with considerable justification, that no one really owned time-share condos. Units were fully furnished and equipped, managed by the developer or an agent, and indistinguishable from rental units except that there was no identifiable owner. condominiums. Thus time-shares severed the link between ownership and a sense of responsibility for property and commitment to community. And for those who blamed developers collectively for what was happening to their island, there was the fact that time-shares were introduced not by some fast-buck operator from the big city but by Charles Fraser in Sea Pines. Hard-pressed for cash during the financial crunch, Fraser brought the first time-shares to Harbour Town in 1975. Sea Pines residents hated Fraser's time-shares, which thus became one more nail in the coffin of a community of interest between settlers and developers.

Condos and time-shares intensified pressures for making Hilton Head more a resort serving a wide range of incomes and tastes and less a residential community catering to affluent retirees and second-home owners. After the local economy recovered from the recession of the mid-1970s, a flood of condos washed across Hilton Head, built by newcomers on land unprotected either by covenants or by the interests of the plantation companies. Among the new "resorts" outside the plantations were ghastly projects that confirmed settlers' worst fears about developers and uncontrolled growth. Islanders dubbed them "stack-a-shacks." They were high-density prefabricated units that came on trucks and were piled like building blocks; the barren barracks looked more like minimum security prisons than vacation resorts. Most notorious was the Four Seasons Centre, erected in 1982 along the main highway next to Palmetto Dunes. Similar projects had equally impressive names—Hilton Head Beach and Tennis Resort, Sea Cabins, and the Spa on Port Royal Sound—and similarly unattractive features.[17] In stack-a-shacks, large numbers of housing units were squeezed onto undersized sites with little concern for aesthetics, effective site planning, or their impact on adjacent areas. All units were furnished and equipped with linens, dishes, and utensils right down to butter knifes. Owners need not come to Hilton Head to outfit their apartments, and many never did, since units were sold primarily through off-island advertising and telemarketing. By the end of 1983 almost 2,000 units were in place. With the stack-a-shacks, the dreams of Charles Fraser and Fred Hack had turned into ugly nightmares for most islanders.

BENEFITS OF GROWTH

While the introduction of stack-a-shacks was dramatic and important—revulsion against the Four Seasons Centre pushed Hilton Head toward home rule—the road that led to them was only part of the growth picture. Hilton Head did not grow simply because developers pursued profits; growth came also because people needed services. To think of development only as the product of greedy profit seeking is to miss the reality that businesses either serve needs or perish. Merchants and providers of services came because people needed food, clothing, repairs, insurance, banks, information, and entertainment. Because Hilton Head had practically no local economy in the early 1950s, many business opportunities existed. A growing population provided the critical mass for the medical clinic, library, schools, churches, clubs, art galleries, and cultural activities as well as for additional shops and restaurants, more and more of which stayed open all year. Increasing numbers of retired residents created a need for specialized care for the elderly, a service that had not figured in the planning of plantations, which were oriented toward resort and recreation rather than geriatrics.[18] More people provided enough customers for a radio station, cable television, direct dialing for long-distance calls, and a movie theater that opened in 1972, showing Walt Disney's *Song of the South* as its premiere attraction. (*Gone With the Wind* presumably would have struck a discordant note on a Dixie isle once again overrun with Northerners.)

Of all the facilities and services that came with growth during the first boom, probably the most important was the Hilton Head Island Hospital, which opened in 1975. Increased population made the hospital feasible; its actual development was made possible largely by the efforts of a single individual, Dr. Peter LaMotte. LaMotte trod a familiar path in making his mark on Hilton Head: he was successful, smitten by what he found on a visit, and determined to live and work on the island. His dream was a hospital that would attract other doctors who wanted to enjoy the good life. LaMotte was well equipped to turn his particular dream into reality; he was an able doctor, an energetic organizer, and wealthy. His father was Louis LaMotte, one of the founders of IBM, and his family underwrote a substantial chunk of the $7 million initial investment in the hospital. Like many other facilities and services on Hilton Head, the hospital was both a product of growth and a spur to additional development, since having a fine hospital and excellent physicians was an additional attraction to the island, especially for retired people.

With the opening of the hospital, essential infrastructure was largely in place along with an impressive array of economic and social activities. "There was," Charles Fraser explains, "one of everything that anyone needed; every service was being provided. Since then, growth essentially added duplication, increasing competition and choice, and added some range and some exotic services."[19] For many islanders, Fraser's distinction between what was essential and what was duplication would differentiate desirable from undesirable growth. Was one more ice cream parlor or exercise salon or gift shop a benefit or cost of growth? Many of the conflicts over growth that engulfed Hilton Head in the 1980s were over such questions, both small and large.

In 1970 islanders got a newspaper so that they could read all about the benefits and the perils of growth. The *Island Packet* was the first newspaper on Hilton Head since 1865, when the two weeklies that served occupying Union forces ceased publication. The paper was founded by Ralph Hilton, a journalist, diplomat, and Sea Pines pioneer who bought a lot from Fraser in 1959, built a house near the ocean, and retired to the island five years later. Hilton and his wife had an active retirement; both wrote while he worked part-time doing public relations for Fred Hack.[20] As Hilton Head grew, Hilton thought a weekly newspaper was feasible and found a few people who shared his enthusiasm for the project.[21] One was Thomas Wamsley, who had come to Hilton Head in 1964 to sell real estate for Fred Hack and had moved into resort development; the others were Jonathan Daniels, the former editor of the *News and Observer* in Raleigh, who volunteered to write a column, and his wife, Lucy Daniels, who joined Wamsley in underwriting the venture.[22]

At the outset, the *Packet* voiced many of the early settlers' worries about growth. Yet the paper, as Daniels said, "suffered like the whole island from schizophrenia" of "worrying about development while benefiting from growth."[23] The paper's fortunes, like those of all community newspapers, were intimately tied to the local economy. The *Packet* was concerned about the adverse effects of growth, but its well-being depended on development to boost circulation and advertising revenues. Straddling these conflicting interests, the paper sought to protect the island while celebrating growth. "The *Packet* shall always be alert to the needs of the community, and ready to fight—against whatever pressures— for its welfare," readers were told at the beginning of 1973 in an editorial that also welcomed the island's expected expansion to "a city of respectable size within the next decade" and indicated that the paper "intends to be in the van- guard of our march, and to help determine the character of the larger commu- nity to come."[24] With the march to a larger community came a more prosperous newspaper as the *Packet* rode the boom of the early 1970s to a stable financial footing.[25] At the beginning of 1973 the thriving weekly moved to its own build- ing in one of the new office plazas; a few months later it joined the list of island firms passing from local control when it was acquired by the News and Ob- server Publishing Company of Raleigh.[26]

Growth was good for business but troubled readers, a reality that led the *Packet* to thread its way around development issues during its early years. Op- ponents of expanding the airport were extravagantly supported in a 1972 edito- rial that saw "little to be gained on the island by importing these poisonous exhaust fumes, shrieking airflows, thundering motors, and destruction of vast areas of beautiful woodlands."[27] A few months later, however, inauguration of scheduled air service was welcomed as "a marked stimulus to Hilton Head Island's burgeoning tourist industry."[28] Dealing with growth, of course, meant making the connection between the "burgeoning tourist industry" and "thundering motors" and the destruction of natural beauty. The paper preferred to avoid this confrontation, as did most of the developers and associated business interests, arguing that growth and quality were compatible, that their synergism was what Hilton Head was all about.

For the *Packet,* concerns about growth were increasingly focused on the implications of development for island facilities and services. Surging development in Forest Beach in the early 1970s was worrisome to the newspaper primarily because the road system could not handle the traffic that growth would bring. "The island is large enough to support many more hotels without the threat to the natural beauty of its setting," dubious readers were assured, "but its roadways cannot accommodate the traffic flow that looms just ahead. The island traffic problem is one that demands attention without delay."[29] Like the rest of the development industry, the newspaper responded to growth by promoting infrastructure that inevitably stimulated more development. While residents talked about blowing up the bridge, the paper was strongly endorsing "a four-lane road the length of the island" and "a four-lane bridge to replace the present drawbridge."[30]

The *Island Packet* would grow with Hilton Head. With more readers and advertising, the paper expanded from a weekly to a biweekly in 1973, grew to three issues a week in 1982, became a daily three years later, and added a Sunday edition in 1988. Shopping malls, department stores, specialty shops, supermarkets, and multiscreen movie theaters filled the additional pages with ads, along with the real estate, resort, and restaurant advertising that was the paper's stock-in-trade from the outset. Growth also turned a lively community billboard into a good newspaper, one that improved over the years, combining detailed local coverage with a steadily enlarging diet of national and international news, financial information, sports reporting, and features—a paper that dominated its market.[31] Its readership was remarkably devoted and spread across the country; the paper was the lifeline to paradise for thousands of sometime islanders. But the *Packet* was not the voice of the people; it was a multimillion-dollar business that flourished on growth.[32] When the chips were down, the paper bet on more development—well planned and sensitive to the environment, it was hoped, but more growth nonetheless. As growth issues increasingly separated residential and business interests in the 1980s, many readers would be alienated by the paper's commitment to the resort industry and to more roads and other large public works. For many islanders, a bigger *Packet,* like so many other things they loved about Hilton Head, was not necessarily better.

FRAGILE ENVIRONMENT

Growth involves more than preferences of residents, developers, businesses, and newspapers. Everywhere development changes nature, altering land, water, air, and all living things. People may differ about whether changes are desirable or undesirable, more or less harmful, and thus worth or not worth their impact on nature. Amid these issues, which arise because people have conflicting interests and priorities about development and the natural setting, is the reality of altered natural states. On Hilton Head, concerns about the natural implications of growth were heightened by the setting. Barrier islands are especially fragile environments, surrounded by water, flanked on one side by transient beaches and on the other by intricate wetlands. They are sandy and low-lying, prone to flooding and vulnerable to tropical storms. Within this delicate setting, environmental sensitivities were intensified by Hilton Head's natural beauty, the standards set by the major developers, the kind of people attracted to the island, and the local economy's dependence on resort and retirement development.

Two forces were affecting the fragile environment of Hilton Head: those of nature and those wrought by man. As the island developed, they increasingly interacted. Tides, ocean currents, rain, wind, and other natural forces constantly reshaped the pile of sand that was Hilton Head. Man's hand was heavier, from antebellum plantation masters who cleared forests and cut waterways to irrigate their indigo, rice, and cotton fields to modern plantation developers who carved the landscape to make nature conform to their dreams and designs. Lagoons were dug and harbors dredged; building sites were cleared, roads cut, and parking lots paved. Golf courses were routed through woods, swamps, and meadows and were cultivated with an alchemist's brew of fertilizers, herbicides, and pesticides. Wetlands—complex networks of water and land that support plant and animal life, store runoff, recharge groundwater, and filter pollutants and sediment—were "routinely ditched, dredged, impounded, lagooned, diverted, dammed and paved."[33]

Development substantially increased flooding on an island that receives 50 inches of rainfall annually, both by altering the natural drainage system provided by wetlands and by covering more of the island's surface with impervious buildings, roads, and parking lots. Lagoons dug by developers were supposed to retain runoff, but their capacity was constantly outstripped by new construction. Heavy rains increasingly produced flooding in low areas, especially in heavily developed Forest Beach. Rainwater also became more polluted as a result of accelerating development. Man-made lagoons worsened the dangers posed by polluted runoff, since they concentrated in their sediment toxic substances that were flushed into surrounding waters during heavy storms. Sewage and dredging added to pollution of the clear waters that were one of Hilton Head's prime attractions.

Risks from hurricanes were also increased by development. While tropical storms would threaten Hilton Head regardless of what was built on the island, their potential impact was greatly affected by construction. Severe storms could be expected every decade, with lesser ones annually and devastation every century or so. As was the case all along the Atlantic and Gulf coasts, development on Hilton Head created more structures to be battered or flooded and thousands of people to be evacuated to escape the screaming winds and surging sea. Development also reduced the natural cushion that absorbs the blows of wind and water, as beaches were built up, dunes leveled, wetlands altered, and drainage blocked. More residents and tourists complicated the problems of evacuation in the event of a major tropical storm, which would be most likely to occur in the late summer, when Hilton Head was crowded with visitors.

Beaches were perhaps the most striking illustration of the interplay of nature and man in a fragile environment being developed largely because of its physical attractions. The beach was Hilton Head's most important asset—the main drawing card, the foundation of the tourist economy and real estate industry. Oceanside development inevitably pits man against natural forces that produce constant flux in the size and location of beaches. Development draws lines in the sand in the form of structures and property rights, and nature does not respect those lines. Compared with most seaside areas, Hilton Head was developed with more concern for beaches—dunes were preserved on most of the oceanfront and structures set well back from the ocean along the beach in Sea Pines and the other plantations. Still, development was accelerating beach erosion. And the unhappy combination of fixed development and migrating beaches prompted countermeasures, ostensibly to retain eroding sand but in fact to save beachfront property. Thus development produced not only buildings that were too close to the water but also groins, revetments, and other structures designed to retain sand and protect property. Barricades further hardened the line development draws between land and sea, a fixed line that does not exist in nature; they also accelerated natural movement of sand. In these ways nature and man combined to produce steady erosion of a substantial portion of Hilton Head's beaches, to the growing consternation of more and more people as the island developed.

Beaches and wetlands were special problems for a growing barrier island. Water and wastes posed more common dilemmas that were complicated by Hilton Head's fragile environment and the nature of its development. Water appeared to be the least of the island's problems in the early years, coming in seemingly inexhaustible quantities from the aquifer that served Hilton Head and adjacent areas. Use was well above the national average, largely because so much water was consumed in irrigating landscaping and golf courses in addition to the annual rainfall. Symptomatic of Hilton Head's profligate use of potable water were automatic sprinkler timers, which dutifully watered lush greenery at programmed times, rain or shine. Growth brought more showers and baths, flush toilets, washing machines and dishwashers, gardens to water, and fairways to irrigate. By the early 1980s, rapidly rising water use led to the first signs of salt water intrusion in the aquifer and restrictions on water use.

More people and businesses also meant more wastes, both solid and liquid. Outside plantations, garbage and construction debris was too often dumped in woods and marshes, increasing the contamination of groundwater and runoff. Garbage, however, could be hauled off the island—out of sight, out of mind. Sewage was less easily disposed of on an island surrounded by relatively clean water. Growth initially replaced reliance on septic tanks with conventional sewage treatment; continued development outran the capacity of sewer plants and complicated disposal of treated wastes, which were pumped into waterways or sprayed on golf courses and other open areas. Rapid growth on Hilton Head coincided with rising environmental concerns nationwide, which produced tighter federal and state regulation of water quality and waste disposal. Problems came to a head after the resurgence of Hilton Head's economy following the 1974–1976 recession. Building quickly outstripped the treatment capacity of the island's utility districts, and this led state officials to close shellfish beds, restrict sewage connections, and impose, in 1983, a general moratorium on new development until the island had a comprehensive wastewater plan. Many residents welcomed the ban, which lasted for more than a year, while developers fumed and utility officials scrambled to patch together an acceptable scheme to increase treatment capacity. More treatment, of course, would bring more growth and eventually more sewage to be treated, as infrastructure and growth reinforced each other at the expense of a fragile and increasingly beleaguered natural setting.

Roads posed problems similar to those associated with sewers as the links between growth and congestion, and additional capacity and more development, were complicated by the island setting. Natural features, particularly the single connection with the mainland and the cleaving of the island by Broad Creek, forced the main road to follow a circuitous route. Alternative routes were precluded by development of the plantations as closed private communities. As a result, everyone traversing Hilton Head had to use U.S. 278, and the road became increasingly congested and dangerous as the island grew and attracted more residents and tourists. Dependence on a single road, moreover, could be life-threatening in a hurricane, and for a long time most islanders lived in Sea Pines at the end of this lifeline. Also frequently inconvenient and occasionally hazardous was the aging two-lane drawbridge to the mainland. Passing boats on the Intercoastal Waterway caused short delays and frayed tempers. Malfunctions and accidents were more serious, the worst occurring when a runaway barge put the bridge out of commission for a month in 1974. Local demands for a stationary four-lane span intensified, and the state eventually responded with a new bridge, thanks to funds made available by Karl Bowers, a South Carolina native who headed the Federal Highway Administration under President Jimmy Carter. The bridge was completed in 1982 and named appropriately for Wilton Graves.

Growth produced traffic, congestion generated pressures for more highway capacity, and better roads fueled more development, which in turn added to the number of vehicles crowding island roads. Travel across the bridge steadily rose as Hilton Head attracted more residents, tourists, and business. From 250 vehicles daily when Sea Pines began in 1957, traffic over the bridge reached 1,000 vehicles in 1962 and more than 10,000 by 1981.[34] The main highway was widened to four lanes, but improvements brought little relief to motorists forced to use the crowded and dangerous road. Six times as much traffic was counted on the improved highway in 1981 as on the two-lane road in 1970.[35] For many, especially among developers and other business leaders, the answer was additional road capacity in the form of an alternative route to the south end. For others, another major road inevitably would facilitate more development, which would further erode the island's beauty and fragile environment.

PRESSURES ON LAND

Roads, resorts, commercial development, and parking lots consumed land at an accelerating rate as Hilton Head grew. More and more of this land was outside plantations after 1970. Land beyond the plantation gates was not protected by covenants, except for those parcels originally owned by the major development companies. Minimal county controls and loosely enforced state health regulations were the only constraints on most of this land. These outparcels, as properties outside the domain of the plantation companies were called (in a telling reflection of how the island was defined in terms of plantations), became increasingly attractive to investors as development spread. Here land was cheaper and controls were negligible, offering irresistible opportunities for lower costs, higher densities, and bigger profits. Lying beyond control of the plantations and the target of a new breed of developers, outparcels would be the main battleground of most of the struggles over growth on Hilton Head after 1970. Complicating this conflict was the fact that a good deal of this land was owned by local blacks.

As long as development was confined to plantations and adjacent land owned by the major companies, blacks were minor players in Hilton Head's dominant industry, confined largely to marginal roles in service trades. With the spread of growth, they finally saw opportunities to profit from the forces that were transforming the island. Their land, particularly holdings along the highway and parcels adjacent to plantation properties, was increasingly valuable and the object of growing interest to developers. For many native islanders, however, the pressures of growth were a mixed blessing. Their property represented more than a good to be sold for the highest price. This land had strong emotional and family ties; it was the legacy of their slave forebears, their haven in a century of hardship and broken hopes. Substantial numbers of African Americans had no interest in selling their land, and others were fearful that developers who wanted their land would cheat them. And whether they wanted to keep or sell their land, blacks were faced with rapidly rising taxes as property values soared, raising for many the specter that they would be taxed off their property.

Whatever black owners wanted to do with their land as growth pressures mounted was clouded by legal complications. Black landholdings were a jumble of murky titles, multiple owners, and missing documents. Records of federal land sales and surveys were destroyed after the Civil War. Later, many black landowners on the remote island had registered neither deeds nor wills, so there were uncertainties about who owned particular properties. Lacking clear titles, African Americans could neither mortgage nor sell their land. A substantial effort to clarify titles was launched in 1972 by the local NAACP with help from the Sea Pines Company.[36] Blacks both welcomed and worried about efforts to clear title to their land. With clear title, land could be sold, but native islanders distrusted outsiders who participated in this process. Getting Sea Pines involved in clarifying titles, some feared, "might merely clear the way for the sale of those properties to established developers."[37]

As legal impediments diminished and development pressures increased, blacks could no longer be easily ignored by other residents. They owned much of the land that new developers wanted for the kinds of projects that most white settlers dreaded— small tracts that could be turned into high-density developments with minimal concern for environment or aesthetics. The most visible stack-a-shacks project was built on property acquired from a black landowner. Outraged settlers responded by seeking effective public controls over undeveloped land, and their efforts led to the incorporation of Hilton Head and controversy over master planning, development regulations, and growth moratoriums. Native islanders resisted all these measures, which they viewed as efforts by rich white people to deny poor African Americans an opportunity to benefit from the forces that were transforming their island.

Along with all its other growing pains, Hilton Head would be afflicted with conflict between blacks and whites as the struggle over growth shifted from private to public arenas. Those arenas were both local and beyond the bridge that connected the island to Beaufort County, South Carolina, and the rest of the United States. The interplay between growth on Hilton Head and development in the surrounding area can be examined in the context of the setting provided by county and state government. As Hilton Head searched for a new political order in the wake of changes that eroded the power of plantation companies, conflicts over industrial development, county development controls, and incorporation of the island revolved around growth issues and involved shifting alliances of settlers, development interests, and black residents.

NOTES

1. The 1970 enumeration of 2,546 was widely disputed as being too low; estimates of the actual population ranged as high as 4,200. See Fleming, "Reorganizing Local Government," 106.

2. An interim census conducted in April 1975 reported 6,511 inhabitants.

3. The census count in 1980 was 11,344.

4. The 1972 data are from the Sea Pines Company. The 1980 figures were collected for the Hilton Head Island Chamber of Commerce by a local marketing firm, T. Gardo and Associates.

5. Bowers and Bowers, "What Does the Future Hold for Hilton Head Island?"

6. Benjamin M. Racusin, quoted in ibid. Racusin was president of the Hilton Head Island Community Association in 1973.

7. Daniels, "Sojourner's Scrapbook," January 25, 1973.

8. Richard A. McGinty, quoted in Bowers and Bowers, "What Does the Future Hold for Hilton Head Island?"

9. Gene Martin, quoted in Hilton, "Personality Profile: Martin Remembers and Welcomes Island Changes," 30. Martin was the owner of the Red and White Supermarket in Coligny Plaza. Between 1969, when he moved to Hilton Head and acquired the grocery, and 1985, Martin's business expanded from 6,000 square feet to 21,000 square feet and from 14 to 42 employees.

10. McCaskey, "Sea Pines Plantation Alumni," 18.

11. Quoted in "McCrary Plans New Role," 33.

12. Joseph B. Fraser Jr., interview.

13. Arthur Schultz, president, Carolina Bay Company, quoted in Stuart, "Hilton Head, Seen as Island Paradise, Is Straining under Big-City Problems."

14. Normally, two weeks were left unsold to allow time for major maintenance.

15. By 1990 Hilton Head had 1,000-time sharing units with more than 40,000 owners. In addition to weekly time-shares, quarter-share projects were developed. These offered four equally priced shares divided among the owners in various ways.

16. Weeks were differentially priced according to demand, with the week of the Heritage Classic usually the most expensive and the mid-winter weeks the least.

17. The Spa on Port Royal Sound was constructed traditionally rather than with modular units, but it was otherwise similar to the other projects.

18. Seabrook, Hilton Head's first facility for the aged, opened in 1982. The facility, a condominium with health care and meal service, was developed on land acquired from Sea Pines on favorable terms.

19. Charles E. Fraser, interview, August 15, 1987.

20. Ralph Hilton was the author of *Worldwide Mission: U.S. Foreign Service.* Mary Kendall Hilton wrote *Old Homes and Churches of Beaufort County* and the informative "Islander of the Month" column for the *Islander* magazine.

21. At the time, the island's publications were the Chamber of Commerce's monthly magazine and a mimeographed newsletter distributed by the Women's Association.

22. Daniels had also served as press secretary to President Franklin D. Roosevelt and as an adviser to President Harry Truman. Daniels wrote more than twenty books. His columns in the *Island Packet* were published in Daniels,

The Gentlemanly Serpent and Other Columns from a Newspaper in Paradise.

23. Jonathan Daniels, quoted in "Executives Discuss Ad Topics; Daniels Is Banquet Speaker."

24. "The Island Packet in Its Own Home."

25. During its first thirty months, the paper's subscribers rose from around 450 to more than 4,000, and its advertisers from fewer than 50 to more than 300.

26. The purchase price was $900,000, providing a hefty return on the original investment of $10,000. The News and Observer Publishing Company was owned by Jonathan Daniels' family, and he remained a vice-president of the company after his retirement to Hilton Head. Daniels continued to write his column for the *Island Packet* until shortly before his death in 1981. Ralph Hilton remained as editor through 1975; Wamsley, who had been president, was soon replaced by a News and Observer Publishing Company official who became publisher of the *Packet*.

27. "Airport in the Island Environment."

28. "Air South Comes to the Island."

29. "More Hotel Rooms."

30. "The Traffic Mess."

31. The *Hilton Head News,* published weekly by the *Savannah Press* beginning in 1970, never came close to the *Island Packet* in terms of local news coverage, readership, or appeal to local advertisers. The *Hilton Head Report* was introduced in 1986 as a weekly newspaper concentrating on local affairs by the publishers of a business newsletter with the same name. The paper was renamed the *Hilton Head Sun* and expanded to two issues a week in 1987, but it was unable to pull readers or advertisers away from the *Packet,* and the venture folded in 1989.

32. The *Island Packet,* along with two other newspapers and some minor publications, was sold by the News and Observer Publishing Company to McClatchy Newspapers of Sacramento for $74 million in 1989. The *Packet* was the most valuable piece of the package, accounting for about $30 million of the purchase price.

33. Ballantine, "Nature Got Her Revenge by Flooding Us Last Week." Ballantine's columns are a valuable source of information on the interplay between development and Hilton Head's natural setting.

34. Traffic counts were of vehicles traveling both ways.

35. Traffic counts were made at the end of U.S. 278 at the Sea Pines Circle and showed 4,200 vehicles in 1970, 27,500 in 1981.

36. Sea Pines provided $36,000, and the program was directed by a black attorney on the Sea Pines staff.

37. "NAACP Officials Tour Island Fri."

Chapter Eight

Across the Bridge

*A certain irony results since the development of the island
provided the resources to fight off industrial development in the
name of preserving a pristine environment.*

—Orion D. Hack, Interview, July 17, 1987

On Hilton Head Island, as in every other place, growth inevitably involved
outside parties and developments. Despite its prevalent local image as an isolated paradise, Hilton Head was ecologically and economically connected to its
hinterland and tied politically to the rest of Beaufort County and South Carolina. Growth on Hilton Head created jobs and business for inhabitants of the
surrounding area as well as generating traffic along the roads feeding the resort
island. Commercial and residential development spilled over the bridge into
adjacent communities. In turn, Hilton Head was affected by what happened off
the island in an area that was poor and had been eager to attract industries that
might not be kind to the environment. Physically, Hilton Head was relatively
small, and more than most localities, it was a prisoner of its environs. It was a
vulnerable island in a fragile environment; its fate was largely determined by
the surrounding Atlantic Ocean, Calibogue Sound, Port Royal Sound, and the
rivers that flowed into these bodies of water. Especially problematic was the
Savannah River, which emptied into the Atlantic a few miles beyond the southern tip of Hilton Head. Savannah's poorly treated sewage and industrial wastes
had decimated shellfishing in the river's estuaries. Paper mills in Savannah
wafted noxious fumes across Sea Pines when the wind was blowing the wrong
way, while industrial wastes threatened water supplies from the aquifer shared
by Hilton Head and Savannah. Ninety miles upstream was the Savannah River
nuclear processing facility, where atomic weapons were manufactured with
highly toxic products. Its potential for destroying the river and its coastal waters was awesome.

Hilton Head was also vulnerable politically. Like many developing places
in the South and West, the island was not organized as a municipal government;
instead it was an unincorporated portion of Beaufort County, which collected
local taxes and provided rudimentary public services. More important than the

county in Hilton Head's early years was the state, which played a critical role in securing ferry and bridge access. Continued state help widened Hilton Head's main highway, improved road connections to the island, and secured a new bridge. The state agencies got into the act with increased regulation of water quality, coastal zones, and wetlands. As a result, state as well as federal officials played steadily larger roles in growth issues on Hilton Head.

In dealing with the state, Hilton Head was handicapped politically and economically. Despite Charles Fraser's carefully cultivated connections with many state leaders, his island did not carry much weight in state political affairs. Most of its inhabitants were Northerners and Republicans in a state that remained one of Dixie's Democratic strongholds well into the 1970s. Moreover, legislators and state officials had little inclination to help an island that was widely seen as populated by fat cats who cared little about South Carolina—a perception enhanced by Hilton Head's insularity and disdain for the state and its people. In a poor state with too few resources to meet too many demands, Hilton Head was easy to ignore, especially since islanders were often seen as out of step with the rest of the state—fussing about the environment, worrying about aesthetics, and questioning the desirability of growth.

Economically, Hilton Head was discounted because South Carolina undervalued the island's resort and retirement development. For decades, little importance was given to Hilton Head's economy in creating jobs, generating increasing tax revenues, and attracting affluent outsiders to a state few had previously been interested in visiting. Not until the 1980s would South Carolina begin to understand that Hilton Head was engaged in a real business and that tourism, recreation, and retirement constituted a key sector of the state's economy.[1] As long as the state did not value the kind of economic development occurring on Hilton Head, Fraser emphasizes, "we didn't count politically."[2] What counted in South Carolina was industry. Tourism and resort communities were a nice sideline, but the state's political and business leaders wanted "real" economic development—textile mills, chemical plants, automobile factories. South Carolina was poor, ranking near the bottom in most measures of personal wealth and economic health. State leaders devoutly believed that salvation lay in industrial development; factory jobs were the key to rising incomes, better education and public services, and a prosperous South Carolina. To lure new industry, the state government was ready to make substantial commitments and more than willing to sacrifice the environment. Polluting industries that other states increasingly shunned were pursued with industrial revenue bonds, water and sewer grants, infrastructure inducements, and tax incentives. Pollution standards were low and enforcement was lax for valued industries.

Growth multiplied Hilton Head's connections with state government while amplifying its differences from South Carolina's political and economic mainstream as more outsiders migrated to the island. Development bolstered Hilton Head's contributions to the state economy and tax coffers and pushed islanders to seek more revenue from the state government for roads, public facilities, and a variety of other local needs. Hilton Head benefited from the political clout of Beaufort County's state legislators, especially Beaufort's James M. Waddell Jr., who parlayed seniority and political skill into a dominant role in the state legislature.[3] Support from influential legislators neutralized some of the antipathy in Columbia to Hilton Head, insuring that many island concerns received attention in the state capital. Legislative delegations play a pivotal role in South Carolina politics, controlling state funds for county governments, state appointments to local agencies, and state legislation addressed to local needs. As a result, backing from the county delegation was sufficient to insure that island developers got legislation to establish their public service districts and accommodate condominium ownership.

Hilton Head, however, was only a relatively small part of the constituency represented by these legislators. The rest of Beaufort County had little in common with the island, and the legislators, all Democrats until 1982, did not identify closely with Republican Hilton Head.[4] When the chips were down, as islanders would discover during a protracted struggle over industrial development, their legislators' loyalties lay with the state and county, not with the exotic curiosity that was Hilton Head.

CARPETBAGGERS AND GOOD OLD BOYS

Hilton Head was locked in an uneasy embrace with Beaufort County. Neither the county's government nor its leading citizens had much interest in the island, its residents, or resort development. Locals were skeptical when the Georgians arrived in 1950 and remained dubious when Fraser and Hack began to develop the island. Their world was centered around Beaufort, the county seat, which had a proud history dating from the early eighteenth century. One of the garden spots of the Old South, a place where planters spent the summer enjoying the cool breezes and riverfront vistas, Beaufort was a world apart from Hilton Head. Physical distance was magnified by the geography of the Carolina Lowcountry, with its broad waterways and numerous islands.[5] From Hilton Head to Beaufort, only 15 miles across Port Royal Sound, required a circuitous 55-mile drive. Psychologically and culturally, the distance was even greater between the traditional and tightly knit world of old Beaufort and Hilton

Head, whose new residents were outsiders—a "'foreign' and obviously unique population" with different lifestyles.[6] Most came from Northern cities, built big houses and drove expensive cars, and made their lack of interest in the rest of the county condescendingly clear. They dismissed Beaufort County as an unsophisticated Southern backwater, full of jealous hicks interested in Hilton Head only for the money to be made off rich Yankees.

Beaufort County's government was also a product of an earlier era, providing minimal services to a largely rural population. The county government was ill equipped to deal with surging growth in an exotic place filled with outsiders, a game with much higher stakes and more sophisticated actors than those familiar to Beaufort County politicians and public officials. In the beginning the county did not try; it simply permitted plantation companies a free hand to develop as they pleased and welcomed private provision of public services. Over time, however, Beaufort County had to respond to development on Hilton Head. Police were added, schools enlarged, health and welfare services expanded, a library opened, and a landfill provided for the island's garbage. Timorous steps were taken to control development and regulate building on Hilton Head. Seed money was provided for the island's public service districts to begin a comprehensive water and sewer system, and tax-free bonds were authorized to finance construction of Hilton Head's hospital. Growth on Hilton Head involved county officials in the contentious airport issue and in provision of bus services that linked low-income blacks in Beaufort and surrounding counties with island jobs.

In terms of South Carolina's norms, Beaufort County's response to Hilton Head was noteworthy. What was exceptional for a rural Southern county, however, did not impress most islanders. Their expectations typically exceeded county capabilities and interests. Successful and sophisticated, used to dealing with local governments that were responsive to their concerns, migrants to Hilton Head were frustrated by the deliberate pace and wary evasiveness of county officials. Everything happened slowly or not at all in a political world that often seemed impervious to island needs. And when the county took action, islanders typically found the results inadequate, incompetent, and tainted by a governmental system that fostered "mismanagement and greed."[7] Exacerbating tensions was the widespread feeling among newcomers that Beaufort County was exploiting Hilton Head, since the island contributed an ever increasing share of county tax revenues. By 1974 Hilton Head accounted for more than 50 percent of the property taxes collected by the county, compared with only 2 percent when the Sea Pines Company was founded in 1956. Islanders endlessly complained that they were getting precious little for the taxes Beaufort County reaped from growth on Hilton Head.

Across the bridge, this grumbling was widely perceived as evidence of the selfishness of well-off islanders and their insensitivity to the sharp differences in wealth and advantage that separated most of the island from the rest of the county. Hilton Head was reminded that the political system was a democracy rather than a plutocracy—"It's not one dollar, one vote; it's one person, one vote."[8] Most island newcomers evidenced little understanding of the county's political, social, or economic context. When a county politician suggested that islanders were isolated, the *Island Packet* tartly reminded Beaufort that "isolated" Hilton Head was "one of the desired points on one of the world's main roads and nobody has to go by dear, sweet, little old Beaufort to get here."[9]

Existence of two worlds did not prevent Beaufort County from benefiting from the development of Hilton Head. Some of the good old boys did quite well dealing with the new carpetbaggers who needed lawyers and bankers and other knowledgeable local folk. Joab Dowling was a shrewd Beaufort attorney who was involved with Hilton Head's developers from the beginning and prospered along with the new plantation builders. For years, the Bank of Beaufort was the island's only bank, providing most of the mortgages for newcomers and other banking services. More general benefits for Beaufort County also came from the transformation of Hilton Head by Fraser and other developers. In 1950, per capita income in the county was 50 percent of the national average. Twenty years later, Beaufort County was the only county in South Carolina to exceed the national median per capita income. These striking gains resulted primarily from Hilton Head's booming economy as well as the county's expanding military installations. Yet much of Beaufort County remained severely disadvantaged, especially among the one in three county residents who was black. Substantial numbers of blacks were poor and illiterate and lived in bad housing.[10] The striking rise in average incomes masked a bimodal distribution of wealth, with bulges at the top produced by Hilton Head and a clustering at the bottom representing large numbers of poor blacks.

County leaders were eager to diversify the local economy, which they saw as excessively dependent on military installations and resort development. Almost half the work force was employed by the military, thanks primarily to the remarkable ability of Mendel Rivers, longtime chairman of the Armed Services Committee of the House of Representatives, to bring home the bacon to his Beaufort County constituents. Bases were lifesavers in an area as depressed as Beaufort County, but their long-run economic contribution was subject to the vagaries of military priorities and congressional politics. Officials in Beaufort, like those in Columbia, saw the future in industrial terms, and they labored to attract real jobs to their corner of South Carolina.

On Hilton Head, little attention was given to the county's economic problems or to its hopes for diversification. The only part of Beaufort County that most islanders cared about was Hilton Head, and perhaps the immediate area across the bridge where development would have direct impact on the island and surrounding waters. The commanding feature of this area was Port Royal Sound, one of last relatively unpolluted estuaries on the east coast. As the 1960s drew to a close, Port Royal Sound would prove as attractive to industrial developers as it once had to explorers and naval strategists. Efforts to bring heavy industry to sites on Port Royal Sound a few miles north of Hilton Head would pit island developers and settlers against state and county leaders. Industrial development posed unacceptable risks to Hilton Head's way of life, its resort economy, and its natural setting. In the battles over growth, islanders would find fighting outside threats easier than coming to terms with their internal disagreements on development—not an unusual experience for an American community.

BEATING BASF

The industrial threat to Hilton Head suddenly materialized in the fall of 1969. At the beginning of October, Badische Anilin and Soda Fabrik AG, a German chemical firm, announced plans to build a $100 million plant at Victoria Bluff in Beaufort County.[11] More than 600 jobs would be created at the planned industrial complex, which the firm wanted to locate on 1,800 acres 3 miles from Hilton Head. South Carolina's political and business elites enthusiastically welcomed BASF as a stunning victory in their campaign for new industries. It would be one of the state's largest industrial facilities and could be expected to stimulate additional development of industries using plastics and other raw materials produced at Victoria Bluff. To snare this prize, extremely generous locational benefits were offered to BASF. Land for the plant was assembled by the county, with a large chunk coming from the state at a bargain price.[12] Water would be furnished through canals from the Savannah River, and an estimated 2.5 million gallons of wastes daily would be treated by a utility district created for BASF. Public funds would develop a deep-water port at the site, including 10 miles of channel dredged into Port Royal Sound. Also promised were a rail line to the site, new roads to the plant, training programs for workers, and five-year exemptions from state and county taxes.

With the public announcement, the deal was done as far as state and county officials were concerned. Negotiations with BASF had been secret, with no public involvement. Everyone was expected to welcome or at least accept what had been done by the state's political establishment. Wilton Graves was certain that "the announcement that BASF will locate in Beaufort County will be hailed by all of our citizens."[13] Neither Graves nor other political leaders were prepared for the hornet's nest stirred up by the decision to locate a massive chemical complex next to Hilton Head. Confident of their constituency's support of the venture, they had prepared neither themselves nor the Germans for controversy. No studies had been made of the probable effects of pollution from the plant or its implications for other economic activities in the area. All state and county officials had was their eagerness to lure industry and BASF's assurances that all would be well. As concern mounted on Hilton Head, Governor Robert McNair told island leaders that "we have assurances from BASF that the company is vitally concerned about the ecology and beauty of the area and that steps are being taken to satisfy all legal, environmental, and industrial requirements in safeguarding the air and water from pollutants."[14]

The claim that a huge chemical plant would have no adverse impact on the surrounding area was not credible. "I've never seen a chemical plant that didn't pollute," Charles Fraser said in voicing the views of those unconvinced by the official cheerleaders.[15] Equally dubious was the contention that South Carolina's pollution controls would safeguard air and water. The state continually reaffirmed that BASF would be held to state standards, while the company solemnly pledged to obey all state laws. Opponents were not reassured, pointing to the state's abysmal record of controlling wastes—a result of weak regulations, lax enforcement, and large loopholes for industry.

Environmental considerations were the most powerful elements in the case against BASF in terms of attracting attention, broadening the base of political support, and challenging the decisions that had been made by state and county officials. Those who opposed BASF stressed pollution, particularly the threat posed to the pristine waters of the Port Royal estuary by a massive chemical complex. Environmental concerns broadened BASF from a local to a national issue, drawing journalists from New York and Washington and other media centers. As the news spread, scientists and environmental activists came from near and far to fight for Port Royal Sound and Victoria Bluff. Americans were rediscovering the environment in 1969, and the BASF controversy was an early skirmish in a series of battles that would underscore the perils of industrial pollution.

Certainly environmental concerns were serious; at stake was the last relatively unpolluted estuary system on the east coast, a thriving ecosystem and beautiful natural setting bound to be destroyed by chemical processing and port facilities handling immense quantities of toxic materials. Environmentalists also discovered Victoria Bluff, previously unknown to almost everyone who whizzed by on the way to Hilton Head. The BASF site was a jumble of forest and ponds, marshes and tidal flats, with palmetto, pine, cypress, and gum trees along with clusters of wild holly and placid ponds covered with pink water lilies. The natural wonders of Port Royal Sound and Victoria Bluff, however, were not the primary issue in this battle. Developers and residents were most interested in protecting their environment on Hilton Head. Heavy industry was incompatible with Hilton Head's resort and recreation economy, its beaches and other natural attractions, and the way of life its developers were selling and its affluent residents were enjoying.

At the heart of the controversy over BASF were competing economic visions, two completely different mind-sets about economic development and the road to prosperity, mutually incompatible and involving very different environmental assessments. The BASF fight was fundamentally about what kind of an economy would prevail in lower Beaufort County and what its impact would be on the environment. Hilton Head was firmly committed to resort development with a strong emphasis on environmental amenities, which precluded heavy industry. The state was equally devoted to industrial development, which would surely undermine Hilton Head's cachet. Though each of these kinds of development would change the environment, heavy industry would be more destructive than condominiums, golf courses, and marinas.

Resorts and heavy industry created different kinds of opportunities for different people, with potential winners and losers on either side. BASF and associated industry, according to one estimate, would have created "5,000 to 7,000 new jobs," while "employment at Hilton Head Island, surrounding resorts, and fishing industries is minuscule in comparison with the projected BASF complex alone."[16] Many blacks saw the issue in much the same terms. For the director of Beaufort County's poverty program, there was "just no question, we need jobs, and BASF will bring in jobs."[17] Moreover, advocates of BASF insisted, heavy industry would bring better jobs as well as more jobs, given the preponderance of low-wage resort workers. Not so, argued the plantation companies, emphasizing the wide range of employment opportunities they were creating in construction, real estate, finance, and services. Because the stakes were clear and high, the BASF conflict was both bitter and far-ranging, and the outcome was heavily influenced by those with the most to lose on Hilton Head: Sea Pines Plantation and the Hilton Head Company.

Despite the substantial stakes, Fraser and Hack were reluctant contestants.

For the development companies, BASF was an unwelcome intrusion, both threatening their businesses and posing the difficult question of whether they wanted to contest the chemical plant with state and county officials whose help they would need on other matters. Whatever had to be done, Fraser decided, more needed to be known before any effective action could be taken. He orchestrated a research effort that carefully scrutinized BASF and the state's pollution control activities. The other major developers held back at first, not sure they wanted to antagonize BASF and thus jeopardize their prospects for selling plantation homesites to the chemical firm's executives. Hack soon changed his mind, deciding that BASF was not worth the profits from a few lot sales. Not so Palmetto Dunes, whose owners remained on the sidelines throughout the fray, "saying they had already made plans with BASF employees," according to one report, "and did not wish to jeopardize their position."[18]

Complementing Fraser's research efforts were the activities of the island's retired residents. Two weeks after the BASF announcement, the Hilton Head Island Community Association formed a task force to examine the proposed chemical complex. The more islanders learned, the more troubled they became. Hilton Head, they realized, would be faced with a huge chemical plant that would pump millions of gallons of largely untreated industrial wastes into Port Royal Sound. BASF was quickly revealed to be a world-class polluter, dumping 90 million gallons of highly acid effluent into the Rhine River daily and fouling the air with noxious emissions. Paradise, more and more islanders became convinced, was going to be engulfed in a vast industrial wasteland of "smudged bleary skies, slag heaps, rank winds, and vile waters."[19]

Turning anxieties into effective action requires leadership, resources, and political skill. In the battle against BASF these essentials were provided largely by Sea Pines and the Hilton Head Company. Charles Fraser threw both his formidable personal skills and the resources of the Sea Pines Company into the fray. Fred Hack became a passionate foe of the chemical plant. The companies paid for staff, hired lawyers, convened environmentalists, financed advertising, supported allied groups, and dispatched emissaries to Washington. Fraser and Hack skillfully led a cause widely supported by islanders; and their resources, to the tune of more than $600,000, enabled Hilton Head to draw national attention and create a political atmosphere in which the project could be killed. At the outset, the odds for success were not promising—somehow Hilton Head would have to find a way around the solid phalanx of support for BASF among the state's public officials, business leaders, newspapers, and television stations. Necessity dictated the strategy of expanding the contest beyond South Carolina by using the courts, mobilizing environmental interests, securing national publicity, and lobbying federal officials.

The legal attack was pursued by a passel of lawyers hired by Sea Pines to do battle with BASF, including an expert in environmental law from New York and the retired chief counsel for Shell Oil Company.[20] Early in 1970 the opening legal salvo was fired when Fraser's lawyers sought a federal injunction against BASF on behalf of local fishermen, contending that the plant's wastes would destroy Port Royal Sound's shrimp, oysters, and crabs. Environmental and scientific support was organized by Orion Hack, Fred Hack's younger brother and an official of the Hilton Head Company. A naturalist and environmentalist who loved Hilton Head's waters and woodlands, Orion Hack hit on the idea of convening scientists and environmentalists, and Fred Hack agreed to underwrite the effort. Predictably, the fifty-odd participants at the symposium recommended a moratorium on construction and called for further study of the BASF project.[21] More important, the conference and Hack's tireless efforts broadened the issue, attracting attention, alerting environmentalists around the nation, and establishing the proposed BASF operation as a serious environmental issue with national ramifications.

Another element of the campaign involved nurturing the diverse collection of interests that joined forces under such banners as "Progress, Yes—Pollution, No!" and "BASF—Bad Air, Sick Fish!" Settlers on Hilton Head were the largest component of the alliance, providing time, knowledge, resources, and connections that proved invaluable as the conflict evolved. Most island businesses lined up behind Fraser and Hack, convinced that whatever benefits smokestack development might bring would be more than offset by the adverse effects of heavy industry on the local resort economy. Environmental groups expanded the coalition's base beyond Hilton Head's development industry and affluent settlers. So did support from opponents from the rest of Beaufort County. Local fishermen were valued partners in the fight. Their adamant opposition to industrial development diluted the racial aspects of the issue and enlarged the economic arguments against BASF. Hilton Head needed African American allies in a conflict that divided white islanders from most blacks in the area. The suit filed by Fraser's lawyers was in the name of the black Hilton Head Fishing Cooperative, and the shrimp boat that sailed from Hilton Head to Washington in the final stage of the campaign came from that cooperative's fleet.

Lawsuits, conferences, advertisements, demonstrations, and petitions—all were designed to attract national attention, thus broadening the base of opposition to BASF and mobilizing pressures to change the outcome. Plantation resources were critical to the publicity phase of the campaign, providing not only money but also Sea Pines' sophisticated public relations skills. Mailings were sent to people who had visited Sea Pines and other island resorts, asking them to help save Hilton Head by urging their representatives in Congress to oppose BASF. The best was saved for last in the public relations campaign: the voyage of the *Captain Dave,* bearing freshly harvested shrimp from Port Royal Sound and petitions protesting BASF signed by more than 35,000 people. A crowd of reporters and television cameras shared the dock in Washington with Secretary of the Interior Walter Hickel, who was looking for ways to dramatize the need to strengthen national environmental policies. The secretary and the shrimp boat were a natural, and their coming together signified that Hilton Head had won the war of images on BASF. Soon the war itself would be won.

In the end, Washington was the decisive battleground in the struggle over BASF. Publicity, petitions, and letters set the stage, and political clout carried the day. Charles Fraser had excellent connections in Washington, and many of his retired customers also had links to federal agencies, the White House, and the national Republican Party. When the chips were down, Hilton Head held better cards in Washington than BASF's promoters. Six months after the project was announced, Secretary Hickel declared that BASF had to prove that the plant would not pollute the surrounding waters in order to get a permit. State officials and South Carolina's congressional delegation were furious, crying that Hickel exceeded his authority. Hickel, however, threatened rather than acted, later admitting he was trying to "bluff" BASF out of Port Royal Sound.[22] The bluff worked; BASF officials decided to abandon the site after Hickel's intervention. Grudgingly, South Carolina admitted defeat, buying the land back from BASF while assailing the "selfish people" who killed the project.[23]

BASF and its political sponsors lost because they had picked the wrong place for heavy industry, both environmentally and politically. Port Royal Sound was inappropriate because of its natural setting and the quality of its waters. After BASF withdrew, a company official was reported to have said, "It's a good thing we were not permitted to proceed with our plans for Victoria Bluff. . . . We would have killed everything in the sea for 50 miles around."[24] Victoria Bluff was also too close to Hilton Head for political comfort. "Those people wondered what happened to them," noted an influential retired islander. "They were hit by a juggernaut of people with know-how."[25] For islanders, good had triumphed over evil; David had slain Goliath.

MORE BATTLES OVER THE BLUFF

Beating BASF did not end the industrial threat to Hilton Head. Over $2 million in public funds were at stake, along with considerable political capital and prestige for state and county leaders who remained committed to industrialization at Victoria Bluff. Eager to avoid a reenactment of the BASF fiasco, state officials promised that any industrial development at Victoria Bluff had to be "ecologically compatible" with "higher standards than ordinary."[26] Higher standards, however, did not mean electronics and research firms in park-like settings or the sporting goods manufacturers suggested by island developers as an alternative to BASF.[27] Instead, the state lured another heavy industry to Victoria Bluff in 1972. Brown & Root of Houston, the nation's largest construction firm, would invest $30 million in a plant to build off-shore drilling rigs, the largest of which would be 240 feet high and 400 feet long and would be towed to sea through a new channel in Port Royal Sound. Then Chicago Bridge & Iron Company acquired 775 acres next to Brown & Root for a plant that would fabricate shipping spheres for liquefied natural gas as tall as ten-story buildings. Victoria Bluff had apparently been saved from BASF to become the mammoth floating structure capital of the eastern seaboard.

Conservationists and settlers mobilized against the new industrial threats to Hilton Head and Port Royal Sound. This time, however, the battle would be less conclusive. The environmental threat from these proposed plants was not so compelling as BASF's had been, although the necessary dredging would surely adversely affect marine life and possibly threaten the aquifer that supplied Hilton Head with fresh water. Publicity and outside support were much harder to secure the second time around in an America that had moved on to other causes in different places. And fewer resources were available for these new fights, since Hilton Head's principal developers wanted to avoid another costly public brawl. They had made their point with BASF, indicating in the process that they were opposed only to unsuitable industry. Once the threat of BASF had passed, the plantation companies lost interest in Victoria Bluff. Sea Pines, in the midst of its massive expansion, "had more important things to do than endlessly battle the state government."[28] By 1974 Sea Pines was struggling to survive financial disaster while the other companies were severely buffeted by recession; now the major developers had little time for such matters at this point.

State officials also behaved differently, working to build support locally, consulting with island leaders before the announcement of projects, and holding public meetings on them. Governor West created an advisory committee chaired by Sea Pines' Joseph Fraser to harmonize industrial and resort development with residential and environmental concerns. Impact studies were undertaken by the advisory committee and financed by the state and county, the industrial firms seeking to locate facilities in the area, and the plantation companies. With the studies came a pause in the headlong rush to industrialize Victoria Bluff. The Hilton Head Company finally decided to oppose industrial projects in 1974, calling for "more determined efforts to enhance coastal South Carolina as a superb vacation and retirement destination, rather than as an industrial area."[29] Delay provided foes additional opportunities to block the projects as various state and federal agencies reviewed the proposals and environmental impact statements. The stalled plants were also the victims of changing economic and political conditions. Obstacles to oil drilling on the Atlantic coastal shelf caused Brown & Root to abandon its plans for Victoria Bluff. Chicago Bridge & Iron persevered longer, fending off opponents in the federal courts, accepting restrictive covenants, and finally securing federal permits to dredge the channel before falling demand for ship containers ended the second round of battles over industrial development at Hilton Head's doorstep.

Over the following years, the threat of industrial development faded. Environmentalists who demonstrated against BASF at Victoria Bluff savored a special kind of victory in 1979 when a 1,200-acre portion of the site was turned into a wildlife preserve. Also located on the BASF land was the Waddell Mariculture Center, dedicated to advancing the local fishing industry and named for one of the most fervent supporters of industrial development at Victoria Bluff. Ironic too was the fate of Chicago Bridge & Iron's land, which was sold in 1989 to developers for a Hilton Head-style development, Colleton River Plantation, with a golf course designed by Jack Nicklaus. What better indication of the triumph of Hilton Head and its private community builders over heavy industry than Colleton River Plantation? Instead of gantry cranes and freighters, the banks of the Colleton would harbor expensive homes and lush fairways; instead of the clank of metal fabrication there would be the thwack of golf clubs and tennis racquets.

Industrial dreams for the area, however, were never abandoned. Almost twenty years after BASF, state and county officials courted an Indiana boatbuilder who planned a $15 million plant at Victoria Bluff. The new industrial scheme triggered another bitter fight, with many echoes of the past. State and county officials offered attractive inducements amid confident promises of no pollution at the Colleton site. Petitions were circulated, lawsuits filed, charges exchanged, and disagreements aired at crowded hearings about the economic benefits and environmental risks. Blacks allied with the proindustry forces, while resort and residential interests insisted that boatbuilding was incompatible in an area specializing in recreation and planned communities. Islanders, however, did not play a central role this time around, although many were distressed by the proposal and cheered the eventual withdrawal of the boatbuilder in favor of

156

public use of the land. The principal opponents were from Bluffton and other settlements near Victoria Bluff, and their numbers and vehemence reflected the growth of the area across the bridge, with its own interests and priorities.

ON HILTON HEAD'S DOORSTEP

Development of Bluffton and its environs was strongly influenced by Hilton Head. Commerce was attracted to the highway corridor leading to the island, while residential and other activity spilled into adjacent areas. Growth on Hilton Head created an expanding army of people who worked on the island and lived across the bridge by necessity or choice, generating increasing demand for housing and services in a widening hinterland. Housing was cheaper, reflecting lower land costs and, after Hilton Head's incorporation in 1983, less stringent public controls on development. Growth brought traffic as well as people and business to nearby areas, and the need to improve the roads serving the resort island. As this process unfolded, a miniature metropolitan area spread outward from Hilton Head in which more and more growth could be expected to occur at the periphery as the core filled and changed. With these developments came increasing tensions, as Hilton Head often looked across the bridge to solve problems while its immediate neighbors blamed islanders for the changes that growth brought to their alluring medley of woods and water.

One of Hilton Head's most important influences on the mainland and adjacent islands was the plantation concept. Rising prices and diminishing amounts of land led developers off the island, where large tracts of attractive Lowcountry real estate could be assembled at relatively low cost. The basic formula was pure Charles Fraser—golf courses and other amenities enhancing residential property values in a pleasant natural setting. Typically the off-island plantations were residential rather than resort communities; most homes were single-family, and densities were lower than on Hilton Head. Some emphasized lower prices than Hilton Head, with marketing targeted on home buyers with island jobs. Others sold seclusion and exclusivity. All promised Hilton Head living with a quieter lifestyle away from the traffic and tourists. Moss Creek Plantation, the first of the off-island planned communities, was launched in 1973 because Hilton Head was "too resort-oriented and too crowded."[30]

Moss Creek was the closest of the off-island planned communities, located just across the bridge on the site of three antebellum plantations. Smaller than most of the island plantations—approximately 1,000 acres—Moss Creek featured two excellent golf courses, lovely vistas of marsh and water, abundant wildlife, and easy access to Port Royal Sound. Six miles further inland was

Rose Hill Plantation, whose 2,000-odd acres offered golf, boating, a large equestrian facility including polo, and homesites 40 to 50 percent cheaper than comparable properties in island plantations. More distant and more secluded was Callawassie Island, boasting one of the finest golf courses in South Carolina in a beautiful uncrowded setting and aimed at a more upscale clientele than the other off-island plantations. Begun by a West German financier in 1981, the property was acquired four years later by two Sea Pines alumni who expanded the project to include adjacent Spring Island with its deep forests and views of Port Royal Sound.[31] Here golf and tennis were stylishly packaged to enhance luxury living in lush surroundings by developers who, in the words of one, had "learned careful land-use planning under Charles Fraser."[32]

Developers were also inevitably drawn to isolated Daufuskie Island, a mile across Calibogue Sound from Hilton Head. First on the scene was Charles Fraser, enticed by the island's natural attractions and its location adjacent to Sea Pines. Fraser acquired more than 700 acres on the ocean opposite South Beach in 1972, but nothing came of this venture because he lost his foothold on Daufuskie during the financial crunch. In 1979 half of the island was acquired by developers who planned to sell plantation living in an idyllic setting, a retreat without automobiles or a bridge to civilization and its intrusions. Turning this concept into reality, however, required more financial resources than the developers could command, and part of their holdings was sold to the International Paper Realty Company in 1984.

Now Daufuskie was ready for the bulldozers as International Paper laid out Haig Point Plantation on its 1,000 acres across from Harbour Town. Featured were a magnificent golf course along Calibogue Sound, homesites with vistas of woods and water, and freedom from automobiles and paved roads within its gates. Haig Point's market niche was the affluent vacation-home buyer who wanted something different, someone "with an average income of $250,000 a year" looking for "a second or third home."[33] Next to Haig Point Plantation was the Melrose Club, which represented yet another approach to attracting wealthy customers to an isolated island. Along with a dazzling golf course designed by Jack Nicklaus, tennis, two miles of beach, and attractive homesites, Melrose peddled memberships in a private club with emphasis on lodgings. For $35,000 initiation plus an annual membership fee, members had unlimited access to the recreational facilities and two weeks at the Melrose Inn and adjacent cottages.

Like much of the development that spilled over, the off-island plantations were an extension of Hilton Head rather than indigenous to their immediate locale. Many of their developers were from Hilton Head and used the island's plantations as their model. Melrose's principals, for example, had worked together at Hilton Head Plantation, and the covenants, design guidelines, and architectural review board for their Daufuskie projects were all adapted from those at Hilton Head Plantation.[34] Customers for these communities lived on Hilton Head or had visited an island resort or had been attracted through advertising aimed at the Hilton Head market. A sales office for the Colleton River Plantation was in a Hilton Head shopping plaza, and advertisements heralded the development as "Hilton Head's Rare Private Club Community."[35] Moreover, the fortunes of all these off-island ventures were heavily dependent on Hilton Head's economic health; in the words of one developer, "As Hilton Head goes, so goes Haig Point!"[36]

Another kind of off-island development that depended heavily on Hilton Head was daily-fee golf courses. For three decades, every golf course on Hilton Head and its environs was built to attract customers and enhance land values. By the 1980s Hilton Head was drawing more visitors than could be accommodated on the resort courses at Sea Pines, Shipyard, Port Royal, and Palmetto Dunes. As a result, freestanding golf courses became an attractive investment, and the only practicable place to build them was on the mainland, where land was available, relatively inexpensive, and easily accessible to Hilton Head's golfers. The first freestanding course was opened in 1989 just over the bridge on U.S. 278; it was named Hilton Head National and marketed as part of Hilton Head with tie-ins to most of the island resorts. Next to Hilton Head National was Old South Golf Links, which advertised "Hilton Head's newest and most spectacular golf design."[37] Seven miles inland, but with a name that underscored the Hilton Head connection, was the Island West Golf Club at Hilton Head.

Hilton Head's ubiquitous presence in all these off-island developments fed mainland resentment of islanders. Bluffton in particular chafed in the shadow and path of its larger neighbor, which local residents regarded as arriviste and gauche. Bluffton had been a resort when Hilton Head was an isolated enclave of black farmers and fishermen. Now Bluffton was Hilton Head's hinterland, a place to dispose of wastes, house workers who could not afford to live on the island, or provide a site for a larger airport to serve the resort industry. For Blufftonians, being on Hilton Head's doorstep was bad enough; being treated like Hilton Head's doormat added injury to insult. They resisted moving the airport, treating island sewage, and providing housing for low-wage island workers. Opposition was particularly intense when a black developer proposed to build 180 inexpensive housing units near Bluffton to serve the Hilton Head labor market and the growing number of workers, mostly black, who traveled long distances to their jobs.

Rapid growth on Hilton Head in the 1980s heightened these tensions, as both positive and negative effects of spillover increased development pressures on neighboring areas. Extensions of water and sewer lines on the mainland accelerated the pace of development, producing a flurry of projects and plans for shopping centers, office complexes, apartments, roadside commerce, and additional large-scale residential communities. With all of this development came rising property values, higher housing costs, and mounting property taxes. More expensive housing pushed poorer people further from Hilton Head's immediate environs. These trends were bound to accelerate in the wake of the 1993 decision by the Del Webb Corporation to develop one of its Sun City retirement communities on 5,100 acres 9 miles inland from Hilton Head. As many as 8,000 homes would be built for 14,000 residents, along with three golf courses and an assortment of other facilities. The new community was, in the words of one local official, "the biggest thing since Sea Pines."[38]

Growth on the mainland also increased pressures on Beaufort County for more effective public control of private development. County officials relied on land use and building regulations that restricted neither the amount nor the location of development. Application and enforcement of these standards, moreover, was weak, with minimal attention given to the impact of development on public services, natural resources, and adjacent areas. Private developers usually got what they wanted in Beaufort, as on Daufuskie Island, where the county's plans gave way to the private designs of International Paper and Melrose. Concerns and complaints on the mainland about ineffective growth controls echoed the rising chorus of dissatisfaction with county land use regulation on Hilton Head more than a decade earlier, a conflict that led in 1983 to the further separation of islanders from the rest of Beaufort County through the establishment of the Town of Hilton Head Island.

LEGACIES

Hilton Head's struggle with Beaufort County for effective development controls and ultimately local autonomy lasted more than a decade. Begun in the aftermath of BASF, the conflict was fueled by the animosities of the battles of Victoria Bluff. For islanders, the industrial controversies intensified concerns about planning, underscored the absence of county development controls, and multiplied worries about Beaufort's indifference toward Hilton Head's economy and way of life. Slowly but surely, these feelings would pull Hilton Head and Beaufort County further apart as they were repeatedly reinforced by the county's failure to respond to mounting island concerns about growth. Beaufort County, more and more islanders became convinced, was another world with different priorities and standards.

Another legacy of Victoria Bluff was a misleading sense of unity among islanders. "The pleasure in these battles was the fact that the island fought as one unit," Orion Hack fondly remembered years later in talking about BASF; "the island pulled together to block that project."[39] From these remembered pleasures would come the persistent myth that Hilton Head needed only to pull together once more as a single community to solve its multiplying growth problems. What was forgotten over the years was that Hilton Head was a relatively simple place in 1969, and the sense of community that emerged during the BASF fight reflected that simplicity. As Charles Fraser emphasizes, "There is no way to recapture the intimacy and power of the community that existed then."[40]

Victoria Bluff was an external threat, the kind of growth issue that communities coalesce about most easily. Internal growth controversies, on the other hand, divided and subdivided islanders. Moreover, the only consensus among the components of the anti-BASF coalition was that industrial development was undesirable. Fraser and Hack were not opposed to building at Victoria Bluff, only to development incompatible with their businesses. They endorsed Disney-type development or substantial light industry for the BASF site, although nothing ever came of their suggestions. Neither theme park nor industrial park, however, would have been welcomed by settlers and environmentalists, who were increasingly opposed to all kinds of development on Hilton Head and its environs. Unity could not be maintained in the lengthy contest with the county over development controls and local autonomy, and it would be illusion rather than reality once Hilton Head had to fight most of its growth battles on its side of the bridge.

NOTES

1. In 1991 tourism surpassed textiles as the state's largest industry.

2. Charles E. Fraser, interview, June 30, 1990.

3. Waddell was elected to the South Carolina House of Representatives for two terms from 1954 to 1958 and to the state Senate in 1960 until his retirement in 1992.

4. No island resident was elected to the state legislature until 1982, when Bill Cork, a Republican and former Sea Pines executive, defeated Wilton Graves.

5. The Lowcountry of South Carolina is defined in various ways (and also

spelled Low Country, with or without capitals). The Lowcountry Council of Governments encompassed Beaufort, Colleton, Hampton, and Jasper counties.

6. Fleming, "Reorganizing Local Government," 113.

7. "On Becoming a Municipality."

8. Charles Baggs, Beaufort County Joint Planning Commission, quoted in Breland, "JPC Expresses Doubts about Island Commission Idea."

9. "Isolated."

10. A wealth of data for Beaufort County and the adjacent area is presented in Oliver G. Wood Jr., "Economic Profile of the Beaufort Economic Area," 23–43.

11. Badische Anilin and Soda Fabrik AG was the parent firm; its American subsidiary was BASF Corporation. Throughout this discussion, the name BASF is used to refer to the two entities, which were one and the same in the battle of Victoria Bluff.

12. BASF paid $200 an acre for 866 acres that had been acquired by the state a decade earlier, while the 639 acres that the county purchased for BASF cost $1,164 an acre. The remainder of the site was marshland that the state planned to sell to BASF for $20 an acre.

13. Quoted in "Local House Members Give Quick Response on Plant."

14. Quoted in "McNair Assures Pollution Control."

15. Quoted in "BASF Backs Off from a Beachhead."

16. Rosen and Pender, "Economic Impact of the Proposed BASF Project and Satellite Plants," 60–61.

17. Charles Simmons, Office of Economic Opportunity, Beaufort County, quoted in Simon, "Battle of Beaufort," 13.

18. Albert, *Private Sector Reaction,* 53.

19. Frady, "The View from Hilton Head," 105.

20. David Sive, of Winer, Neuberger and Sive, and William T. Kenney. Sive, one of the pioneers of environmental law, had recently represented local and environmental interests in a successful court fight against a proposed six-lane expressway along the Hudson River north of New York City.

21. Among the groups and institutions represented were the American Academy of Environmental Engineering, American Horticultural Society, American Littoral Society, Clemson University, Friends of the Earth, Garden Club of South Carolina, Georgia Conservancy, Isaac Walton League, League of Women Voters, National Audubon Society, National Wildlife Federation, Sierra Club, and Wildlife Management Institute.

22. Quoted in Albert, *Private Sector Reaction,* 133.

23. Governor John C. West of South Carolina, quoted in "BASF With-

drawal Aftermath." West was elected in November 1970 and succeeded McNair at the beginning of 1971.

24. "BASF Official Reportedly Admits Pollution Problem."

25. Franklin Rouse, quoted in Albert, *Private Sector Reaction,* 170.

26. Governor John C. West, quoted in "Industry for Victoria Bluff."

27. During the BASF fight, Sea Pines and the Hilton Head Company had offered to find compatible industries that would generate at least as much employment as BASF would have generated. Among the possibilities were an industrial park for manufacturers of sporting equipment and attire and, more grandly, a $50 million "Seven Flags Over Port Royal" theme park that might generate 5,000 jobs during the tourist season.

28. Charles E. Fraser, interview, June 30, 1990.

29. Roy M. Whitehead, senior vice-president, Hilton Head Company, quoted in Cathcart, "Hilton Head Company Opposes CBI Plant."

30. G. Stewart Smith, quoted in "Off-Island Plantation Comes Full Circle." Smith was one of the founders of Moss Creek Plantation, developed primarily by Northwestern Mutual Life Insurance Company, which acquired the property in 1975.

31. James W. Light, former president of Sea Pines Company, and James J. Chaffin Jr., once Sea Pines' vice-president for marketing.

32. James W. Light, quoted in Richards, "Developers Purchase Spring Island."

33. Jack Barry, vice-president, sales and marketing, International Paper Realty Corporation of South Carolina, quoted in "Islander Interview: Jack Barry," 44.

34. The Melrose Company was composed of James P. Coleman, Steven B. Kiser, and Robert T. Kolb.

35. Colleton River Plantation, advertisement.

36. Jack Barry, quoted in "Islander Interview: Jack Barry," 44.

37. Old South Golf Links, advertisement. Old South opened in 1991.

38. D. P. Lowther, chairman, Jasper County Council, quoted in Millard, "Del Webb Project 'a Wonderful Thing' for Jasper County." The site of the planned retirement community straddled Beaufort and Jasper counties.

39. Quoted in Callahan, "Orion Hack Shifting Gears in Public Service."

40. Charles E. Fraser, interview, June 30, 1990.

Chapter Nine

In Their Own Hands

The straw that broke the camel's back was the county's approval of the stack-a-shack on U.S. 278. We saw that we had no control over development on the island.

—Michael J. Malanick, quoted by Dean Foster
in the *Hilton Head Report,* August 22, 1986

Rising concerns about growth inevitably prompted questions about the arrangements under which Hilton Head had developed. Less and less willing to leave the fate of their community to a changing cast of private developers, islanders pondered public growth controls. Unable to secure effective development restraints from county officials, Hilton Head sought to master its own destiny. For a decade, islanders wrestled with these two interconnected objectives—public control over private development and local control over the vital parameters of community life. Reining growth was the primary goal; governmental change offered an instrument for public regulation of private development that was responsive to local interests.

In seeking local autonomy, Hilton Head would tread an often traveled and revered path, one redolent with the Jeffersonian virtues of home rule, community control, and government close to the people. Incorporation as an independent municipality with elected officials promised more responsive government than distant and often indifferent Beaufort County. Tensions between Hilton Head and Beaufort County were symptomatic of stresses wherever development has brought rapid change to rural areas. Such conflicts are intensified in resort and retirement communities whose primary appeals are natural features and amenities. Breaking away from the county offered islanders more voice in decisions that intimately affected their lives as well as the means to shape the forces that were threatening their community and its singular attractions. Home rule would provide elected leaders in place of the private figures who dominated public affairs on the developing island.

Independence also promised to confer political identity on a fragmented community. The yearning for community was an important part of the appeal of a local government encompassing the entire island rather than municipalities incorporating separate pieces such as Sea Pines or Forest Beach. A single local government would offer "representation of all sections and all communities on the island in one governing body, and municipal officials and agencies . . . accessible to all residents."[1] The divisions that enhanced the attractions of an island-wide public realm, however, structured conflict over controlling growth and local autonomy. Wide differences separated blacks and whites on the inter-related issues of regulating development and creating an island government. Plantation gates further divided islanders into those who lived within private communities and those who lived outside them, reinforcing class and racial differences and shaping distinctive perspectives on growth, public services, and local government.

Private development set the stage for the quest for growth controls and a responsive local political system. Successful private planning spawned demands for public controls outside the realm of the plantation companies, while con-cerns about the durability of private restrictions spurred interest in public checks on plantation developers. Service provision by community developers created different perspectives on the role of local government inside and outside plan-tations. Moreover, the nature of the private communities largely determined what sort of people were drawn to Hilton Head and the kinds of political inter-ests they would articulate. Affluent, educated, experienced in civic affairs, and with time for public activities, plantation dwellers wanted more control over their communities and island. Privately, they pursued these goals through cre-ation of property owners' organizations; publicly, they settled on local autonomy as the way to protect their paradise. But home rule was attractive only within the context of preserving private communities: settlers wanted private control over their plantations and public control over the rest of the island.

Business interests too were shaped by the plantation system. The major companies insisted on retaining private control over their domains but wanted public regulation of the outparcels, the large tracts of land outside plantation gates, preferably by Beaufort County rather than a municipal government re-sponsive to residential concerns. Smaller developers favored no public restric-tions. Other island businesses evolved distinctive interests by the early 1980s, reflecting the lessened role of plantation companies and the local economy's decreasing dependence on land development. Eventually Beaufort County's failure to respond to the resort industry's fears about the adverse economic effects of uncontrolled development pushed business into an uneasy alliance with settlers in support of local autonomy.

Sorting out these conflicting interests would take more than a decade of debate and dispute about growth and government. At the outset, growth was far more evident on Hilton Head than government. In the absence of any public standards, county building permits were issued for many years by the Hilton Head Island Chamber of Commerce, and the county government's role was limited to registering developed property on its tax rolls. Minimal land use control was hardly unique to Beaufort County; none of South Carolina's coastal counties employed zoning in 1970. This minimalism reflected widespread distrust of land regulation, a common perspective in rural areas, where property owners passionately believe in their right to do what they want with their property. Reinforcing this attitude has been the general desire of rural officials to encourage development that bolsters the local economy and enhances the tax base. Beaufort County welcomed rather than regulated anyone who wanted to build anything, from a convenience store on Hilton Head to BASF's huge plant at Victoria Bluff.

PRIVATE LAND USE CONTROL

With no public restraints on land use and building, growth was essentially a private matter. Developers on Hilton Head were free to do as they wished in pursuing profits, following the dictates of their consciences and their reading of the market. For a long time, the only constraints were self-imposed, in covenants, master plans, and agreements among major developers. Plantation plans were the sole blueprints for development on Hilton Head, delimiting residential, commercial, and recreational areas. Private plans, however, were not reliable guides to what would in fact be developed. Company plans were primarily marketing devices. Only Sea Pines after the 1974 accords with property owners had a covenanted limit on the total number of dwelling units and condominiums that could be built. Elsewhere, housing mixes and densities projected in plans were not legally binding; instead, plans were subject to changing economic circumstances and management objectives.[2] Even in Sea Pines, amendments of the master plan that did not affect the 1974 agreements were made unilaterally by the company, to the dismay of property owners opposed to changes which they feared would alter the character of nearby residential areas. Moreover, whether legally binding or not, plans covered only a single plantation. No overall design for the island's development and infrastructure emerged from private plantation plans.

Complementing private planning was private land use control through covenants. Deed restrictions imposed constraints on all property conveyed by the plantation companies. By the early 1970s, close to 80 percent of the island was affected by private restrictions of one kind or another. Covenants were only as effective as their provisions, which reflected private rather than public goals. Different plantations and developments provided varying degrees of protection to property owners. Deed restrictions also were inflexible, best able to shield property from known risks and externalities and unhelpful when dealing with the unexpected. Time-shares, for example, were not covered by the 1974 or earlier Sea Pines restrictions, which limited condominium construction but were silent on time-shares because "when these covenants were written, no one even thought of time-sharing."[3] As a result, Sea Pines' revised covenants failed to deal with a kind of development that was particularly troubling to many residents.

Private covenants had to be enforced in the courts, a system that raised problems. First was the question of whether South Carolina courts would uphold Fraser's covenants, an issue that was not finally resolved until thirty years after the first restrictive deeds were executed at Sea Pines.[4] Further, the system's effectiveness depended on judicial enforcement; thus, the integrity of covenants rested on the willingness of private parties to take court action against violators. Thus in turn required that someone oversee conformance with covenants and have the resources to underwrite potentially substantial legal expenses. When monitoring was lax, covenants were easily breached, as was the case in Forest Beach, where many multifamily dwellings were erected despite deed restrictions permitting only single-family homes. Compliance with covenants was more closely watched within plantations; development companies and architectural review boards reviewed plans, inspected projects, and were prepared to defend deed restrictions in court. But these efforts were expensive, especially when covenants were challenged by obdurate property owners with deep pockets.

Whatever their strengths and weaknesses, private controls protected only part of Hilton Head. A quarter of the island was outside the web of restrictions created by plantation companies, its development subject to neither private nor public regulation. Much of this land was owned by blacks, none of whom had adopted private restrictions on development. In the absence of private or public controls, outparcels could be developed without any restraints on location, size, density, quality, aesthetics, or incompatible land uses. Five-story condos would be plunked next to single-family homes; large projects were crowded on small sites, trees sacrificed for parking lots, hazardous connections made to the main highway, and substandard sewage treatment facilities installed.

Uncontrolled development of outparcels eroded faith in private land use restrictions. As growth spread, more islanders wanted public controls on the quantity and quality of development. Doubts about private controls were enhanced by the transfer of company properties during the mid-1970s to large banks interested primarily in maximizing their return. With taller buildings, massed condominiums, and higher densities came increasing talk of the necessity for public measures to guide, slow, or stop growth. Public controls, concerned islanders insisted, would provide a means of both regulating unrestricted land and reinforcing the protection afforded by private covenants and master plans.

Plantation companies also were troubled by uncontrolled development. Their business was based on selling the good life in a high-quality setting, an atmosphere that was not degraded by cheap, poorly planned, and overcrowded projects built on unrestricted outparcels by developers indifferent to environmental and aesthetic considerations. Private controls within the plantations, however, were an article of faith to the companies—they needed restrictive covenants to market their communities successfully. Plantations were understandably reluctant to share control of their land and development plans with public officials. Private controls, they argued, offered the surest protection against unsuitable development and the best guarantee of planned growth. The major companies wanted government to control only lesser developers and thus protect their business environment and the quality of life for their customers. Their choice for the job was Beaufort County, a familiar arena in which they had considerable influence and one that, despite Victoria Bluff, could be trusted to be sympathetic to plantation companies.

For Hilton Head's blacks, development involved both threat and opportunity. It imperiled native islanders' way of life while dangling before them the prospect of higher land values. African Americans distrusted everybody—government, plantation companies, and the newcomers drawn to their island by development. Public restrictions, they were convinced, would drive them from their homes, prevent them from selling their land, or cheat them of its true value. Black resistance to public land controls emerged soon after the Hilton Head Company began selling lots in the early 1950s. Concern about haphazard building by early landowners prompted the company to propose a zoning commission for the island to protect the company's interest in orderly growth. Wilton Graves secured state legislative approval for limited zoning in 1955, but what Graves thought was a noncontroversial accommodation of an influential constituent quickly escalated into fiery conflict. Outraged blacks dramatically underscored their opposition by setting fires on company property. Backpedaling furiously, Graves got the legislation repealed.

Almost two decades would pass before land use control finally resurfaced. Black holdings again were the primary target of those who supported public regulation, and black landowners remained intense. They denounced "zoning slavery," which favored "the rich residents of the island at the expense of poor blacks."[5] Restrictions, many insisted, were aimed at squeezing out small black holdings to make way for resort developers. Regardless of the motives of settlers and developers, black areas, a 1974 study concluded, "would experience the most direct harm from enforcement of zoning and building code restrictions. In these areas, single-family dwellings are situated in close proximity to each other and in violation of most reasonable zoning restrictions in force in other cities in South Carolina."[6] Understandably, blacks feared any kind of public controls, whether by Beaufort County or by an independent Hilton Head.

WAITING FOR BEAUFORT COUNTY

Those interested in regulating growth on Hilton Head initially turned to Beaufort County; there was nowhere else to go. The county's first halting steps in the direction of regulating land use came in the wake of BASF as county and state officials promised a plan to guide anticipated industrial development. At the time, the county had no planning staff, no land use or building regulations, nor any idea of what was needed. A frantic effort ensued to prepare guidelines for the avalanche of building that would come with BASF. Zoning was cribbed from Columbia, the state's largest city, with nothing changed but the name of the jurisdiction. This ill-conceived initial venture was a harbinger of things to come from Beaufort County, a series of ineffective responses that lacked credibility on Hilton Head.

With BASF out of the picture, two years passed before county planners unveiled their proposed zoning scheme. What resulted from these labors embraced the existing pattern of development on Hilton Head. Plantations were classified resort-residential; the rest of the island was zoned according to current or adjacent uses—commercial along U.S. 278, marshland in conservation zones, a scattering of residential districts, and the remainder designated forest and agricultural. Reaction from Hilton Head was overwhelmingly negative. At a public hearing on the island, almost everyone was opposed—settlers because the proposals did not go far enough, blacks because they were too restrictive. County officials were repeatedly shouted down before the jeering crowd walked out, protesting both the substantive proposals and foolish procedures that allowed no discussion. In the aftermath of the debacle, the local NAACP threatened legal action, while the Hilton Head Island Community Association advised the planning commission to go back to square one.

Under attack from all sides, county planners retreated, belatedly consulting locals and attempting to respond to their demands. Providing black landowners with more freedom of action, however, conflicted with the interests of settlers who wanted stricter development controls. Accommodating developers angered citizens who urged zoning for "the protection of all already here and not merely for the profit of those anxious to attract others to this place."[7] What finally emerged in 1974 was minimal regulations that permitted almost anything to be built on Hilton Head. An even freer hand was dealt to plantations, since all development proposed in private master plans prepared before the regulations went into effect was exempted from any county review.

Dissatisfaction with these ineffective controls rose as growth accelerated after Hilton Head emerged from the recession. Beaufort County responded in 1978 with new rules that addressed neither what could be built nor where projects would be located. Absent were any restrictions on density, building heights, setbacks, or buffers. In practice, almost anything a developer proposed anywhere passed muster with the county's feeble development standards, and the including the prefabricated condos of the Four Seasons Resort stacked next to single-family homes in Palmetto Dunes. Plantation master plans predating county regulations continued to be exempt from review, and new plantation plans were routinely accepted, as were requests for amendments to existing plans. Extensive changes in the master plan for Port Royal Plantation were approved by the county planning commission despite protests from unhappy residents, as were amendments to Sea Pines' plan that were bitterly contested by property owners.

In effect, county rules provided public blessing for private planning, adding the authority of government to the already formidable power of developers. As the pace of development on Hilton Head intensified, growth overwhelmed the county's limited land-use review capabilities. An understaffed planning agency fought a losing battle against a rising tide of applications and pressures from developers chafing at the delays. Weak laws, powerful developers, and a beleaguered agency produced a system that issued permits, rarely rejecting anything or enforcing even its minimal standards. For most settlers, involving Beaufort County in growth control made things worse: now private developers could obtain a public license to defile their piece of paradise.

For plantation companies, lax county land use regulations were a mixed blessing. While they freed major developers to implement and alter their plans as they pleased, the county's failure to regulate development on the outparcels decreased the appeal of Hilton Head and its planned communities. Moreover, unless the county responded to mounting dissatisfaction over uncontrolled growth, Hilton Head would surely incorporate in order to regulate developers, and this outcome would be fraught with uncertainty for the companies. What the companies needed was a means of sustaining the county, restraining the new breed of developers, and mollifying troubled islanders while reassuring blacks that their interests would be protected. One possibility was to treat development on Hilton Head separately from the rest of the county, an idea that had been bouncing around for years. Special rules could deal with Hilton Head's distinctive situation while retaining county authority over land use.

Leadership in this effort came from Charles Fraser, who proposed the application of plantation standards to all development on Hilton Head. Density and building heights would be restricted for hotels and condominiums, and projects occupying more than 15 acres would have to dedicate land for open space and recreation. Strip development along the main highway would be tightly regulated. The answer to black concerns about development controls was to "leave any 'rural' residential or farm area 1,000 feet or more removed from US 278 and more than 1,000 feet from the Atlantic beach unregulated, until the residents of such areas seek land use controls for their ancestral lands."[8]

The proposal was welcomed by the *Island Packet* as "an imaginative stroke characteristic of the man who set the tone for development on Hilton Head."[9] Fraser's approach appealed to settlers and businesses that wanted to restrict development on the outparcels. Common interest brought the plantation companies, Chamber of Commerce, and residents together to turn Fraser's ideas into specific proposals for special land use controls for Hilton Head. Differences between settlers and developers complicated negotiations, and many residents were unhappy because the resulting compromise failed to deal with general growth caps or restrictions on plantations. Nonetheless, proposed supplemental development standards for Hilton Head were submitted to the county council in 1981 with the general endorsement of business and settler groups.

Beaufort County responded in characteristic fashion, ignoring Fraser's original proposals and repeatedly delaying consideration of special island standards. Officials blamed Hilton Head for the delays, pointing to the lack of agreement among islanders about growth and development controls. Blacks opposed any kind of regulation. The companies wanted controls only on others. Settlers, on the other hand, demanded overall growth caps, density controls, less commercial development, and limits on hotels and time-sharing projects in plantations. County planners also had doubts about many of the specific measures, particularly the legality of restricting development in designated zones and the effectiveness of open space requirements and density limitations.

Conflicts on Hilton Head, unreasonable expectations, and legal complications only partially explain Beaufort County's reluctance to embrace effective growth controls. More important for county leaders were the attractions of growth on Hilton Head. Growth bolstered the county's tax base and created more jobs. Beaufort saw Hilton Head as a cash cow to be milked for maximum gain; the more rapidly the island grew, the greater the county benefits would be. Growth also fostered more profitable relationships between politicians and developers.

Figure 9.1 - Building Permits, 1975–1983

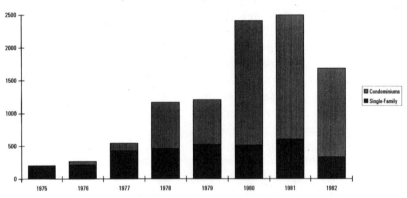

Public and private roles were blurred in the growth machine that dominated Beaufort County; symptomatic was the hiring of a council member by the developer of the stack-a-shacks to assist in securing permits from the planning commission.[10] Special island development standards were finally approved early in 1983, but density controls, building limits, and many other restrictions were gone. Hilton Head was also going, in the midst of a successful campaign for incorporation in 1983, with supporters pointing to the county's unwillingness to control growth as the most compelling reason for islanders to take their future into their own hands.

DEAD ENDS

Beaufort County's repeated failure to regulate development steadily bolstered the appeal of local autonomy on Hilton Head. Key decisions had to be made by officials responsive to local concerns, needs, and conditions. Growth control was the most powerful argument for local autonomy but not its only attraction. Many islanders came from independent communities and valued local self-government. Business boosters hoped the island would be more visible if it was incorporated as a city or town. Those unhappy with public services saw political independence as a means to secure municipal police, water, and other functions. These strands of interest were played out in the context of rapid and uncontrolled growth; they were influenced by the existing framework of county government and local public service districts as well as by the private power of the development companies; and they were shaped by the state's rules for creating municipal governments.

Calls for autonomy were heard first in 1970 in Forest Beach, where rapid growth fueled dissatisfaction with existing governmental arrangements. Poor drainage was getting worse as more of the area developed. County police protection was inadequate to cope with the problems that came with more residents and tourists. Water and sewer charges were rising to finance utility extensions to hotels and condominiums. What Forest Beach needed, concluded two businessmen, was its own local government—a municipality of Hilton Head Beach encompassing the southern portion of the island lying outside Sea Pines, Shipyard, and Palmetto Dunes.[11] The proposal tapped a wellspring of interest in local autonomy but attracted little support because the issues it covered were framed too narrowly for most islanders.

Home rule was a good idea, many agreed, but Hilton Head needed a single government. Creating a group of small villages would duplicate services and magnify differences while providing no controls over growth beyond municipal boundaries. Out of the discussion following the Forest Beach proposal came a general consensus that autonomy should be cast in an island-wide frame of reference. Ideas about incorporating parts of the island continued to surface periodically. Company officials and residents flirted with creating a municipality in Sea Pines. Property owners in Port Royal Plantation studied the possibility of incorporating their community. The local NAACP considered incorporation as a means of securing black control over part of Hilton Head. But the idea of a single government was more persuasive to most islanders, promising the means to solve uncontrolled growth and other island-wide problems as well as provide an inclusive political system that would bridge differences among plantations and other communities.

Once autonomy was on the agenda, home rule was linked primarily to controlling growth and its consequences. "A plague has descended on our land" was the complaint in 1971 of a prominent settler who called for "the necessary steps to be taken to establish all Hilton Head Island as a municipality with

elected officials and local laws and adequate law enforcement."[12] This statement struck a responsive chord; islanders rushed to endorse incorporation as a
means of securing zoning restrictions, limiting condos, and getting a building
code. They found, however, that South Carolina's legal requirements posed
insuperable barriers to incorporating Hilton Head. An area seeking to become a
municipality had to have 15,000 residents or 300 persons per square mile, standards far in excess of Hilton Head's official 1970 population of 2,546 and 60
people per square mile. Areas within 2 miles of the ocean were exempted from
these requirements, provided they encompassed 1 dwelling unit for every 3
acres. But Hilton Head Island was more than 6 miles from the Atlantic at its
widest point and had fewer than half the needed dwelling units. Hilton Head
was in the ironic position of having to grow more before being able to incorporate to control growth.

Other complications emerged as autonomy was discussed. While local control over development was appealing, settlers worried about costs. One of Hilton
Head's attractions was low taxes. Despite grousing about unfair treatment by
the county, most newcomers recognized that Beaufort County's taxes were a
bargain, and many were not enthusiastic about the prospect of financing a new
municipality. Heightening these concerns was the fact that plantation residents
were already paying for services provided by the companies and public service
districts. Autonomy would be less desirable if it required plantation residents to
underwrite substantial improvements in public services for the rest of the island. For some settlers, the whole idea of more government was anathema:
Hilton Head was paradise, an escape from politics and conflict, a place where
government was unnecessary.

Despite these discordant notes, substantial numbers of islanders considered autonomy to be Hilton Head's best bet, albeit one that probably could not
be realized immediately. More and more settlers were wary of depending on
private companies for services or development controls; they wanted an authoritative role in decisions about high-rise hotels, expanded airports, and new
highways. While some settlers wanted as little government as possible, others
were convinced that Hilton Head had to have popular government, a political
focus, and legitimate leadership. Who, asked a frustrated resident in 1973, can
say that "I represent the people on Hilton Head Island, and this is our position"?
The answer: "Nobody and everybody. . . . Nobody really speaks for anybody
else on the island, but then everybody tries to."[13]

The development companies, of course, had been speaking for the island
for years and were still the dominant force on Hilton Head in the early 1970s.
They did not want to deal with another level of government, which inevitably
would impinge on their freedom of action and increase costs. An elected local

174

government could be hostile to the companies, aggregating the interests of disgruntled plantation residents, other settlers, and blacks. Under the worst-case scenario, the gates would come tumbling down, private roads and security guards would disappear, and private planning would succumb to public zoning. What the plantations needed was an alternative to island-wide municipal government that would protect their interests. With talk of autonomy filling the air in 1971, Sea Pines searched for an approach that would insure "continuing Sea Pines as a private community, self-governed with restricted access."[14]

The solution, concluded Sea Pines and the other companies, was to use the island's public service districts as proxies for municipal government through a council empowered to deal with island-wide problems. As indicated in chapter 5, most of the districts had been created by the plantation companies and were responsive to the needs of the major developers. The districts embraced the council proposal; they were not enthusiastic about sharing their turf and tax base with a municipal government. They were also under growing federal and state pressure to coordinate the provision of water and sewers. Proponents of the council plan argued that Hilton Head had been well served by public service districts that provided familiar, flexible, and economic means of meeting local needs. Retaining the districts system, supporters emphasized, would assure islanders of continuing to be taxed primarily for services they were using, in contrast to what would happen under municipalities, which would tax all property owners for services that only some might receive or want.

Announcement of the proposed council triggered heated debate. Opponents objected to placing the island's future in the hands of appointed rather than elected officials. The idea of an appointed council, with six of its nine members from public service districts, raised the hackles of islanders who favored home rule as a means of reducing the influence of the companies.[15] Local self-government, critics insisted, required elected officials responsible to their constituents rather than appointed commissioners not easily accountable to the public. For advocates of local autonomy, the council plan offered much less local control than incorporation. The proposed council's only clear-cut authority was for water and sewer planning; building and zoning codes, fire and safety regulations, and better police protection could be undertaken only in collaboration with the county government.

For those who believed that growth was the central issue, Hilton Head's public service districts were curious candidates to control development. Their mission was to serve rather than regulate development. New districts had been created as growth generated demands for utilities, fire protection, and health care. Existing districts expanded their domains by extending water and sewer lines to new residential and commercial developments; their relationship with developers was symbiotic, each accommodating the other's activities. In this process, developers had the upper hand since utility districts were obligated to extend their boundaries to adjacent properties whose owners petitioned for inclusion.

Blacks were even more disturbed by the council plan than supporters of autonomy. As usual, blacks were not consulted until the plan was formulated, which increased their distrust of whatever was proposed. Native islanders would be excluded from the new governmental arrangements since they lived outside existing utility districts. Talk of the council's exercising land use controls was even more alarming, and African Americans emphatically registered their strong objections to any arrangements—municipal, public service council, or county— that involved zoning and building controls on their land. To make matters worse, blacks would pay higher taxes to finance the council so that utility districts that did not serve black Hilton Head could secure more federal aid.[16] Such an insensitive approach was guaranteed to reinforce black suspicions that white Hilton Head wanted control over their land under a local government system that would perpetuate inequality.

What finally emerged from the council controversy was a watered-down version of the original proposal too feeble to offer a real alternative to incorporation. Gone were any taxing authority in response to black objections and most of the specific powers that bothered advocates of municipal government. Whatever legitimacy the council might have claimed was lost when county political leaders turned aside demands for an elected body.[17] Without funds, powers, or constituency base, the council lacked resources to plan, depended on voluntary compliance by the member districts, and was easily ignored by county officials.

The debate about governmental alternatives produced, in addition to the ill-fated public service council, a comprehensive formal appraisal of Hilton Head's options. Many people felt that the island was rushing headlong into the future with insufficient knowledge about complex and contentious issues. Further study also the Hilton Head community, a place full of well-educated and informed people who believed in the value of information and analysis. Knowledge had been a key weapon in the successful campaign against BASF. An unbiased outside appraisal also, it was hoped, would defuse conflict and distrust, particularly among blacks. Engaged for the task was Horace Fleming, a political scientist at Clemson University. With the development companies picking up most of the tab, Fleming spent the summer of 1973 on Hilton Head, collecting material and interviewing more than 150 people.

Hilton Head wanted information and options, and Fleming provided both— an exhaustive 340-page study replete with maps and tables, along with thirteen alternative approaches to organizing local government.[18] With Fleming's findings in hand, islanders pondered their options. In typical Hilton Head fashion, the process was cumbersome, replete with commissions, committees, and large casts representing everyone under the island's bright sun.[19] From all this talk emerged agreement that local government must control growth. Following up on this agreement, Hilton Head's leaders opted to proceed within the framework of Beaufort County, asking the county to establish an island commission with elected members, taxing authority, and planning staff.[20]

County officials were not thrilled by the idea of an agency that could undercut their authority, pave the way to Hilton Head's independence, and jeopardize potential future profit from the island's tax base and development. Reluctantly, the county council authorized an advisory referendum on Hilton Head, in which 53 percent voted for the commission.[21] Not good enough, concluded the county, pointing to the narrow margin and adamant black opposition. Months of research and study and endless hours of discussion, conflict, and compromise left Hilton Head back at the beginning, dominated by what one local leader termed a "county political establishment" determined "to retain as long as possible absolute control over its most important financial resource, Hilton Head Island."[22]

Hilton Head had run out of options. Incorporation was legally out of reach, the public service council ineffective, and the island commission seemingly stillborn. For some islanders, the only alternative was to secure more political influence in Beaufort by running candidates and winning elections. By 1976 enough Republicans had migrated to Hilton Head to elect Gordon Craighead, a former Sea Pines executive, to the county council. Craighead's election was the first step in a political progression that led to eventual Republican control of the council and to the appointments of more islanders to county boards and agencies. Depending on internal political change in Beaufort County, however, was a problematic answer to Hilton Head's problems. Only 20 percent of the county's registered voters lived on Hilton Head in 1979. Moreover, islanders elected and appointed to county posts did not form a cohesive bloc on matters affecting Hilton Head. From Hilton Head's perspective, the changing cast of characters in Beaufort did not have much effect on policies or attitudes, particularly on the central issue of growth. Again and again, county officials moved slowly and grudgingly, only in response to pressure and usually with too little, too late.

Disenchantment with Beaufort County mounted rapidly as growth accelerated in the late 1970s. Ineffective county land use regulation fueled interest in governmental change, convincing more and more islanders that Hilton Head had to secure some control over its future. Business interests were particularly restive. They questioned whether or not Beaufort County was capable of maintaining a favorable business climate as Hilton Head's economic base shifted from development to resort activities. The Chamber of Commerce reexamined Hilton Head's governmental options in 1978, a process that led back to the idea of the island commission.[23] In this incarnation the commission would have neither legislative powers nor tax base, and thus, it was hoped, it might be more acceptable to county officials. Beaufort responded by ignoring the proposal for more than a year before agreeing to establish an appointed body rather than an elected one. Over 98 percent of island voters endorsed the commission in 1982 in an election boycotted by blacks, who remained deeply suspicious of white Hilton Head's governmental schemes.[24]

Eight years after the idea surfaced, Hilton Head finally had an island commission, but the group had no power, no funds, no electoral base, and no influence on county officials, who ignored it. By now Hilton Head was awash in unwanted development, and the new commission sought without success to convince the county to tighten development regulation. "Somebody ought to listen to us," complained one member in the wake of futile efforts to persuade the county planning commission to stop approving projects lacking sewage plans acceptable to state health officials.[25] A powerless advisory body that no one heeded while a new breed of developers did as they pleased, the island commission was the perfect metaphor for Hilton Head's relationship with Beaufort County.

BREAKING AWAY

Island commissions, special development standards, public service council—each failure convinced more islanders that Beaufort County could not be trusted with their future. Time and again Hilton Head's efforts to work with the county had been rebuffed or reduced to impotence. County rule meant ugly condos, massive hotels, commercial overbuilding, and cozy relationships between developers and politicians. Only autonomy could offer public control over private developers by responsive local officials. Still, substantial numbers of island residents remained dubious about independence; they worried about duplicating existing services, feared higher taxes, and desired to avoid racial conflict. Then came Beaufort County's most spectacular failure in dealing with growth on Hilton Head, the infamous stack-a-shacks. As trucks rumbled across the bridge with the prefabricated sections of the Four Seasons Centre in the summer of 1982, the tide turned decisively in favor of autonomy. Enough! cried angry islanders as cranes began piling up the boxes—"Some people were determined right then to incorporate and never let that happen again."[26]

At this point incorporation was not only more appealing but finally feasible. Results from the 1980 census confirmed that Hilton Head had grown enough to meet the state standard of 1 dwelling unit for every 3 acres.[27] Now the island could cut loose from Beaufort; nothing had to be approved by county officials. Incorporation was a state responsibility that involved meeting legal requirements; once state standards had been satisfied, autonomy would be in the hands of islanders. Hilton Head's voters alone would decide whether to incorporate, not the county council. The campaign could be focused on local issues; supporters needed only local political resources. For the first time, Hilton Head's future was dependent on decisions made by island residents.

Before Hilton Head could decide on incorporation, autonomy had to be transformed from an appealing concept into specifics that satisfied state requirements and addressed local concerns about costs, services, plantation gates, and property rights. Much of this effort was devoted to the nuts and bolts of incorporation that previous studies had not addressed, including legal requirements, governmental structure, finances, programs, and petitions of incorporation.[28] Leadership in this work continued to come from the Chamber of Commerce, which organized committees, financed research, and played a major part in the final campaign for incorporation. Reflecting the growing diversity of the island's economy, none of the leading business advocates were developers; instead they managed resort housing, practiced law, operated a restaurant, and published the local newspaper.[29] Major developers remained ambivalent about incorporation; they still worried about public encroachments on their private realms. But they too had lost patience with what one called "an inept county government."[30] With new business leaders out front, however, neither the resources nor the views of the plantation companies played an important part in the campaign for incorporation.

Keeping the plantations in the background also facilitated coalition on incorporation between residential and business interests. By the early 1980s, *developer* was a dirty word on Hilton Head; developers were lumped together in most people's minds as greedy and uncaring. Working with settlers was essential for the Chamber of Commerce in order to insure support from the island's largest bloc of voters. With the Chamber and Community Association leading the way, property owners' organizations and environmental groups joined forces with merchants and builders to support incorporation—hardly the usual alliance in efforts to control growth. Underlying this unexpected coalition was widespread agreement that "bad" development had to be regulated. Beyond easy targets like the stack-a-shacks, however, growth control meant different things to different people. Business people wanted to restrain undesirable development, not growth in general. Settlers favored strict restrictions on all development; they wanted to incorporate to "protect Hilton Head Island from uncontrolled growth and all the attendant problems of increasing density."[31]

Common interests held the coalition together during the campaign for incorporation; but once local autonomy was achieved, differences over growth would sunder this fragile alliance.

Incorporation also posed dilemmas for plantation residents. Most wanted growth controls but were troubled by the implications of municipal government for private communities. Change might jeopardize restricted access and force plantations to open their facilities and beaches to the public. Plantation residents were repeatedly assured that private roads and private communities were no more incompatible with municipal government than private property. Those living in the private communities were also reluctant to be taxed for services they were already buying. To quell these concerns, the architects of an independent Hilton Head offered limited service government, a municipality concerned primarily with planning and development control that would depend heavily on the county, utility districts, and private plantations to meet service needs.[32] Limited service government promised settlers just what most wanted: control over development without having to pay for additional public services.

As 1983 began, incorporation supporters staged the final act of a drama that had started more than a dozen years earlier. In February the last in a long series of study committees recommended incorporation to an enthusiastic crowd of over 700 gathered at the Marriott Hotel in Shipyard Plantation. More than 1,500 signatures were quickly gathered on petitions requesting that the state hold a referendum on home rule. The petitions went to South Carolina's secretary of state along with hundreds of pages documenting that incorporation was feasible, that alternative solutions had been considered, and that citizens had been involved in this action. Mastery of the technical details of the complicated process by proincorporation forces led to the state's speedy determination that its requirements had been satisfied. On May 10, 1983, Hilton Head's voters would finally get a chance to decide whether islanders wanted local control.

Opposition was less vocal than the well-orchestrated efforts of proincorporation forces. A number of prominent island pioneers did not embrace political change. Architects Pete McGinty and Doug Corkern believed that home rule and public regulation were more likely to impede good design than restrict bad development. Orion Hack feared that independence would "intensify conflict among the island's various constituencies or tribes."[33] Also opposed were Hilton Head's members of the county council. Gordon Craighead denounced the rush to home rule as unnecessary, costly, and divisive.[34] Island needs, Craighead insisted, could be satisfied by Beaufort County; islanders could "control their destiny substantially at the ballot box" within the county political system.[35] But Beaufort County had run out of credibility by the spring of 1983. County politicians never took home rule seriously until the issue was out of their hands, blithely assuming that contentious islanders could never agree on anything as important as local autonomy. As with BASF, notes a central figure in the push for incorporation, the county underestimated the island, once again overlooking "Hilton Head's political potential in the form of lots of able and experienced people with political know-how."[36]

African Americans, on the other hand, never underestimated the political clout of the white newcomers. Any kind of local autonomy would dilute black political influence. In Beaufort County, these islanders formed part of a substantial bloc of black votes that influenced political outcomes and public policies. On independent Hilton Head, blacks would be swamped in a sea of white votes, most of them cast by affluent plantation residents.[37] For island blacks, Beaufort County was an ally rather than an enemy, widely viewed as "their protector in many instances and as their last line of defense locally against arbitrary action on the part of their white neighbors."[38]

Autonomy might have been more palatable were a full-fledged municipality being created, one that would extend water and sewer lines, improve police protection, build housing, and develop recreational facilities. But limited service government promised African Americans higher taxes rather than improved public services. The same political arithmetic that had produced the proposal for limited service government would erect formidable obstacles to improving public services for blacks in the new municipality. "If a majority of them have services already," predicted one black leader, "don't expect them to vote to extend services to outsiders."[39] And this government that offered so little to blacks was being created primarily to regulate black land. Blacks were just as opposed to losing control over their land in 1983 as they had been three decades earlier. White settlers, they worried, would impose standards that would force blacks off their land. "What are standards?" asked one black islander; "I can just see one of the first city ordinances outlawing trailers. Most blacks can't afford new homes. They live in trailers."[40]

In the end, blacks had little impact on incorporation. They were consulted, their complaints were heard, and their objections were noted. But the architects of local autonomy did not respond substantively to black concerns. Close to 200 blacks turned out for a presentation of the incorporation plan at the First African Baptist Church two weeks after the proposal was unveiled to white Hilton Head at the Marriott; speaker after speaker criticized the endeavor and demanded changes. Nothing, however, was modified, because the backers of incorporation were going through the forms rather than the substance of consultation.[41] Blacks wanted different outcomes, which supporters of autonomy were unwilling to consider. Abandoning minimal government in favor of substantial municipal services would imperil plantation residents' backing for incorporation.

In the view of most blacks, race was the reason they were treated differently from whites on incorporation. Home rule advocates insisted that "race was never really an issue."[42] And for white islanders, race was not a central concern; growth control and local autonomy were their interests. Incorporation and land regulation, whites contended, were not designed to disadvantage African Americans politically or economically, even though their effect was detrimental to blacks. Whatever the intent, however, white benefits and black costs made autonomy a racial issue for native islanders. Perhaps no other outcome was possible, given the way Hilton Head was divided by race, class, and private communities. Nonetheless, white insensitivity to black Hilton Head intensified racial conflict in the process of creating a new political community that was supposed to bring islanders together.

ENDGAME

A few days before the home rule referendum, an advertisement appeared in the *Island Packet* picturing the Four Seasons Centre and asking, "Is this what you want Hilton Head to be? Help save your island. Vote for incorporation."[43] Sixty percent did just that on May 10, 1983, creating the Town of Hilton Head Island in an election that attracted barely half the island's registered voters.[44] As expected, support for incorporation was strongest in the plantations and weakest among African Americans. Autonomy was favored by three to one in the district encompassing most of Sea Pines, while the adjoining district with the rest of Sea Pines and Shipyard Plantation produced a two-to-one majority. Areas with the most blacks registered the heaviest votes against incorporation: the three election districts where over 99 percent of Hilton Head's blacks lived accounted for 63 percent of the negative vote.

Five other questions on the ballot dealt with basic governmental arrangements in case incorporation was voted in, and all were approved by larger margins than autonomy. Over 77 percent agreed to name the new municipality the Town of Hilton Head Island, *town* having a nicer connotation than *city* to the suburban refugees who had come to Hilton Head to escape urban America. Islanders favored council-manager government and nonpartisan elections by large margins, opting for expert leadership rather than partisan politics in the quest for growth control. Two-year terms were strongly preferred; after the long struggle for responsive local government, Hilton Head would keep elected officials on a short leash. And most voters wanted a combination of ward and at-large elections for the town council to insure that the island's diverse communities would be represented in the new political system.

Table 9.1
Results of the Incorporation Referendum: May, 1983

	In Favor	Opposed	Percent in Favor
Sea Pines—southern portion	653	224	74.5
Sea Pines, Shipyard, Forest Beach	776	381	67.1
Palmetto Dunes and mid-island	384	306	55.7
Port Royal and mid-island	262	496	34.6
North end and Hilton Head Plantation	393	304	56.4
Absentee	157	38	80.5
Total	2625	1749	60.0

Source: Jordan and Fleming, "Organizing Local Government," chapter 10, 8–11; and "Incorporation Election Results."

Optimists hoped that the new government would be a rallying point, that a sense of community would be created that would transcend the divisions between residents and developers, retired and working islanders, plantation dwellers and others, blacks and whites. Blacks, however, were not through fighting the government whose creation they had overwhelmingly opposed at the polls. Incorporation was challenged in state and federal courts by the NAACP. The South Carolina suit alleged that Hilton Head failed to qualify for incorporation because hotel rooms and vacation rental units had been counted in meeting the state requirement of 1 dwelling unit per 3 acres. In the federal action, the NAACP contended that creation of the new town diluted black representation in local government and that incorporation had not been cleared by the Justice Department as required by the Voting Rights Act of 1965. Both of these efforts failed to block incorporation. South Carolina's Supreme Court was "convinced that the Legislature intended to include within the provisions of the requirement dwelling units other than those occupied by permanent residents."[45] A federal district court found that the new town was established in compliance with the Voting Rights Act, and this ruling was sustained by the U.S. Court of Appeals for the Fourth Circuit.[46]

Hilton Head now had its destiny in its own hands—to a certain extent. Beaufort County would still be providing police and other public services, and the county's land use controls would regulate development until the new town devised its own plans and standards. Public service districts remained in charge of water, sewer, and fire protection; and state and federal rules affecting water quality, waste disposal, and beach management were more important than ever. Moreover, the private realms of the plantation companies still encompassed

Table 9.2
Results of Referendum on Governmental Structure, May 1983

	Vote	Percent
Town of Hilton Head Island		
In favor	2917	77.5
Opposed	845	22.5
Form of government		
Council-manager	2468	69.9
Mayor-council	771	21.9
Council	289	8.2
Type of election		
Nonpartisan	3046	87.7
Partisan	428	12.3
Term of office		
Two years	2857	81.0
Four years	669	29.0
Council constituencies		
At-large and wards	2140	62.0
Districts	889	25.8
At-large	442	12.2

Source: "Incorporation Election Results."

most of Hilton Head, their plans blessed by existing laws, their land protected by deed covenants, their services and facilities reserved for residents and guests. The first years of Hilton Head's new government would also be a time of change on the plantations, marking the departure of Charles Fraser from Sea Pines, the consolidation and subsequent collapse of many plantations under single owner-ship, and acquisition of Sea Pines by a group of residents. At the same time, Hilton Head was changing rapidly, doubling its population in the 1980s, at-tracting ever more tourists, and shifting from a development-based economy to a resort-based one. Amid these changes, the new local government struggled to find its way in an increasingly plural political setting beset by the turmoil of rapid growth.

NOTES

1. Fleming, *Hilton Head Island Government: Analysis and Alternatives,* 262.
2. In 1984, in a case involving a dispute over the Sea Pines forest pre-

serve, the South Carolina Supreme Court ruled that plantation master plans were not enforceable in the courts. See *Butler v. Sea Pines Plantation Co.*

3. John Swartout, president, Association of Sea Pines Plantation Property Owners, quoted in Richards, "Residents Concerned about Timesharing Neighbors."

4. South Carolina courts upheld private covenants in cases involving Palmetto Dunes and Sea Pines in 1985 and 1987. These decisions are discussed in chapter 14.

5. Bowie, "Zoning Hearings Create Much Heat, Little Light."

6. Fleming, *Hilton Head Island Government: Analysis and Alternatives,* 265.

7. Daniels, "Sojourner's Scrapbook," May 11, 1972.

8. Charles E. Fraser, "A 1979 Action Plan," 6.

9. "Action Plan."

10. William Bowen, a lawyer and Hilton Head resident, represented the U.S. Capital Corporation, the developer of the Four Seasons Centre, while serving on the Beaufort County Council.

11. The proposal originated with Wilbert Roller, perhaps Forest Beach's most ardent developer, and merchant Louis McKibben.

12. Goddard, letter to the editor. Goddard was the island's first physician.

13. Quoted in Fleming, *Hilton Head Island Government: Analysis and Alternatives,* 189.

14. Sea Pines Plantation Company, "Political Subdivisions for Hilton Head Island." The study was undertaken by Robert B. Killingsworth, a retired Mobil executive who had organized the Sea Pines Public Service District for the company and then served as its chairman.

15. Eight of the nine members of the proposed council would be appointed. In addition to the representatives of the six public service districts (the Forest Beach Public Service District, Hilton Head Fire District, Hilton Head Medical District, Hilton Head Public Service District No. 1, Palmetto Dunes Public Service District, and the Sea Pines Public Service District) were two appointed members residing outside the jurisdiction of the four subisland utility districts. The sole elected official was the member of the county council from the Hilton Head–Bluffton district. Council members would be appointed by the governor on the advice of the county's legislative delegation, the same process used for public service district commissioners. In practice, legislators solicited nominees from the island's leaders, including, of course, the plantation companies. In the Sea Pines district, an unofficial referendum enabled residents to indicate their preferences, which were honored in recommending nominees to the governor.

16. A four-mill tax ($4 per $1,000 of assessed value) on property on Hilton Head was proposed to finance the public service council.

17. The bill approved by the state legislature in mid-1973 enlarged the council to eleven members to accommodate the newly created public service district for Hilton Head Plantation and an additional representative from the areas not included in the utility districts. All three representatives of the outside areas appointed to the council were African Americans.

18. The report treated in detail the legal framework of local government in South Carolina, Beaufort County's governmental system, Hilton Head's public service districts, and local assessments of public services as well as examining the social and economic structure of Hilton Head and Beaufort County. See Fleming, *Hilton Head Island Government: Analysis and Alternatives.* Fleming summarized his findings in "Reorganizing Local Government."

19. A fifty-member Commission for Island Government, established by the Hilton Head Island Community Association, represented the Hilton Head Island Community Association; property owners' groups from Sea Pines, Port Royal, and Spanish Wells; the three development companies; public service districts and the new public service council; the Clemson study liaison group established by the Community Association; the local NAACP and community action organization; the League of Women Voters, Woman's Association, Association of University Women, and National Organization of Women; the Hilton Head Island Chamber of Commerce, Junior Chamber, Lions, and Rotary; and both political parties, the bar association, the Association of Architects, the rescue squad, the Human Relations Council, the Progressive Club, and the island representative on the Beaufort County Council.

20. A 1972 amendment to the state constitution authorized counties to create special commissions to provide services to part of their jurisdiction. Counties determined the area, taxing authority, powers, and membership of such commissions and retained all legislative authority. Half the members of the proposed Hilton Head commission would be elected, half appointed by the county council. The commission would be supported by a tax on island property not to exceed five mills.

21. The vote was 936 in favor, 817 opposed.

22. Robert B. Killingsworth, quoted in "Public Service Official Blasts County Authorities."

23. Fleming was engaged to update his study. See Fleming, *Hilton Head Government: Analysis and Alternatives II.*

24. The vote was 2,411 to 46.

25. Frederick Hack, Hilton Head Island Commission, quoted in Bender, "Lack of Communications with JPC Cited at Meeting."

26. Willis Shay, quoted in Hill, "Island Issues Come to Full Boil in Summer of '82."

27. The additional state requirement that limited special oceanside standards to areas within 2 miles of the ocean had been modified to include all islands bordering the Atlantic.

28. Outside assistance was secured from the Bureau of Governmental Research and Service at the University of South Carolina to assess Hilton Head's viability as a municipality as required by state law. The new study concluded that independence was both feasible and desirable. See Bureau of Governmental Research and Service, "Incorporation as an Option for Hilton Head Island."

29. John F. Curry, who cochaired the incorporation campaign, ran Sand Dollar Management, which operated rental properties in Palmetto Dunes. Michael L. M. Jordan, the principal architect of incorporation, was a partner in a leading island law firm. Brian Carmines, who owned the island's largest restaurant, and Ben T. Banks, publisher of the *Island Packet,* worked closely with Curry and Jordan.

30. Robert Onorato, president, Palmetto Dunes Resort, quoted in Breland, "Conflict Erupts over Procedures of Development." See also Charles E. Fraser, "Time for a Vote on the City of Hilton Head Island," 45–49.

31. Association of Sea Pines Plantation Property Owners, Letter to Property Owners.

32. In reexamining Hilton Head's options in 1978, Fleming emphasized that creating a "municipality with limited powers" offered islanders "an opportunity to structure their local government to suit their own particular needs without assuming some responsibilities and costs that they do not wish to undertake." See *Hilton Head Island Government: Analysis and Alternatives II,* 205–6. The 1982 study by the Bureau of Governmental Research and Service at the University of South Carolina echoed Fleming in suggesting that Hilton Head adopt "minimum service" government. See "Incorporation as an Option for Hilton Head Island, S.C." 16.

33. Orion D. Hack, interview.

34. Craighead and Edward Smith, publisher of a prodevelopment newsletter, headed the Committee to Question Incorporation.

35. Quoted in Fran Smith, "Craighead to Battle against Incorporation."

36. Baker, interview. Thomas F. Baker was president of the Hilton Head Island Community Association and cochair of the Committee for Incorporation.

37. In 1980, 32.8 percent of the population of Beaufort County was black, compared to 13.1 percent on Hilton Head Island.

38. Jordan and Fleming, "Organizing Local Government," chapter 5, 9.

39. Perry White, president, Hilton Head chapter of the NAACP, quoted in Plumb, "Black Islanders Lambast Idea of a Municipality."

40. Herb Campbell, quoted in "Hilton Head Islanders Split Racially over Incorporation Vote."

41. Michael L. M. Jordan, who helped present the case for incorporation at the First African Baptist Church, later wrote, "While no positions were changed by this meeting with the Black community, it was clear that their views and opinions were sought." Quoted in Jordan and Fleming, "Organizing Local Government," chapter 8, 36.

42. Michael L. M. Jordan, quoted in Hill, "Incorporation Controversial, but Islanders Say 'Yes.'"

43. Advertisement, *Island Packet,* May 5, 1983.

44. Turnout was 51.6 percent.

45. *NAACP v. Town of Hilton Head,* 287 S.C. 254, 335 SE2d 808 (1985).

46. See *NAACP v. Town of Hilton Head Island,* U.S. District Court, District of South Carolina, Charleston Division, Civil Action No. 83–1707–8, and *NAACP v. Town of Hilton Head Island,* U.S. Court of Appeals for Fourth Circuit, No. 83–2029. An attempt to bring the issue before the U.S. Supreme Court failed because of technical deficiencies and delays.

Port Royal Sound and Hilton Head Island circa 1562 as depicted by Jacques Le Moyne (*De Bay's Grand Voyages*, Amsterdam, 1591)

The first wave of Yankee visitors to Hilton Head Island, November 7, 1861 (*Harper's Illustrated Weekly*)

Charles Fraser hunting quail with businessmen at Honey Horn Plantation, 1955 (courtesy Charles E. Fraser)

Construction crew at Sea Pines Plantation, 1964 (courtesy Charles E. Fraser)

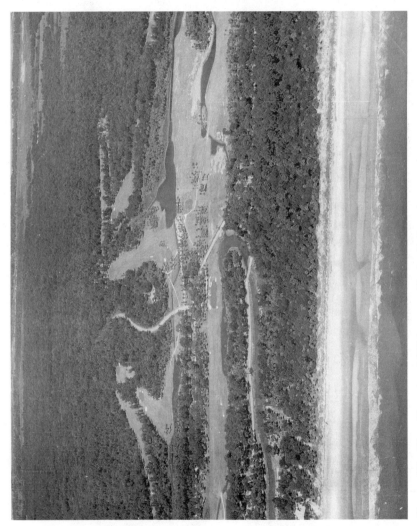

Center of Sea Pines Plantation, 1960 (courtesy Charles E. Fraser)

Charles Fraser accepts a check for a million dollars from Bessemer Securities, 1961 (courtesy Charles E. Fraser)

The fifteenth hole of Hilton Head's first golf course, overlooking the Atlantic Ocean (courtesy Charles E. Fraser)

William Hilton Inn, the island's first full-service hotel, after expansion in 1964 (courtesy Charles E. Fraser)

Charles and Joe Fraser with a model of Harbour Town after receiving the Urban Land Institute's certificate of excellence for private-community planning (courtesy Charles E. Fraser)

Typical Sea Pines home nestled in natural surroundings (photograph by the author)

Charles Fraser with Jack Nicklaus, Pete Dye, and Donald O'Quinn laying out Harbour Town Links in 1968 (courtesy Charles E. Fraser)

Arnold Palmer accepts the winner's trophy at the first Heritage Golf Classic, 1969, with the lighthouse at Harbour Town under construction in the background (courtesy Charles E. Fraser)

Aerial view of Harbour Town (courtesy Harbour Town Yacht Club)

Harbour Town (courtesy Lafayette Cowart, #671–6016)

One of the many man-made lagoons that increased the attractiveness of interior property at Sea Pines (photograph by the author)

Shrimp boat in Skull Creek, part of the fleet of the Hilton Head Fishing Cooperative, which opposed the BASF plant (courtesy Charles E. Fraser)

Interior Secretary Walter Hickel accepts petitions with 35,000 signatures from David Jones of the Hilton Head Fishing Cooperative and John Gettys Smith of the Sea Pines Company (courtesy Charles E. Fraser)

"Captain Dave" at Harbour Town after his return from delivering petitions protesting the BASF plant (courtesy Charles E. Fraser)

Charles Fraser discusses Sea Pines with Atlanta developer Blaine Kelly, 1968 (courtesy Charles E. Fraser)

William Stevens, president of the Sea Pines property owners' association, and Joe Fraser after agreeing on the location of 1,280 acres of parkland and open space at Sea Pines (courtesy Charles E. Fraser)

Condominium development at Sea Pines (courtesy
Charles E. Fraser)

The modern span that replaced the original bridge linking Hilton
Head to the mainland (courtesy Charles E. Fraser)

Chapter Ten

Second Fall of the Plantations

I'm not Charles Fraser. I don't mean that in a negative way. He's extremely educated; he's very fluent; he's very elegant. I'm not any of these things. I'm not trying to build any empires over here.

—Bobby Ginn, quoted by Margaret Greer
in the *Hilton Head Report,* March 1985

The first plantation system on Hilton Head Island lasted more than a century. The collapse of the domains of the Popes, Stoneys, Baynards, and Lawtons commenced with the landing of the Union forces in 1862 and was completed when Robert E. Lee surrendered at Appomattox in 1865. Hilton Head's second plantation system had a much shorter existence, beginning with the arrival of the Frasers and Hacks in 1950 and falling apart after Charles Fraser sold Sea Pines a third of a century later. Sea Pines was acquired in 1985 by a reckless local speculator who gathered most of the island's plantations into a shaky financial structure. This flawed empire soon passed into the hands of disreputable characters from the netherworld of real estate development. And the ignominious final blow to the proud creations of Charles Fraser and Fred Hack came when the jerry-built successor to Sea Pines and the Hilton Head Company collapsed into bankruptcy late in 1986. With this second fall came the end of another era in which Hilton Head's fate was determined largely by the masters of the plantations.

Rogues and bankruptcy demonstrated with a vengeance the fragility of communities organized and operated by private enterprise. Owners came and went—Sea Pines and the Hilton Head Company changed hands three times between 1980 and 1986. With new owners came new plans, policies, and uncertainties. Private ownership put planned communities at the mercy of outside events that could rapidly change the fortunes, interests, and names of their owners. External developments affected large companies as well as small, venturesome and conservative, locally-led and owned by outsiders, successful and less so. A corporate takeover led to a decision to sell the Hilton Head Company in 1985, and the company that acquired Sea Pines from Fraser was compelled by its principal owner to liquidate. For plantation dwellers, this game of musical chairs underscored the fact that their communities were someone else's commodities, assets with dollar signs rather than places where people lived, to be bought and sold with little concern for residents' interests.

Last and most convincing in the indictment of privately owned communities was the devastating combination of leveraged buyouts, savings and loan hanky-panky, and bankruptcy in the mid-1980s. What began with local community builders ended in the hands of glib speculators and shady bankers who cared little about the plantations or Hilton Head. What happened to Sea Pines and the Hilton Head Company was dramatic but not particularly unique in the 1980s, when markets were magic and greed was good. Hilton Head was a microcosm of the dark side of privatism, a world of ever more dubious deals, bankers eager to test the limits of deregulation, lawsuits and indictments, foreclosures and bankruptcies, and the collapse of the savings and loan industry. That Hilton Head's business was development increased its vulnerability since real estate in the 1980s attracted so many quick-buck artists who left the American landscape littered with unfinished projects, defunct banks, and bankrupt companies. Hilton Head would survive, sustained by the durable attractions of the place, the resources of local residents, the land-use covenants, and the strength of the island's expanding resort economy. In the process, however, any legitimacy private companies still had as proxies for more accountable realms disappeared.

SEA PINES IN TRANSITION

Ironically, the plantation system collapsed during prosperity, not during economic adversity. Development companies led the sustained boom that followed the recession of the mid-1970s, selling land for new housing, adding resort facilities, attracting large numbers of customers, and undertaking new plantations. Although the major companies were slipping politically, they still dominated Hilton Head's economy. In 1982 plantations accounted for 90 percent of the island's single-family housing starts and 75 percent of the multifamily units under construction. They also captured the lion's share of Hilton Head's rapidly expanding market for tourists, conventions, and meetings. New resort hotels were developed in Palmetto Dunes, Port Royal, and Shipyard; and another generation of planned communities was launched by the Hilton Head Company, Palmetto Dunes, and former Sea Pines executives.

190

Table 10.1
Housing Units in Plantations, 1982

Plantation	Total	Single-Family	Multi-Family
Sea Pines	3,688	2,062	1,626
Palmetto Dunes	1108	177	931
Shipyard	633	181	452
Port Royal	411	377	34
Hilton Head	344	326	18
Spanish Wells	39	39	0
Total	6,223	3,162	3,061

Source: Beaufort County Joint Planning Commission, "Hilton Head Island Land Use Survey."

Among the plantations, Sea Pines remained the most important despite the mid-1970s financial disaster, wrenching contractions, and substantial debts. Sea Pines' durability was a testament to Fraser's underlying accomplishment. His company was by far the island's largest, and his plantation the most developed. In 1982 Sea Pines was the leading employer on Hilton Head, with 1,200 on the payroll. Almost 60 percent of the housing constructed in plantations through 1981 was in Sea Pines, as were two-thirds of plantation home sales between 1978 and 1983. Real estate in Sea Pines was more valuable; in 1983 its ocean-front property commanded 60 percent more than comparable sites in Port Royal and twice the price of those in Palmetto Dunes. And Sea Pines, with $125 million in sales in 1982, was the largest real estate broker in South Carolina.

Sea Pines also had Charles Fraser. As his plantation recovered, Fraser was eager to return to his first love, community planning and development. But Sea Pines no longer had much to develop. Fraser had lost control over most of the undeveloped land in the plantation in the wake of his company's financial problems. Along with the lost opportunities within Sea Pines, Hilton Head Plantation was gone, which left the company with very little land to sell and nothing large enough to challenge Fraser's restless intellect. Development activities also were constrained by creditors, who kept the company on a short financial leash to protect their $20-odd million stake.[1] Revenues from Sea Pines could not be used for new undertakings, nor could properties be sold to raise investment capital without the consent of the creditors. These restrictions prevented Fraser from pursuing the purchase of Palmetto Dunes in 1979, an acquisition that would have afforded Sea Pines major new opportunities since much of Palmetto Dunes was still to be developed.

Lacking land and largely blocked from new ventures, Sea Pines had become primarily a resort operator. By the early 1980s, resort activity was producing two-thirds of company revenues, while less than one-fifth was from real estate development. Operations once ancillary to selling real estate were now the company's principal business—Harbour Town's shops and marina, golf courses and tennis clubs, condo rentals, the Hilton Head Inn, and the Plantation Club. Unfortunately for Sea Pines, resort activities had never been profitable; they were loss leaders for the sale of land that Sea Pines no longer owned. What was tolerable to help market real estate became punishingly inefficient in a company that derived so much of its revenues from the resort business.

Table 10.2
Sea Pines Revenues from Operations, 1980–1982

	Annual Revenues 1980 (000)	Annual Revenues 1981 (000)	Annual Revenues 1982 (000)	Average 1980–82 Percent Share
Resort operations	24.5	30.0	28.7	67.1
Real estate development	3.1	13.3	6.3	18.4
Real estate brokerage	4.5	6.7	6.9	14.5
Total	32.1	50.0	41.9	100.0

Source: Sea Pines Company, "Notice of Special Meeting of Shareholders to Be Held June 9, 1983," 40.

Sea Pines was also facing increasingly stiff competition from Hilton Head's newer resorts. Harbour Town Links was still a premier attraction for golfers, but Ocean and Sea Marsh slipped as new courses were built. With condominium fever gripping the island, Sea Pines was no longer the principal supplier of resort accommodations. Moreover, in an overstocked market, many of the plantation's older condos were difficult to rent at Sea Pines' luxury rates. Another disadvantage was the absence of a resort hotel within Sea Pines. The Hilton Head Inn was outside the plantation and showing its years. Palmetto Dunes and Shipyard had major resort hotels inside their gates, with Palmetto Dunes adding a second hotel in the early 1980s and the Hilton Head Company planning an oceanside luxury hotel at Port Royal. In addition, the competition had the advantage of combining resort facilities with plenty of land to develop. And while Sea Pines was tightly controlled by creditors, the other major companies had deep pockets to reach into to develop land, build hotels, and market their properties aggressively. The Hilton Head Company was now backed by the resources of Marathon Oil, while Palmetto Dunes was owned by the textile barons of Greenwood Mills.

Sea Pines' evolution from community builder to resort operator also did not suit Fraser's interests or talents. "I have," he readily admitted, "no passion for restaurant or hotel management."[2] As the twenty-fifth anniversary of the founding of the company approached in mid-1982, he concluded the time had come for him to move on to new endeavors. Another factor in Fraser's decision to sell was the deterioration of his relations with property owners. Residents were understandably distressed by the consequences of financial adversity for their community—maintenance, services, and investment suffered as Sea Pines struggled to stay afloat. Adversity also sharpened worries about the durability of agreements between property owners and Sea Pines. By 1979 these concerns were being advanced by a new cohort of grassroots leaders. Less closely connected to the company than their predecessors, they brought new demands and a confrontational approach that radically altered the terms of discourse between Sea Pines and property owners.

Sea Pines was less willing than ever to subsidize plantation services for residents. The company sought to shed responsibility for security, landscaping, maintenance, bike paths, and other facilities. Property owners, argued Fraser, should underwrite more of these expenses because they now owned most of the plantation. When residents resisted, Fraser blasted them for not shouldering their fair share. Heightening Fraser's ire was his conviction that many of his customers were ingrates who wanted the company to pay the bills while they reaped the lion's share of benefits from appreciating property values.

Fraser and the owners' association locked horns over gate policies, plantation operations, golf course maintenance, development plans, and the 1974 agreements. Differences over policies were exacerbated by personal conflicts that poisoned relations between Fraser and the people who ran the association after 1979. The new leaders aggressively asserted residential interests and claims on the company, accusing Fraser of bad faith and worse. Fraser excoriated the association's officers for waging "guerrilla warfare," charging that they "misrepresented facts, distorted the covenants, and repeatedly sought to take over effective control of the assets of the Sea Pines Plantation Company."[3] Charges and countercharges filled the air. Lawsuits were threatened and filed, and conflicts were escalated and personalized.

193

Most acrimonious was a dispute over hotel development rooted in the tension between resort operations and residential interests. Fraser was convinced that Sea Pines needed luxury hotel accommodations to compete with Palmetto Dunes and the Hilton Head Company in attracting groups and conferences. Most residents did not want Sea Pines to attract more tourists, particularly hotel guests who would make heavy demands on golf courses and other recreational facilities. Hotels had been indicated on all Sea Pines master plans and were permitted under the covenants that accompanied the 1974 agreements between the company and property owners. But the agreement itself did not specifically mention hotels. Fraser insisted that the covenants were the last word, while property owners wondered what kind of protection was offered by documents that seemed full of loopholes. "We could have as many as 10,000 motel rooms within the gates," fretted the association members in a wild exaggeration.[4] With neither side willing to compromise, the association sued to prevent Sea Pines from proceeding with its hotel plans.

For Fraser, the hotel dispute was the last straw. Battling with property owners added to the personal wear and tear of keeping the company afloat. Late in the fall of 1982 Fraser would describe the decision to sell as "an uncharacteristic . . . 'to hell with it' response to three years of unjustified harassments by a tiny handful of lusting-for-power . . . leaders."[5] Perhaps Fraser would have sold even if good relations had been maintained with property owners—residents, after all, had little to do with Sea Pines' debts, creditor restrictions, limited land resources, or weakened competitive position. Still, these bitter conflicts soured Fraser's last years at the helm and reinforced the attractions of freeing himself from the burdens of running a private community in tandem with contentious property owners.

In the fall of 1982, Sea Pines was sold for $10 million to Vacation Resorts, an operator of resort housing in Colorado and Hawaii. Fraser thought he had found in Vacation Resorts a purchaser who treasured his plans and shared his values. The company was controlled by E. F. Heizer Jr., a venture capitalist who had known Fraser since Yale Law School and had been involved in Sea Pines' financial dealing with Allstate Insurance Company in the 1960s.[6] Under the deal, Sea Pines Company became a wholly owned subsidiary of Vacation Resorts, with Fraser receiving $6 million in notes in return for his 57 percent share of Sea Pines.[7]

Absent from any involvement in the sale were Sea Pines residents. Fraser made no effort to see whether they might be interested in buying the plantation; nor were they consulted about potential purchasers. Residents were excluded in part because of the bitter conflict between Fraser and ASPPPO. But they were also not regarded as key parties with a legitimate interest or role in the transaction. The deal, according to the company's directors, was "in the best interest of Sea Pines and its shareholders."[8] That determination was made solely by the Sea Pines Company, particularly its chairman and dominant stockholder, Charles E. Fraser, and his brother, Joseph Fraser Jr., who owned the second-largest share of the company. Despite the considerable influence that residents had amassed over the years, Sea Pines Plantation Company was a privately owned firm, a commodity that could be bought and sold with no involvement by the plantation's inhabitants.

Fraser officially turned the plantation over to Vacation Resorts in June 1983 after the transaction was approved by Sea Pines stockholders. An era had ended, a quarter of a century in which Fraser had crafted a new kind of community and transformed Hilton Head from a sleepy backwater into a thriving resort. "It's going to be difficult to think of Sea Pines—or Hilton Head for that matter—without Charles Fraser being the leader," wrote a local journalist echoing local feelings; "it was his ability to dare and to dream that brought most of us this gem among the world's most beautiful communities."[9] No one, however, anticipated that the sale of Sea Pines would set in motion a chain of events destined to imperil Fraser's plantation and Hilton Head generally.

At the outset, the new owners paid homage to Fraser's legacy. "We will always . . . do our very best to do the right thing for Sea Pines," pledged Vacation Resort's president, "and to act as stewards for this fantastic community."[10] An olive branch was extended to residents in the dispute over hotel development, even though Sea Pines had the better side of the legal argument over the covenants. Not wishing to prolong the conflict, Vacation Resorts negotiated a settlement that limited hotel development in Sea Pines to 160 rooms, about half of what Fraser had planned to build. The company also agreed to give property owners control of the plantation's architectural review board while promising to improve maintenance, continue restricted access to Sea Pines, and be more responsive to residents.[11] Vacation Resorts hailed these developments as marking "a renewed spirit of cooperation between the Company and the Property Owners of Sea Pines Plantation which would lead to a better community and an improved resort."[12]

Cooperation, a better community, and an improved resort, however, all proved to be illusory under Sea Pines' new masters. Vacation Resorts inherited the problems that led Fraser to sell, along with more financial burdens and constraints added by the purchase. Vacation Resorts brought to Sea Pines limited experience in the resort business and none in community development. Going from managing condominiums at Colorado ski resorts to operating an enterprise as large and complex as Sea Pines was a big step, and it quickly proved to be beyond the capabilities of the newcomers. Marketing was neglected, with national advertising cut to the bone. Little attention was paid to real estate development, which contributed less than 3 percent to Sea Pines' revenues in 1984.[13] Fewer resources were devoted to maintenance, and the reputation of an increasingly shabby Sea Pines plummeted. In 1984 the company that had been profitable when Fraser sold it was losing $4 million.

Among Sea Pines residents, no one was more troubled by Vacation Resort's inept regime than Charles Fraser. His concerns were both paternal and financial; Sea Pines was his creation, and Vacation Resorts owed him more than $6 million. He did not like the way the new owners were treating his people, running his plantation, and ignoring his advice. Fraser's financial stakes intensified his concerns about having most of his assets sunk in Vacation Resorts: their value depended on what happened to the company. Vacation Resorts was also heavily burdened by debt: carryover obligations to Sea Pines creditors, the acquisition notes, and $6.7 million in revolving credit from Heizer at punishing interest rates. This murky picture was further clouded at the end of 1983 when the Heizer Corporation decided to liquidate, a process that federal law required to be completed in twelve months.[14] Heizer's unexpected action effectively pulled the financial rug from under Vacation Resorts. Awash in debt and with unpaid bills accumulating, the company was in no position either to repay its loans from Heizer or to buy out Heizer's 75 percent share in the firm. Vacation Resorts had to be sold or dissolved. Suddenly Sea Pines was on the market again, and something had to happen quickly under the terms of the Heizer liquidation.

Among the parties interested in purchasing Sea Pines was Charles Fraser, a possibility not welcomed by many Sea Pines residents. Fraser's endeavors also conflicted with a belated effort by the property owners' association to buy the plantation from Vacation Resorts.[15] In the end, neither Fraser nor the property owners fashioned an offer that was acceptable. As the deadline for the liquidation approached in February 1985, Heizer decided to sell to an island developer who patched together a complex set of deals that combined Sea Pines and the Hilton Head Company and thereby set the stage for disaster.

THE HILTON HEAD COMPANY MAKES ITS MOVE

Ironically, Sea Pines and the Hilton Head Company were brought together at a time when Sea Pines, the leader for a quarter century, was declining, while the Hilton Head Company, the perennial follower, was bursting with energy, plans, and resources. The Hilton Head Company had struggled through the 1970s with inadequate funds and inexperienced management under Oxford First Corporation, a personal finance company never comfortable in the land development business. Recession, rising energy costs, and high interest rates had battered the Hilton Head Company and Oxford First's other real estate ventures in Florida and Hawaii. Mired in debt, Oxford First survived only by the good graces of its creditors and by selling off pieces of the Hilton Head Company, including large parcels that were later developed as planned communities.[16] Oxford First finally closed the door on its costly Hilton Head adventure in 1980, selling the Hilton Head Company and its remaining 4,600 acres to a subsidiary of Marathon Oil Corporation for $28.6 million.

With Marathon came access to bountiful resources for the first time in the history of the Hilton Head Company. Oil companies had plenty of cash in 1980, and Marathon was eager to expand its real estate operations. The Hilton Head Company owned thousands of acres of undeveloped land in a premier location, and Marathon had the money to turn plans into reality. Marathon poured more than $20 million annually into its island holdings, building new facilities, redesigning Port Royal and Shipyard, developing two new plantations, and marketing their properties aggressively.

Marathon reworked the Hilton Head Company's plans and overall development strategy to serve a variety of resort, recreational, and residential markets. Resort activities would continue to be heavily emphasized at Shipyard Plantation, the most intensively developed of the company's properties, with more than 1,000 condos, scores of time-share units, and a resort hotel. At Port Royal, Marathon planned resort development centered on a luxury hotel on the ocean and including condominiums, posh clubhouses, a tennis center, and a third golf course. This scheme sparked the same kind of controversy as Fraser's hotel plans at Sea Pines, with property owners arguing that residential values at Port Royal were being sacrificed for resort development and tourist dollars. After a lot of give and take, Marathon and the homeowners compromised on a new master plan for the plantation that separated the residential area from golf, tennis, and resort lodgings. Now Marathon could market two Port Royals, a glitzy new Port Royal Resort and Port Royal Plantation, a private single-family residential community with no condos, hotels, restaurants, shops, or tourists.

The Hilton Head Company's remaining properties offered a different set of opportunities and challenges. In contrast to Shipyard and Port Royal, where Marathon was elaborating previous plans, the slate was clean at the company's other two substantial sites. The opportunity to start from scratch, however, resulted in large part from the planning and marketing challenges posed by these pedestrian interior properties. One parcel consisted of 500 acres on swampy land bordering Broad Creek opposite Shipyard Plantation; the second was piney woods across from Hilton Head Plantation on the northern end of the island. As Marathon's plans evolved, these sites would emerge as Wexford and Indigo Run Plantations, and each would require special efforts to turn it into salable real estate.

Wexford was designed to capitalize on the dissatisfaction of Sea Pines' settlers with resort activities by developing a private upscale residential golf community. A private plantation would prevent conflict with resort activities while offering its developers an opportunity to enhance substantially the value of less attractive land. Building a private golf community in the middle of Hilton Head was such a good idea, however, that the developers of Long Cove Club, next to Wexford, came up with it too and quickly attracted large numbers of buyers from Sea Pines who were eager to live and play golf in a truly private community. Marathon then decided to retarget Wexford on the top end of the market. Wexford would be the priciest of private communities, with lavish amenities: an elaborate harbor and canal system, an excellent golf course, and luxurious club facilities. Wexford became the plantation for the 1980s, the place on Hilton Head for ostentatious displays of wealth. Here affluence was boldly proclaimed in huge homes, a palatial British colonial clubhouse, and 23-karat gold leaf lettering on the signs. In striking contrast to Sea Pines, where understated houses in muted colors blended into the natural setting, Wexford's massive dwellings were out of scale on lots no larger than those in Sea Pines. In Wexford, man was no longer married to nature as in Sea Pines; here nature was overwhelmed by money.

Table 10.3
Planned Development in Hilton Head Company Plantations: 1982–1984

	Acres	Single-family	Multi-family	Hotel Rooms	Total Units	Density (Units per Acre)
Shipyard	838	304	1,508	338	2,150	2.57
Port Royal	1,266	1,021	132	450	1,603	1.27
Wexford	500	429	96	0	525	1.05
Indigo Run	2,040	884	4,500	0	5,384	2.64
Total	4,644	2,638	6,236	788	9,662	

Source: Beaufort County Joint Planning Commission, *The Hilton Head Island Land Use Plan,* 16.

Indigo Run was designed for the other end of the Hilton Head spectrum—those who wanted plantation amenities but could afford only smaller and less expensive housing. This market was expanding rapidly as Hilton Head's economy surged forward in the early 1980s. Indigo Run's 2,000-plus acres would be intensively developed, with five times as many condos as single-family homes, along with two golf courses and other recreational facilities. As an added attraction to a mundane site, Marathon offered land for a town center at Indigo Run. Clustering government, cultural, educational, and recreational activities in a town center, many islanders believed, would help forge a sense of community by providing a counterweight to the centripetal pull of the plantations. Of course, building the town center at Indigo Run would also benefit the Hilton Head Company by increasing land values in the new plantation, particularly for the substantial commercial development planned for the center.

With this ambitious agenda, backed up by significant investments and aggressive marketing, Marathon appeared to be more committed to Hilton Head than the other outside firms that had dabbled in plantation development. But Marathon turned out to be another bird of passage, a sojourner whose stay was determined by distant forces. In 1982 U.S. Steel acquired Marathon Oil, and the Hilton Head Company passed to yet another set of outsiders. Now the Hilton Head Company was an even smaller part of a far larger operation, one that had neither interest nor comparative advantage in resort community development. And when corporate officials in faraway offices decided to get out of the land business in 1984, the Hilton Head Company went on the block, providing an upstart developer with an ill-fated opportunity to recombine the realms of Fraser and Hack.

A DEAL TOO BIG

Bobby Ginn lived to make deals. "It is the deals that make things go for me," the young developer confided a few years before acquiring Sea Pines and the Hilton Head Company.[17] Ginn was a positive thinker with enormous confidence in himself and his deals. He learned the development business from the bottom up, dropping out of college at nineteen to lend a hand in his father's construction business in a small town 50 miles from Hilton Head. From building federally subsidized housing in rural South Carolina, he moved on to Atlanta, taking on bigger projects and making the kind of financial and political connections necessary to get himself into increasingly larger deals. Ginn arrived on Hilton Head in 1976, one of the new breed of developers who flocked to the island after the recession. He developed housing at Sea Pines, put together a resort project at Singleton Beach next to Palmetto Dunes, and—off the island—built condos at seaside communities in Florida, Georgia, and other parts of South Carolina.

With U.S. Steel's decision to unload the Hilton Head Company, Ginn saw a golden opportunity to move into the developers' big leagues by acquiring Hilton Head's biggest package of real estate, now even more valuable than before because of the money pumped into it by Marathon. As Ginn worked to put together a deal for the Hilton Head Company, Sea Pines also became attractive. For Ginn, Sea Pines' appeal was primarily financial: its $6 million carryforward tax losses from the 1970s offered a means of sheltering profits that Ginn expected from the sale of Hilton Head Company assets. Despite its award-winning plans, worldwide reputation, and proud residents, Fraser's Sea Pines was reduced to a tax shelter for a speculator who wanted to buy the Hilton Head Company in order to sell off its properties.

Ginn's deals for Sea Pines and the Hilton Head Company were leveraged buyouts in which the assets of the two companies were used as collateral to finance the purchases from Heizer and Marathon. In the case of Sea Pines, $16 million was paid to Heizer, with Ginn assuming obligations in excess of $30 million to Fraser and other creditors. For the Hilton Head Company, Marathon took $39 million in cash and $31 million in notes and turned over $14 million in debts to Ginn. Ginn borrowed all the money for these exchanges through a complicated set of transactions with two Florida savings and loan associations and a group of collateral investors. Ginn had Sea Pines, the Hilton Head Company, and $80 million in new debt in what he triumphantly called "one of the largest, if not the largest, real estate purchases in the history of South Carolina."[18] Approximately $25 million, the difference between the $80 million raised by Ginn and the $55 million paid to Heizer and Marathon, went to the deal makers. A substantial hunk stayed with Ginn and his associates, including $1.5 million to the Ginn Corporation for arranging the transaction, another $750,000 in fees to Ginn's firms, $335,000 in legal fees to Ginn's partner, and $2 million for working capital. The rest went to banks, lawyers, brokers, consultants, accountants, appraisers, creditors, and other involved parties.[19]

Once the deals were done, the mortgages sealed, and the fees collected, Sea Pines and the Hilton Head Company were reunited, now under the banner of Ginn Holdings. Bobby Ginn was master of Sea Pines, Port Royal, Shipyard, Wexford, and Indigo Run—including nine golf courses, two resort hotels, tennis clubs, Harbour Town, and Sea Pines' Compass Rose logo. Ginn also had four real estate companies that employed 40 percent of the island's agents and accounted for over 70 percent of its property sales.[20] Ginn Holdings was Hilton Head's largest employer, its biggest purchaser of goods and services, and responsible party for the private covenants executed over three decades by Sea Pines and the Hilton Head Company.

Who, islanders asked, was this fellow who appeared out of the blue to own the plantations where most residents lived and many worked? Although Ginn had lived on Hilton Head for almost a decade, he remained on the periphery, neither part of the local business elite nor a visible participant in the struggles over growth or incorporation. To many islanders, Ginn was suspect simply because he was a developer, one of that lot that by 1985 were considered the prime villains on Hilton Head. More troublesome to those familiar with Ginn were his checkered past and shaky financial condition. Involvement in a banking scandal in Tennessee had burdened Ginn with over $50 million in debt.[21] Rumors, most of which proved to be true, hinted that he owed millions more on loans, mortgages, and unpaid taxes and that he was under investigation for fraud and other illegal practices.[22]

Despite these worries, most islanders suspended disbelief and hoped the companies were back on track. After the inept Vacation Resorts interlude and the anxiety of seeing almost half of Hilton Head on the market, finally someone was in charge, and a local boy at that. Ginn emphasized his Lowcountry origins and his commitment to the island where he lived, trumpeting the fact that Hilton Head's most important holdings were back in islander hands. Charles Fraser, perhaps seeing something of himself in the brash young developer, reminded those who hesitated about jumping on the Ginn bandwagon that "there were at least as many skeptics as to whether I would be able to get a golf course built on this jungle island as there are that Bobby Ginn will ever be able to succeed with his purchase."[23]

Unlike Fraser, who built Sea Pines, Ginn the salesman was mostly talk, spinning webs of words about his grand business plans that centered on combining the two companies and their plantations into a single operation, Sea Pines' reputation and trademark would be used to market real estate and resort facilities, Harbour Town would be the jewel in the crown, and Indigo Run's town center would be bigger and better than anything envisaged by Marathon. Precious little resulted from any of these promises. Ginn apparently was neither planner nor builder nor manager. What resulted was chaos rather than coordination as two companies and five plantations scattered across the island were forced into an uncomfortable embrace. Comprehensive marketing, cross-utilization of resort facilities, and merged brokerage operations never materialized. Nor did the renewal of Harbour Town or the promised town center or good relations with residents. Instead, Ginn left a trail of broken promises, angry property owners, and dashed hopes. The honeymoon at Sea Pines was short-lived, as Ginn's desperate need for cash inevitably led to conflict with plantation residents. To service his debts, Ginn had to increase resort revenues as well as enhance the value of property he could sell—both courses of action bound to exacerbate resort-resident frictions.

Deteriorating relations came to a head over Ginn's decision to develop a 250-room hotel at Harbour Town despite the 160-room ceiling accepted by Vacation Resorts and assurances that Ginn accepted the agreement between the property owners and the previous management. Residents fought back in a battle that raged for months, replete with arcane disputes over what should be counted as a hotel room, flip-flops on the part of Sea Pines' architectural review board, and threats of legal action. In the wake of the bitter hotel dispute and worsening financial problems, whatever goodwill existed on the part of plantation residents went the way of Bobby Ginn's promises.

Commitments were even more elusive and money woes more punishing at Indigo Run, where lot sales began just as Ginn acquired the Hilton Head Company. During 1985 more than $9 million worth of real estate was sold to buyers seeking a sliver of paradise at Indigo Run's bargain prices. Purchasers were reassured by all the trappings of a Hilton Head plantation: a fancy gate with security guards, winding roads and private cul-de-sacs, and a golf course, newly planted and green with promise. Water and sewer lines were in place before Marathon transferred the property to Ginn, as was a preliminary agreement with the local utility district for sewage treatment. On the basis of this tentative arrangement, state officials certified the availability of water and sewers, which in turn led the town government to issue a building permit for the plantation's first house. Unfortunately, none of this assured that water and sewer lines were connected, since Ginn Holdings did not have $3.5 million to finance its share of the extension. More than 180 lots were sold, and none got water or sewers from Ginn or anyone else for years. No more building permits were issued for Indigo Run, and the one completed house sat empty since the town government would not grant a certificate of occupancy without water and sewer connections.

Ginn also failed to deliver on Indigo Run's promised town center, to the sharp disappointment of many of Hilton Head's leading citizens. Under Marathon, planning for the center was advanced, involving company officials, planning consultants, the town government, local organizations, and key figures from the island's major resort and development firms. As usual, Ginn was long on dreams and short on action; he kept talking about donating more land, grandly mentioning more than 400 acres late in 1985. But no land was transferred because title to the site was encumbered by the mortgages that propped up Ginn Holdings. With the delays came flagging commitment from organizations that planned to locate at the town center. Other sites looked increasingly attractive for an arts complex, island museum, and town hall, and another dream faded.

In reality, Ginn and his plans were doomed from the outset by the terms of the deals that brought Sea Pines and the Hilton Head Company together. To finance the transactions, Ginn assumed too much debt and lost control over too many assets. At the heart of his financial problems were his arrangements with two small Florida thrifts, Southern Floridabanc and Intercapital Savings and Loan Association. Neither of these banks was a financial pillar; both were newly organized, undercapitalized, and soon to be tainted by scandal.[24] Together, the two banks provided Ginn with the $80 million he needed; in return each received a substantial interest in Ginn Holdings. To advance these funds, however, it was necessary to circumvent federal limits on loans to a single borrower; otherwise, no more than $11 million would have been available to Ginn from the two thrifts. The way around these restrictions was to have additional borrowers, thus permitting the banks to keep each loan within the limits. These additional investors were recruited by Ginn and the bankers. Parcels were transferred to them, 100-percent mortgages were issued by the two banks, the proceeds of the loans went to Ginn to buy the two companies, and Ginn completed the deal by leasing the properties from the new "owners."

Now Ginn owed money to a diverse group of investors as well as the two banks; he also did not own the properties that had been transferred to the collateral investors: the Sea Pines Racquet and Plantation Clubs, a big chunk of Harbour Town, parts of Port Royal and Wexford, and much of Indigo Run. Because he owed too much and controlled too little, Ginn's financial problems steadily mounted through 1985. Cash flow problems intensified, unpaid bills piled up, and anxieties mounted among plantation residents, company employees, and local businesses. "Honk if Bobby owes you" bumper stickers appeared by fall, and local banks stopped honoring paychecks from Ginn's companies. Whatever could be sold to raise cash went on the block: $3.3 million was raised from the obliging Florida bankers by selling a golf course in Sea Pines to Fraser (who leased it back to the company), and $5 million was realized from peddling Ginn Holdings' share in the resort hotel in Port Royal.[25] But Ginn had too little unencumbered property left to trade for time. With the end of the tourist season, resort revenues took their annual plunge, cutting further into Ginn's inadequate income stream.

As 1986 began, Ginn faced pressures that could not be easily deflected. Mortgage holders were threatening court action—Oxford First filed notice after Ginn failed to make payments due on loans carried over from the sale to Marathon. The following month one of the collateral investors began eviction proceedings because of rent arrears on properties in Sea Pines. Also unraveling were Ginn's deals with the Florida thrifts, which had come under the scrutiny of federal regulators. Both banks were found to have inflated the real estate backing their loans to Ginn, which necessitated reducing the value of the mortgages on their books and establishing reserve funds to cover the shortfall. Unable to comply, Intercapital Savings and Loan was closed by federal regulators in February 1986, and its assets were taken over by the Federal Savings and Loan Insurance Company. Southern Floridabanc survived but was increasingly nervous about its embrace with Ginn's collapsing empire.

Last but hardly least among Ginn's troubles was the formidable figure of Charles Fraser. Once an ally, Fraser became the most dangerous of Ginn's creditors, a master of arcane financial and legal combat who knew where all the bodies were buried. Fraser attacked where Ginn was most vulnerable, charging violations of the trust agreements attached to the Vacation Resorts acquisition notes. Fraser's concerns were partially financial; he had over $4 million tied up in the obligations Ginn inherited from Vacation Resorts, secured by a bank trust holding 100 percent of the voting stock of the Sea Pines Company. He was also appalled by what was happening to Sea Pines and Hilton Head. Moreover, he wanted Sea Pines back; he was more convinced than ever that selling the plantation had been a mistake, that new owners could not be trusted to preserve his masterpiece.

As the dispute with Fraser moved toward a showdown in court, Ginn's options were grim: he could either pay off the notes with $5.8 million he did not have or lose Sea Pines to Fraser. Meanwhile, other creditors were beating at Ginn's door and, more ominously, going to court to get their money or their collateral. By the time the controversy over the notes was heard in federal court in Charleston, Ginn was ready to file for bankruptcy. Judge Solomon Blatt Jr., however, was concerned that bankruptcy would have adverse consequences for Hilton Head, especially with the island's major golf and tennis tournaments only a few weeks away. Couldn't a way be found, the judge wondered, for the company, creditors, and other interested parties to sustain Hilton Head's most important enterprise until the situation improved? While various alternatives were being considered in Blatt's court, a new investor materialized by way of Southern Floridabanc.

FROM BAD TO WORSE

By March of 1986, Southern Floridabanc was inextricably intertwined with Ginn Holdings. Loans to Ginn and his proxies placed the bank well over its legal lending limit, and Ginn's financial condition precluded retiring any of this debt in the foreseeable future. To complicate the situation, federal regulators were pressing Southern Floridabanc to recall inflated loans from the original deal with Ginn. And the bank itself, like many other overextended thrifts, was in turmoil; the management that had engineered the Ginn transactions was gone, and the new ownership was searching for a way to avoid being dragged under with Bobby Ginn's sinking ship. Rather than let the bank's fate be determined by Ginn, Southern Floridabanc decided to take charge of its destiny by securing a controlling position in Ginn Holdings.

Orchestrating these moves was Luke M. Taylor, a Palm Beach developer with close ties to Southern Floridabanc. Taylor had been one of the collateral investors in Ginn's original deal, acquiring parts of Harbour Town, the Plantation Club, and other properties in Sea Pines. Providing the money was Philip B. Schwab, a New Yorker who had acquired a controlling interest in Southern Floridabanc at the end of 1985. Taylor convinced Ginn to join forces with Schwab. An agreement was hammered out in Judge Blatt's court by which Fraser and the other note holders would be paid the $5.8 million they were owed, Ginn Holdings' $6 million tab to local vendors would be squared, and Ginn would get $5 million in exchange for various properties.[26] Beyond these transfusions, Taylor held out the prospect of millions more from Schwab's deep pockets. Everyone emerged from court with smiles; the crisis was over, bankruptcy was averted, and new money was on the way.

Bobby Ginn thought he was getting new partners and new capital for his company, but instead he got the gate. Ginn Holdings disappeared, replaced by the Hilton Head Holding Company with Taylor as president and Schwab as majority stockholder. Ginn took an extended leave of absence and was gone, to the relief of almost everyone on Hilton Head.[27] Islanders hoped the new owners, about whom they knew even less than they had known about Ginn, had the resources to save the companies. Unfortunately, Hilton Head Holdings brought neither capital nor stability. Despite Taylor's expansive promises, Schwab never intended to invest substantial sums in his new company. Instead almost all of the money needed to pay off the note holders and local creditors was raised by new borrowing; thus old debts were replaced by new ones. Schwab was badly overextended on a host of shaky business deals, and his reputation was hardly an improvement over that of Bobby Ginn; as one reporter noted, Schwab and his Cuyahoga Wrecking Company had "left a 15-year trail of bankruptcies and lawsuits stretching from Detroit to Buffalo to southern Florida."[28] Schwab himself was invisible, avoiding publicity and shielded by employees who deflected inquiries into his background, which included a federal indictment, various state and federal investigations, and rumors of mob connections.

Luke Taylor, on the other hand, was all too visible, a constant reminder to islanders that things had gotten worse rather than better. Taylor had no experience in resort operations or community development, no sense of public and customer relations, and certainly no appreciation for the place and its residents and distinctive attractions. More often than not, Taylor went out of his way to alienate islanders, most notably in the case of the bronze alligator that graced the Plantation Club in Sea Pines. Taylor personally owned the Plantation Club, having acquired it as one of the collateral properties in Ginn's original deal. He liked the alligator and moved it to his home in Florida. When residents protested, he told them to mind their own business. "I own the property," he said; "I do with it as I see fit."[29] Like the stack-a-shacks, the purloined alligator became a rallying point for residents. Property owners had enough of a succession of owners who did not care about them and treated their communities as properties to be mortgaged, sold, and milked for all they were worth. In retaliation for the alligator, the Sea Pines property owners' association postponed a referendum on raising assessments, thus delaying implementation of an agreement worked out in the last days of the Ginn regime to boost funding of maintenance and capital improvements.

With Schwab's promised millions an illusion, Hilton Head Holdings could not escape from the financial morass that ensnared Ginn. Loans kept coming due, new investors were hard to find, and local banks remained reluctant to extend credit. Island radio stations began announcing when funds had been deposited so that employees of Hilton Head Holdings could cash paychecks. Prize checks bounced at a senior's professional golf tournament staged at Harbour Town Links in the fall of 1986. Suppliers stopped delivering goods to Hilton Head Holdings, including golf balls to the pro shops at the company's courses. Without money to pay contractors and suppliers, development activities ground to a halt.

Hilton Head Holdings was also fending off a torrent of lawsuits arising from the buyout of Ginn Holdings and related deals. Ginn secured an injunction to protect his interest in Hilton Head Holdings' assets; he also sued Hilton Head Holdings for not paying what was promised in the takeover deal, which prompted a countersuit as charges of fraud, swindles, double-dealing, and bad faith were exchanged. Charles Fraser was back in court, complaining about

Hilton Head Holdings' failure to pay off the note holders and seeking to have the company evicted from his golf course because lease payments were overdue. Lawsuits were costly and time-consuming, and they further encumbered the dwindling resources of Hilton Head Holdings and contributed to the erosion of the company's image and credibility. In May—a glorious month on Hilton Head, when skies are blue, breezes are gentle, and tourists crowd the golf courses and tennis courts—the Harbour Town Racquet Club was abruptly closed because of a dispute between Hilton Head Holdings and one of the collateral investors in the original deal. Company employees took down the nets, cleared merchandise from the pro shop, and even removed the water fountains before a judge ordered the courts reopened. Such follies further battered the image of Sea Pines and its resort business, to say nothing of the morale of company employees, plantation residents, and islanders more generally.

Hilton Head Holdings came apart during the latter half of 1986. Schwab supplanted Taylor with new management from his gambling casino in Reno. Truth was hard to separate from fiction as stories buzzed around Hilton Head: prostitutes from Las Vegas had been installed at the Hilton Head Inn; the new bosses packed revolvers in shoulder holsters and were accompanied by beefy bodyguards; company executives carried suitcases of cash and were stealing Hilton Head blind. What was indisputable was a combination of chaos and incompetence, along with the reality that once again things had gone from bad to worse.

THE BOTTOM LINE

In November Hilton Head Holdings was back in the same federal court where the ill-fated venture had been born eight months earlier. Once again Judge Blatt tried to unravel the tangled litigation and financial complexities of Hilton Head's largest enterprise. Dozens of lawyers and corporate executives were on hand, representing creditors, potential purchasers, and the beleaguered company. Marathon Oil, claiming that Hilton Head Holdings had defaulted on $38 million in debts carried over from the sale to Ginn, sought control over its collateral in Port Royal, Shipyard, and Wexford Plantations. Another interested party was the Federal Deposit Insurance Company, which had won a $30 million judgment against Ginn growing out of his involvement in the Tennessee banking scandal and was in court to safeguard the federal government's claims against his assets.

Among a clutch of potential purchasers of parts of Hilton Head Holdings, the most serious was Avron Fogelman.[30] A flamboyant Memphis real estate developer and co-owner of the Kansas City Royals baseball team, Fogelman built and managed apartment complexes. His interest in Hilton Head was personal as well as professional; he and his wife had fallen in love with the island and with Sea Pines on a visit. In 1981 the Fogelmans bought a condominium in Harbour Town overlooking the boats, including their own 70-foot yacht. When Hilton Head Holdings hit the skids, Fogelman decided to combine business with pleasure by buying Sea Pines. His first step was to acquire Luke Taylor's personal holdings from the Ginn deal, a $5.85 million package that included Harbour Town marina, the Plantation Club complex, and the Sea Pines reception center. The next step was to acquire the rest of the plantation from Hilton Head Holdings.

Fogelman might have been the light at the end of the tunnel, a purchaser who finally cared about Sea Pines and the island. But instead of rescuing Hilton Head, he precipitated the final crisis that plunged Hilton Head Holdings into bankruptcy. Sea Pines could not be sold to Fogelman without a court hearing because of the injunction that Ginn had obtained to protect his assets. In addition, foreclosure actions were pending against Hilton Head Holdings by Marathon and Southern Floridabanc. As the story unfolded in Judge Blatt's court, the depth of the company's financial problems became painfully clear. Debts far exceeded projected revenue flows, and creditors, unsurprisingly, had lost all confidence in the company's management. A few days after the hearing in Blatt's court, Hilton Head Holdings was forced to file for bankruptcy in the wake of involuntary bankruptcy proceedings in New York against Schwab, his wife, and fifteen of their companies.[31] Hilton Head's largest employer and landowner was bankrupt; many local businesses were owed large sums of money; and an island built on the good life found its reputation tarnished and its future clouded. Sea Pines and the other private communities had hit bottom, victimized by spectacularly unsuccessful quests for profit. What went wrong was fairly easy to understand. How to secure local control over the salvage and rebuilding operations posed more difficult problems for plantation residents and for Hilton Head generally.

NOTES

1. The principal creditor was Travelers Insurance, which was owed $11.3 million in 1978.

2. Quoted in Putnam, "Savannah to Charleston: A Good Life in the Low Country," 813.

3. Fraser, "Appendix A to the 1988 Jubilee Year Plan for Sea Pines Plan-

tation," 1. Donald V. Bennett, a retired general, was Fraser's principal adversary. In 1979 Bennett succeeded William J. Stephens, who had served as president of the Association of Sea Pines Plantation Property Owners from its inception in 1973.

4. Association of Sea Pines Plantation Property Owners, "Newsletter and 1982 Annual Report," 5.

5. "Appendix A to the 1988 Jubilee Year Plan for Sea Pines Plantation," 2.

6. Heizer operated through the Heizer Corporation, which was incorporated in 1969 and had assets of $347 million in 1983. Heizer created Villas International Corporation in 1971 and reorganized the firm as Vacation Resorts Holdings in 1976.

7. Sea Pines' other stockholders were given a choice of taking two dollars a share, $6.44 in notes per share, or a combination of cash and bonds. Since Sea Pines stock was selling for substantially less than the offered price and notes were backed only by Sea Pines common stock, most shareholders, including Joseph Fraser, took the cash. About 100 shareholders opted for notes amounting to approximately $2 million.

8. Sea Pines Company, "Notice of Special Meeting of Shareholders," 11. Some residents were parties to the deal because they owned stock, which they were now able to sell at a higher figure than the market price, albeit far less than the $18 per share most had paid in 1973 when Sea Pines went public.

9. Donnell, "From the Editor," 9.

10. John B. Platt III, quoted Sea Pines Company, "Special Meeting of Shareholders," 10. Platt, an attorney, had headed Vacation Resorts since 1978. He became president of Sea Pines Company.

11. Four of the seven voting members of the architectural review board represented property owners, and the other three were appointed by the company.

12. Sea Pines Company, "Press Release," 2.

13. Revenues in 1984 were $40.7 million: $32.7 million from operations (80.4 percent), $6.7 million from real estate sales (16.9 percent), and $1.1 million from real estate development (2.7 percent). Vacation Resorts Holdings, *Annual Report,* 20.

14. The liquidation was under Section 331 of the Internal Revenue Code. Liquidation offered substantial tax advantages as well as freeing Heizer from federal security regulation affecting business development corporations.

15. The activities of the Association of Sea Pines Plantation Oroperty Owners in connection with purchasing the plantation from Vacation Resorts are discussed in the next chapter.

16. One 660-acre parcel became Long Cove Club. Most of another 250-odd acres on Jenkins Island, at the northern tip of Hilton Head, was developed as Windmill Harbour. Both of these enterprises are discussed in chapter 12.

17. Quoted in McGregor, "B-Ginn the B-ginner B-gins A-gin," 28.

18. Quoted in Williams and Bender, "Ginn Purchases Hilton Head Co. for $100 Million."

19. See Rutter, "Dozens Get Fees in Transaction." This article provides a detailed account of the fees and payments associated with Ginn's purchase of Sea Pines and the Hilton Head Company.

20. Sea Pines Real Estate Company, Hilton Head Company Realty, and Lighthouse Realty Company were acquired in the purchase. The fourth firm, Nexus Properties, was owned by Ginn before the deal.

21. Banks controlled by Jake Butcher and his brother C. H. Butcher Jr. were Ginn's primary funding source. The Butcher banks were closed by the Federal Deposit Insurance Company in 1983. After federal officials unraveled the tangled skein left by the Butchers, Ginn wound up owing $52 million.

22. More than twenty debt collection suits were pending against Ginn at the time he acquired Sea Pines and the Hilton Head Company. The following year, federal banking officials charged Ginn with fraud, negligence, and diversion of corporate assets.

23. Quoted in John C. Williams, "Fraser Sees Sale as Passing of Torch."

24. Intercapital's chairman and principal stockholder, B. Roy Norton III, was forced to resign by the Federal Home Loan Bank Board in May 1985 and was later sued by Intercapital for fraud. Robert V. Gibbs, Southern Floridabanc's chairman and majority stockholder at the time of the Ginn deal, was convicted in 1987 of federal racketeering, wire and mail fraud, and interstate transport of stolen property in connection with a Maryland thrift that he had controlled before moving to Florida.

25. In the deal with Fraser, the price for Sea Pines' Club Course was $5.15 million, financed by a $3.3 million mortgage from Southern Floridabanc and a $1.85 million promissory note by the company. As with the deals with other collateral investors, Fraser leased the course back to the company for operation, leaving Ginn with the proceeds of the mortgage and Fraser with title to a golf course in which he had invested a token $10.

26. In addition, $7 million went to Southern Floridabanc to cover the shortage created by the overvalued property backing loans in Ginn's original deal.

27. Ginn filed for bankruptcy in 1988 in the face of suits by creditors for around $140 million.

28. Scardino, "A Gust of Bankruptcy and Scandal Rattles Elegant

Hilton Head Island."

29. Taylor, letter to Haworth, July 31, 1986.

30. Others hoping to pick up the pieces of Hilton Head Holdings were Atlantic Coast Equity Group, a New Jersey firm interested in the golf courses and other revenue-producing property; U.S. Shelter of Columbia, S.C., which had owned Moss Creek Plantation and had its eye on Indigo Run; Investors Management Group of Columbia, Md., which wanted to buy Wexford; and the PGA Tour, with an interest in adding Harbour Town Links to the golf courses owned by the touring golf professionals.

31. The estimated debt of the Schwabs and their enterprises was $500 million.

Chapter Eleven

A Friend in Court

I'm not going to supervise the demise of Hilton Head Island when I can stop it.

—Judge Solomon Blatt Jr., quoted by Janet Smith
in the *Island Packet,* January 7, 1987

Bankruptcy clouded Hilton Head in a pall of uncertainty. Islanders wondered whether this state of affairs signaled a new beginning after the plague of bad deals, broken promises, unpaid bills, lost jobs, inept managers, legal wrangling, and damaging scandals or whether insolvency was another depressing chapter in the decline and fall of Hilton Head. Few were familiar with bankruptcy and its arcane procedures. But everyone was unsettled by the collapse of plantations that encompassed one-third of Hilton Head's land, population, and work force. Plantation residents worried about covenants, amenities, security gates, and property values. Employees feared for their jobs, while many local firms were imperiled by the burden of past debts and the loss of future business with Hilton Head Holdings. Resort operators, developers, and realtors were concerned about negative publicity and damage to the island's image. Complicating these economic worries was the fall of Sea Pines and the future of the Heritage Classic golf tournament, Hilton Head's foremost assets in attracting visitors and potential residents.

Bankruptcy involved a sense of failure for the community as well as the company, and failure brought an unwelcome and uncomfortable feeling for Hilton Head. Most islanders wore the badges of success—good jobs, nice homes, comfortable retirement—and they lived in a place whose brief history was a quintessential American success story. Bankruptcy was a stigma, calling "into question the very integrity of Hilton Head Island and threatening to topple it from its proud standing among the world's premier resorts."[1] The sense of failure was strongest for residents in the affected plantations, and nowhere was this feeling more intense than in Sea Pines. People in Sea Pines were especially vulnerable—they were the pioneers, the elite; their community was the finest place on the island to live.

Adding to the fears was Hilton Head's apparent lack of control over the situation, which was particularly frustrating for a place filled with influential people who resented being at the mercy of outsiders. Bankruptcy proceedings were controlled by federal courts and implemented by court-appointed trustees. High stakes in the bankruptcy did not guarantee islanders a role in decisions that would affect their future. Bankruptcy laws were designed to protect creditors and insolvent firms rather than local interests. What most islanders wanted was new owners who paid their bills, maintained their properties, and understood "what makes Hilton Head Island special"—owners "whose words we can trust, whose hands we can hold, whose interest in us is long-term."[2] What was not clear was whether anyone would pay attention to these desires or whether caring mattered when the time came to auction off the properties.

Despite these legitimate fears, Hilton Head survived bankruptcy relatively unscathed. In part, bankruptcy was less disruptive than expected because the island's enduring appeal was sufficiently strong to offset the negatives. Hilton Head was still a great place to live. The beach was as beautiful and uncluttered as ever, especially in Sea Pines. Palms and pines, lagoons and marshes, golf courses and tennis clubs—all continued to attract visitors and home buyers to the plantations. Hilton Head's population increased 34 percent between 1985 and 1990, and tourism was 16 percent higher in 1987, during the bankruptcy, than it had been in the previous year.[3] Even more striking was the buoyancy of the local real estate market: total sales in 1987 reached new heights and were 50 percent greater than sales the year before. Increasing numbers of residents and tourists cushioned the effect of bankruptcy on merchants, restaurants, contractors, and other local businesses.

The impact of the collapse of Hilton Head Holdings was also mitigated by the nature of the plantation system. Most property at Sea Pines, Port Royal, and Shipyard belonged to home owners rather than Hilton Head Holdings; only at Indigo Run and Wexford were large amounts of residential land ensnared in the bankruptcy. Property owners were further insulated by a formidable web of covenants and other agreements. At Sea Pines, deed restrictions insured that density limits, open space, and master plans could not be altered unilaterally by a Bobby Ginn or a Luke Taylor or a trustee.

A final and critical element in the equation that eased Hilton Head through the crisis of bankruptcy was powerful champions. As in the case of BASF, Hilton Head's interests wound up being protected to an unusual degree because of the influence of people who had been attracted to the island. Key roles were played by a federal judge and a former governor of South Carolina, both of whom owned homes on Hilton Head and were highly supportive of island interests. A prominent local resort executive was appointed bankruptcy trustee, and he enlisted business leaders in shaping outcomes sensitive to Hilton Head's needs.

With the bankruptcy in friendly hands, the worst fears of islanders never materialized, and Hilton Head emerged changed but hardly crippled by the downfall of its most important enterprises.

JUDICIAL ACTIVISM

Solomon Blatt Jr., chief judge of the U.S. District Court for South Carolina, was the central figure in the complex drama triggered by the insolvency of Hilton Head Holdings. Beginning in March of 1986, when he engineered the replacement of Ginn with Schwab and Taylor, Blatt adopted an interventionist approach that emphasized his concern for Hilton Head. The dispute between Fraser and Ginn, he told reporters, "hangs like a dark cloud over Hilton Head." He stopped Ginn from filing for bankruptcy because he "felt it would be a terrible thing" for the island; and his goal was a solution in the "best interest" of the "parties and the entire Hilton Head community."[4] Bankruptcy, he feared, would drive away the Heritage golf and Family Circle tennis tournaments, at enormous cost to the island's prestige and economic prospects.

After his efforts to fend off insolvency failed, Blatt moved swiftly to insure that the case was handled in his court, even though there was a stronger claim to lodge the matter in New York as part of the Schwab bankruptcy. Blatt's retention of the case was unusual because federal district judges normally do not oversee bankruptcy cases, especially judges with no experience in bankruptcy. Blatt later explained that he wanted the case because Hilton Head's interests would have been lost in the Schwab morass: "If this little island had been involved in a bankruptcy of over half a billion dollars, I hate to think what would have happened."[5] Blatt had strong ties to "this little island;" he had owned a home in Palmetto Dunes for eighteen years, enjoyed Hilton Head's beaches and golf courses, and made no secret of his desire to keep the bankruptcy in friendly hands.

One of Blatt's primary objectives was seeing that the plantations wound up with responsible owners. He "had a lot of misgivings" about his own role in inflicting Taylor and Schwab on Hilton Head: "I couldn't have searched the world over and found a worse man to bring to this island than Taylor" because of "his personality and temperament."[6] Determined that his earlier mistakes would not be repeated, Blatt warned potential buyers that they would be carefully scrutinized: "Before this court agrees to any sale, it will conduct a thorough examination of the financial responsibility and the management record of any buyer." Plantation residents, he insisted, "are not going to go through again what they've been through."[7] As far as Blatt was concerned, the most respon-sible buyers would be the property owners themselves. His views both encour-aged residents to explore the purchase of their plantation and discouraged other potential buyers.

To safeguard Hilton Head, Blatt needed help from people who shared his concerns. Most critical was choice of a trustee, who under federal bankruptcy law would bear primary responsibility for protecting the assets of Hilton Head Holdings. Blatt tapped John F. Curry, a resort official with strong ties to the plantation system, the local political scene, and the island's business leader-ship. Curry came to Hilton Head in 1973 to run Sea Pines' resort operations, leaving in 1976 to organize a firm that managed rental properties in Palmetto Dunes. He had served as president of the Chamber of Commerce, led the fight for incorporation, and run unsuccessfully for mayor in the first municipal elec-tion in 1983. Curry lived in Sea Pines, understood the plantation business, and was a vigorous spokesman for the island's resort industry. Like Blatt, Curry defined his mission broadly; his basic goal was "to preserve and protect the quality of life for the island and thereby ensure that its values and economic contribution to the region and the state are maintained."[8]

Working closely with Curry was John C. West, a lawyer and politician with a home in Palmetto Dunes. West was not hired as general counsel for his exper-tise in bankruptcy or his legal talents; he freely admitted that he "didn't know anything about bankruptcy" and hadn't "been in a courtroom in ten years."[9] What West brought was excellent political connections in Columbia and Wash-ington and a close personal relationship with Blatt. He had served as governor of South Carolina and ambassador to Saudi Arabia.[10] Blatt and West had been close friends for twenty years; both were products of the state's closely knit political establishment, one of whose most powerful figures was Blatt's fa-ther.[11] While governor, West had been an antagonist of Hilton Head in the battles over industrialization at Victoria Bluff; now he was an ardent supporter of his adopted island, prepared to do what he could to help Blatt save Hilton Head. West played a key role in insuring that the bankruptcy would be handled in the friendly confines of South Carolina, persuading a federal judge in New York that the Hilton Head Holdings portion of the Schwab bankruptcy should be handled where the assets were.[12] As the bankruptcy unfolded, West was the center of a series of complex negotiations, fund-raising efforts, and legal ma-neuvers.

Judge Blatt's hands-on approach to bankruptcy was not welcomed by par-ticipants who did not share his concern for Hilton Head's welfare. Creditors, particularly those from off the island, wanted to get as much of their money back as possible. The most insistent critics were the federal banking agencies, particularly the Federal Savings and Loan Insurance Corporation, which held mortgages on substantial chunks of Hilton Head Holdings' property. Their lawyers wanted Blatt removed from the case, arguing that his concern for Hilton Head was prejudicial to creditors and precluded federal agencies from getting a fair hearing. The U.S. Court of Appeals for the Fourth Circuit eventually agreed, ruling in one case that "Judge Blatt, a Hilton Head homeowner, has amply demonstrated an abiding and declaredly paramount interest in the economic well-being and reputation of Hilton Head Island" that could be misinterpreted and deciding in another that "Judge Blatt's participation has created an appearance of impaired impartiality."[13] Blatt made no apologies for worrying about Hilton Head: "Everybody was represented in the case but the people," he said. "I guess I was the people's lawyer."[14]

KEEPING AFLOAT

Support from Judge Blatt was essential but not sufficient to insure that bankruptcy would be responsive to island interests. Curry's most urgent need was cash. Failure to meet Hilton Head Holdings' payroll would shift the bankruptcy from the relatively permissive environment of reorganization under Chapter 11 of the federal bankruptcy laws to the draconian world of liquidation under Chapter 7, an outcome that would have put one-third of the island on the auction block. Avron Fogelman, still eager to acquire Sea Pines, offered to lend Hilton Head Holdings $400,000 and take over plantation and resort operations as well as the Heritage and Family Circle tournaments. Curry accepted the proposal under an arrangement that gave Fogelman first right of refusal on the company's assets, 6 percent of gross receipts, and a priority lien for his $400,000 loan. This deal, however, was promptly rejected by Hilton Head Holdings' secured creditors, the big lenders with the largest financial stakes, in a move that underscored the necessity for Curry to craft solutions that were acceptable to these parties.[15] After torpedoing Fogelman, the creditors provided some help, but their $673,000 loan would carry Hilton Head Holdings only through the end of January.

Curry and West then turned to local banks to get the company over the hump. Island bankers were sympathetic since their interests would be served by minimizing the adverse impact of bankruptcy on developers, resort operators, and merchants. Still, loans had to be backed by collateral, and this need prompted a hectic search through Hilton Heads Holdings' jumbled records to identify unencumbered properties. Enough were found to secure a $3 million loan, which provided financing into the summer tourist season, when a positive cash flow was expected.[16] By late summer, the loan was paid back, but the financial situation was touch and go throughout the bankruptcy. A rainy Labor Day weekend was sufficient to push the fragile operation onto the financial ropes, necessitating a hastily arranged $300,000 loan to tide Hilton Head Holdings over the last few weeks until the plantations were sold at the end of 1987.

As pressing as the financial situation was the threat bankruptcy posed to the Heritage Classic golf tournament. Saving Hilton Head's foremost attraction was one of Judge Blatt's chief concerns in rescuing the company in March and arranging the bankruptcy eight months later. For Curry and other business leaders, as well as many residents and local organizations, loss of the Heritage would be a staggering blow with adverse effects on tourism, property values, charities, and the island's reputation and pride. Over 100,000 visitors were attracted to Hilton Head by the Heritage. They pumped an estimated $15 million into the local economy, making the week of this tournament the best week of the year for merchants, restaurants, and realtors. By the time Curry was in charge, prospects for retaining the Heritage seemed slim. The PGA Tour had wearied of an increasingly unsatisfactory situation at Harbour Town Links and Sea Pines. The course had steadily deteriorated because of too much use and too little maintenance by a succession of financially crippled owners. Even more troubling than the course were the escalating financial problems as Sea Pines lurched from Vacation Resorts to Ginn Holdings to the Schwab-Taylor fiasco. For the PGA Tour, the final straw came when purse checks bounced at a tournament held at Harbour Town in the fall of 1986.

Curry hurriedly organized a last-ditch effort to persuade the PGA Tour to reconsider. One thing that helped was that many players wanted the tournament to remain on Hilton Head, one of the more attractive stops on the tour for golfers and their families. Another was CBS, which had been televising the event for years and valued Harbour Town's dramatic eighteenth fairway, framed by Calibogue Sound and the lighthouse, as a great setting for television. But Hilton Head's entreaties, players' sentiments, and even television's preferences were not enough; the PGA Tour demanded ironclad assurances that the purse would be backed, that a stable organization was in place to manage the tournament, and that Harbour Town Links would be restored to tour standards. To meet these conditions, Curry turned to the parties with the greatest interest in saving the Heritage, the leaders of the island's resort industry. Pledges from Palmetto Dunes, the major hotels, and other resort interests backed the prize money and immediate improvements to the golf course. Local banks and the town government provided loans for operating funds for the tournament. Ownership of the event was shifted from Sea Pines to the Heritage Classic Corporation, with a board of directors drawn from Hilton Head's business and civic elite.

In addition to obtaining essential financing and retaining the Heritage, Curry's efforts broadened local participation in the bankruptcy. Banks, resorts, and development companies backed up their stakes with financial commitments and personal involvement. The business community was tapped for people to help operate the bankrupt company. A successful restaurateur took over the company's troubled food service operation; a local advertising man handled marketing; an executive in Charles Fraser's development firm came aboard to manage assets; and Joseph Fraser handled community relations and club facilities.[17] Curry was especially attentive to residents of the affected plantations, whose stakes were substantial and anxieties understandable. Curry appeared at their meetings, played up the fact that he lived in Sea Pines, answered questions, eased worries, and advocated acquisition of the plantations by property owners. These efforts were encouraged by Judge Blatt, who wanted islanders involved in defending their interests in the bankruptcy. He appointed an advisory committee that included local officials, business people, civic and black leaders, and residents from the affected plantations. Local government was part of this supporting cast, loaning $150,000 in town funds as part of the Heritage rescue mission.[18] But the town government was less involved than bankers and business leaders in the bankruptcy; its expertise and financial resources were limited, and their use was legally and politically constrained.

As Curry turned to his central task of dealing with the company's assets, his overriding objective was to maintain the integrity of the plantation units. Preserving plantations as units, Curry was convinced, was essential for residents, local businesses, and the island as a whole. Keeping plantations whole, he argued, also served creditors' interests because selling off the best parts would sharply reduce the value of the remaining properties. In line with this policy, Curry deflected offers for flagship properties such as Harbour Town Links, profitable golf courses and tennis clubs, and certain restaurants. Preservation of the plantations, however, did not entail keeping the major units under single ownership. Curry emphasized that he "would very much like to see the plantations split up once again so they can operate on their own and not be a part of a giant mass of plantations."[19] Hilton Head was now as wary of concentrated economic power as of outside owners.

Keeping individual plantations together was more easily said than done. At every turn there were problems—deferred maintenance, demoralized employees, overburdened managers, missing records, unfiled tax returns, and purloined supplies. Marketing was almost nonexistent; Hilton Head Holdings spent only $75,000 on marketing in its last year, about one-tenth of the combined outlays of Sea Pines and the Hilton Head Company before the disastrous round of deals. At the center of efforts to sustain the plantations was Sea Pines. Though it was aging—not always gracefully after some hard years—Sea Pines was still Hilton Head's principal attraction; its national reputation remained the key to selling the island to potential visitors. For marketing purposes, Hilton Head Holdings, a name that meant nothing off the island, was replaced by Sea Pines Resorts, which had instant recognition. Half a million dollars of the company's scarce funds was invested in marketing in 1987. By March, resort booking at Sea Pines and Shipyard were 25 percent higher than they had been the previous year. Visitors found golf courses and tennis courts in better shape, more flowers and fresh paint, good food and attentive service, and a brisk real estate market, all a testament to the remarkable turnaround engineered by Curry and his staff. Not only was business better and property more attractive to buyers, but Hilton Head was healing, regaining its confidence, and thinking hard about the big question: who was going to buy the plantations?

SELLING PLANTATIONS TO RESIDENTS

For Blatt and Curry, the official answer was that the buyers would be the highest bidders. But they made no secret of their hope that residents would emerge as owners of their communities. Property owners had a powerful interest in preserving the integrity of plantations. They also had a strong stake in maintaining and improving community facilities, both to enhance their quality of life and to increase property values. Most residents wanted to be free of the vagaries of private ownership of their communities. Their financial interest was far greater than that of the company in fully developed plantations such as Sea Pines and Port Royal; they owned over $1 billion in property at Sea Pines, compared with perhaps $50 million held by the company.

Bankruptcy offered residents an opportunity to act on their widespread desire to take control of their communities. In past sales, residents had been marginal players; now they were full-fledged participants. They had the advantage of a judge and bankruptcy trustee who were encouraging them to acquire their plantations. Bankruptcy also made acquisition more feasible financially for property owners by lowering plantation values that had been inflated through financing deals. Of course, bankruptcy posed threats as well as opportunities. Outsiders might well outbid property owners, if indeed residents were even able to organize and finance an offer. And for many residents of Sea Pines, outsiders were not the only threat, because Charles Fraser made no secret of his desire to reacquire the plantation. All of these concerns reinforced the determination of those residents who said, "We're not going to take it anymore. We're going to take control."[20]

Taking control, however, was an idea that had to be turned into action; information had to be gathered, expertise tapped, organizations created, and money raised. Complicating the problem, property owners faced five distinctive situations because the five plantations differed in their stages of development, proportion of permanent residents, and mix between resort and residential activities. Sea Pines and Port Royal were largely settled, while Indigo Run had no residents, and almost half of Wexford's lots were held by the company. Most of Port Royal's property owners lived on the plantation, in contrast to Shipyard's high proportion of absentee owners. At the outset, property owners on all the plantations except Indigo Run expressed an interest in purchasing. But the effort at Shipyard was stillborn—the price was too high because of the heavy volume of resort business, and the plantation had too few permanent residents to share the burden. Wexford's affluent residents overwhelmingly supported acquisition despite daunting costs resulting from the large amount of undeveloped land on the plantation. Port Royal and Sea Pines, the most settled communities, with substantial residential populations, appeared to be in the best position to take advantage of the opportunity offered by bankruptcy. Property owners in Sea Pines, however, proved far more able than those in Port Royal to muster the human and financial resources needed to organize a viable purchase offer.

Residents of Sea Pines had already failed in one purchase attempt, and an influential group of settlers was determined not to repeat the mistakes that had undermined the earlier effort. The first endeavor was undertaken by the Association of Sea Pines Plantation Property Owners after Vacation Resorts went on the block in 1984. An offer was prepared involving $3 million in cash and assumption of the company's debt, which was rejected by the sellers, who eventually got a better deal from Bobby Ginn. Many residents, however, were uncomfortable with this effort, including people who favored purchase by property owners. Critics argued that ASPPPO—with its large board, complicated committee structure, and surfeit of retired executives who loved to dabble in plantation business—was the wrong instrument to purchase or operate Sea Pines. All property owners would have been involved in the acquisition regardless of whether or not they wanted to participate, and increased annual assessments of $600 to finance the purchase would have to be approved by 75 percent of the property owners. A large number of residents vociferously opposed the purchase plan, making it unlikely that the proposal would have been endorsed in a referendum and certain that some property owners would go to court to block the scheme.

When the question of purchasing resurfaced during the bankruptcy, activist residents began looking for a more viable approach. The need, they concluded, was for a new instrument organized around the objective of acquisition rather than another attempt to adapt ASPPPO to the task. Their alternative was a private company, organized and financed by Sea Pines residents, and they had the advantage of having already created a suitable vehicle. The possibility of purchasing one of Sea Pines' courses led a group of retired residents to organize Country Club Associates a few months before the bankruptcy. Negotiations to purchase the course ended with the bankruptcy and Curry's determination to keep plantation assets intact. Now the group's attention turned to purchasing the plantation. After extensive discussions with interested and knowledgeable parties, they concluded that Country Club Associates in a new incarnation as Sea Pines Associates could be the appropriate instrument to acquire the plantation for its property owners.[21]

Leading the potential purchasers' efforts was Peter Bauman, a corporate lawyer from Pittsburgh who had retired to Sea Pines in 1978. Bauman was soon enmeshed in plantation affairs, serving as vice-president of the owners' association and chairman of its long-range planning committee. An outspoken critic of the succession of owners, Bauman believed "the only solution to Sea Pines' current problems" was "for the property owners to acquire the plantation's assets and henceforth operate the plantation."[22] Bauman and his associates brought considerable business experience, legal knowledge, and financial expertise to the complex process of bidding for part of a bankrupt company, but they had no experience in acquiring a residential community. Nor did many models exist, since buyouts of large planned developments by residents were few and far between.[23] To help chart a course, Sea Pines Associates engaged expert assistance, including an Atlanta attorney who specialized in residential takeovers.[24] What emerged from this advice was a for-profit corporation to be capitalized through the sale of shares to Sea Pines residents, with stockholders limited to legal residents of South Carolina in order to avoid the expense and delay involved in registering with the federal Securities and Exchange Commission.

Selling shares was the key to the venture. Although most of the organizers were well-off, few had the means to underwrite a large chunk of the $7–10 million that had to be raised as part of an estimated $25 million acquisition cost. Nor did they want any individual or small group to obtain a commanding financial position; the rationale for the endeavor was collective ownership by Sea Pines residents, or at least by as many residents as were able to invest. Maximum shares were set at $500,000; the minimum purchase was $10,000, less than recommended by the outside advisers but more than some Sea Pines residents could afford.[25] The pool of potential investors was also limited by the necessity to restrict sales to South Carolina residents, which excluded almost two-thirds of the potential participants, including many affluent nonresident owners eager to invest in the acquisition. Sea Pines residents enthusiastically endorsed the purchase plan; more than three-quarters of the 600-odd people attending an owners' association meeting in March indicated that they were ready to invest in acquiring the plantation. Led by the directors of Sea Pines Associates, who bought the first $1 million in stock, over 650 of 1,800 eligible residents purchased shares, a far higher proportion than the organizers' outside experts thought likely.

While the organization and financial plans were being elaborated, Bauman's group began negotiating with Curry for the purchase of Sea Pines. A tentative agreement was reached at the end of March: Curry accepted in principal the residents' offer of $24.9 million, to be financed with $7 million in cash and the rest with long-term debt, and agreed not to solicit other offers while the money was being raised by Sea Pines Associates. Curry, however, could not sell Sea Pines on his own; any sale of Hilton Head Holdings' assets had to be acceptable to the court-appointed creditor committees, approved by Judge Blatt, and able to withstand review in the federal courts. Creditors protested that the Sea Pines deal was not the way to sell to the highest bidder. Particularly unacceptable was the exclusivity of the arrangement, which froze out other offers. The creditors also objected to the financing plan; they wanted cash on the barrelhead for Hilton Head Holdings' assets. Understandably, the creditors' overriding objective was to get as much of their money back as possible. They did not share Curry's concerns for Hilton Head, his desire to preserve plantations as units, or his interest in selling to residents.

Rejection of the deal by the creditors was a substantial setback for Sea Pines Associates. They had lost the inside track; now they had to compete with other purchasers and back up their bid with cash. They grumbled about broken commitments but had no choice but to accommodate this more perilous process. Blatt and Curry had done as much as they could to keep residents in the game. Now Sea Pines Associates had to refashion their bid, revitalize their demoralized supporters, and renew their funding efforts. Raising money was now more difficult; most who intended to buy shares were already in the fold, and those who were undecided were not encouraged by these setbacks. Almost all of the additional money came from people who had already invested. On the brighter side, Sea Pines Associates bolstered its chances for a successful bid by securing an $18 million loan from a local bank, thus assuring that the next offer would satisfy the creditors' demand for a cash purchase.

COMPLICATIONS

For Curry, the false start with Sea Pines Associates was only part of an unruly whole. Unraveling the affairs of Hilton Head Holdings was a Herculean task involving hundreds of properties, thousands of creditors, and eventually over $2 billion in claims. Affecting almost everything was the fact that Blatt, Curry, and West were neophytes in bankruptcy, while the attorneys representing the other major parties were intimately familiar with federal bankruptcy law. As a result, there were missteps and setbacks such as the Fogelman and Sea Pines deals. A major complication was the involvement of federal banking agencies through the collapse of the two Florida thrifts that had financed Ginn's original deals. None of Hilton Head Holdings' creditors was more zealous than the Federal Savings and Loan Insurance Corporation, which pressed at every turn to make certain all assets were sold at the highest possible price, regardless of the impact on Hilton Head's residents, economy, or future.

Following the early setbacks at the hands of the secured creditors, Curry and West decided to use litigation aggressively to enhance their bargaining position with Marathon and the Federal Savings and Loan Insurance Corporation, the largest and most truculent creditors. Marathon was charged with fraud and conspiracy in connection with the original sale to Ginn in a lawsuit that sought to set aside $25 million of Marathon's mortgages. Actions against the Federal Savings and Loan Insurance Corporation challenged the liens acquired by the Florida thrifts and other financial transactions. After much bickering and legal maneuvering, agreements were hammered out with the federal regulators and Marathon. The Federal Savings and Loan Insurance Corporation settled for $15.6 million of the proceeds from the sale of Sea Pines, along with $1.4 million from Indigo Run. Marathon agreed to buy the properties on which it held mortgages if bids did not reach specified minimums, in effect providing the trustee and creditors with a guaranteed price of $61.5 million for Hilton Head Holdings' largest block of assets.[26]

With these agreements, the stage was set for the sale of the plantations under Curry's reorganization plan. Indigo Run had been broken out from the rest of the properties and sold under emergency procedures because of deteriorating conditions on the abandoned development. Port Royal, Sea Pines, Shipyard, and Wexford would be auctioned to financially qualified bidders. As Curry had insisted, plantations were packaged as units, with minimum bid prices for each, and the sale was advertised in the *Wall Street Journal, New York Times,* and *Atlanta Constitution.*

Table 11.1
Minimum Prices for Major Assets of Hilton Head Holdings, September 1987

Property	Price ($)	Assets Included
Port Royal Resort	12,085,000	Three golf courses, racquet club, food and beverage operations, and assorted facilities
Port Royal Plantation	15,000,000	26.5 acres of oceanfront property
Sea Pines	24,300,000*	Four golf courses, food and beverage operations, resort rental business, other resort activities and facilities, real estate companies
Shipyard	12,325,000	27-hole golf course, racquet club, food and beverage operations, and maintenance activities
Wexford	18,665,000	186 single-family lots, maintenance areas, riparian rights to build boat slips

Source: Curry, Advertisement.

*The price for Sea Pines in the advertisement was $23 million, but it was increased to $24.3 million with the addition of the real estate companies to the package.

Plantation residents anxiously awaited the outcome of the bidding. Tensions were highest in Sea Pines, which was the only plantation in which property owners were able to muster sufficient resources to back their desires with a firm bid. Wexford came the closest of the other communities, creating an acquisitions committee and making a preliminary offer. In the end, however, Wexford's residents were dissuaded by the $18.7 million price tag; the plantation had too much undeveloped property and too few property owners to make purchase financially feasible. Settlers at Port Royal also wished to acquire their plantation but were unable to assemble an acceptable offer. They pinned their hopes on a deal under which residents would acquire Port Royal without additional investment. As part of the settlement in the hotel controversy in 1981, Marathon had promised to transfer Port Royal's roads and open spaces to property owners. Now residents proposed to trade the value of this agreement for the plantation, but Curry rejected the offer because the roads and open spaces did not come close to meeting the price that had been set for Port Royal. With property owners unwilling to invest their own money, Port Royal residents retired to the sidelines, wondering who was going to possess their community next.

At the outset, the list of potential buyers was extensive; resort operators, community developers, and real estate investment firms from near and far looked over the offerings.[27] Many were attracted to Sea Pines; some were interested only in the golf courses and others in the undeveloped properties or the real estate companies. Also in the hunt were Avron Fogelman and Charles Fraser, who together owned most of Harbour Town as well as the Plantation Center, a golf course, and a tennis club in Sea Pines. Fogelman had been disappointed when his earlier offer had been rejected by the creditors; now he joined forces with Fraser to explore the possibilities offered by the open bidding.

Potential buyers worried about residents. Blatt and Curry clearly preferred residential ownership, which scared off some interested parties. Residents repeatedly expressed their antipathy to outside buyers, whether they were respected resort companies, established developers, highfliers in search of a fast buck, or the often rumored Japanese and Arabs. Japanese investors lost interest in Sea Pines when they learned that property owners would not greet them with open arms, and settler antagonism was an important factor in dissuading a developer who believed that a good relationship with property owners was "a fundamental prerequisite to success."[28] An additional deterrent at Sea Pines was the property owners' well-organized and well-financed effort to purchase the plantation. Not only would Sea Pines Associates be difficult to outbid, but the intensity of the residents' commitment to acquiring the plantation would make life difficult for anyone who snatched Sea Pines away from its property owners.

But residential antipathy was not the only deterrent to potential outside buyers. Curry's insistence that plantations remain whole deterred purchasers interested in particular pieces such as Harbour Town Links or wary of taking on unattractive operations such as food service and property management. Others were leery of buying plantations from which key pieces were missing as a result of the various deals. Sea Pines in particular had been dismembered—much of Harbour Town, both tennis clubs, and the conference center were not part of the package. A further disincentive was the web of agreements with residents, time-share operators, and hotels that tied up substantial slots on the resort golf courses and tennis courts. Prospective purchasers also could not help noticing that the resort plantations were run-down and showing their years. Last, and particularly persuasive in light of the other negative factors, the plantations were no bargain; the minimum acceptable bids were "retail prices," and, as Curry noted after the bidding, "the retail buyers were not out there."[29]

WINNERS AND LOSERS

In fact, the only plantation buyer was Sea Pines Associates. The big prize was won with a minimum bid of $24.3 million, and the absence of competing bids obviated the planned auction.[30] With no bidders for the other plantations, Port Royal, Shipyard, and Wexford went back to Marathon for $61.5 million. Sea Pines residents breathed a collective sigh of relief, "giving prayers of thanks and appreciation to the board and founding group of Sea Pines Associates . . . for their faith in the attempt to give the residents control of the fate of their homes and properties."[31] And, as a fitting bonus, Sea Pines got the famed alligator back through the efforts of John Curry. The 4-foot statue was the featured guest as 1,000 people gathered at the Plantation Club to celebrate the purchase; the alligator was back and so was Sea Pines.

Curry and West resigned a few months after the sale, and Curry was finally able to become a stockholder in Sea Pines Associates. As the loose ends of the bankruptcy were wrapped up, the unsecured creditors got fifty cents on the dollar for their substantiated claims and almost $3 million in back taxes was paid to the county, state, and federal governments. Lawsuits were settled with Charles Fraser, Luke Taylor, and various other participants in the Hilton Head follies of 1985–87. Those at the end of the creditors' line got nothing, including Ginn and Taylor, whose claims on Hilton Head Holdings' assets proved as insubstantial as their visions of profit and glory. On the other hand, those who managed the bankruptcy did very well indeed, winding up with over $4.5 million in administrative and legal fees.

One important loose end dangled for months, as federal lawyers disputed transfer of common properties to property owners under the reorganization plan. Roads, open spaces, lagoons, and security facilities were not included in the assets that were packaged for sale; instead they were to be deeded to plantation residents under separate arrangements. In proceeding in this fashion, Curry advanced his general objective of giving plantation residents more control over their communities. Separating these properties and activities also increased the attractiveness of the plantations to commercial buyers, since community facilities and services were unprofitable operations. But the Federal Savings and Loan Insurance Corporation, as indifferent as ever to Hilton Head's interests, objected because no determination had been made of the value of these assets. After a year of legal wrangling, communal properties were finally transferred in return for some token concessions, ending an unnecessary dispute that benefited lawyers far more than federal taxpayers.[32]

Along with these happy endings for Hilton Head and plantation residents generally, bankruptcy left casualties. One was the Hilton Head Inn, the island's first modern hotel and its premier resort lodging for many years. By the time Vacation Resorts arrived in 1983, the aging inn was already buffeted by competition from newer hotels offering more modern accommodations, better convention and meeting facilities, and locations within Palmetto Dunes and Shipyard. Mounting financial troubles added to the hotel's liabilities, as maintenance was deferred and improvements were postponed. Ginn fell behind in lease payments to the company that had purchased the hotel from Sea Pines, jeopardizing its continued operation.[33] Next came Schwab and Taylor, who sealed its fate as the collapse of Hilton Head Holdings led to the abrupt closing of the inn and to bankruptcy.[34] An effort to auction the bankrupt hotel drew no bidders, and the holder of the largest mortgage reopened the inn with great fanfare in mid-1987 in the hope of attracting a buyer.[35] But this last fling only postponed the inevitable, as the frayed hotel attracted neither customers nor purchasers. Then the bank failed, bringing in the Federal Deposit Insurance Corporation and causing the eventual sale of the property and its 1,000 feet of prime beachfront to Marriott, which planned to replace the inn with a time-sharing and condominium project. So ended the Hilton Head Inn, gateway to Sea Pines for thousands of vacationers and home buyers and long-time center of the island's social and business life. Lots had been sold, deals sealed, and romances pursued at the inn, which had also housed church services, conventions, art exhibits, and homeowners' meetings as well as two presidents, cabinet members, governors, and other luminaries.

Far sadder was the fate of Indigo Run. While the Hilton Head Inn had enjoyed its place in the sun for years, Indigo Run was stillborn. After the bankruptcy ended, Indigo Run remained a ghostly place, its unfinished golf course reclaimed by the jungle, its lone house vandalized, and its grand gates covered with graffiti. A forlorn sign proclaimed, "Welcome—Indigo Run Plantation Real Estate Information Center. Center temporarily closed." Indigo Run had become Indigo Ruin, the most visible scar from the painful years of Ginn, Schwab, Taylor, and bankruptcy. The biggest losers were the people who invested $8.4 million in lots that were sold before reality caught up with real-estate hype. Unlike the residents of the established plantations, Indigo Run's lot buyers had little influence on the bankruptcy. As one bitterly noted, "There was more interest in bringing the alligator back than in helping us."[36]

Bankruptcy kept Indigo Run in limbo. The trustee had no funds to secure utility connections or renew construction activities or maintain deteriorating facilities. Nor was Curry able to revive the moribund town center, since land could not be given away without the permission of the creditors. What Curry could do, with Blatt's consent, was move Indigo Run out of bankruptcy quickly in order to preserve its rapidly deteriorating assets. Four months before the other plantations went on the block, 1,285 of Indigo Run's 2,040 acres was packaged for sale; the plantation's remaining land belonged to collateral investors and lenders. In a bizarre twist, the winning bid of $12.3 million came from the successor to the defunct Southern Floridabanc, the organization whose irresponsible lending practices had triggered the chain of events that produced Indigo Ruin. The new thrift, Southern Floridabanc Federal Savings and Loan Association, looked impressive on paper; it was managed by a subsidiary of a developer of posh golf communities in Palm Beach and California and already controlled 330 acres of Indigo Run as a result of past deals and foreclosures. Nothing, however, happened under the new owners; utilities were not connected, facilities were not renovated, and nature continued to reclaim Indigo Run. The rush to sell turned fiasco into farce as the plantation continued to molder for another four years.

Poor Indigo Run, betrayed by Ginn, abandoned by Hilton Head Holdings, and peddled by the trustee, was now trapped in the Kafkaesque world of the savings and loan bailout. Southern Floridabanc Federal was a creature of the federal government, controlled by bank regulators and unable to undertake anything without approval from Washington. While Indigo Run was the largest tract of real estate in the Southeast to come into federal hands from failed thrifts, property was only a small piece of a large puzzle. It was also caught up in a bureaucratic maze as Washington organized and reorganized to cope with the mushrooming thrift disaster. Early in 1989 Southern Floridabanc Federal was passed to the Federal Deposit Insurance Company, which brought new federal officials into the picture along with more reviews and delays. A few months later the newly created Resolution Trust Corporation closed the insolvent bank and took over its assets, including Indigo Run. Another set of masters brought fresh rules, additional appraisals, and further delays.

As this game of musical chairs was played, sporadic efforts were made to sell Indigo Run. Under federal direction, Southern Floridabanc Federal resolved the water and sewer problem. Even with the sewer deal finally in place, Indigo Run remained unattractive to potential buyers at the $45 million price set by federal regulators. Each delay dashed the hopes of Indigo Run's property owners, who kept paying taxes and mortgage obligations for land they could neither use nor sell, since no lender could get title insurance. The long-delayed utility connection was only the beginning of an answer to their problems. Before building permits could be issued, the town government had to recertify everything from water pressure to streets. Even if these hurdles were cleared, property owners were dubious about building without some assurance that the golf courses and other amenities were going to be provided so that Indigo Run would be a plantation, a real piece of Hilton Head, rather than a bunch of homesites in scruffy woods. By 1989 many of Indigo Run's property owners were fed up with relying on other people to turn their nightmare back into the promised dream. They organized and went to court, suing the federal government and everyone else with a hand in the mess for $7 million in damages.

Meanwhile the ponderous machinery of the Resolution Trust Corporation finally got around to selling Indigo Run. Real estate agents were engaged to market the property, and they peddled Indigo Run by selling Hilton Head. Wide beaches and green golf courses, brilliant sunsets and mauve marshes—the tried and true images of island marketing were reworked to put Indigo Run back in the paradise portfolio. Advertisements in the *Wall Street Journal, National Real Estate Investor, Tokyo Business Today,* and *Financial Times* of London rhapsodized about "the last plantation on prestigious Hilton Head Island," a "glorious tract of land" whose "possibilities . . . are limited only by the imagination."[37] After years of neglect, Indigo Run was spruced up for potential buyers, made into a tidy Potemkin village with new plantings, a freshly painted gate, and twenty-four-hour security to discourage vandals.

For all its troubles, Indigo Run was an attractive parcel, the last major undeveloped land on Hilton Head and located in the heart of the island's most rapidly growing section. Still, its plans were dated and its commercial dreams unrealistic. With the condo market on Hilton Head glutted, no one was going to develop 80 percent of the Indigo Run housing in multifamily units as Marathon had planned. During the development's years in limbo, a blizzard of commercial development had swept across Hilton Head, spreading around the island office buildings, stores, and motels that might have located in Indigo Run. Most of the facilities that might have formed the nucleus of Indigo Run's town center had gone elsewhere. In the end, Indigo Run proved most attractive to a local firm. The winning bid of $24.8 million came from the Melrose Company, whose portfolio included Hilton Head Plantation and two resorts on Daufuskie Island. Hilton Head breathed a sigh of relief: "They are a known quantity," emphasized the *Island Packet;* "they are known to bring class to whatever they do."[38] Finally, more than six years after Bobby Ginn had bought the two companies, Indigo Run was back in the fold, and Hilton Head was whole again.[39]

Bankruptcy and its aftermath at Indigo Run underscored the wide net of interests created by private community development. Hilton Head Holdings was not merely a bankrupt firm, lost jobs, and unpaid debts. The company controlled resort facilities and real estate that were critical to the island's economic health and future, and it owned and operated communities in which a substantial number of islanders lived. Bankruptcy facilitated its broadening control over key elements of these private communities. Hilton Head's most valuable resort attraction, the Heritage Golf Classic, was moved into the public sector under a nonprofit corporation. Sea Pines, still the premier resort destination, was acquired by residents likely to be more sympathetic to the island's general interests than the succession of owners that followed Charles Fraser. And bankruptcy provided the means by which community facilities and services on the other plantations were transferred to residents.

That bankruptcy facilitated such sweeping changes in the shape of the local political economy, rather than presiding over the transfer or dismemberment of Hilton Head Holdings, was a testament to the island's political clout and business competence. Experience, business savvy, and political sophistication were also essential for the successful navigation of Sea Pines Associates through the largely uncharted waters of acquiring a large resort community, as were the dedication and financial resources of the 650 property owners who invested over $12 million in their community. Last but hardly least was the influence of the individual best placed to advance Hilton Head's interests. Certainly Hilton Head did not forget the importance of its friend in court; at the end of 1987, 200 islanders honored Judge Blatt at a dinner sponsored by the Chamber of Commerce, Community Association, and town government as Hilton Head celebrated Sol Blatt Day.

NOTES

1. Bright, "Back from the Brink," 1.
2. "Please, Santa, Buyers Who'll Straighten It Out."
3. Population rose from 17,622 in 1985 to 23,694 in 1990, an increase of 6,072. Between 1986 and 1987 the number of visitors rose from 950,000 to 1.1 million, with each year marking a new annual high in tourists.
4. Quoted in Rutter, "Ginn, Fraser: Solution Is Close at Hand," and in Janet Smith, "Judge Had Key Role in Legal Saga."
5. Quoted in Janet Smith, "Blatt Leaves Bankruptcy Case, Lashes Out at FSLIC Lawyer."
6. Quoted in Janet Smith, "Judge Had Key Role in Legal Saga."
7. Quoted in Janet Smith, "Federal Judge Sets Oct. 1 Sale Deadline."
8. Quoted in Young, "Island Residents Seek to Purchase Assets of Hilton Head Holdings' Developments."
9. Quoted in Janet Smith, "Hilton Head Holdings: The Bankruptcy Saga."

10. West was governor from 1971 to 1975 and had previously served as lieutenant governor between 1966 and 1971. He was ambassador to Saudi Arabia during the Carter Administration, from 1977 to 1981.

11. Solomon Blatt Sr. and his fellow Barnwell County legislator Edgar A. Brown were the leaders of the Barnwell Ring, which dominated the South Carolina legislature for more than three decades.

12. Under normal federal procedures, jurisdiction over Hilton Head Holdings would belong to a federal court in New York because the Schwabs and Cuyahoga Wrecking had filed for bankruptcy in New York before Hilton Head Holdings' filing in South Carolina.

13. The first ruling applied to the Ginn component of the bankruptcy; see Janet Smith, "Judge Blatt Leaves Case after Ruling." The second ruling applied to the bankruptcy itself; see Smith, "Court Orders Blatt off Bankruptcy Case." All the major issues in the bankruptcy were resolved months before Judge Blatt was removed from the case in mid-1988.

14. Quoted in Janet Smith, "Judge Had Key Role in Legal Saga."

15. Secured creditors had claims on Hilton Head Holdings that were backed by collateral, in contrast to unsecured creditors whose claims were not. The major secured creditors were Marathon, Southern Floridabanc, and the Federal Savings and Loan Insurance Corporation. Southern Floridabanc was closed by the Federal Home Loan Bank Board and placed in receivership in April 1987.

16. Four commercial banks and eight savings and loan associations put up $250,000 each: Citizens and Southern National Bank of South Carolina, Hilton Head Bank and Trust, NCNB National Bank, South Carolina National Bank, American Federal Bank, Federal Saving Bank, First Federal of Greenville, First South Savings Bank, Palmetto Federal Savings and Loan, Palmetto State Savings and Loan Association, Standard Federal Savings and Loan Association, and United Savings and Loan of Greenville.

17. In addition to Joseph Fraser, Curry recruited, for food service, Brian Carmines, owner with his wife of Hudson's Seafood, one of the island's most popular restaurants and tourist attractions; for marketing, John David Rose, a partner in Gardo, Doughtie and Rose, the island's largest advertising firm; and for asset management, Mark Puntereri of the Fraser Group.

18. The money was advanced from the town's accommodation tax revenues, which were dedicated to tourism-related expenditures. It was repaid as soon as tickets were sold.

19. Quoted in Eyre, "Court Places Inn in Bankruptcy, Curry Sees It Opening by Summer."

20. Charles Flynn, president, Sea Pines Associates, quoted in Felder, "Axene:

Sea Pines Associates, Inc. Alive and Well." Sea Pines Associates was the instrument through which residents acquired Sea Pines, as discussed in detail below.

21. Sea Pines Associates was not incorporated until May 1987; before that the group operated as Country Club Associates. To avoid confusion, the name Sea Pines Associates is used throughout the rest of the chapter.

22. Quoted in Janet Smith, "Group of Sea Pines Residents Makes Offer to Purchase Company."

23. Two years earlier, property owners had purchased Moss Creek Plantation on the mainland from U.S. Shelter Corporation, whose plans to build condos and increase residential densities were vehemently opposed by residents. With an average investment of $70,000, they raised $3 million and borrowed the remainder from a local bank to finance the $9 million purchase of the golf courses, marina, infrastructure, and undeveloped land.

24. Wayne Hyatt of Hyatt and Rhodes, the author of *Condominium and Homeowner Association Practice.* Legal fees and other expenses were underwritten by $50,000 in seed money invested by the organizers, with each of the twenty-five associates putting up $2,000.

25. Sea Pines Associates offered 1.2 million preferred shares and 1.8 million common shares, which were sold in units of 500 preferred shares and 750 common shares at $5000 each. The smallest purchase permitted was 2 units (a minimum investment of $10,000), with a 5 percent discount to purchasers of 5 units and a 10 percent discount for those who bought 10 units.

26. Forty-three million dollars was for the assets in Port Royal, Shipyard, and Wexford plantations and the remaining $18.5 million for other properties. Thirty-six million of the $61.5 million was in mortgages held by Marathon, while $17 million was in notes to other creditors.

27. Among the interested companies were American Golf Corporation of Los Angeles; Country Club Corporation of America of Dallas; Coventry Investment Group of Houston; East West Partners of Fripp Island, S.C.; National Financial of Louisville; U.S. Shelter of Greenville, S.C.; Valley Isles Partners of Maui in Hawaii; and Nomura Securities, Japan's largest investment firm.

28. Harry H. Frampton III, East West Partners, quoted in Smith, "New Offer Made for Sea Pines, Other Assets." Frampton, a former real estate salesman at Sea Pines, met with Sea Pines residents before deciding not to pursue an offer for the plantation.

29. Quoted in Janet Smith, "Sea Pines Associates, Marathon Only Bidders."

30. The only other bid was $5 million from Fogelman for some property in

Harbour Town that was offered separately from the plantation.

31. Winston Roberts, letter to the editor.

32. Sea Pines Associates, the Association of Sea Pines Plantation Property Owners, and Fogelman Properties paid a grand total of $10,000 to the bankruptcy estate. Curry's successor as trustee transferred a few minor parcels to the Federal Savings and Loan Insurance Corporation.

33. The hotel was purchased for $2.45 million by Holyoake N.V. of the Netherlands Antilles in 1977. Under the purchase agreement, Sea Pines would continue to operate the inn under a ten-year lease.

34. Schwab and Taylor acquired the inn outside the framework of Hilton Head Holdings. When Hilton Head Holdings failed, lease payments to their hotel company ceased, and the hotel company also was forced into bankruptcy.

35. First American Bank and Trust of Florida held a mortgage for $5.65 million. The other major mortgage holder was Wachovia Mortgage Company of Winston-Salem, N.C., which had lent $4.6 million. First American assumed the other mortgages and paid $500,000 to Hilton Head Holdings, $300,000 to Taylor's Hilton Head Island Holding Corporation, and $250,000 to Schwab.

36. Joseph Nicolini, quoted in Janet Smith, "Legal Battles Keep Plans on Hold."

37. Indigo Run Plantation, advertisement.

38. "Indigo Run Rescue Welcome at Last."

39. Completion of the sale was delayed for months because of the pending lawsuit filed by Indigo Run property owners. In the end, the Resolution Trust Corporation had to agree to protect the interests of the property owners whose lawsuit was pending by putting funds in escrow to cover possible damages.

Chapter Twelve

The New Hilton Head

*The resort business is the backbone of the whole economy on
Hilton Head.*

—Charles Pigg, quoted by Carolyn Grant
in the *Island Packet,* January 26, 1990

Hilton Head was changed by the demise of the major development companies. Sea Pines and the Hilton Head Company, the most influential players for
the first three decades of the island's modern history, were pale shadows of
their former commanding presences by 1987. Private communities that were
the base of company power were now wholly or substantially in the hands of
property owners. Accompanying these shifts were sweeping general changes in
the 1980s. Population was expanding rapidly, increasing numbers of visitors
vacationed on the island, and the economic base was in transition from land
development to tourism. A new Hilton Head was emerging, bigger and more
diverse—a place with more permanent residents, a greater variety of economic
interests, and complex political conflicts. Growth was transforming Hilton Head
and its environs into a bustling urban area, a reality that clashed with the image
of paradise, a place apart from the troubles of the "real world."

Diversity softened the impact of the long slide into bankruptcy. Two-thirds
of Hilton Head's land, residents, and labor force were outside the realm of Hilton
Head Holdings. Other development companies had become prominent in the
local economy, and their roles were enhanced by the troubles of Sea Pines and
the Hilton Head Company. The Melrose Company was a leader in both residential and resort development; its Hilton Head Plantation paced the island in housing starts while two new Melrose resorts were taking shape on Daufuskie Island.
Greenwood Development was completing Palmetto Dunes and building an adjacent resort as well as launching a new plantation. Additional firms were developing smaller residential communities, resort villages, and a variety of
commercial projects.

Within this diversifying array of developers, the traditional dominance of
the plantation companies was diminishing. They were still the biggest set of
enterprises, and plantations continued to house most island residents and guests,

but their relative importance was steadily declining. Population growth and increased tourism fueled more development outside plantations than inside their gates. By 1985 almost half of Hilton Head's residents lived outside planned communities, and the proportion was increasing. Similarly, more hotel rooms and resort condos were built outside than inside plantations in the 1980s. Smaller developers were less dependent on plantation companies; their options were greater, with more plantations to chose from and increased opportunities on the rest of Hilton Head, Daufuskie Island, and the mainland.

Development in general also accounted for a declining share of local economic activity. This smaller portion was a natural consequence of the diminishing supply of land on Hilton Head. The lessened role of development also reflected the vitality of the resort sector. Originally stimulated by plantation companies as a means of enhancing property values and selling real estate, resort activities displaced development as the fundamental pillar of the local economy in the 1980s. Increasingly, resort operators were not directly connected to the development business. All the resort hotels were independently operated, in contrast to the inns developed by Fraser and Hack to support their real estate operations. Developers and realtors continued to rely on the resort trade for customers, but resort operators no longer needed developers to succeed. The island's attractions combined with aggressive promotional activities to bring increasing numbers of tourists to Hilton Head. With more guests to house, feed, recreate, and service, the resort sector rapidly expanded its share of the island's businesses, employment, and income.

Figure 12.1 - Economic Growth, 1975–1990 (1990 Dollars)

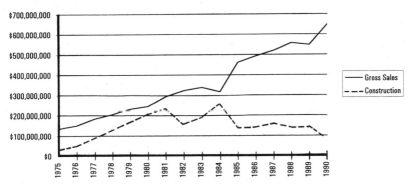

THE CHANGING DEVELOPMENT BUSINESS

Among the many significant companies on the new Hilton Head, the most influential was Greenwood Development, whose portfolio included Palmetto Dunes, the adjacent resort and commercial development at Shelter Cove, and a new 750-acre residential plantation called Palmetto Hall. Greenwood owned substantial amounts of developable land as the 1980s began, and much of it was strategically located. Greenwood was in both the development business and the resort business. Its flagship property was Palmetto Dunes, which was successfully marketed as Hilton Head's ideal resort, with luxury hotels, hundreds of condos and time-share units, fine golf courses, and a lavish tennis center. Behind Greenwood Development were the deep pockets of Greenwood Mills, one of the largest textile companies in the world. Greenwood Mills was owned by the Self family of Greenwood, South Carolina, which had a long-standing interest in Hilton Head beginning with James C. Self's backing of Charles Fraser in the early years. Greenwood acquired Palmetto Dunes and other island properties from Phipps Land Company in 1979.[1]

Greenwood built its Hilton Head operations on a strong base, since Palmetto Dunes had weathered the lean years in better shape than Sea Pines or the Hilton Head Company. During the 1970s, more than 1,000 single-family lots were sold and 700 condos built; a second golf course was finished; and the ten-story Hyatt Hotel, which so dismayed islanders, opened as the resort's showcase. Compared to most large-scale developers, Greenwood was in a strong position. The company owned all the undeveloped land and resort facilities on its properties, was not encumbered by debt, and was backed by the formidable resources of its parent firm.

Across the main highway from Palmetto Dunes, Greenwood developed Shelter Cove with the help of Charles Fraser and Robert Onorato.[2] Fraser and Onorato were an odd couple, competitors and controversialists who shared little except for large egos and years of experience in development. Onorato, however, thought they were a perfect match, "two developers who totally complement each other—Charles, the idea man, sensitive to environmental aesthetics and architectural styles, and I, a strong manager, an operations person who makes things happen."[3] Shelter Cove was Harbour Town redux, only much grander, with three times as large a boat basin, more than 1,400 condos, and a 240-room hotel. Bigger, however, was not necessarily better; Shelter Cove had little of the charm and intimacy that Fraser had created at Harbour Town, offering instead a vast concrete expanse with massed buildings and too little foliage.

Shelter Cove was the most resort-oriented of any planned community built on Hilton Head. All of its housing was multifamily and was marketed primarily as second homes and investment rental property. A significant number of units were time-shares. Shelter Cove was also the most intensively settled development on the island, with residential densities almost ten times higher than the plantation average and more than fivefold greater than in Palmetto Dunes (see table 12.1). Shelter Cove combined resort intensification with the largest concentration of commercial activity on Hilton Head, including a shopping center and the island's first covered mall in addition to shops and offices around the harbor. Development at Palmetto Dunes proper under Greenwood also heavily emphasized resort lodgings and facilities. Another oceanfront hotel was built; this time Palmetto Dunes respected the informal five-story limit, spreading the 344-room Mariners Inn across 13 acres. The southern end of the plantation offered over 400 virgin acres for additional intensive resort development, including almost 1,400 condos and a golf course for resort guests. When these developments and other projects were completed, Palmetto Dunes would have 78 percent of its housing in condominiums, more than twice the proportion in Sea Pines, and the highest residential densities of any planned community except its spin-off at Shelter Cove.

Greenwood's ambitious program at Palmetto Dunes and Shelter Cove marked the end of major resort-oriented developments on Hilton Head, at least

Table 12.1
Planned Densities in Plantations, 1982

Plantation	Acres	Dwelling Units	Density (Units per Acre)	Multi-Family	Percent Multi-Family
Hilton Head	3,995	5,950	1.5	3,420	57.5
Long Cove	614	850	1.4	200	23.5
Palmetto Dunes	1,670	4,511	2.7	3,500	77.6
Port Royal	1,266	951	.8	122	12.8
Shelter Cove	93	1,401	15.1	1,401	100.0
Shipyard	780	1,470	1.9	1,119	76.1
Sea Pines	4,511	5,890	1.3	2,100	35.7
Spanish Wells	366	189	.5	0	0.0
Windmill Harbour	172	470	2.7	414	88.1
Total	13,467	21,682		12,276	

Source: Adapted from Beaufort County Joint Planning Commission, "State of the Island Report—Land Use," 3–4.

on virgin land. By the time Shelter Cove was ready to offer to the public, the market for condominiums was very soft in the wake of the 1986 federal tax reforms, which eliminated shelters for rental properties. Now most buyers were looking for primary dwellings or second homes in which they expected to live permanently some time in the future. Driving the market for primary homes was the doubling of the island's population during the 1980s, from 11,336 to 23,694, an average annual increase of over 1,200, which translated into 530 new households per year.[4] As population grew, the proportion of primary homes in the overall housing stock expanded, increasing from 43 percent to 48 percent between 1985 and 1990. Most primary-home buyers preferred single-family dwellings despite the glut of bargain-priced condominiums; typically they were seeking more space, separation from tourists, and a better investment than that offered by the overstocked condo market.[5] Responding to these changes, developers shifted to single-family homes and lowered residential densities. After acquiring Indigo Run, Melrose cut densities in half, from 2.7 to 1.3 units per acre, and emphasized single-family homes rather than condos, thus departing from Marathon's plan.

Table 12.2
Population Change on Hilton Head Island, 1970–1990

Year	Population	Total Change	Average Annual Change	Annual Percent Change (Compounded)
1970	2,546	—	—	—
1975	6,511	3,965	793	20.7
1980	11,336	4,825	965	11.7
1985	17,622	6,286	1,257	9.2
1990	23,694	6,072	1,214	6.1

Demand for single-family homes was spread through a wide price range. At one end was a growing corps of wealthy buyers in the market for posh beachfront houses in older plantations and large homes in new plantations catering to the carriage trade. By 1991 properties on the beach in Sea Pines were selling for as much as $2 million, as were the grandest houses in Wexford, a plantation that had by design the island's largest collection of expensive homes. Less spectacular but more important to developers was the sharp increase in demand for moderately priced single-family housing generated by the growing ranks of working islanders. Greenwood's Palmetto Hall was aimed primarily at younger families seeking less expensive detached housing but with the added attraction of plantation amenities including guarded gates, private security, golf, and tennis.

Palmetto Hall also reflected the enduring appeal of golf for real estate development on Hilton Head and its environs. Despite an increasing number of residents interested in healthier pastimes than riding around a golf course on an electric cart, by the time Palmetto Hall was planned, more people than ever before wanted to play golf on Hilton Head. As a result, golf remained "the main marketing tool for real estate developments. . . . You've got to have that golf course to sell that dirt."[6] And putting fairways in backyards meant that lot prices could be jacked up, a lesson learned at Sea Pines and zealously applied throughout Hilton Head and its environs. Privacy was as important as golf on the new Hilton Head in selling real estate for primary homes and to prospective retirees. Many permanent residents, working and retired, preferred truly private communities whose amenities were for residents in contrast to the resort-residential mix that was the basis of Sea Pines. They wanted purely residential plantations with private golf and tennis, guarded gates to insulate them from tourists and transients, no short-term rentals or time-shares, and preferably no condos. Many islanders wanted even greater privacy with respect to golf and thus created a market for private golf clubs. Demand for purely residential communities and private clubs created opportunities for developers to fill a variety of niches. With the best locations already claimed by older seaside plantations, they had to work with what was available, mostly interior property of the kind that became Wexford and Indigo Run.

Next to Wexford was Long Cove Club, the most striking example of niche development on the new Hilton Head. Long Cove's developers capitalized on the market for private golf and the willingness of affluent islanders to pay a premium for well-planned and carefully executed privacy. Developed by three partners who had worked together at Sea Pines and Hilton Head Plantation, Long Cove had the look and feel of Sea Pines, but a Sea Pines with only single-family homes, private golf, and neither tourists nor commerce within its gates.[7] Long Cove Club's 660 acres of initially unpromising interior land, acquired from the Hilton Head Company and similar to adjacent Wexford Plantation, was thoroughly reworked; its developers extracted as much as they could from nature and moved earth wherever necessary to transform swamp and scrub into a lovely setting.[8] The pièce de résistance was the golf course by Pete Dye, the designer of Harbour Town, who was by 1980 world-renowned for his singular layouts. Modeled on the classic links courses in Scotland, Dye's Long Cove course was quickly recognized as one of the best in the nation.[9]

Long Cove Club found an enthusiastic market from the outset, selling almost all of the first 100 lots on the day they were offered. Most initial buyers were island residents, and many were Sea Pines owners who jumped at the chance to relocate in a Sea Pines–like setting without tourists, time-shares, and traffic. Attracting so many buyers at the outset saved marketing money, and selling the initial land offerings quickly generated a favorable cash flow that permitted internal financing. Long Cove's developers designed a high-quality product for an expanding affluent market, and they maintained complete planning and financial control. Their customers enjoyed remarkable stability during a period of turmoil on Hilton Head, dealing with the same company and owners throughout with no threats to their peace of mind or property values from leveraged buyouts, unhappy lenders, or bankruptcy. When Long Cove was completed, the developers departed, turning the plantation over to its residents in accordance with their covenanted agreements with property owners. For their success in responding effectively to the desire for a different kind of private community, Long Cove's trio left with fat profits and considerable goodwill, both rarities among Hilton Head's plantation builders.

Another example of adjustment to a changing market through specialization was Windmill Harbour, a boating community on Calibogue Sound off the northwest tip of Hilton Head. The 172-acre site was acquired in 1979 from the Hilton Head Company by investors who teamed up with Sea Pines to develop the property.[10] With 2 miles of frontage on Calibogue Sound, the location was ideal for a water-oriented community, offering seascapes and magnificent sunsets. Windmill Harbour's centerpiece was a sheltered marina with moorings for more than 300 boats and an innovative lock system that tamed strong tidal flows. Despite the advantages of a splendid location and excellent marina, Windmill Harbour failed to carve out a niche among boaters and others attracted to a waterside community. One problem was a changing housing market gone sour on condos, which predominated in the original design; another was the series of ownership changes at Sea Pines. Together they left Windmill Harbour with a plan based on the wrong kind of housing and a stalled project with substantial operating costs for the harbor and infrastructure. Windmill Harbour was rescued through radical restructuring by its developer, who acquired Sea Pines' interest and redesigned the community, reducing the number of housing units and switching from condominiums to lots for single-family homes.[11] Also added was the South Carolina Yacht Club, complete with a $3 million Charleston-style clubhouse to cash in on Hilton Head's blossoming love affair with private clubs. In its new incarnation, Windmill Harbour found an enthusiastic market and was sold out by 1992.

Of all the island's planned communities, Hilton Head Plantation played the most important role in responding to demographic change and shifting housing demand. Hilton Head Plantation was extensive, at 3,995 acres second to Sea Pines among the island's planned communities; and the plantation was largely undeveloped as the second boom began. From the start, Hilton Head Plantation was aimed at permanent residents whom Charles Fraser foresaw becoming an increasingly important market as Hilton Head grew. After Sea Pines lost the property in 1975, Fraser's basic marketing and planning strategy was further refined, targeted on "a clientele that wanted larger lots, safe streets for children, and easy commuting to local professional jobs."[12] The plantation would also appeal strongly to retirees who wanted Hilton Head's climate, lifestyle, and golf without the tourists and bustle of Sea Pines. Hilton Head Plantation was quieter and more familiar; its feel was more suburban hometown than exotic resort, and that was just what many permanent residents, working and retired, wanted for their piece of paradise.

Ownership of Hilton Head Plantation passed from Sea Pines to Citibank of New York and First Chicago Bank in 1975, with the banks hiring Sea Pines to manage the property until it could be sold. Dissatisfaction with the arrangement with Sea Pines led the banks to bring in their own manager, Howard Davis, a retired general and land developer.[13] Marketing was Davis's forte, and he moved aggressively to heighten the plantation's appeal to home buyers. He stressed single-family houses and cut back on condos. Davis turned the plantation's model home program into a highly successful marketing device, attracting customers by demonstrating how inexpensively houses could be built at Hilton Head Plantation. By 1982 Hilton Head Plantation had surpassed Sea Pines in single-family housing starts, and it continued throughout the decade to capture more residential growth than any other planned community. Rapid development of Hilton Head Plantation and its strong appeal to permanent residents were primarily responsible for the shift in the center of economic and political gravity from the southern to the northern half of Hilton Head.

In 1985 Citibank and First Chicago sold Hilton Head Plantation for $30 million to Melrose, which had been organized the previous year to develop land on Daufuskie Island. Melrose's trio of partners was intimately familiar with Hilton Head Plantation, all having worked for Howard Davis.[14] For Melrose, the acquisition of Hilton Head Plantation was the stepping stone to further expansion on the island. Next came the successful bid for Indigo Run, which provided the best setting in which to extend strategies that had proved so successful at Hilton Head Plantation. "We'll be doing Hilton Head Plantation all over again" was how a Melrose official summarized the company's plans for Indigo Run.[15]

Table 12.3
Population Change by Section, 1980–1990

	1980	1990	Percent Change
Port Royal and Hilton Head Plantation	2,161	7,036	225.6
Rest of northern Hilton Head	2,250	4,121	83.2
Long Cove, Palmetto Dunes, Shelter Cove, Shipyard, and Wexford	2,278	5,423	138.1
Forest Beach and Sea Pines	4,647	7,114	53.1

THE NEW ECONOMIC ELITE

With the acquisition of Indigo Run, Melrose's plantations encompassed one-fifth of Hilton Head Island. The company also controlled 20 percent of Daufuskie Island with its two resort clubs. Melrose and Greenwood Development were the preeminent players on the new Hilton Head; they owned the most land, were the largest developers, and operated major resorts. The two firms were also now the prime benefactors among island businesses, using their landholdings, as Fraser and Hack had done in the past, to advance public and private interests. Greenwood provided property at Shelter Cove for a visitors' center and cultural center. Like other island developers, Greenwood was hoping to do well by doing good. Donating land for the visitors' and cultural facilities drew more people to Shelter Cove's shops, restaurants, and real estate offices. Melrose too mixed civic and business interests, providing land for churches and Hilton Head's museum in Main Street, a commercial development just outside the entrance to Hilton Head Plantation. When Indigo Run was acquired, Melrose talked about additional marriages of community and business development. Land donations for government facilities, a public park, or a college campus would bolster Indigo Run's commercial area as well as complement Main Street, just across the highway.

For all their resources, however, neither Greenwood nor Melrose possessed the kind of power wielded by Charles Fraser and Fred Hack when they controlled most of the island's real estate and almost all of its development. Economic diversity dispersed political influence among a variety of business interests on the new Hilton Head. The island no longer had a major employer or dominant economic actor, as it had in the years when Sea Pines was riding high. Most of the new economic elite came from larger development and resort firms, and the influence of the latter grew with the shift to a resort-based economy.

242

After Greenwood and Melrose, the most influential resort operators were the luxury beachfront hotels, but the hotels had smaller local stakes then the locally based firms. They were links of national or international chains, so Hilton Head was only a small part of their overall operation, and hotel officials were birds of passage assigned to the island for relatively short tours of duty. Banks, normally an essential element of the local economic elite, never had a significant role on Hilton Head. The Bank of Beaufort, the island's first bank, was not big enough to play an important part during the heyday of the plantation companies. By the mid-1980s, regional banks dominated the local banking scene. Affluent and booming Hilton Head was a profitable locale for these banks, but the island was not a central focus of outside bank corporations; and bankers, like hotel executives, were transients with few incentives to maintain continuous involvement in local affairs.

An interesting contrast with hotels and banks was provided by the *Island Packet,* also owned by a large outside corporation but deeply absorbed in local affairs. The newspaper covered Hilton Head in detail with a degree of sophistication rarely found in a newspaper in a town of 24,000. The *Packet* sought to influence outcomes on a wide range of issues through its editorial page and its energetic publisher's direct involvement in civic and business affairs during the 1980s. The paper grew with Hilton Head, expanding its advertising, circulation, and coverage as resort business soared. The *Packet* and the locally owned telephone company were the most valuable economic assets on the island as the 1990s began. Bolstered by growth, it was the apostle of the resort economy, strongly supporting a bigger and better Hilton Head.

Like the *Island Packet,* the Hilton Head Island Chamber of Commerce flourished with growth and the diffusion of economic influence. During its early years, the Chamber depended heavily on the dominant plantation companies. As the companies declined, it played an increasingly autonomous role in business, civic, and governmental affairs. Its promotional activities steadily expanded; the Chamber marketed all of Hilton Head as a resort, in contrast to its earlier peddling of individual plantations when the companies reigned supreme. With more members and resources, the Chamber emerged as a champion of the island's economy, especially its burgeoning resort industry.

RESORT TOWN

Hilton Head was a boom town in the 1980s, and the driving force behind robust economic advance and rapid population growth was the steady rise in visitors. Between 1980 and 1990 the number of tourists more than doubled, from 648,000 to 1.58 million, while their spending on Hilton Head increased from $121 million to $583 million. Over three-quarters of the island's businesses were services, and one-third of its workers were employed in resorts and restaurants.[16] Visitors accounted for approximately nine out of every ten dollars collected by local businesses. Tourism sustained Hilton Head through the recession in the mid-1970s and the crash of its largest development companies a decade later.

Table 12.4
Visitors to Hilton Head Island and Estimated Expenditures, 1980–1990

Year	Visitors	Index (1980 = 100)	Total Expenditures	Expenditures per Visitor
1980	648,000	100	121,051,000	187
1981	700,000	108	133,785,750	192
1982	680,000	105	149,164,800	219
1983	750,000	116	200,297,400	267
1984	825,000	127	250,570,650	304
1985	875,000	135	314,457,500	359
1986	950,000	147	371,972,000	392
1987	1,100,000	170	410,801,000	373
1988	1,200,000	185	485,000,000	404
1989	1,400,000	216	529,000,000	378
1990	1,580,000	244	583,000,000	369

Source: Hilton Head Island Chamber of Commerce and Town of Hilton Head Island, "Hilton Head Island Commercial Information Packet," pt. 4, 4. These data are derived from information collected by the South Carolina Division of Tourism.

Increasing numbers of tourists stimulated a surge in hotel and motel construction. Luxury hotels came first—the Mariner's Inn and Marriott's Hilton Head Resort in 1983, followed by the Inter-Continental in Port Royal in 1985.[17] This round of construction saturated the market for resort hotels that offered ocean views, restaurants, room service, and convention facilities. The motel business too was jumping as more and more visitors crossed the bridge, many looking for a relatively cheap place to sleep. Soon they could choose from among the familiar names advertised on the highway interchanges—Comfort Inn, Days Inn, Knights Inn, Quality Suites, Red Roof Inn, and Super 8. Most motels offered few services beyond the requisite soft drink machine, ice dispenser, and tiny swimming pool, but all, even Super 8, played one important part of the Hilton Head game—they offered a golf package to their customers.

Golf packages everywhere underscored the fact that most visitors came to Hilton Head to play games. Certainly the island's broad beaches, tropical scenery, gentle climate, and posh plantations were powerful attractions; but golf and tennis were the lifeblood of its resort economy. Golf was the more important game, attracting affluent vacationers, second-home purchasers, and well-off retirees. Twenty-seven courses graced the island and its immediate environs in 1991, and over a million rounds were played at the cost of countless balls whacked into lagoons, marshes, jungle, and backyards. People came to watch golf and tennis as well as play. Heritage week was the crowning glory of the resort and real estate industries, filling hotels, condos, restaurants, and shops with over 100,000 visitors, most of them affluent. The second-best week was the week of the Family Circle tennis tournament.

Golf and tennis also drew associated enterprises that bolstered the resort economy. Dennis Van der Meer's renowned tennis center enrolled 10,000 students annually, each staying an average of five days. In 1986 two island resorts organized spring break tennis, which brought college teams to Hilton Head throughout March for practices and matches.[18] Four years later the event was attracting more than 200 college teams with 2,000 players, coaches, and trainers, who, along with parents and friends, spent more than $175,000 on lodgings alone. Like most people who came to Hilton Head to play games, college tennis players tended to be affluent; they could afford good restaurants, and they bought a lot of merchandise in local shops.

Keeping them coming and spending required constant promotion. Tastes for leisure activities and vacations were in constant flux. Island resorts relentlessly promoted Hilton Head, spending increasingly large sums to compete with upscale vacation spots in Florida, Hawaii, and the Caribbean. Affluent visitors were the primary objective of Hilton Head's resort leaders. Especially valued as tourists were executives and professionals who might return with business colleagues. Corporate and professional meetings were more attractive than family tourists; participants had higher incomes, spent more, and booked resort hotels and luxury villas. By 1986 such groups accounted for 25 percent of the island's 1.2 million visitors.[19] At the resort hotels, which concentrated on businesses and groups, over half of all guests came for meetings and conferences or with tours.

Another objective of resort promotion was extending the tourist season. A longer season brought more visitors, who could be accommodated without enlarging capacity. Expanding the season furthered the goals of attracting more affluent visitors and booking more meetings. People who came in the spring and fall to play golf and tennis tended to have higher incomes than families drawn by the beach in the summer. Golf and tennis were central to lengthening the resort year; both games could be played all year on Hilton Head, and golf in particular drew visitors throughout the mild winters. Professional golf and tennis tournaments in spring stretched out the resort season. Sports, festivals and other promotions, and generally changing vacation patterns combined to flatten out the seasons substantially. Summer tourists dropped from 51 percent of the annual total in 1976 to 31.5 percent in 1991, while winter visitors rose from 7.4 percent to 15.4 percent (see table 12.5).

Table 12.5
Percent of Annual Visitors by Season, 1976 and 1991

Season	1976	1991	Change 1976–1991
Spring (March–May)	19.7	28.9	+9.2
Summer (June–August)	51.1	31.5	-19.6
Fall (September–November)	21.8	24.2	+2.4
Winter (December–February)	7.4	15.4	+8.0

Source: Hilton Head Island Chamber of Commerce and Town of Hilton Head Island, "Hilton Head Island Commercial Information Packet," pt. 4, 2.

Despite Hilton Head's preference for visitors from the corporate and professional worlds, the reality of the resort business moved the island in the opposite direction in the 1980s. Vigorous promotional efforts increased the its visibility, luring tourists of more modest means to add exotic Hilton Head to the list of sights they had seen. Extending the season with bargain rates inevitably attracted people with less to spend. Lower-cost lodgings were developed both in response to this market and in anticipation of its growth. Along with the motels came more shops catering to budget vacationers, inexpensive restaurants, tour buses, and outlet malls, adding another dimension to the new Hilton Head. Many resort leaders were troubled by these developments. Mass and class were not complementary in the resort business; budget motels, chain restaurants, and outlets detracted from the island's ambiance and distinction. Businesses catering to budget travelers, on the other hand, resented the elitism of established resort operations, insisting that they had as much right to make a living on Hilton Head as the owners of the Hyatt or Harbour Town's elegant shops and established restaurants. Motel operators pressed the Chamber of Commerce to "sell Hilton Head Island to get more visitors here so all will enjoy a good business."[20] Operators of inexpensive eateries and stores also expected that their interests would be reflected in efforts to attract customers to Hilton Head. Responding to its diversifying membership, the Chamber of Commerce plugged for less affluent tourists as well as upscale visitors, marketed all kinds of accommodations, and promoted Hilton Head as "a shopper's dream come true."[21]

Neither dreams of shopping nor life in a bustling resort was the primary appeal of Hilton Head to its retired residents. Most were troubled by the explosion of hotels, motels, malls, crowds, and traffic that came with more tourists. Almost everyone who retired to Hilton Head was initially attracted by the resort, but once settled in, the typical retired resident valued privacy, nature, and uncrowded amenities. Retirees constituted an important component of the island economy; most were affluent and generated substantial demands for goods and services. Retirement income was relatively stable, providing a welcome cushion to a local economy based on development and tourism and sustaining many businesses during the slack winter season. Still, retirees constituted a far smaller share of the island economy than tourists, and much less was heard about a retirement industry than the heralded resort industry. In contrast to many places eager to attract retirees, the Hilton Head resort industry devoted little of its formidable promotional energies to this market. Retirees, complained one critic, were "brushed aside as mere 'extras' in this economic production."[22]

Local business saw the retirement and resort sectors as interdependent. Everyone benefited from tourism, insisted resort leaders; tourists spent money, created jobs, paid taxes, and used few public services. Because Hilton Head was a resort, settlers had more golf and tennis, restaurants and shops, and choices among goods and services than would be possible in a local economy based on retirement. Many retirees, however, were not persuaded that their interests were served by headlong resort development. Private communities with excellent amenities could thrive without resort activities, as demonstrated by the success of Long Cove Club. Added choices for diners and shoppers and moviegoers were nice, but retirees questioned the cost in terms of more development, traffic, and people. Retirees worried about the growing demands tourists placed on finite water supplies and other public services as well as the burdens that local taxpayers would have to shoulder to support more visitors.

For many settlers, soaring commercial development became the symbol of the excesses of a tourist-driven economy. New developments sprang up everywhere in a bewildering variety of centers, malls, parks, plazas, squares, and villages. By 1988 Hilton Head had thirty-six shopping areas totaling over 1.5 million square feet of retail space and ranging from small strip developments to the island's first enclosed mall. Settlers saw trees felled, buildings erected, and acres of asphalt laid in what most regarded as an orgy of excessive development driven by resort intensification. Commercial overbuilding generated pressures for more customers, priming the pump for energetic efforts to attract additional tourists. The new Shelter Cove Mall, with a quarter of a million square feet of retail space, had to bring in shoppers to survive in a town with fewer than 25,000 permanent residents. "The more shops that come on the island," explained a commercial real estate broker, "the more customers must come from off the island."[23]

Enlarging the resort sector through broadening the tourist base was also dismaying to settlers. What attracted them to Hilton Head was being eroded by a flood of fast-food restaurants, tacky T-shirt shops, and cheap motels. They raised the familiar bugaboo of Myrtle Beach, Hilton Head's favorite place to disdain, and decried the damage wrought by mass tourism to the island's image, property values, and future development patterns. They had no interest in resort activities; they lived in Long Cove, Wexford, Hilton Head Plantation, and other developments that were not resorts. Many were against anything that promised more tourists—motels, commercial development, new roads, airport improvements, beach rebuilding, cultural attractions, and sporting events.

PROPERTY OWNERS AND PLANTATIONS

While Hilton Head grew and settlers became unhappier, plantation residents were dramatically increasing control over their communities. The most striking case, of course, was Sea Pines, which was acquired in 1987 by property owners. Elsewhere residents had more power than ever before, operating community services or sharing the direction of plantation activities with development companies. Increases in the influence of property owners further diminished the power of plantation companies on the new Hilton Head, lessening their freedom of action and reducing the scope of matters under their authority. Private control by profit-seeking companies was supplanted, in most instances, by transfer of communal responsibilities to property owners' associations. Property owners at Port Royal, Shipyard, and Wexford emerged from bankruptcy owning roads, lagoons, bike paths, and open spaces as well as providing security, architectural review, and enforcement of covenants. At purely residential Wexford, homeowners also acquired the golf course, tennis courts, and clubhouse, leaving only unsold property in private hands.

Shifting activities from private companies to property owners reflected business considerations as well as residential desires for more authority. Maintaining infrastructure and operating services generally was an unprofitable headache for plantation companies and became an increasing liability as land sales moved toward completion. To insure that burdens would be assumed by property owners, and to avoid the disputes that plagued Sea Pines, developers organized the newer plantations under arrangements that progressively increased residential responsibilities as the community developed. Covenants at Hilton Head Plantation provided greater representation of property owners and transfer of community services as the number of residents grew. By 1988 residents controlled the community association board and had taken over security, roads, and common spaces. Long Cove Club provided for transfer of communal facilities as part of basic agreements once a specified number of lots had been sold.

For property owners, taking over these activities brought increased costs—about a million dollars annually at Wexford, for example—which dampened the enthusiasm of some residents for community control. Still, most residents were eager to assume community services. They wanted control over access to their plantations and security within the gates; they wished to operate recreational facilities in the interest of members rather than according to company needs; and they wanted to determine priorities for services and improvements. These new arrangements were not the dawn of a new age of harmony in Hilton Head's private communities. Residents disagreed among themselves on all sorts of matters, and conflicts were common as property owners sought to set priorities, fees, and policies. Nevertheless, most residents strongly preferred to make their own decisions about community life rather than have them made by private companies.

Ownership brought residents the fullest measure of control. Residential ownership was most advanced at Moss Creek, on the mainland, where property owners collectively held the plantation through their association. By contrast, at Sea Pines, only those who had invested in Sea Pines Associates shared in ownership of the plantation's nonresidential properties. Sea Pines Associates had development and resort interests that were not shared by all residents or every shareholder. Nonetheless, the Sea Pines Associates was a residents' organization created to secure control over the plantation by property owners. Almost half of the plantation's permanent residents owned stock in Sea Pines Associates, and the new regime emphasized that "the plantation truly is under the control of the property owners."[24]

Once in control, Sea Pines Associates concentrated on restoring the plantation. Maintenance was upgraded, landscaping reworked, and an ambitious program of capital improvements launched. For the first time in years, money was invested in Sea Pines by an organization whose principal concern was operating the plantation. Restoring the plantation was designed to benefit both residents and Sea Pines' resort business. Income from resort activities was essential to repay Sea Pines Associates' $18 million debt and generate funds to reinvest in the plantation. To bolster its resort business, Sea Pines Associates built a new stadium for the Family Circle tennis tournament and pondered developing another golf course to attract more visitors. Also included in the resort plans was the controversial hotel that had aroused passions in the past; and here residential concerns clashed most directly with resort needs. Sea Pines Associates proceeded cautiously. Shareholders were assured that "if any inn is to built, it would be low-key, low-profile, high-quality."[25]

Many residents were unconvinced that this new recipe was any more palatable than previous versions served up by Charles Fraser, Vacation Resorts, and Bobby Ginn. Now, however, residents owned the plantation. Criticism was muted because Sea Pines Associates, unlike previous owners, was not interested primarily in resort operations or real estate development. A new hotel, larger resort facilities, and more tourists were means to the end of residential control of the plantation. Because residents owned the company, Sea Pines was more sensitive to residential concerns; because they were owners, many residents were more sympathetic to the need for resort operations. Opposition to decisions that troubled residents was further diffused by the abundant evidence that the new regime was devoted to making Sea Pines a better place to live. Money was being poured into the plantation; Sea Pines looked and functioned better than it had before. Among the improvements was a new $4.6 million Sea Pines Country Club for residents, complete with spacious clubhouse, tennis courts, swimming pools, and exercise facilities.

Sea Pines demonstrated the feasibility of residential ownership of an established large-scale planned community with extensive resort activities. Sea Pines Associates not only survived but prospered; by its second year the company was operating in the black, showing a net income in 1989 of $277,000 on revenues of $29.5 million.[26] The new Sea Pines was conservative, predictable, and responsive, which was what most residents wanted. The approach was derivative rather than original; restoration was the goal, and the new owners represented a logical progression from the creative founder to conserving residents. The overriding goal was to put Sea Pines in the hands of its residents; beyond that the new regime was content to be caring caretakers, moving cautiously to preserve and modernize within the framework of what Charles Fraser had created. Sea Pines was also a much diminished player on Hilton Head. Once the most expansive and outward looking of the island's enterprises when Fraser ruled the roost, Sea Pines was now preoccupied with minding the store. As a result, the new Sea Pines had limited influence on the island's business community and little political clout on Hilton Head or beyond.

Aside from Moss Creek, where property owners controlled everything, changes on the plantations produced mixed systems of ownership. At Sea Pines, Charles Fraser and Avron Fogelman owned substantial chunks of the plantation as a result of deals with Ginn, Hilton Head Holdings, and others. Fraser's continued role at Sea Pines was a source of conflict and controversy. Residents successfully opposed his proposal for a private beach club at the site of the only public facilities along the southern half of Sea Pines' beach. Fraser's next venture was miniature golf on land within the plantation that he had been trying to sell to the Sea Pines Community Services Association. Property owners predictably went berserk at the thought of miniature golf in Sea Pines. Over 200 marched in protest, carrying signs that said, "Just Say No to Charles," and cheered as the organizer read a manifesto that proclaimed, "We, the owners and residents, don't want this to happen. We . . . are the stockholders of Sea Pines Associates," and we "want this development stopped."[27] Fraser wound up selling both properties to the Community Services Association; his proposals, although unsuccessful, demonstrated the threat posed by outside control of the remaining developable land, even in a plantation that residents owned.

More substantial were the holdings of Fogelman Properties, including much of Harbour Town and the Plantation Center in the middle of Sea Pines. Fogelman concentrated on Harbour Town and invested far more in the plantation's centerpiece than was feasible for Sea Pines Associates.[28] He pumped $25 million into dredging the harbor, replacing the docks, installing wave and siltation barriers, and renovating shops and other properties. Sea Pines Associates and plantation residents were delighted with the rebirth of Harbour Town and with Fogelman, who assured property owners that "each associate of Fogelman Properties in Sea Pines knows they have a responsibility to the entire community—to you the homeowner."[29] But soon Fogelman was giving cause for concern as the real estate market went sour in 1989 and debts and obligations to investors, estimated at $290 million, caused a sharp contraction in his operations. Gamely, Fogelman held on to Harbour Town, but the uncertainty that was an inherent part of private real estate operations was unsettling to Sea Pines residents, who thought they had insured a stable future when they acquired the plantation.

Entanglements with private firms were even more troublesome on the former Hilton Head Company plantations. Marathon wound up as the reluctant owner of substantial properties at Port Royal, Shipyard, and Wexford. Lingering disputes arising from the bankruptcy prevented Marathon from selling these properties until the fall of 1988; the new owner then turned around and resold them in a profitable move that indicated that musical chairs were still part of the real estate game on Hilton Head.[30] After the players were back in their seats, Wexford's 185 lots and some other assets belonged to Gaelic Properties. Most of the principals in the $20 million purchase were Wexford property owners, who promised residents stability after six changes in ownership in six years. Gaelic Properties embarked on a $400,000 campaign to market Wexford to rich people and sold one-third of the lots in its first four months of operation. Still, the arrangement was less satisfactory than having control vested more widely in residents as at Sea Pines.

Marathon's properties at Port Royal and Shipyard went to Fogelman, who paid $30 million to expand his foothold in the booming resort business on Hilton Head with the plantations' golf courses and tennis clubs. As he had done at Harbour Town, Fogelman planned to finance Port Royal and Shipyard by selling limited partnerships, then to make money for his partners by raising rates, increasing resort use, and negotiating more lucrative golf and tennis contracts with hotels and rental agencies. But the $37 million issue went on the market as Fogelman's financial problems were intensifying, forcing him finally to abandon the deal and sell his holdings. This round of musical chairs left the properties in the hands of a new owner, from Charleston, who arrived with familiar words of reassurance: "Hilton Head Island has some of the finest golf and tennis facilities in the country and we intend to make sure it stays that way. All our efforts will be concentrated on long-term objectives."[31] With three owners in a year, residents of Port Royal and Shipyard could be forgiven for being skeptical about talk of long-term objectives. Constant turnover and uncertainty increased the attractions of owner control at both plantations. Shipyard's property owners sought to buy the golf course and racquet club from Marathon, but their $8 million offer was not "even in the right league."[32] At Port Royal, owners tried unsuccessfully to block the sale by Fogelman in court, arguing that the plantation's covenants gave the owners' association the right to match the highest bid for properties; but they remained unwilling to muster the resources needed to buy more complete control over their community.

Control over plantations was only part of what residents—particularly retired residents—wanted as the new Hilton Head grew. They also sought to check growth, using the new municipal government that islanders created in 1983 to provide public regulation of private development. The public agenda was determined largely by surging resort and commercial growth along with a rapidly expanding population. The major development companies were less influential in this economy, supplanted by resort businesses and plantation residents in the more plural politics of the new Hilton Head. Settlers, however, found that controlling local government was a good deal more difficult than running their plantations. "Residents of Sea Pines are in a state of euphoria now that they have taken over their plantation," wrote one resident four years after incorporation. "Now, if island residents can only take over town government."[33]

NOTES

1. Phipps Land Company, as noted in chapter 4, was a subsidiary of Bessemer Securities Corporation.

2. Onorato and Fraser had hoped to purchase Phipps' holdings for themselves but had been unable to finance the deal, so they arranged the purchase by Greenwood for a fee of $400,000. Not long after the purchase, Onorato resigned from Palmetto Dunes.

3. Quoted in Callahan, "'The Godfather' of Palmetto Dunes," 22–23.

4. The number of households was calculated by the 1990 ratio of 2.29 people per household.

5. There were 17,740 occupied dwelling units in 1985, 7,551 of which were occupied more than six months of the year. In 1990 the totals were 21,470 and 10,256.

6. Jack Barry, vice-president of sales and marketing, Haig Point Plantation, quoted in Sander, "Driving Force."

7. Long Cove's principals were David Ames, Joseph Webster III, and Weston Wilhelm, all of whom had been vice-presidents at Sea Pines. After leaving Sea Pines, they formed Development Associates in 1976, working on Hilton Head Plantation and some projects in Sea Pines and Forest Beach. Ames was the planner; Wilhelm was the builder; and Webster was in charge of finance, marketing, and operations.

8. The partners paid $6.6 million for the property in 1980, with 20 percent down and the rest on a note to Oxford First that was paid off in five years. Ames, Wilhelm, and Webster created Long Cove Club Associates Limited Partnership to develop the property. Of the 660 acres, 614 were developed as Long Cove Club and the rest as commercial property along the main highway.

9. *Golf Digest* consistently ranked Long Cove Club as the best course in South Carolina and among the top twenty-five in the United States.

10. The site for Windmill Harbour, along with 84 additional acres on Jenkins Island and two parcels in Shipyard Plantation, cost $4.9 million.

11. James N. Richardson ran the Windmill Harbour Company. Richardson, the son of island pioneers Lois and Norris Richardson, also operated the family's Coligny Plaza shopping center.

12. Ames, interview. David Ames was involved in planning Hilton Head Plantation while he worked for Sea Pines and afterwards as a consultant.

13. Davis was hired at the end of 1976. The relationship with Sea Pines was terminated in 1978. Before coming to Hilton Head Plantation, Davis had been involved in developing seaside properties in Mexico, a ski village in Colorado, and a large residential community in Bloomfield Hills, outside Detroit.

14. James P. Coleman had been a senior vice-president of Hilton Head Plantation; Robert T. Kolb had been vice-president of marketing; and Steven B. Kiser had been with Sea Pines and Hilton Head Plantation.

15. Bob Gerhart, vice-president, Melrose Corporation, quoted in Hill, "Melrose Plans Change in Name for Indigo Run."

16. The data are for 1984, but the proportions remained relatively constant throughout the decade. See Gardo, Doughtie and Rose, "Hilton Head Business and Employment Survey."

17. The Inter-Continental was acquired in 1988 by Westin Hotels and Resorts and renamed the Westin Resort at Port Royal Plantation. The Mariners Inn became part of the Hilton chain in 1992; its name was changed to the Hilton Head Island Hilton Resort. Also in 1992 the Marriott was sold to Holiday Inn-Worldwide Corporation and became the Crystal Sands Holiday Inn Crowne Plaza Resort.

18. The program was organized by promoters at the Port Royal Racquet Club and the Hilton Head Beach and Tennis Resort and was sponsored by Rossignol Tennis USA, a French manufacturer of tennis equipment, whose marketing and sales operation for the United States was located on Hilton Head.

19. See Hilton Head Island Chamber of Commerce and Town of Hilton Head Island, "Hilton Head Island Commercial Information Packet," pt. 4, 6.

20. Albert Branham, manager, Red Roof Inn, quoted in Van Amberg, "Budget-Priced Island Lodging."

21. Hilton Head Island Chamber of Commerce, "Media Facts."

22. Bernier, letter to the editor. Carol Bernier was president of the Resident Home Owners' Coalition, a group dominated by retired residents. It is discussed in the next chapter.

23. Al Ceratti, quoted in Eyre, "The Quest for the Perfect Mall."

24. David N. Axene, president, Sea Pines Plantation Company, quoted in Felder, "ASPPPO Announces Steps to Collect Delinquent Fees." Axene had run the Hilton Head Company for Marathon; Sea Pines Plantation Company was the operating arm of Sea Pines Associates.

25. Axene, quoted in Felder, "Axene: Sea Pines Associates, Inc. Alive and Well."

26. In 1988, its first full year, Sea Pines Associates registered a loss of $174,000 on revenues of $28 million. Profits were $714,000 in 1990 and $672,000 in 1991.

27. LaVera Nagle, quoted in Richards, "Ralliers Decry Sea Pines Mini-Golf."

28. Fogelman sold the Plantation Center to Sea Pines Associates for $2.8 million soon after residents purchased the plantation.

29. Avron Fogelman, "No Plans to Sell Major Assets."

30. The purchaser was Robert A. Kathary, whose firm was R.A.K. Development in Pittsburgh.

31. George S. Way Jr., president, the Beach Company, quoted in Richards, "Kiawah Partner to Buy Amenities from Fogelman." The Beach Company was involved in developing Kiawah Island and the Wild Dunes Resort outside Charleston.

32. Charles Duggan, Shipyard Plantation Landowners Association, quoted in Richards, "Shipyard Approaching 'Build-Out.'"

33. Grush, letter to the editor.

Chapter Thirteen

Preserving Paradise

Incorporation is not going to solve, by itself, the problems of growth. Don't look to incorporation as the answer to all our maiden's prayers.

—Donald Bennett, quoted by Chris Porter
in the *Island Packet,* November 9, 1982

The Town of Hilton Head Island was created to control growth. Those islanders who supported incorporation wanted a limited government whose raison d'être was preserving their paradise. The new municipality was launched in the midst of the sweeping changes that were shaping the new Hilton Head. Tourism was booming, population was expanding rapidly, and new construction was everywhere in the summer of 1983. Spawned by dissatisfaction with Beaufort County's response to surging development, the town government would be preoccupied with growth. Islanders expected their officials to employ planning and land use controls to check ugly development, impose high standards, maintain natural beauty, and preserve the environment. Their model was the plantations—well-planned private communities with pleasing landscapes, tasteful buildings, and high architectural standards. They sought to extend the rigid private controls imposed by development companies into the public realm.

These expectations were unrealistic, especially given the economic and political forces that were changing Hilton Head. Planning, design, and environmental standards on plantations were higher than those resulting from public controls almost anywhere in the nation. The Town of Hilton Head Island was a government rather than a private landowner. Its top officials were elected by and responsive to a diverse constituency. The town was also constrained by state and national law, especially by the constitutional protections afforded private property. Moreover, growth pressures unleashed by the burgeoning tourist economy created insistent demands for more intensive development outside plantations. Under the most favorable circumstances, Charles Fraser and the private standards set by Sea Pines would be tough acts for Hilton Head's new government to follow.

Incorporation also came fairly late in the development of the island, as is often the case in areas undergoing rapid growth. Hilton Head's future had been determined largely by private developers and complacent county officials. On the eve of the island's incorporation, almost 11,000 of its 23,000 usable acres were developed; another 8,600 acres were covered by private plans ratified by the county planning commission (see table 13.1).[1] Over 36,000 approved residential units, more than twice as many as had existed on Hilton Head in 1983, were inherited by the town, along with large amounts of approved commercial space. The new town was also bound by covenants attached to property that had been developed by plantation companies. Thus the government created to control growth inherited a limited set of opportunities; only one-sixth of the developable land on the island—less than 3,600 acres—was up for grabs.

Table 13.1
Status of Developable Land on Hilton Head Island, 1982

	Amount in Acres	Percent of Total Acreage
Developed	10,772	46.9
Undeveloped: covered by plantation master plans	8,619	37.5
Undeveloped: outside plantations	3,583	15.6
Total	22,968	100.0

Source: Beaufort County Joint Planning Commission, *The Hilton Head Island Land Use Plan*, 35.

Beyond these constraints, expectations were based on unrealistic assumptions about consensus on controlling growth. Many islanders believed they could overcome internal differences through creation of their own municipality. The alliance between settler and business interests that secured local autonomy enhanced the notion of consensus on growth policy. Plantation residents, development companies, and major resort operators did agree on the desirability of good design, environmental sensitivity, and control of externalities. Consensus, however, quickly dissipated when it came to translating general preferences into specific policies. The main difference was over whether growth was desirable; the central issues were whether Hilton Head should grow more or less and whether growth should be accommodated or restrained by government. Growth became the fundamental political fault line in the newly independent town, dividing Hilton Head into two general camps: those who wanted to use local power to limit development and those who saw government's primary role as harmonizing growth. Many retired residents were in the first group; most working residents, landowners, the local newspaper, and businesses were in the second.

Conflict over growth was intensified by the pace of change. The new government inherited a boomtown with a rapidly increasing population, rising numbers of tourists, a blizzard of new development, sharp increases in traffic, and mounting demands for more public services. New residents poured onto Hilton Head, increasing the diversity of the population, diluting the influence of established leaders, and straining further the tenuous connections between residential and business interests, retirees and working islanders, whites and blacks. Settlers who had escaped from cities and suburbs to what they believed to be a paradise were dismayed that accelerating growth had turned Hilton Head into an urban area with urban problems, and they were appalled at predictions that the island's population could exceed 50,000 by the turn of the century.

CONFLICTING INTERESTS

Among islanders, retired plantation residents were the most troubled by rampaging growth and the most insistent that town government restrict development. Incorporation was their victory. They looked on the new municipality as their instrument, and their primary political interest was in using local autonomy to control growth. Few settlers were against all growth, but the vast majority wanted less growth and careful regulation to insure high-quality development. Retired plantation dwellers did not agree on how to slow growth or insure quality development; still, they had the most unambiguous stake in strict controls, and they formed the core of the slow-growth movement on Hilton Head.

Retired residents also formed a potent political force in the new municipality, even though their portion of the electorate declined as a booming economy increased the ranks of working residents. Settlers were better organized, more involved in local affairs, and more likely to vote than other islanders. Retirees had experience and time to get involved; they dominated community organizations and homeowners' associations; they were overrepresented among candidates for local office and were active participants in the plethora of commissions, committees, boards, and task forces spawned by the new government. Each of Hilton Head's first four mayors was a settler whose political base rested on fellow retirees, as was the sixth, who was elected in 1993. Sixty percent of the individuals elected to the council between 1983 and 1993 were retired or semiretired.[2]

Growth issues were retirees' principal interest in local politics. Retired residents on Hilton Head were not organized politically around a "gray" agenda dealing with issues of particular concern to the elderly.[3] What was special about their political role was their intense interest in maintaining what had attracted them to Hilton Head. Politics in the new town was shaped by the disappointment of many retirees with the government they had created to preserve paradise. They were unhappy about the failure of town officials to move swiftly to restrict growth and outraged by the responsiveness of local officials to business interests. Many retirees saw business influence behind everything, a sinister, all-pervading web of interests that tainted the town council, planning commission, and candidate selection. "The island, since it was incorporated," insisted an outspoken settler, "has been in the hands of special interest groups," and "the town is basically controlled by the Chamber of Commerce."[4]

Settlers demanded strict land use controls accompanied by development standards that would protect the island's natural beauty, fragile environment, and special character. Retirees strongly opposed additional commercial development, motels, and outlet stores. Some rejected the need for a cross-island expressway, arguing that more road capacity would only intensify growth pressures. They attacked projects that would bolster the resort industry, including the cultural center, museum, and beach restoration. Disaffected settlers began to organize soon after incorporation to advance their political interests. Of the new organizations, most durable was the Resident Home Owners Coalition, which attracted members primarily from retired plantation residents.[5] The organization closely monitored town meetings, published a newsletter, polled its members on growth and other issues, and endorsed candidates in town elections. The coalition represented itself as the voice of residents, though its membership never exceeded 700, few working islanders joined, and the group did not speak for retirees of more moderate persuasion.

Growing frustration with local officials turned many settlers to plebiscitary politics. "Let the people decide" became their motto, and their activism led to a series of campaigns for referendums on growth controls and related issues. Soon after incorporation, impatient residents circulated petitions in an unsuccessful effort to put a proposal on the ballot to halt building until new development rules were adopted. Three years later the town's seemingly endless process of crafting growth controls spurred a referendum on a temporary moratorium on new construction. The campaign was organized by a Sea Pines settler who "felt the council and the government were not controlling growth and that was the whole reason for incorporation."[6] Approved by island voters in 1986, the moratorium had its intended effect as the town council quickly enacted comprehensive land use legislation. Emboldened by this success and disappointed with the new controls, antigrowth activists sought public approval for a general moratorium on development. A long and bitter struggle ensued that divided Hilton Head into warring camps and resulted in defeat for the no-growthers by a coalition of business interests, elected officials, blacks, working islanders, and moderates among retirees. Despite this setback, dissident settlers continued to insist that the public should decide important questions. Growth politics became a struggle over process as well as policies as opponents fought unsuccessfully for public votes on a lengthening list of issues.

Business interests were the principal adversaries of slow-growth settlers as Hilton Head wrestled with development issues in the years after incorporation. Developers, resort operators, and the *Island Packet* emphasized the benefits of growth and the need for balanced policies that would sustain the island's economy. Business, however, was neither a cohesive force nor an omnipotent one. The resort industry was divided between its class components and mass components, with plantation and hotel operators favoring public restrictions on motels and other development that would dilute Hilton Head's cachet as an exclusive resort. Developers also had conflicting interests; home builders sought to differentiate their projects from large commercial and condominium schemes that troubled residents, arguing that it was "grossly unfair to penalize local builders" when "the tourist industry . . . is mostly responsible for the strain on our roads and environment."[7] Many merchants and professionals were reluctant to offend their retired customers by supporting pro-growth policies; moreover, many people were in business on Hilton Head because of its residential attractions and favored more stringent public controls to protect the environment and quality of life.

Business also labored under the burden of unpopularity, which made anything supported by developers and the Chamber of Commerce suspect for many residents. Once the heroes of Hilton Head, developers had become the enemy. "Greedy developers touched down here like the plague," wrote a settler sounding a common theme; "everything they touched turned into a motel, hotel, fast-food restaurant, shopping plaza or mall and asphalt."[8] Business expected more understanding in a place populated by thousands of retired capitalists, but many settlers changed their identification when they began their new life on Hilton Head. Once former industrialists had tirelessly battled BASF to protect their paradise from outside invaders; now retired bankers and lawyers fought developers and resort operators who threatened their domain from within.

Distrust of business strongly influenced local electoral politics. Despite his central role in the business-settler coalition that engineered incorporation, John

Curry was decisively whipped in 1983, garnering less than a quarter of the votes as retirees overwhelmingly supported a fellow settler.[9] According to Curry, "the initial election set the pattern in which those perceived to favor growth were at a substantial political disadvantage."[10] Business leaders fretted over the success of settlers at the polls and the predominance of retired residents on town commissions and committees. In practice, however, electoral handicaps were a minor annoyance rather than a major obstacle to business's influence on growth policies in the new municipal government. Developers, landowners, resort executives, builders, lawyers, and architects infested the planning commission and other local agencies, where they supported more development, less stringent standards, and a regulatory system that accommodated rather than constrained growth.[11] This outcome was not surprising in a community where development and tourism were the major industries, despite the dismay of antigrowth settlers over having foxes mind the henhouse. Business owners, executives, professionals, and other working people had as legitimate a stake in local growth policies as retired residents, although settlers insisted that economic self-interest was incompatible with service local government agencies.

Business influence was further legitimated by the nature of the American political economy and the interdependence of public and private spheres. As in most jurisdictions, Hilton Head's elected officials sought to maintain a good business climate in order to attract investment, create jobs, and generate taxes. "Growth is the natural order of things," insisted one settler elected to the council in 1987. "Managing it, control, those are the issues—not whether to have it."[12] The business-growth-taxes link became increasingly important as the town government took on expanded responsibilities. Visions of big tax dollars helped convince officials to plan for a regional shopping center on the island's north end despite widespread opposition to commercial development.

Business also benefited from the fact that developers and resort operators had produced good as well as bad effects on Hilton Head. The image of greedy developers raping the island was a blatant oversimplification at variance with the reality of Sea Pines and other plantations. More than in most places, private enterprise on Hilton Head had planned well, designed attractively, and preserved a good deal of the natural setting. Fair-minded settlers wanted less growth and more effective controls on ugly development, but they also understood that much of what they loved about Hilton Head was the work of Charles Fraser and other gifted private entrepreneurs. As a result, many settlers listened when business warned that excessive controls would drive away the kind of developers who had created Sea Pines, Long Cove, and the other planned communities.

Economic interests were championed by a relatively small proportion of the working population. The most active participants were company executives, owners of larger firms, and successful professionals. Other working islanders were no more active in the local public arena than were ordinary citizens anywhere in the United States, and perhaps less so, considering the pleasant diversions offered by the ocean, golf courses, and tennis courts. Relatively few working residents voted or attended public meetings, certainly in comparison with the high participation rates of retirees. Many were newcomers, lacking connections to the island's civic, community, and political circles. As a result, working residents were a sleeping giant politically, not easily roused but steadily increasing in size and voting potential as the population doubled during the 1980s.

Standing apart from both settlers and business interests, as they had from the earliest efforts of the Frasers and Hacks, were Hilton Head's blacks. They had unsuccessfully opposed development regulation and incorporation; now they feared they would lose control over their land in a new political system in which their influence was steadily diluted as Hilton Head's population grew and an economy dominated by whites expanded rapidly. In 1980 African Americans accounted for 13 percent of the island's permanent residents; a decade later, the proportion had dropped to 8 percent. Yet this diminishing minority owned about two-thirds of the land not covered by past permits, and it was thus most affected by land use controls imposed by the town. Native islanders continued to see development issues and growth politics in racial terms. Whites had taken their profits and fenced off the plantations; now the white majority was using its political muscle to deny blacks their rightful share of the island's development bounty.

White Hilton Head sought to mollify black concerns about being frozen out of the new governing and planning arrangements. District lines were carefully drawn to insure that blacks would be able to elect a member of the town council, and blacks were represented on the planning commission and other agencies.[13] But black islanders did not play leading roles in the new town government or in formulating land use policies. Plantation residents and business interests dominated the commissions and committees that studied problems, set agendas, and recommended policies and programs. Blacks were on the outside looking in, as they had feared they would be under incorporation. They were dealing with people who often viewed them as inconvenient or obstructionist. And they were faced with a complicated governmental system that proliferated agencies, rules, fees, and bureaucracy, in the process stacking the deck against poor people, many of whom had little formal education and had only muddled titles to their land. "Now we live in a town where we seem not to exist," complained a black leader. "About the only thing you can get plenty of from the Town of Hilton Head is red tape."[14]

Blacks favored an expanding local economy and opposed growth controls. On the town council and planning commission, African Americans generally supported developers and resort expansion. They joined working islanders and business interests in opposing growth moratoriums supported by plantation dwellers. Their primary political concern, however, was retaining control over their land. Settlers' pressure on the town government for strict controls brought black owners together to defend their interests collectively. Under the banner of the Parallel Property Owners Association, they hired a planner and attorney to prepare a development scheme for their 3,100 acres, permitting high-density residential and commercial development. Uniting behind the plan, black land-owners gained the upper hand in the bargaining that produced the town's land management law. Surprised by the black initiative and unwilling to use raw political power to prevail over native islanders, white leaders accepted their zoning plan. In so doing, local officials defused the most explosive racial issue facing the new town government. At the same time, the town acquiesced in development of the outparcels at relatively high densities, thus undermining one of the prime purposes of incorporation and further frustrating settlers who wanted their town to stop growth.

GRAPPLING WITH GROWTH

Hilton Head's new municipality attempted to sort out the conflicting demands of settlers, business, and blacks under difficult circumstances. A government had to be organized and growth policies devised as developers continued to unveil new projects. Everything took longer than expected. Elected officials were political neophytes who had to learn on the job; they spent three months choosing a town manager from hundreds of applicants, and then more time passed before the manager hired a planning staff. Until planners were on board, work could not begin on a comprehensive plan that was required under state law before the town could enact land use controls. Meanwhile, Hilton Head attempted to cope with growth by using interim controls based largely on the inadequate county development standards that had prompted incorporation.

The town also inherited developments that the county had approved before incorporation, some in the mad rush for permits that preceded creation of the new municipality. Residents, expecting rapid action to halt undesirable development, were dismayed by the unwillingness of town officials to reverse county actions. The town's impotence in dealing with projects approved by the county fueled the impression that local officials were betraying their constituents, failing to carry out the mission of the new government, and caving in to developers. Town officials reinforced these impressions when they continued to approve new projects under weak interim development controls. Critics questioned whether incorporation made any difference, especially since the town appeared as permissive as the county in applying minimal standards.

Bogged down in processing complicated and contentious projects, town hall had little time for developing comprehensive land policies. Work on a comprehensive plan did not begin until well into 1984. Further delays became inevitable when town officials decided to engage outside consultants to prepare the plan and then opted for a complicated approach to development regulation requiring extensive research. As months stretched into years without the promised controls on development, Hilton Head's elected officials found their position increasingly uncomfortable. Most owed their office to the support of retired residents who expected growth to be slowed, and they had run on platforms that promised action. Once ensconced in town hall, they found that regulating development was much more difficult than Hilton Head had anticipated. Government moved slowly. State laws had to be obeyed and constitutional rights respected. They were particularly impressed by legal constraints on public regulation of development. Residents, impatient with the pace of government and legal complexities, chafed at repeatedly being told that government cannot deprive property owners of the right to develop their land without a valid constitutional reason. They asked, "We read about the rights of developers who purchased property as an investment and wish to develop it. Does that mean the residents have no rights?"[15]

Efforts to respond to these constituency concerns underscored the difficulties of devising effective measures that were legally and politically acceptable. By mid-1984, residents were clamoring for measures to stem the flood of development that was being permitted by town government. Support came from the Hilton Head Island Community Association, the League of Women Voters, the Resident Home Owners Coalition, and property owners' organizations in plantations. Reacting to these demands, the council considered an emergency zoning ordinance that would sharply reduce residential densities.[16] The measure was adamantly opposed by the Chamber of Commerce, plantation companies, and other resort and development interests that insisted that any changes should await completion of the comprehensive plan. Black landowners were outraged by the efforts of white plantation residents to restrict their property rights. By the time the smoke cleared, the density restriction was eliminated, as was a time limit on permits, which developers also opposed. What was left were new requirements for commercial developments in residential areas and other minor changes, a package that fell far short of satisfying those who had pressed for stringent regulations.

Grappling with issues like the emergency ordinance made elected officials far more sensitive to Hilton Head's political, economic, and social diversity than their constituents in the plantations. Business, working residents, and black landowners had to be taken into consideration in developing growth controls; and doing so made issues more complex, politics more conflictual, and solutions less satisfactory to retired plantation dwellers. Dealing with these realities made local political life more arduous than most islanders had anticipated. Dropout rates for elected officials were high, especially among retirees who began their political careers at advanced ages.[17] Rapid turnover and contentious constituencies produced a local government that tended not to shape events but rather to be shaped by them.

The promised means of molding the future was Hilton Head's comprehensive plan. To devise the blueprint, town officials hired John Rahenkamp, an innovative planner based in Philadelphia. For Rahenkamp and his associates, Hilton Head offered a unique opportunity to plan on the basis of carrying capacity. Growth would be limited by the capacity of the island's natural systems and public services to support additional development. Rahenkamp's comprehensive plan was approved at the end of 1985. Then, working from his concepts, the town's planners proposed growth management regulations featuring impact zoning and growth caps that substantially reduced development permitted under existing rules. Doubts about the legal viability of this approach led the town council to seek advice from lawyers familiar with the treatment of land use regulations by the courts in South Carolina. Try something more conventional, they counseled; impact zoning would be very risky because the conservative state courts had no experience with such measures. Town officials were also advised that cutting back development that was covered by plantation master plans and county preliminary approvals would be highly vulnerable to judicial challenge. Their fears confirmed, town officials abruptly switched gears, embracing growth controls based on the capacity of the road system.[18] Packaged with the growth controls was conventional zoning that bolstered the legal credibility of the land management ordinance, presenting the courts with a familiar method of regulation backed by a substantial body of case law.

Throughout this process, developers and other business people pressed for weaker growth controls. Never happy with Rahenkamp, business argued that his carrying capacities were defined so strictly that future growth would be severely limited and that his approach was too subjective for developers who needed "definite rules to play by."[19] What they really wanted was rules designed by developers, and business persistently pressed for weaker regulations. Developers and their lawyers helped convince town officials that impact controls were too risky, and the land law was rewritten by a joint town council–planning commission committee top-heavy with development people.[20] The business segment was much more comfortable with the final product than it had been with earlier versions, especially since the town's preferred controls included neither water and sewer capacity and failed to cover commercial development.

As the land law was drafted and redrafted, the rank and file in the plantations grew increasingly restless. Residents were troubled by repeated delays that permitted developers to continue to operate under the old rules and disturbed by changes that had progressively weakened the growth controls proposed by Rahenkamp. Out of this anxiety came the Grass Roots Amendment, designed to stop development until new growth controls were enacted.[21] More than 2,400 islanders signed petitions supporting the amendment, and hundreds crowded town hall demanding action on the proposal. But the council brushed the amendment aside, insisting that the measure was neither needed nor defensible in court. Rebuffed and angered by the town's cavalier attitude, amendment supporters sought to override the council through a referendum and in the process to send a message to elected officials to pay attention to their constituents.

Underlying the campaign for the Grass Roots Amendment, as proclaimed in an election eve advertisement, was "a profound belief among Hilton Head residents island-wide that better controls are needed to slow down the run-away growth on our island."[22] Supporters of the amendment ignored arguments about legality, effectiveness, or adverse impact on business, working residents, and the island's economy. Instead they were concerned about doing something, and right away. Over two-thirds of the 4,653 islanders who turned out for the referendum in early December voted for the amendment.[23] The message had been sent. "It was a shocker," emphasized one activist, "like putting a burr in the saddle of the guy who wasn't paying attention."[24]

Seven hectic weeks after the referendum, Hilton Head finally had its comprehensive growth controls as council members unanimously approved the 252-page land management ordinance. The audience applauded, champagne was uncorked, and toasts were offered to the large cast of characters that had played parts in the long-running drama. For the *Island Packet,* the land law was "basically what incorporation was all about. It gives us self-control."[25] The new law superseded the development standards ordinance as amended by the Grass Roots Amendment; the controversial measure passed into the island's folklore, taking its place with the BASF fight and the incorporation struggle as landmarks in the struggle of good against evil.[26]

SAYING NO TO NO GROWTH

The concerns that prompted the Grass Roots Amendment persisted after enactment of the land management ordinance. Passage of the measure was supported by a wide range of interests, including the Chamber of Commerce, development companies, black landowners, the Hilton Head Community Association, the League of Women Voters, the Resident Home Owners' Coalition, and property owners' associations. But consensus on the new growth controls was thin, with different interests having very different expectations. Those who wanted more stringent regulations were least comfortable, but they decided to endorse the measure because the new law would provide more control than existing rules. Hilton Head, they concluded, would be better served by a flawed law that could be amended than by delaying further while development continued to be approved under the old ordinance.

Dissatisfaction was greatest over the treatment of commercial development in the land management ordinance. Belief that the island was overstored was widespread, and this impression was bolstered by Rahenkamp's studies, which concluded that Hilton Head had excessive retail floor space and recommended that future commercial development be keyed to the number of residential units. Caps on commercial development, many groups concluded, clearly were needed. But town officials demurred, arguing that regulating commercial building through traffic capacity could not be justified. Commercial development did not generate traffic, they asserted, but merely rearranged traffic patterns depending on the location of stores and offices. Sensitivity to potential legal challenges reinforced official reluctance.

Large numbers of residents were not persuaded by these arguments. Their daily driving adventures on Hilton Head's congested roads convinced them that commercial development affected traffic. More stores would bring additional travel as shoppers patronized more places and additional employees drove to and from work. Furthermore, overbuilding of stores would lead merchants to lure more customers to the island. Commercial development was a major issue in the 1987 campaign, with most candidates assuring unhappy voters that something needed to be done. After the election, however, the council continued to drag its feet, worrying about the legal risks in extending rate-of-growth caps to commercial development and claiming that more information was needed. Meanwhile, commercial projects continued to be approved while settlers fumed, and their frustration fueled another uprising and a growth moratorium disarmingly called the Traffic Safety Amendment.

Critics connected growth control and traffic because Hilton Head had chosen to regulate development through traffic capacity. Caps on residential and hotel building in the land law were justified by road congestion, and further restrictions were possible if traffic movement was not maintained at "level of service D," a widely used standard that translated into a wait of two traffic lights at an intersection sufficiently congested so that traffic was moving at no more than fifteen miles per hour.[27] Legally linking growth and traffic increased the political significance of worsening road conditions. Despite the new growth controls, traffic increased more rapidly than anticipated by town planners, exceeding level D at some intersections during the summer of 1987 and adding to the clamor for action. But the increased traffic did not trigger additional building controls, since the use of level D as an explicit regulatory standard had been rejected on administrative and legal grounds. All the land law required was study by the planning commission to determine what action was needed to rectify the situation, which led to the conclusion that road improvements rather than additional development controls were the appropriate way of dealing with traffic congestion.

For those who wanted less growth, this system was useless without a mechanism for halting development when traffic congestion fell below the standard. To put teeth in the land law, a group of settlers proposed a moratorium on building permits when traffic exceeded level D. Thus was born the Traffic Safety Amendment, which was to monopolize the political stage on Hilton Head for more than a year. Its principal architect was Don Hook, a retired teacher who had served on the planning commission and town council, where he had advocated more stringent development restrictions. Hook's proposal got short shrift from town officials, who rejected the Traffic Safety Amendment. Disappointed but undaunted, Hook and his followers took their case to the people, collecting over 2,500 signatures on petitions to put the amendment on the ballot. Islanders signed petitions because they were troubled about growth, commercial development, and traffic congestion; many were disappointed with the town's efforts and wanted to send another message.

In the ensuing war of words, the amendment's opponents were easy winners. Whatever the attractions of doing something about growth and sending a message to elected officials, Hook's proposal was badly flawed. So shaky were its legal prospects that proponents were never able to find a local attorney to endorse the amendment. Compounding the measure's legal shortcomings was the risk that the town could be held responsible for financial losses resulting from denial of a development permit, a possibility that loomed large in the wake of a decision the previous year by the U.S. Supreme Court.[28] The Traffic Safety Amendment could be a very expensive message, involving huge legal costs and substantial damages, all of which would have to be underwritten by island taxpayers. Supporters of the amendment dismissed these criticisms, warning that the establishment was again foregoing effective growth controls by conjuring up the judicial bogeymen. Outside the large corps of true believers, however, the legal debate seriously damaged the amendment's credibility with people who wanted to do something about growth but shied away from a proposal that seemed likely to be laughed out of court.

Doubts multiplied as critics hammered away at the substance of the amendment. The notion of stopping all development because of traffic congestion at an intersection was effectively portrayed as overkill. Halting building was also unfair; lot owners could not build houses, homeowners would not be able to improve their dwellings, and churches and other community projects would be halted. Blacks, as usual, saw themselves as most injured because they owned so much undeveloped land, and they felt betrayed because the amendment jeopardized the guarantees they had won in the land law concerning development of their property. Critics also accused amendment advocates of recklessly imperiling the island's economy, threatening thousands of jobs and hundreds of businesses as well as the town's tax base and its ability to borrow money. Some of the harshest criticism of the amendment and its supporters came from town officials. Hilton Head's mayor used words like *unreasonable, preposterous,* and *frivolous* to describe the proposal.[29]

Opponents were gathered under the banner of the Concerned Citizens Coalition, organized and financed by the Chamber of Commerce, the Board of Realtors, and the Home Builders Association. The coalition easily outgunned proamendment forces, registering more voters, mobilizing more supporters, circulating more advertising, and spending more money. Particularly active were home builders who supplied field workers and secured help from their national association in the campaign against what Washington called "the worst damn thing we've ever seen."[30] This judgment was shared by almost all the island's most prominent citizens. The Hilton Head Cultural Council, which included many community leaders, urged members to vote against a moratorium that could prevent construction of its arts center.

Almost two-thirds of Hilton Head's voters went to the polls on May 9, 1989, and rejected the Traffic Safety Amendment by a 6,369 to 2,995 vote.[31] The proposal lost in every precinct, garnering as much as 45 percent in only one district in Sea Pines and being buried by 93 percent or more in three heavily black precincts. Traffic safety proponents were unable to enlarge their base beyond disaffected settlers on the plantations. A poll commissioned by the *Island Packet* ten weeks before the election indicated that 29 percent favored the amendment, 30 percent were opposed, and a huge 41 percent undecided, with those in favor being older, retired or semiretired, and plantation dwellers.[32] These undecided voters overwhelmingly rejected the amendment; fewer than one in ten apparently supported the moratorium. In part, this outcome reflected the political resources of the opposition as well as the weight of the arguments against the amendment. But the defeat also resulted from political weakness and miscalculation. Despite their numbers and fervor, the stop-growth forces were a minority, albeit a noisy and active one. Islanders had supported the Grass Roots Amendment because they were frustrated by governmental inaction. When faced with a more radical and problematic proposal, they balked.

After the fight over the Traffic Safety Amendment, conflict over growth shifted to the cross-island expressway. Local opposition had killed a proposed highway in 1974 that would have connected the southern portion of the island directly with the bridge to the mainland. The road proposal was revived after a study by Beaufort County indicated that additional capacity was needed to handle anticipated growth. The town government folded the highway into its comprehensive plan and staged its rate-of-growth controls over the five years needed to build the road. The commitment to build the expressway, town officials argued, was essential to protect growth controls against legal challenges, as was the promise to remove the growth quotas once the highway was completed. The uninitiated could be forgiven for being puzzled by growth controls that appeared to be right out of *Catch-22:* the expressway had to be built to insure that growth caps could be maintained, but quotas would be removed once the road was completed, thus permitting more growth that might not have occurred if road capacity had not been increased.

Underlying the conflict over the cross-island highway was the question of whether roads solved or caused growth problems. For town officials and many islanders, new roads were critically needed because of increasing congestion on the island's only artery. Growth had not been kind to U.S. 278; on an island full of carefully planned private communities, the highway was a testament to weak public development controls. Once a pleasant drive through fields and woods to the plantations on the southern end, the road became a gasoline alley of strip development, helter-skelter intersections, unplanned curb cuts, and hair-raising left turns. A growing population and more tourists overloaded the highway during rush hours and throughout the lengthening tourist season. Though the congestion was not severe compared to that in larger urban areas, this was beside the point for residents who saw traffic jams as the most obvious manifestation that their paradise was being lost to galloping urbanization, excessive development, and too many visitors. Preoccupation with traffic was reinforced by the rate-of-growth system, which emphasized the connection between road capacity and development and turned traffic worries into an obsession for some islanders, who tracked vehicle counts as nervously as hypochondriacs charting their vital signs.

On Hilton Head as elsewhere, many of those troubled by traffic congestion were understandably convinced that the answer was road improvements. Backing for the cross-island project was bolstered by concern about the need for an alternative route for hurricane evacuation and medical emergencies. The new highway appealed especially to those living on the southern portion of the island—about half the population of Hilton Head. They had the longest drives to the bridge, hospital, and public schools on the other end of Hilton Head. Because of these considerations, many residential organizations threw their weight behind the cross-island expressway, including the Community Association and homeowners' groups from Sea Pines, Shipyard, and Forest Beach.

Numerous islanders, however, came to different conclusions about roads and growth. An expressway would make Hilton Head more urban and less attractive as a resort and retirement community, they believed. The way to use roads to control growth, critics insisted, was not to build them. Intensifying these concerns was the scale of the planned cross-island expressway—6 miles of four-lane highway cutting through 175 acres of wood and marsh, soaring over Broad Creek on a bridge 65 feet high and connecting with the existing highway in a maze of ramps and elevated crossings. "What we are facing now with the proposed cross-island expressway," an irate islander warned, "makes the stack-a-shacks seem relatively insignificant."[33] And, angry opponents insisted, this was all for the benefit of developers and "business groups represented by the Chamber of Commerce that want to see more and more people pour onto the island."[34]

Certainly business interests strongly supported the cross-island expressway. By the time the climactic struggles over the cross-island were fought in 1990, the road had been endorsed by the Chamber of Commerce and local organizations representing resort operators, rental agents, home builders, mortgage lenders, insurance underwriters, architects, lawyers, and accountants. For business, the cross-island promised more tourists, better jobs, higher property values, and less time wasted in traffic jams. And best of all, as a town official explained to the local Home Builders Association, "the cross island provides an alternative to restricting growth."[35]

Basing growth control on road capacity, however, meant heavy dependence on the South Carolina Department of Highways and Public Transportation, which would build the road and thus deal with a complex bureaucracy that played its game by its own rules. Islanders found the highway agency unreliable, especially concerning the projected completion date for the expressway, the magic number on which town officials had based the rate-of-growth system. In fact, both state and town were unrealistically optimistic about the time that would be required to build the road. Local officials needed an early and firm completion date to justify their growth controls, while the Department of Highways made upbeat guesstimates to calm the impatient folks on Hilton Head even as the beginning of construction fell further behind schedule.

Every step in the complicated planning process took longer than anticipated. Locating the road was a particularly painstaking job, involving extensive hearings, negotiations, and alterations. Initially state engineers proposed plowing through black neighborhoods and widening a local road next to Sea Pines from two to seven lanes. African Americans vehemently objected to the destruction of their homes, businesses, and churches to accommodate more tourists and settlers. Sea Pines residents whose homes flanked the two-lane road collected over 1,700 signatures on petitions protesting the state's plan. Elected town officials plunged into the disputes over location, determined to minimize the road's adverse impact and reduce opposition to it. One end of the planned highway was relocated to spare most native islanders, and the road widening was limited to four lanes. Working out these changes took time, as did quibbles over the height of the bridge, preservation of trees, bike paths, and toll plazas.

By 1988 it was clear that the cross-island expressway was not going to be finished in 1991 as promised. Pushing back the completion date jeopardized the legal viability of the rate-of-growth controls. Amid talk of a possible development freeze or abandonment of caps if construction of the expressway was further delayed, the town compromised by spreading the rate-of-growth allocations over six instead of five years. To meet the new schedule, supporters pressed to tie up the loose ends of the plan and unleash the road builders. New barriers, however, were erected by the 1989 municipal election, which changed the complexion of the town council on growth issues. State plans for right-of-way acquisition still had to be locally approved, and only three of the seven members of the new council clearly favored the road.

As the council pondered plans for the road, Hilton Head's establishment lined up solidly behind the expressway, as they had against the Traffic Safety Amendment. Everything, political and business leaders insisted, had been studied, discussed, and negotiated. The island's three former mayors warned that "a retreat from the concept of the cross-island parkway will unquestionably undermine the legal basis" for the rate-of-growth controls.[36] When the council finally voted, the cross-island squeaked through by a 4 to 3 margin. To make the highway more palatable, approval was conditioned on lowering the speed limit, adding bike paths, and preserving trees and historic sites. And to protect Hilton Head's image from the tarnish of an urban expressway, the highway would be called the Cross-Island Parkway.

For opponents, the cross-island road by any name was unacceptable. Foes continued the fight in a series of actions that further delayed beginning the project. The Coalition of Expressway Opponents brought together adversely affected property owners, backers of the Traffic Safety Amendment, environmental groups, and other residents troubled by the prospect of more roads and growth.[37] The coalition sought to block the highway with a referendum. Enough islanders signed petitions to force a vote, but the town checked the referendum in court, prompting an appeal by antiexpressway forces that was eventually rejected by the state supreme court. These moves and countermoves were played to the accompaniment of another emotional debate, which polarized Hilton Head once more over growth issues. The middle of 1991, initially the projected completion date for the cross-island, passed with no ribbon-cutting ceremonies for the new parkway. A year later, following a municipal election in which supporters of the road won the mayoralty and five of six council seats, the Department of Highways began acquiring rights-of-way, but delays in obtaining permits and funds pushed the completion date for the road to 1998 or later.

ADJUSTING THE BALANCE

These disputes heightened town officials' concern over growth. Some of the response was political, as officeholders sought to demonstrate to unhappy constituents that they were listening. The town administration sought to undercut the Traffic Safety Amendment with tighter regulation of commercial development, hastily enacting a measure just before the referendum so that council members could claim that they had fulfilled their campaign commitments to do something about commercial growth. More than politics, however, was involved in the promises and proposals. The costs of servicing the amount of planned development loomed ever larger, as did the implications of increased demands on water supply, sewage capacity, and drainage. Property rights, legal worries, and business pressures could not change the reality that Hilton Head was an island with a limited area and a fragile environment. Its distinctive character resulted from the success of private developers in managing growth and imposing high standards on what was built inside the plantations. Agreement, at least in principle, was widespread that town government had to devise better public controls than a land management ordinance that permitted as much residential development as the old rules.

Hilton Head's revised comprehensive plan foresaw about 30 percent less residential development than the 57,000 units envisaged in the 1985 plan. Most of this reduction resulted from changing market conditions, along with lessened amounts of land available for development because of highway construction, additional parking requirements, and stricter building regulations. The plan also recommended purchase of land and development rights to reduce future growth, as well as stricter controls on new motels. In 1993 Hilton Head replaced its rate-of-growth controls with tougher rules that tied regulation of most private development to road capacity.

Town officials were strengthening what, despite insistent local criticism, were already the most restrictive development regulations in South Carolina and one of the more innovative approaches to growth management in the United States. The town government had adopted and revised an imaginative and wide-reaching comprehensive plan, set high public standards for building and landscape design, enacted strict sign regulations, and approved one of the most advanced tree ordinances in the country.[38] Clearly, Hilton Head had far better control over growth at this point than it had had before incorporation, and much more effective development regulations than Beaufort County's feeble efforts on the other side of the bridge.

That these impressive accomplishments were controversial, however, is not surprising. No amount of study, data, expert advice, and hard work is likely to produce agreement on questions that raise complex political, social, economic, environmental, and legal issues. Moreover, the stakes in growth were higher on Hilton Head than in most rapidly developing places. Because Hilton Head was a world-famous resort and a highly desirable locale for retirees, there were substantial possible profits for successful developers and resort operators as well as strong concerns on the part of affluent residents about preserving the quality of life on the island. Growth increased the number of people who were concerned while widening and intensifying disagreements over land use controls and future development.

Expectations about public growth controls were unrealistic, especially considering how much development had occurred or had been permitted before incorporation. Hilton Head, like so many rapidly expanding places, adopted stringent public controls in response to growth rather than in advance of it. In a familiar pattern, constituency pressures to check growth were fed by development. By the time these pressures were sufficiently strong to secure incorporation and effective local growth controls, the development surge had peaked. This common cycle is a formula for frustration and recrimination, both of which were enhanced on Hilton Head by inflated expectations based on the previous success of private development controls.

Town officials were excessively deferential to legal constraints. Certainly the sensitivity of South Carolina courts to property rights posed a substantial concern for them, but no more so than it had for Charles Fraser when he was devising covenants that constrained individual property rights in favor of collective interests. At the slightest legal qualm, town hall backed away from innovative proposals to limit growth. By placing so much emphasis on insuring that their controls would pass judicial scrutiny, local policy makers ignored, in Fraser's view, "the clear grounds that exist for limiting growth on Hilton Head— evacuation, a limited supply of fresh water, the high cost of building roads."[39] Fear of lawsuits left town officials wary of challenging plantation master plans and other vested rights, unwilling to cap commercial building, and eager to compromise with developers to avoid adverse court rulings. Official timidity enhanced the influence of developers and their attorneys while increasing the frustration of residents who expected more creativity and courage from their elected representatives.

Legal worries were a factor also in persuading town hall to ditch the most innovative aspects of Rahenkamp's work on carrying capacity. Consequently, emphasizes one of Hilton Head's most thoughtful commentators, the plan "lost its soul," the "visionary, yet logical theorem" of "carrying capacity as the sensitivity barometer for determining growth control."[40] Vision is not the strong suit of government in the United States. Charles Fraser was a visionary, and his foresight indelibly shaped modern Hilton Head. Governments, even relatively small ones like the Town of Hilton Head Island, operate on collective agreement rather than individual judgments. They properly are responsive to their constituents, responsible under the law, and bound to respect the rules of state and nation. That people expected more vision than government could possibly deliver was not surprising on Hilton Head. Residents understandably but unreasonably expected the public sector to match the private sphere in terms of planning, aesthetics, and environmental sensitivity as practiced by Charles Fraser. At the same time, islanders wanted government responsive to their interests; and in responding, the Town of Hilton Head Island, like most governments, inevitably disappointed many citizens in its efforts to preserve paradise.

NOTES

1. Some of these plans had been formally approved, others had been exempted under the various grandfather clauses, and still others had been filed with the county before incorporation and thus were subject to consideration under county rules.

2. Of the twenty-three council members, fourteen were retired or semiretired.

3. For similar findings concerning retirees in Florida, see Rosenbaum and Button, "Is There a Gray Peril?" and Button and Rosenbaum, "Gray Power, Gray Peril, or Gray Myth?"

4. Constance Angeletti, quoted in Callahan, "Speaking Out." Angeletti, who retired to Sea Pines in 1968, was a persistent critical voice at town council meetings and in letters to local newspapers.

5. The Resident Home Owners Coalition was founded by Valborg Schaub, who retired to Palmetto Dunes in 1976 and was active in the Palmetto Dunes Property Owners Association.

6. Miriam Muldoon, quoted in Hill, "A Town Was Born, but Instant Happiness Was Not."

7. Tom Peeples, letter to the editor. Peeples was elected to the town council in 1990 and 1993.

8. Connie Fisher, letter to the editor.

9. The tally was 3,281 for Benjamin Racusin to 1,078 for Curry, with a third candidate receiving 103 votes. Racusin had retired to Sea Pines from a career in the Central Intelligence Agency and had served as president of the Hilton Head Island Community Association.

10. Curry, interview.

11. Among the prominent members of the planning commission with business connections were Donald Furtado, a lawyer, developer, and former Sea Pines official; Joe Harden, head of one of the island's largest construction firms; John P. Qualey, a lawyer formerly with the Hilton Head Company; Edward

Pinckney, a leading landscape architect; Charles Pigg, vice-president of Green-wood Development; and Marsha Smelkinson, vice-president of Seinsheimer Companies, a real estate development firm, and a former president of the Hilton Head Island Chamber of Commerce.

12. Russ Condit, quoted in Hill, "Russ Condit: Improve Communications First." Condit, a retired Proctor and Gamble executive who lived in Sea Pines, was reelected in 1989.

13. As required by state law, the initial council was composed of four members elected at large, and one of the four victorious candidates was a black businessman who was supported by whites eager to insure that blacks were represented on the council from the start. The restructured seven-member council had five district seats, one at-large member, and the mayor. After the 1990 census, the town moved to six districts and eliminated the at-large seat in order to maintain one district with a black majority.

14. Thomas C. Barnwell Jr., quoted in Littlejohn, "Businessman, NAACP Head Remembers Island's Past."

15. Frank Barbieri, letter to the editor.

16. The emergency proposal capped densities at 4 units per acre. Under the existing rules, densities of up to 16 units per acre were permitted.

17. Each of the first three mayors, all retired residents, stepped down after serving a single two-year term. The fourth mayor, also a retiree, was defeated in a 1991 reelection bid, as was the fifth, a retired local businessman, in 1993. Turnover on the council was also high, with only three of seventeen members serving more than one two-year term through 1991.

18. Residential building was capped at 4,250 housing units and 800 hotel rooms permitted during the five years needed to complete the cross-island expressway.

19. Walter G. Seinsheimer, president, Seinsheimer Companies, quoted in Younce, "Projections, Projects and Proposals," 32.

20. Two of the four members from the planning commission were developers, while one of the three council representatives was a planner with connections to local developers.

21. The amendment limited residential building to 4 units per acre and prohibited commercial projects within 500 feet of major roads.

22. Grass Roots Group, advertisement.

23. Turnout was 48 percent, compared with 52 percent in the previous municipal election.

24. Jerry Dunn, quoted in Hill, "Jerry Dunn Believes He Can Make a Dif-

ference." Dunn, a supporter of the amendment and president of the Spanish Wells Property Owners Association, was elected to the town council in 1987.

25. "We Must Learn from 1987, Both the Good and the Bad."

26. The Grass Roots Amendment had little affect on development during the short period of time between the referendum and enactment of the land management ordinance. A few projects were turned down because of the 500-foot provision, but the amendment itself was never directly tested in the court, although a state judge who heard a case involving a commercial project affected by the measure expressed "serious doubts that the Grass Roots Amendment could withstand even cursory constitutional scrutiny." Judge Luke N. Brown, 14th Judicial Circuit of South Carolina, quoted in Hill, "Judge Calls Grass Roots Repugnant."

27. The standards in Hilton Head's comprehensive plan were adapted from the *Highway Capacity Manual:* level A was free-flowing; level B was moving with 70 percent volumes; level C was stable with acceptable delays at 80 percent of capacity; level E was near gridlock with the road at 95 percent of capacity during peak periods; and level F was gridlock.

28. *First English Evangelical Lutheran Church v. Los Angeles County.*

29. Baumberger, "Traffic Safety Amendment Flawed in Concept, Language," and Mayor Martha Baumberger, quoted in Schulte, "Mayor Calls Traffic Safety Amendment 'Frivolous.'"

30. Tom Baker, vice-president for political affairs, National Home Builders Association, quoted in Richards, "Building Industry Facing Referendums Nationwide." The National Home Builders Association sent a political action specialist to Hilton Head and assisted with a telephone campaign.

31. Turnout was 65 percent, compared to 54 percent the preceding November and 45 percent in the Grass Roots referendum.

32. The sample was small. Of 157 respondents, only 118 indicated how they intended to vote, and the margin of error was 8 percentage points. The responses of those not intending to vote have been dropped from the percentages reported in the text. See Massey, "Poll: Most Voters Undecided on TSA Referendum."

33. Harold D. Kenney, letter to the editor.

34. Gordon Masters, letter to the editor.

35. Carey Smith, town manager, Town of Hilton Head Island, quoted in Richards, "Smith: Cross-Island Alternative to Restricting Development."

36. Racusin, Malanick, and Baumberger, "Former Mayors: Cross-Island Route is the Right Thing to Do."

37. Organizations supporting the coalition included the Resident Home Owners Coalition, Residents Opposed to the Expressway, the Committee of Concerned Citizens, Citizens for an Alternate Route, Island Community against Road Expansion, and the local chapters of the Audubon Society and NAACP.

38. Architectural controls are discussed in the next chapter. For an appraisal of the effort to preserve Hilton Head's trees, see Gale, "Hilton Head: The Canopy View."

39. Charles E. Fraser, interview, June 30, 1990.

40. Ballantine, "Cut Future Population."

Chapter Fourteen

Private and Public Communities

If we hadn't done what we did as major developers, little of value would have been created on this island. We did it out of a sense of wanting to leave a place better than we found it.

—Charles E. Fraser, Interview, April 4, 1990

One product of the endless public contention over growth and change was nostalgia for private rule by benevolent dictators. Charles Fraser's Hilton Head encouraged creativity, imagination, and spontaneity, all of which were deterred by multiplying rules, cautious bureaucracy, and endless controversy. "You could not build Harbour Town today," complains one of the island's pioneer architects; "you cannot design a work of art under local rules and officials."[1] Private development was flexible, with plans adjusted to meeting changing conditions, demands, and opportunities. Harbour Town's Quarterdeck Lounge, which became a favorite watering hole for islanders, resulted from the realization of a few Sea Pines executives that the view from the partially completed building was too good to be wasted on the harbormaster's office, and the attractive town houses that flank the eighteenth hole at Harbour Town Links were an eleventh-hour replacement for planned condominiums that were not selling. In making the changes, Sea Pines did not need planning approvals, zoning changes, or a new set of permits.

Control of land by "responsible developers," insists Charles Fraser's brother, was "more effective and more predictable than regulation subject to public pressures and changing interests."[2] Without question, conflict over public growth policies fostered uncertainty, leading to repeated land rushes as developers sought county permits before the creation of the town, and town permits under existing rules before the adoption of new controls. Enactment of the land management ordinance triggered a mad rush to reserve rights under the rate-of-growth limits. During the first day of business under the new law, developers filed requests for almost three times as many hotel rooms as would be permitted over the next five years. This "first-come first-serve approach to limiting development," in the view of another long-time island architect who preferred private controls, "undermined good design and discouraged responsible developers since the shoddy fly-by-night operators can get there first."[3]

For many islanders, particularly retirees in plantations, the good old days were also a simpler time of private communities, fewer people, and less commerce. They feared that public programs to expand roads or restore beaches would imperil the privacy of their planned communities. Large numbers were devoted to preservation of the traffic circle outside Sea Pines, an increasingly dangerous but cherished relic of the era of private community builders. Many wondered whether local government was worth the cost and controversy, particularly when the principal public goal of controlling growth proved so elusive. Creating a public realm to encompass the entire island, some argued, was a mistake, leading one unhappy settler to urge his neighbors to "consider the case for seceding from the town of Hilton Head and reforming as Sea Pines Plantation, S.C.—a private community under its own township structure."[4]

That public complexities nourished nostalgia for private realms is hardly surprising in a place so intimately shaped by private visions and power. Going back to benevolent dictatorship or retreating to local governments organized around plantations, however, were not viable options. Benevolent dictatorship failed to encompass the multiplying interests of an increasingly diverse community, and private rule could not provide the legitimacy or authority required to govern. Plantations as governments also could not encompass all responsibilities of managing Hilton Head, where an island-wide polity was a means of forging an inclusive public community from a set of private enclaves. Public Hilton Head would expand rather than contract; its decision-making processes would become more public as the island inexorably evolved its own political styles and governmental imperatives. In this process, public Hilton Head was heavily influenced by its distinctive legacy of private community building. Hilton Head's physical form, population, economy, and communal expectations were far more systematically influenced by private enterprise than in most places because of the extent of private control over community development on the island.

PLANTATION BOUND

Private community development largely set the settlement pattern on Hilton Head. Plantation plans were most influential in determining residential, recreational, and commercial locations. Architectural styles, design features, height limitations, and density patterns were developed by Fraser at Sea Pines and adapted by other plantation builders. Tree preservation, beach setbacks, blending of structures and setting, and other environmentally sensitive practices that shaped the physical character of the community were the result of private planning and design controls. At the same time, plantations chopped Hilton Head into segments that were difficult to connect. All streets within plantations were private, as were the roads built by the companies outside the gates, leaving an island as extensive as Boston with only a single thoroughfare. Plantation boundaries also divided environmentally connected areas into separate private realms, controlled by particular plans and covenants.

Exploiting and preserving Hilton Head's natural attractions, plantation builders created an economy based on development, tourism, and services that did not comfortably coexist with other industries. Much of the island's land was devoted to resort development, leaving little for additional large-scale economic activities. Smokestack industry was anathema to developers, resort operators, and residents, as was dramatically demonstrated during the battles over Victoria Bluff. Most businesses attracted to Hilton Head were closely connected to resort development and recreation. They included conference and seminar operators, diet and exercise enterprises, tennis and golf schools, and sports-related firms like Rossignol, a manufacturer of tennis equipment whose national marketing headquarters moved to Hilton Head because of the island's importance in the world of tennis. Other businesses were located on Hilton Head by people who wanted to enjoy plantation living and were electronically connected with suppliers, customers, and information. Few of these enterprises, however, employed more than a handful of people, compared to hundreds employed by each of the resort hotels or Sea Pines Plantation or the thousands of seasonal workers who served tourists every summer.

Private community development also shaped the social and political makeup of modern Hilton Head. Sea Pines and the other plantations attracted affluent retirees who provided the bulk of the residential population during modern Hilton Head's first quarter century. Plantations organized these newcomers into private rather than public communities, protected by private security guards and private land use controls. These private enclaves made strong claims on the loyalties of their residents, and their connections were reinforced as the plantations developed indigenous grassroots institutions that secured control over a lengthening list of communal activities. Substantially self-sufficient and increasingly self-governed, plantations were the primary point of reference for their residents, a potent centripetal force that influenced every aspect of community life. Private communities were the fundamental political reality on Hilton Head. Sensitivity to the concerns of residents about their private communities was embedded in a political system dominated by people who lived on plantations, as more than half the island's population, a larger proportion of its voters, and most of its political activists did. "We have to live within the constraints of the island," explained Mayor Martha Baumberger; "We have the plantations. That is the way the island is."[5] Living within the constraints meant deferring to plantation residents and companies. Town hall preferred that internal development disputes be settled privately. In the fight over Bobby Ginn's hotel plans, the planning commission refused to get involved until Sea Pines' architectural review board had acted. "We are not going to get in the middle," the commission told property owners, "between you and Ginn."[6] Deferring action on a complicated dispute involving property owners in Hilton Head Plantation, Mayor Baumberger explained that "it is a hard thing for town council to enter into any plantation differences."[7]

The plantation companies were also a powerful legacy of private community building. Greenwood and Melrose were the largest enterprises on the island; Sea Pines, despite its diminished status in later years, remained the keystone of the resort economy and the locus of the major golf and tennis tournaments. The companies maintained substantial control over their turf despite enhanced public regulation following incorporation; they were considered by most local officials to be good corporate citizens whose interests were largely coincident with those of the municipal government. As a result, the town usually accepted plantation plans as givens and deferred to the companies that developed them as designs were implemented and changed.

PRIVATE COMMUNITIES AND PUBLIC SERVICES

Large-scale private development committed Hilton Head to heavy dependence on private services and public utility districts. Paved streets, modern utilities, recreational facilities, and neighborhood policing were primarily a function of private community development. At the time of incorporation, six plantations encompassing half the island employed 100 police officers, compared to 25 county deputies for the rest of Hilton Head. Most of the public service districts and private utilities that provided water and sewers were organized by plantation companies. These arrangements gave plantation dwellers a strong vested interest in designing a local government that did not duplicate existing services. Private rather than public initiative was widely viewed as the appropriate means of providing public services. In discussing how services might be extended to Hilton Head's black neighborhoods, two architects of the town government suggested that "once these undeveloped areas are purchased for development, the funding for water and sewer service will, by necessity, be provided by the new development companies."[8]

Certainly private services and utility districts have many attractions. They tend to be cost-efficient, to match services with needs and ability to pay, and to relate costs to use. Depending on private developers also relieves local government of the burdens of extending and financing services. Such arrangements, however, are fraught with political tensions, particularly when they are used extensively and when they extend to basic public services such as police, roads, water, and sewers. Provision of public services under Hilton Head's arrangements divided the population into a well-serviced majority with access to private and utility district services and a poorly served minority dependent on minimal public services. Blacks insisted that they were being treated unequally by town government. They had no public water or sewers. They had unpaved roads, poor police protection, and severe drainage problems. "The situation is desperate," a black leader argued five years after incorporation. "Some people can't use their water supply. Some people suffer from a lack of water because there are times when their wells are out, not to mention that there's no water for fire protection there."[9]

Proposals to extend municipal services were opposed by those already served privately or by public service districts. African Americans were most affected by this political calculus, but so were white residents and businesses in areas less well served than the private communities. For example, Sea Pines residents argued that drainage improvements in Forest Beach should be financed by special assessments since similar work inside plantation gates was undertaken and funded by property owners. Conflicts over public improvements for particular areas are commonplace, especially in rapidly developing areas; what is instructive about Hilton Head is the degree to which heavy reliance on private services broadens and intensifies conflict, another legacy of private community development for succeeding public realms.

An important consequence of the private origins of public services was a multiplicity of service agencies. Five years after incorporation, nine plantation companies, four water and sewer districts, two fire districts, a rural water district, five private utilities, the county sheriff, the town government, and a few voluntary organizations were providing "municipal" services. Plantation boundaries strongly influenced organization of basic services, both for services provided directly by plantations and for those offered by utility districts or companies. Water was supplied by a different agency in each plantation, with its own wells, pumps, and distribution system. Efforts to furnish water to one of the island's black communities added another agency, the Hilton Head Rural Water District.[10] Fragmentation of public services among a variety of public and private providers is common on the American local scene, especially in rapidly developing areas lacking municipal governments. On Hilton Head, the extensiveness of private services provided by plantation companies prompted incorporation of a municipality with extremely limited service responsibilities.

Limited government and multiple service providers hindered Hilton Head's efforts to control its destiny, the principal objective of incorporation. Controlling growth requires more than land use regulation. Water supply, sewage treatment, and road capacity create development opportunities and set growth limits as much as zoning. Hilton Head, however, had little control over public services and facilities that influence development. To complicate the problem further, the town government based growth management on its ability to service growth, although the means to build roads, provide water, and get rid of wastes were outside its control. A minimal public sector also severely restricted Hilton Head's ability to protect its population since no police officers or firefighters worked for the town of Hilton Head Island during the first decade after incorporation.

Just how little control Hilton Head had over its destiny was exemplified by a wrenching controversy that erupted over the island's water supply. Saltwater intrusion into the aquifer used by Hilton Head led state officials to order the island's utilities to reduce their water use to 9.5 million gallons a day by 1995. Since Hilton Head was consuming 13 million gallons daily in 1990, and up to 20 million gallons on peak summer days, an alternative source of water had to be developed. The town and Hilton Head's ten water utilities created a task force to study the problem; consultants were hired to evaluate alternatives; and a decision was made by the water suppliers to tap the Savannah River.[11] This determination brought a loud public outcry. Drinking Savannah River water was a very distasteful prospect for most islanders. Cities and their sewage, industries with toxic wastes, and farms with fertilizer and pesticide runoff flanked the Savannah, producing what the island's most prominent environmentalist called "functionally . . . a sewer."[12] And looming 90 miles above the proposed intake was the Savannah River nuclear bomb works, which periodically discharged radioactive wastes into the river.

Belatedly, town officials scrambled to get a handle on water policy. Unhappy constituents were demanding that the town do something to reverse a widely unpopular decision. Many islanders also believed matters as important as water supply and projects costing millions of dollars should not be left to an invisible group of water utilities, some with appointed boards, others private companies, and each concerned with a relatively small portion of the island. A coordinated approach was required, argued critics of the utilities, that considered conservation, community needs, and future growth. Town hall, however, was frustrated by the legal reality that the utilities were in charge of water policy.

Council members pondered taking over the public service districts, going into the wholesale water business, or establishing policy control over the utility districts and companies. Additional studies confused the issue, leading to demands for more information, further testing of alternative water sources, and successful efforts to delay agreement on the Savannah River project. All that was clear in the prolonged struggle was how little influence town officials had on critical aspects of Hilton Head's destiny.

Limited service government was politically unrealistic. Government was bound to expand, regardless of the desire to avoid duplicating existing services or the effectiveness of many services provided by plantations, public service districts, and private utilities. A growing population and economy pushed Hilton Head's government to assume additional responsibilities. More people would bring more crime and resulting demands for more public policing and creation of a municipal police force. Constituency pressures were intensified by the increasing proportion of residents living beyond the realm of private plantation services who wanted recreational facilities, bike paths, storm water drainage, and paved roads. Inevitably, elected officials responded to their constituents, while town employees naturally looked for more things to do.

Pressures to enlarge the public sector increased conflict, often reinforcing the differences that divided the community on growth issues. Retired plantation residents were most dubious about expanding public services; they were already paying for police, water, sewer, and other services provided by plantations and utilities. Settlers had wanted limited service government to control growth; instead they seemed to be getting an expanding municipality reluctant to restrict development. Those urging more town activities tended to be less enthusiastic about growth controls. Business wanted local government to accommodate growth, as did the *Island Packet,* which stressed the necessity for the town to provide needed services and facilities. Resort and real estate interests spearheaded the successful effort to involve the town in replenishing sand on the island's eroding beaches. Local elected officials found enlarging the public domain more satisfying than grappling with the thankless task of controlling development.

PRIVATE LAND AND PUBLIC INTERESTS

Public Hilton Head was also significantly shaped by the heritage of private land arrangements crafted by Charles Fraser. Hilton Head's plantations were more than large-scale private developments with extensive private services; they were also organizing units for complex bundles of restrictions, agreements, and standards affecting the use of property within their boundaries. Covenants, obligations to property owners' associations, and agreements between plantation companies and home owners' organizations provided detailed rules for regulating land use, building, design, upkeep, and use of a substantial portion of the island. By and large, these private rules were not subject to direct public regulation; they were deed restrictions on private property or contractual agreements between private parties. As a result, the island's public realm coexisted with a much more extensive set of private controls, and plantation standards both shaped demands for public regulation as restrictive as private rules and limited the reach of town controls within private communities.

Covenants were the most influential private controls. They proved to be durable and enforceable, a testament to Fraser's creativity and legal skill. Judicial blessing for Hilton Head's covenants came in 1985 when the South Carolina Court of Appeals upheld the authority of Palmetto Dunes to apply aesthetic standards under its covenants, indicating that while "people may reasonably differ as to whether a house is aesthetically appropriate, the covenant is unambiguous in leaving this solitary judgment to Palmetto Dunes . . . which is constrained only to exercise its judgment reasonably and in good faith."[13] Two years later the South Carolina Supreme Court swept away any lingering doubts about the enforceability of Fraser's covenants. The case involved a wealthy businessman who ignored Sea Pines' covenants, adding to his $4.5 million oceanfront house a third story that blocked the ocean view of adjacent houses and committing many other violations. Application of the covenants by the Sea Pines architectural review board, the justices ruled, was neither arbitrary nor discriminatory, and failure of a property owner to secure approval by the review board constituted a breach of covenants enforceable in the courts.[14]

Covenants provided more certainty about land use, aesthetics, and externalities than public regulations. "One of the great strengths of land use covenants running with the land," Fraser emphasized, was that, unlike zoning ordinances and other public land use controls, "they are not subject to change by changing political fashions or economic greed."[15] Private controls enhanced Hilton Head's appeal to prospective buyers and increased property values as plantations developed. Covenants, however, had to be enforced to be effective, and the Sea Pines case underscored the difficulty of securing compliance when someone with deep pockets was determined to ignore private rules. The property owner disregarded the architectural review board and a restraining order. The dispute dragged on for more than three years, running up large legal bills for Sea Pines and the property owners' association. Covenants were also complex legal constructions that led to differing interpretations and conflicts, as can be seen in the many disputes between Fraser and property owners over the meaning of various Sea Pines restrictions.

Still, private restrictions provided more control, durability, and stability than normal public rules. The effectiveness of private regulations led Hilton Head's government to extend design controls to areas outside the realm of covenants and architectural review boards. A committee was created in 1986 to review the design, colors, landscaping, and signs within a 1,000-foot corridor along the main roads outside plantations. The corridor review committee's mission was to insure that projects fit the island's environment and architectural character, covering such matters as the use of appropriate materials and colors. Preserving character essentially meant making Hilton Head beyond the plantation gates look like the plantations. Almost all committee members were plantation residents, and a number were architects and other professionals who worked with plantation standards. Public arbiters of taste, however, had less clout than private regulators, since the corridor review committee could be overruled by the planning commission, the town's board of adjustment, or the courts. In this way they were different from the private architectural review boards, whose judgments were final. Nonetheless, adapting private design restrictions to the public sphere enhanced the aesthetics of development along Hilton Head's principal roads—no small accomplishment, considering the discordant jumble of most boomtowns in the Sunbelt.

Private development and covenants also provided almost all of Hilton Head's open space and recreational land. Just before incorporation, Sea Pines alone encompassed 2,400 acres of parks, woodlands, golf courses, and tennis courts, while the public sector provided only two ball fields and a pair of unimproved beach access points. Like private land use controls, private protection of open space resulted from Fraser's foresight and creative use of deed restrictions. A total of nearly 1,300 acres of Sea Pines was eventually dedicated through open space covenants. Other community developers, however, failed to emulate Fraser's open space dedications. Palmetto Dunes contained little covenanted open space. No large parcels in the Hilton Head Company's holdings were legally set aside as wildlife or nature areas. Later developers dealt with smaller parcels and more expensive land, and none protected much open space.

Dependence on private land for recreation, parks, and nature was a mixed blessing. Hilton Head had the benefit of substantial golf, tennis, boating, beach, and other facilities along with some critical natural areas that were preserved, including the extensive forest preserve in Sea Pines. But almost all of this open space was private, located within plantation gates, reserved for plantation residents or guests, and maintained by property owners. Private playgrounds and open space were designed to sell real estate, attract visitors, and satisfy residents, not serve general community needs. Access to Sea Pines required purchase of a daily permit, which did not entitle the holder to use beach parking lots or most recreational facilities in the plantation. Plantation golf courses and tennis courts open to the general public charged substantial fees geared to the resort trade rather than to local players. Plantation companies and property owners rather than public officials decided who could use private open space. The natural area in Hilton Head Plantation belonged to property owners, who in 1989 restricted access to plantation residents and their guests. A proposal by Fraser that a large chunk of Sea Pines' forest preserve be turned into a public park was buried in an avalanche of negative reaction from residents who did not want a public facility in their private community.

Private sustenance of open space was also problematic, as illustrated by the Sea Pines' forest preserve, the island's only large tract of protected undeveloped land. The term *forest preserve* suggests a pristine wilderness, but only about two-thirds of the 605 acres was dedicated as wildlife habitat. The remainder included water and sewage treatment facilities, an incinerator, a firing range for plantation security officers, huge piles of brush and landscaping debris, three man-made lakes, and the remains of the runway for a planned Sea Pines airport that was never built. For years the wildlife area was overgrown and poorly maintained, with deteriorating boardwalks and trails, a victim of progressive neglect in allocation of community service funds. Private open space was further complicated by ambiguities about what was preserved, under what conditions, and for whose use, since the forest preserve was not divided into zones that clearly demarcated the 400-odd acres destined as wildlife habitat until 1987.

Dependence on private open space and recreation lessened interest in developing public programs. No land was preserved by Beaufort County on Hilton Head; nor was any acquired during the first five years of the new municipal government. Most islanders did not want to pay higher taxes for land acquisition, especially since many enjoyed private recreation and open space. Town officials were preoccupied with regulating development, constrained by the limited service concept, and strapped for funds as demands on the meager municipal exchequer multiplied. Meanwhile, land was rapidly disappearing during the prolonged boom, and what remained undeveloped was steadily rising in price. As the land supply diminished, study groups urged the town to act. Public efforts were needed, advocates argued, to meet growing recreational needs and protect sensitive areas. And— the clinching argument for many—public acquisition of land would prevent development. Grappling with the complexities and conflicts of land use regulations and property rights convinced many islanders that the surest way to control growth was to save land through purchase or acquisition of development rights. A 1989 bond issue provided the initial funds for government to follow in Fraser's footsteps, acquiring land for beach access, recreation areas, and public parks.[16]

PRIVATE AND PUBLIC GOVERNMENT

Private development spawned private government on Hilton Head, initially in the form of plantation companies whose founders ruled as benevolent dictators during the formative years of resort building. Creation of property owners' associations complicated the web of private government, as did the acquisition of Sea Pines and Moss Creek by their residents. These private entities provided substantial services, maintained extensive infrastructure, managed communal facilities, regulated land use and design, and taxed residents through assessments. In developing private government, and especially in the emergence of property owners' associations as the principal instrument of private community governance, Hilton Head was on the cutting edge of changes that have swept across the United States. Private governments created by developers and embodied in property owners' associations have multiplied rapidly as condominiums, planned communities, and other common-interest housing has claimed an increasing share of home building over the past two decades. At the time property owners were being organized at Port Royal and Sea Pines, in the early 1970s, fewer than 5,000 of these associations existed across the country. Fifteen years later, there were more than 125,000 serving and regulating perhaps 40 million Americans.[17]

Hilton Head provides an extreme case of the influence of private rule by development companies and homeowners' associations because of the extent of common-interest housing on the island. Private rules cover plantations, other planned unit developments, freestanding condominium projects, and land beyond the gates originally controlled by plantation companies, leaving relatively little outside the realm of one or another form of private government. A wider range of activities is privately controlled on the plantations than is often the case with common-interest housing. This situation reflects the reach of Fraser's covenants, the breadth of services provided, and the extent of communal facilities and property. Many plantation residents are also under the jurisdiction of two levels of private rule: one covering the entire plantation and another with responsibility for condominium complexes or housing subdivisions. The latter organizations, usually called regimes, maintain buildings and common property, provided services, and regulated use of facilities.

This fragmented realm of private entities coexists with local government, both limiting the reach of the town and relieving local officials of responsibility for many activities. Town officials accepted private governments as a given, which was prudent, considering the size of their domain. Private governments in plantations encompassed a substantial majority of island voters. Property owners' associations had a significant voice in decisions about land use, roads, and other community issues, and their private political arenas provided a training ground for municipal officials and other participants in town government. Coexistence was a basic part of the formula under which town government was developed; plantation residents wanted property owners' associations to manage their "communities' affairs separately from the management by island government . . . because of different concerns and interests within and between the private communities."[18] Internal issues and disputes were seen as private rather than public matters. "This council," argued Mayor Baumberger in eschewing involvement in a wrangle between residents and the Hilton Head Plantation Association, "has no right to enter between the property owners" and their association.[19]

Government by property owners' associations have tended to be more effective and less contentious on Hilton Head than is often the case with private rule in common-interest housing.[20] Particularly in plantations, conformance with private regulations has been high. Serious conflicts over policies were infrequent, contested elections for boards were uncommon, and instances of personal harassment of officers or legal actions against associations were rare. Part of the explanation lies in the substantial pool of retired executives and professionals with time and experience to devote to managing plantations; they were able to handle this work in a way that was widely regarded by members as efficient and effective. Hilton Head's modern history and character also eased tensions over private controls. More than most places, the island was a product of private regulations, services, and facilities; and private controls and amenities were widely accepted as critical elements in the appeal of the plantations, preservation of natural beauty, and enhancement of property values. Another contributing factor was socioeconomic homogeneity. The vast majority of settlers during the formative years came from similar backgrounds, shared common interests, and created familiar corporate institutions to operate their communities.

Though these factors lessened conflict in the private realms increasingly dominated by property owners, they hardly eliminated it. Sea Pines was roiled for years by differences over assessment methods that divided those with more expensive homes from those with less expensive ones. Regimes were often at odds with plantation associations, mirroring conflicts between neighborhood groups and community-wide interests over land use and other issues in the municipal public arena. Plantation associations developed interests and perspectives not shared by constituents, as do most organizations and governmental bodies. Leaders of the homeowners' association in Sea Pines antagonized many members by supporting the cross-island expressway, a position that had been unilaterally determined by the board, as was the usual practice of property owners' organizations. Growth and changing demographics also posed problems for private government. At Hilton Head Plantation, conflict erupted over plans to build a ball field on communal land in response to the recreational needs of the plantation's growing number of families with children. Such disputes are sure to recur as Hilton Head grows and changes, and the dominance of retired settlers in property owners' associations is likely to be challenged as younger home owners with different interests and priorities become increasingly important residents of the private realms that cover most of the island.

Clearly, the heritage of private community building left a substantial private tilt to Hilton Head's political economy. Private services, development controls, and property owners' associations are central features of island life. The remaining private development companies continue to play outsize roles in providing services, determining settlement patterns, and regulating design. This rich web of private activities, however, coexists with an expanding public realm. Plantation companies no longer structure community life. Private control over development could not survive the arrival of people who wanted an authoritative role in determinations that affected their community, their lives, and their future. Even in the kind of paradise that Charles Fraser built, people are unwilling to leave all important decisions to private parties, although those private determinations produced attractive communities, preserved nature, and satisfied needs. Islanders wanted a real local government with elected officials responsive to their constituents, an authoritative public realm for the entire island with the legitimacy that private government cannot possess. Despite the persistence and importance of private rules and activities, the primary arenas on Hilton Head after incorporation have been the town council, planning commission, and other public committees and agencies.

Certainly powerful private interests frequently prevailed in these arenas. Developers and the tourist industry remained the mainstays of the local economy, sustaining a growth machine that wants more building and more tourists to make Hilton Head bigger, better for business, and more profitable. On Hilton Head, as everywhere else, private economic interests normally had the initiative in development, deciding what would be built, where, and when. Developers proposed while government largely reacted, applying and adjusting regulations in response to private ventures. Nonetheless, Hilton Head's development companies, resort operators, and other business interests after incorporation have had to operate in the public forums of the town council, planning commission, and corridor review committee. Their plans were contested by residents, antigrowth coalitions, environmentalists, black property owners, and all the other components of the diverse polity that Hilton Head had become. The growth machine has not always prevailed; public controls restricted development, raised costs, and increased uncertainty about what could be built in the future. Hilton Head's experience with private domination may even have enhanced public control, since high private standards provided the model for public land use and design regulations.

Creating a local public realm also provided islanders with far more responsive government than was offered by Beaufort County. Town government was closer to the people of Hilton Head than county government was; residents are more aware of and more involved in local government. The town has been much more open than the county, involving large numbers of people and encompassing a wide range of viewpoints. Even its flaws tend to reflect a constituency inclined toward cumbersome organization and intolerance toward those outside establishment organizations and established wisdom. The result has been a local government excessively complicated for its size, one that often confounded citizens and businesses with bureaucracy, red tape, and delay. Still, Hilton Head has forged a flourishing local democracy on the foundation provided by private benevolent dictators, a public realm with high rates of participation, informed and spirited discussion of the substance of public issues, and innovative solutions to complex problems.

Responsive government, to the disappointment of many islanders, has not been consensual government. Incorporation did not magically create agreement on where Hilton Head was going; what it did was provide a political arena in which the community could struggle with important common concerns. Critics wanted more. "Somehow this island has to develop a consensus about the direction we want to go as a community," insisted one editor. "We need well-defined community goals that most everyone can embrace."[21] Such goals, however, are too general to be useful in dealing with most issues. Most islanders agreed that Hilton Head was a wonderful place to live, but they differed widely on how to preserve their paradise. With a growing and diversifying population and economy, consensus became an increasingly unrealistic goal. Everything in Hilton Head's experience and in that of similar locales demonstrates the conflicts that can be expected when attractive places draw more people and development, which inevitably threatens their appeal. Politics is bound to be difficult in such places. The stakes are high for residents and businesses, and natural resources are painfully finite, especially on a fragile barrier island.

Responsive government also has not served all interests in the community equally well. Hilton Head's public realm was more accessible and responsive to business and affluent settlers than to other islanders, especially blacks. Discussions about expanding the local public sector usually omitted basic services for black areas and affordable housing. Public life on Hilton Head did not pay much more attention to African Americans than had the private realms that had previously dominated the island. Native islanders are largely outside the business and settler networks that strongly influenced growth, service, and other public policies. Moreover, blacks comprise a steadily declining share of the island's population and electorate. Town officials have responded primarily to their most numerous, active, and influential constituents, while limited service government has provided a shield to deflect pressures to extend utility services, pave streets, or build inexpensive housing.

Admittedly, strenuous efforts have been made to insure that blacks were represented on the town council, planning commission, and other town agencies. Blacks also prevailed politically in securing a better deal for native property owners in the land management ordinance and relocation of the cross-island expressway to minimize the highway's impact on black settlements. But African Americans did not see themselves as welcome or influential participants in local politics. Behind the facade of responsiveness to blacks was the "reality of a political system dominated by affluent white plantation residents . . . who have no interest in the island's natives and their needs and problems."[22] Complicated and costly town rules hindered the development of black land despite the concessions in the land law. "How is it that Hilton Head is 70 percent built out, and the town is now implementing an impact fee?" asked a black leader who saw impact fees as one more way white Hilton Head could tell native islanders to "get off your land and get the hell out of there."[23]

Behind these views are deep feelings of anger and anxiety that transcend the immediate issues of land regulations, design standards, and road building. Hilton Head's blacks see themselves as threatened with political, economic, and cultural extinction—as an "endangered species" on a sea island that had been largely theirs four decades earlier.[24] Understandably, they felt overwhelmed by the waves of white newcomers who occupied Hilton Head. Lack of capital, limited opportunities, and racism left African Americans largely on the outside looking in as Hilton Head boomed. They resent a system that consigned them to the shadows, ignored their needs, raised their taxes, and expected them to be grateful for the benefits that came with development. Their rage was vented in local forums as well as to visiting journalists, most notably in the case of a 1991 *60 Minutes* segment on CBS that provided 30 million Americans with images of angry blacks threatened by rising property taxes and the loss of their land.

White Hilton Head was frustrated by black hostility and cries of exploitation. Development, whites insisted, had brought jobs, excellent schools, and a fine hospital. Rejecting the charge that a new plantation system had enslaved blacks, an island leader extolled the "resort-retirement industry which is creating thousands of job opportunities especially for undereducated, unskilled workers."[25] Whites denied that blacks were excluded, pointing to persistent efforts to include them in all phases of public life. In the view of many white islanders, blacks were ungrateful and difficult; their rhetoric was exaggerated, and their demands were unrealistic. A decade before incorporation, Hilton Head had been told that "no form of government on the island is going to be very effective until the black and white communities can reach a position of mutual trust and willingness to participate in working sessions on solving problems affecting both sides."[26] A decade after incorporation, mutual trust and willingness of the races to work together were still in short supply on Hilton Head.

Nothing could reverse the process that transformed life for black islanders. Hilton Head was too attractive not to be "discovered"; development and urbanization were bound to swamp traditional black life. What might have happened, though, was more sensitivity and responsiveness to blacks. The term *plantation* so deeply offended many blacks that Sea Pines dropped the word from its name in 1993; but five other planned communities on the island and three across the bridge remained plantations. Despite the innovations that made Hilton Head distinctive, little creative energy has been expended on incorporating native islanders economically and politically into the emerging new society. Hilton Head might have offered training programs for black developers, resort officials, and local entrepreneurs. Efforts could have been made to improve housing for blacks. What little affordable housing that has been built has resulted from the initiative of black developers such as Thomas Barnwell who persevered despite complicated rules, inadequate utilities, and objections from settlers.[27] Affluent islanders could also have accepted responsibility for improving public services to black Hilton Head as an essential part of building a viable community as well as an equitable quid pro quo for land use controls and the higher taxes incorporation imposed on blacks. Most important, in a place with so many intelligent and concerned citizens, both private and public life needs to be informed with a greater sense of social justice, for doing the right thing for the descendants of the people who were Hilton Head between the original and the modern plantation eras.

A SPECIAL PLACE

Although flawed in many ways, Hilton Head remains a special place more than four decades after the organization of the Hilton Head Company commenced the island's modern development.[28] The stunning natural setting continues to delight first-time visitors and longtime residents. Despite a constant reworking of nature by community builders and other developers, the beach is still spectacular. The sunsets remain gorgeous. Delicate birds wade in marshes, fish leap in lagoons, and dolphins bob in the glittering sea under crystal blue skies. Tropical foliage, brilliant flowers, and the Spanish moss draping live oaks captivate the newest arrival as much as they had charmed the Frasers and Hacks forty years earlier. Most of Hilton Head's built environment is also uncommonly attractive. Though some unfortunate development mars the landscape, most houses blend into their settings, handsome hotels and commercial buildings are the rule, and lush golf courses are scattered like emerald necklaces across the island. Private and public controls on Hilton Head have been among the most stringent in the land. Natural beauty and quality development are Hilton Head's cachet, its comparative advantage in the competition for visitors, retirees, and investment. For all the conflict over growth controls, settlers and major business interests share a common interest in quality, without which Hilton Head would lose its appeal to affluent visitors and home owners.

Hilton Head also has survived growth, retaining its basic character and appeal despite substantial increases in population, visitors, and business activity. Two decades of rapid growth left the island relatively lightly settled, despite widespread fears that conjured images of a Hilton Head resembling Long Island or Miami Beach. Fewer than 24,000 people lived on Hilton Head Island in 1990, less than half its population during the heyday of the Union occupation in 1864. Population density was only 564 residents per square mile, less than one-third of the median population density for the urbanized portion of metropolitan areas in the Southeast.[29] And by the end of the 1980s, Hilton Head's growth surge was over. A diminishing supply of land was available to be developed, and much of what remained would be settled less intensively because of changing market conditions and the imposition of increasingly stringent controls by town government.

Many islanders grumbled that Hilton Head could have done better, both in maintaining its special character and in controlling growth. Certainly growth and diversity reduce the distinctiveness of development, as did substitution of public for private controls. Much of what is singular on Hilton Head resulted from Charles Fraser's innovative development of Sea Pines and his strong influence on the island's other community builders. Over time, Fraser's distinctive Hilton Head inevitably has been diluted by less creative developers, hotel chains, franchise operations, and the pluralism of the public realm, which supplanted rule by benevolent dictators.

Critics could also point to other upscale resort communities that have been more successful in controlling growth. Nantucket Island, for example, has been more aggressive in acquiring land to preclude development. Aspen has applied more stringent growth controls while providing affordable housing for some of its working population. Most often, dissatisfied islanders compared Hilton Head to Sanibel on Florida's Gulf coast, another fragile island whose natural beauty and ambiance had been threatened by overdevelopment. After incorporating in 1973, Sanibel Island adopted land use controls that sharply limited densities and building heights, restricted resort housing, and rationed building permits. Overall development was capped with a projected population of 18,000, compared to the 90,000 that could have been accommodated under the county's plan for the island.[30] Sanibel's experience inspired advocates of incorporation on Hilton Head, many of whom hoped that their island could enact similarly tight controls on development. Hilton Head's choice not to do the same reflects the fact that the two islands were different places in separate states with distinctive interests. Sanibel had no large private communities that became world-famous resorts; its prime attraction was nature—the beach, seashells, and a national wildlife refuge. Residents had greater political clout on Sanibel, while local commercial interests wanted to preserve the natural attractions that brought visitors to the island. From the beginning, Hilton Head was dominated by the private interests that developed the plantations, and their success generated a complex set of local economic interests that had to be accommodated as Hilton Head sought to define and control its destiny.

That destiny was often articulated as "paradise," Hilton Head's shorthand for preserving the island as a special place. Paradise was a state of mind, a vision fostered by the beauty of the place, by the attractions of what Fraser and others built, and by the dreams that real estate salesmen sold customers eager to possess something they believed was special. For some, paradise was a dangerous illusion, creating false and unrealistic expectations. "Islanders who expected town government to legislate Shangri-la are discovering that Hilton Head Island is Hometown USA instead," the *Island Packet* reminded its readers in 1987: "a regular community subject to the same kinds of pressures and the same kinds of individual rights that other communities in this country have."[31] But Hilton Head was not just another place. "Hometown USA" did not attract more than a million visitors or contain world-class resorts and golf courses; and thousands of affluent retirees did not pick up stakes and settle just anywhere. Modern Hilton Head was built on the idea of paradise, and when the island stopped being an approximation of paradise—at least in comparison with most other places—Hilton Head would be just another seaside town that flowered and wilted.

No one understood the interplay of dreams and reality on Hilton Head better than Charles Fraser. His dreams combined with a restless intelligence to create a new kind of resort community in America. Some of the ideas were new, and others were borrowed; but the mix was original, as was the product. Against all kinds of odds, Fraser turned a forgotten corner of South Carolina into a world-renowned resort and in the process significantly influenced development of seaside towns and private community building everywhere. Sea Pines was a triumph of private development, the transformation of a large parcel of land into a planned resort community, with each step in the process tightly controlled by the creator through ownership of the land, private provision of infrastructure, and private regulation of design and building through deed covenants. Fraser's sense of stewardship protected hundreds of acres from development, and his creative approach to developing oceanside property preserved dunes and natural foliage as well as insuring that most building on the island's beachfront would be residential rather than high-rise hotels and condominiums, as is the case in most seaside resorts.

Fraser's approximation of paradise at Sea Pines required control. Despite his striking success in building a new kind of community and transforming Hilton Head, he could not maintain control. Financial reverses undermined his opportunities for expansion on Hilton Head. Demographic and economic change overwhelmed private domination of the island by Sea Pines and the other major companies. Replacing private with public control produced more responsive and accountable rule. But Hilton Head's distinctive character is largely a legacy of the daring and creativity of Charles Fraser. Profit was part of Fraser's goal, as was political power, but both were means to the end of building something worthwhile. Profit-seeking alone would have produced a different kind of Sea Pines and Hilton Head; so would political domination harnessed to purely private goals. What happened to Hilton Head in the end would depend on the fate of Fraser's vision. "Hilton Head is a garden," he reassured islanders as they faced the severe test of bankruptcy. "What makes us happy here is what makes people come here. As long as we maintain this place as a garden, it will remain a happy place."[32]

298

NOTES

1. Richard A. McGinty, interview.
2. Joseph B. Fraser Jr., interview.
3. Corkern, interview.
4. Jack D. Dougherty, letter to the editor.
5. Quoted in Oneufer, "Mayor at Odds with RHOC Position that Council Not Producing Solutions."
6. John Present, acting chairman, Planning Commission, Town of Hilton Head Island, quoted in Dobson, "Ginn Strikes Out with Town Planning Commission."
7. Quoted in Oneufer, "Council Tables Plantation Zoning Controversy Again."
8. Jordan and Fleming, "Organizing Local Government," chapter 15, 8.
9. Emory Campbell, quoted in Schulte, "Water System for North End on the Way." Campbell was a commissioner of the Hilton Head Rural Water District.
10. The Hilton Head Rural Water District. organized in 1980, struggled for much of the decade to finance its plans before patching together federal and state funds to finance a $1.4 million project for 200-odd families.
11. The $41.5 million project would be undertaken by an existing agency, the Beaufort-Jasper Water and Sewer Authority, which would wholesale river water to the island's utilities.
12. Ballantine, "Not the Savannah River."
13. *Palmetto Dunes Resort v. Brown.*
14. See *Sea Pines Plantation Co. v. Wells.*
15. Fraser, letter to the editor.
16. In 1990 Hilton Head enacted a real estate transfer tax to raise additional funds for the purchase of land and development rights. The rate was a quarter of a percent on all transactions except gifts and inheritances.
17. See Dowden, "Governance by Community Association."
18. Fleming, "Reorganizing Local Government," 135.
19. Quoted in Oneufer, "Skull Creek Change OK'd by Town Council."
20. See Stevens, "Condominium Owners Grapple with Governing Themselves," and Bowler and McKenzie, "Invisible Kingdoms."
21. "What Is Our Focus and Who's Promoting It in Columbia?"
22. Barnwell, interview.
23. Eugene Wiley, quoted in Gwen Richards, "Native Landowners Dislike Transportation Impact Fee." The town adopted impact fees in 1990 to help finance road improvements. Fees ranged from $576 per condo unit to $989 for

single-family homes of 1,500 or more square feet and from $2.85 per square foot of office space to $11.45 per square foot for retail building.

24. See Singleton, "We Are Endangered Species."

25. Marscher, "Slavery in the Lowcountry?" Marscher was a member of the town council for four years.

26. Robert B. Killingsworth, quoted in Dowling, "P S Council Deferred Again."

27. Few more than 200 units of affordable housing were built during the decade after incorporation, none with direct involvement of the town government. One project, involving 182 rental units on 25 acres, was underwritten by the state housing authority with federally insured bonds. A 24-unit development was financed by the Farmers Home Administration.

28. No attempt has been made in this study to assess Hilton Head in comparison to similar places. The case that Hilton Head is special is made in the context of its natural features and the quality of its development. For an effort to compare quality of life in 219 "micropolitan areas"—places with cities of 15,000 to 50,000 people in counties with at least 40,000—see Thomas, *The Rating Guide to Life in America's Small Cities* and "Micropolitan America." In making his ratings, Thomas uses measures of climate, diversions, economics, education, health care, housing, public safety, sophistication, transportation, and urban proximity. He ranks Hilton Head in the middle of the pack. As in all such studies of quality of life, the subjective processes of selecting and weighting variables have a substantial impact on results, despite the appeal of precise numerical scores for each place being rated.

29. See Abbott, *The New Urban America,* 65.

30. See Babcock and Siemon, *The Zoning Game Revisited,* 96–118.

31. "RHOC's Poll Sets Stage for 1987 Election Campaign."

32. Quoted in Smith, "Fraser Optimistic about Island's Economic Future."

Bibliography

Abbott, Carl. *The New Urban America: Growth and Politics in Sunbelt Cities.* Chapel Hill: University of North Carolina Press, 1987.

"Action Plan." Editorial. *Island Packet,* May 10, 1979.

Advertisement. *Island Packet,* May 5, 1983.

"Air South Comes to the Island." Editorial. *Island Packet,* June 1, 1972.

"Airport in the Island Environment." Editorial. *Island Packet,* February 10, 1972.

Albert, Howard E. *Private Sector Reaction to Normal Political Institutional Procedures and Outcomes When Water Is an Issue.* Clemson, S.C.: Water Resources Research Institute, Clemson University, June 1973.

"Alive and Well and Dream Intact." Editorial. *Island Packet,* May 27, 1976.

American Institute of Architects. "Citation for Excellence in Private Community Planning to Sea Pines Plantation, Hilton Head Island, South Carolina, Charles E. Fraser, President." May 31, 1968.

Ames, David. Interview by Patricia R. F. Danielson. Hilton Head Island, S.C., April 5, 1990.

Association of Sea Pines Plantation Property Owners, Letter to Property Owners, April 25, 1983.———"Newsletter and 1982 Annual Report." February 1983.

"Atlantis Announces $11 Million Project." *Island Packet,* January 18, 1973.

Axene, David N. Interview by Michael N. Danielson and Patricia R. F. Danielson. Hilton Head Island, S.C., August 14, 1987.

Babcock, Richard F., and Charles L. Siemon. *The Zoning Game Revisited.* Boston: Oelgeschlager, Gunn and Hain, 1985.

Bachrach, Peter, and Morton S. Baratz. *Power and Poverty: Theory and Practice.* New York: Oxford University Press, 1970.

———. "Two Faces of Power." *American Political Science Review* 56 (December 1962), 947–52.

Baker, Thomas F. Interview by Michael N. Danielson. Hilton Head Island, S.C., June 20, 1990.

Baldassare, Mark. *Trouble in Paradise: The Suburban Transformation in America.* New York: Columbia University Press, 1986.

Ballantine, Todd. "Cut Future Population." *Island Packet,* February 11, 1991.

———Interview by Michael N. Danielson. Hilton Head Island, S.C., June 25, 1990.

———. "Nature Got Her Revenge by Flooding Us Last Week." *Island Packet,* September 17, 1987.

———. "Resculpting Landscape Taking Its Toll Here." *Island Packet,* December 10, 1987.

———. "Not the Savannah River." *Island Packet,* December 17, 1990.

Banks, Ben T. Interview by Michael N. Danielson. Hilton Head Island, S.C., June 27, 1990.

Barbieri, Frank. Letter to the Editor. *Island Packet,* March 18, 1990.

Barnwell, Thomas C. Interview by Michael N. Danielson and Patricia R. F. Danielson. Hilton Head Island, S.C., July 24, 1987.

"BASF Backs Off from a Beachhead." *Business Week,* April 11, 1970.

"BASF Official Reportedly Admits Pollution Problem." *Charleston News and Courier,* December 19, 1971.

"BASF Withdrawal Aftermath; What Next for Port Victoria?" *Island Packet,* January 21, 1971.

Bauman, Peter W. Interview by Michael N. Danielson. Hilton Head Island, S.C., June 28, 1990.

Baumberger, Martha. "Traffic Safety Amendment Flawed in Concept, Language." *Island Packet,* May 3, 1989.

Beaufort County Joint Planning Commission,"The Hilton Head Island Land Use Plan." Beaufort, S.C., 1982.

———. "Hilton Head Island Land Use Survey." Beaufort, S.C., 1981.

———. "State of the Island Report—Land Use." January 1982.

Bender, Bob. "Lack of Communications with JPC Cited at Meeting." *Hilton Head News,* October 7, 1982.

Bernard, Richard M., and Bradley R. Rice, eds. *Sunbelt Cities: Politics and Growth Since World War II.* Austin: University of Texas Press, 1983.

Bernier, Carol. Letter to the Editor. *Island Packet,* June 19, 1991.

Bisher, Furman. "The Island World of Charles Fraser." *Southern Living,* March 1970.

Bowers, Doris. "Hilton Head Island." *Islander,* November 1972.

———. Interview by Michael N. Danielson. Hilton Head Island, S.C., June 22, 1990.

Bowers, Doris, and Seward Bowers. "What Does the Future Hold for Hilton Head Island?" *Island Packet,* January 4, 1973.

Bowers, Seward H. Letter to the Editor. *Island Packet,* January 6, 1972.

Bowie, Jack. "Zoning Hearings Create Much Heat, Little Light." *Island Packet,* May 4, 1972.

Bowler, Mike, and Evan McKenzie. "Invisible Kingdoms." *California Lawyer* 5 (December 1985), 54–58.

Breland, Debbie. "Conflict Erupts over Procedures of Development." *Island Packet,* May 15, 1979.

———. "JPC Expresses Doubts about Island Commission Idea." *Island Packet,* May 24, 1979.

Bright, Rick. "Back from the Brink." *Property Owners Monthly,* October 1988.

Bunton, Terry. *The History of the Heritage: 1969–1989.* Bluffton, S.C.: Terry Bunton, 1989.

Bureau of Governmental Research and Service, University of South Carolina. "Incorporation as an Option for Hilton Head Island, S.C.: A Preliminary Analysis." Report prepared by Mike Easterwood, 1982.

"Butera New Hilton Head President." *Island Packet,* August 31, 1972.

Butler, Nancy. "Ancient Country of Lotus-Eaters and Sacred Ibis." *Islander,* November 1973.

Butler v. Sea Pines Plantation Co., 282 S.C. 113, 317 S.E.2d 464 (1984).

Button, James, and Walter Rosenbaum. "Gray Power, Gray Peril, or Gray Myth?: The Political Impact of the Aging in Local Sunbelt Politics." *Social Science Quarterly* 71 (March 1990), 25–38.

Callahan, Katie. "The Godfather of Palmetto Dunes." *Islander,* August 1979.

———. "Orion Hack Shifting Gears in Public Service." *Island Packet,* July 9, 1987.

———. "Speaking Out." *Island Packet,* September 14, 1989.

Campbell, Emory. Letter to the Editor. *Island Packet,* March 1973.

Caro, Robert A. *The Power Broker: Robert Moses and the Fall of New York.* New York: Knopf, 1974.

Adams, Samuel Hopkins, "Carolina Cruise." *Holiday,* November 1953.

Carse, Robert. *Department of the South: Hilton Head Island in the Civil War.* Hilton Head Island, S.C.: Impressions Printing Company, 1987.

Cathcart, George. "Hilton Head Company Opposes CBI Plant." *Island Packet,* January 10, 1974.

"Charles Fraser Looks to the Future He'll Help." In *Charles E. Fraser in Print.* Hilton Head Island, S.C., 1982.

Charles E. Fraser in Print. Hilton Head Island, S.C., 1983.

Clark, Richard. Interview by Michael N. Danielson. Hilton Head Island, S.C., June 22, 1990.

Coleman, Ed. "'Operation Hilton Head' Is Fight against Venereal Disease." *Beaufort Gazette,* October 27, 1949.

Colleton River Plantation. Advertisement. *Island Packet,* May 5, 1991.

Corkern, W. Douglas. Interview by Michael N. Danielson and Patricia R. F. Danielson. Hilton Head Island, S.C., August 4, 1987.

Cornelison, Jimmy. "One Man's Island in the Sun." *Charleston News and Courier,* April 5, 1981.

Coverdale and Colpitts. "Hilton Head Toll Bridge, Beaufort County, South Carolina, First Annual Report, Fiscal Year Ending November 30, 1956." December 28, 1956.

Craighead, Gordon. Interview by Michael N. Danielson. Hilton Head Island, S.C., July 2, 1990.

Curry, John F. Interview by Michael N. Danielson. Hilton Head Island, S.C., July 2, 1990.

———, Trustee, Hilton Head Holdings. Advertisement. *Wall Street Journal,* September 11, 1987.

Dahl, Robert A. *Who Governs? Democracy and Power in an American City.* New Haven: Yale University Press, 1961.

Daniels, Jonathan. *The Gentlemanly Serpent and Other Columns from a Newspaper in Paradise.* Edited by Ralph Hilton. Columbia, S.C.: University of South Carolina Press, 1974.

———. "Sojourner's Scrapbook." *Island Packet,* March 25, 1971.

———. "Sojourner's Scrapbook." *Island Packet,* February 17, 1972.

———. "Sojourner's Scrapbook." *Island Packet,* March 2, 1972.

———. "Sojourner's Scrapbook." *Island Packet,* May 11, 1972.

———. "Sojourner's Scrapbook." *Island Packet,* January 25, 1973.

———. "Sojourner's Scrapbook." *Island Packet,* May 27, 1976.

Danielson, Michael N. *The Politics of Exclusion.* New York: Columbia University Press, 1976.

Danielson, Michael N., and Jameson W. Doig. *New York: The Politics of Urban Regional Development.* Berkeley: University of California Press, 1982.

Davis, Howard. Interview by Michael N. Danielson. Hilton Head Island, S.C., July 7, 1990.

Dey, Richard. Interview by Michael N. Danielson. Hilton Head Island, S.C., June 29, 1990.

"Dick Wallace, among the Eight Palmetto Dunes Founders, Dies Tuesday." *Island Packet,* March 13, 1987.

Dobson, Marguerite. "Ginn Strikes out with Town Planning Commission." *Hilton Head Report,* December 1985.

Dolce, Philip C. *Suburbia: The American Dream and Dilemma.* New York: Anchor, 1976.

Donaldson, Scott. *The Suburban Myth.* New York: Columbia University Press, 1969.

Donnell, Jolie. "From the Editor." *Island Events,* October 9, 1982.

Dougherty, Jack D. Letter to the Editor. *Island Packet,* September 20, 1990.

Dowden, C. James. "Governance by Community Association." *Bureaucrat* 16 (Winter 1987–88), 39–44.

Dowell, David E. "An Examination of Population-Growth-Management Communities." *Policy Studies Journal* 9 (1980), 414–27.

Dowling, Liz. "P S Council Deferred Again." *Island Packet,* August 30, 1973.

Drake, Ross. "Developer Charles Fraser Learns Secret of Turning Beaches into Gold." *People,* June 2, 1975.

"Dunes Asked to Change 'High Rise' Project." *Island Packet,* July 22, 1971.

Eichler, Edward P., and Marshall Kaplan. *The Community Builders.* Berkeley: University of California Press, 1967.

Elkin, Stephen L. *City and Regime in the American Republic.* Chicago: University of Chicago Press, 1987.

"End of Detour: Oxford First Recovers from Land Development Fling." *Barron's,* March 7, 1983.

"Executives Discuss Ad Topics; Daniels Is Banquet Speaker." *Island Packet,* August 31, 1972.

Eyre, William. "Court Places Inn in Bankruptcy, Curry Sees It Opening by Summer." *Hilton Head Report,* February 20, 1987.

———. "The Quest for the Perfect Mall." *Hilton Head Report,* March 17, 1987.

Feagin, Joe R., and Robert Parker. *Building American Cities: The Urban Real Estate Game.* 2d ed. Englewood Cliffs, N.J.: Prentice-Hall, 1990.

Felder, Lynn. "ASPPPO Announces Steps to Collect Delinquent Fees." *Island Packet,* March 31, 1989.

———. "Axene: Sea Pines Associates, Inc. Alive and Well." *Island Packet,* March 5, 1989.

First English Evangelical Lutheran Church v. Los Angeles County, 482 U.S. 304 (1987).

"First Phase Started on $35 Million Island Project." *Island Packet,* August 24, 1972.

Fisher, Connie. Letter to the Editor. *Island Packet,* March 2, 1989.

Fleming, Horace W. Jr. *Hilton Head Island Government: Analysis and Alternatives.* Prepared for the Committee on Community Government Options. Hilton Head Island, S.C., 1974.

———. *Hilton Head Government: Analysis and Alternatives II.* Prepared for the Committee on Community Government Options, Hilton Head Island, S.C., July 1978.

———. "Reorganizing Local Government: The Hilton Head Island, S.C. Experience." *Journal of Political Science* 2 (1974), 105–43.

Fogelman, Avron. "No Plans to Sell Major Assets." *Hilton Head Sun,* March 30, 1988.

"For a Happier Island." Editorial. *Island Packet,* February 1, 1973.

Force, Peter. *Tracts and Other Papers, Relating Principally to the Origin, Settlement, and Progress of the Colonies in North America, from the Discovery of the Country to the Year 1776.* Vol. 4. Washington: William Q. Force, 1846.

Foster, Dean. "Town Turned Three on August 5, Too Much Going On to Celebrate." *Hilton Head Report,* August 22, 1986.

Fowler, Vance. Interview by Michael N. Danielson and Patricia R. F. Danielson. Hilton Head Island, S.C., July 22, 1987.

Frady, Marshall. "The View from Hilton Head." *Harper's,* May 1970.

Fraser, Charles E. "Appendix A to the 1988 Jubilee Year Plan for Sea Pines Plantation." N.d.

———. *The Art of Community Building: The View from Hilton Head Island.* Hilton Head Island, S.C., n.d.

———. "Basic Data on the Sea Pines Development." Sea Pines Plantation Company, July 1, 1957.

———. "Charting the Directions of New Communities and Growth Area Land Use Management in the Era of President Carter and Chairman Burns." Speech for the Urban Land Institute. Washington, D.C., November 17, 1976.

———. "Confidential Policy Statement on Architecture, Design and Construction." Sea Pines Plantation Company, October 20, 1965.

———. "Financial Aspects of Development Activities, 1951–1955." Memorandum for the Stockholders of the Hilton Head Company, 1955.

———. Interview by Michael N. Danielson and Patricia R. F. Danielson. Hilton Head Island, S.C., August 15, 1987.

———. Interview by Patricia R. F. Danielson. Hilton Head Island, S.C., April 4, 1990.

———. Interview by Michael N. Danielson. Hilton Head Island, S.C., June 30, 1990.

———. Letter to the Editor. *Island Packet,* October 30, 1985.

———. "A 1979 Action Plan to Protect the Environmental and Aesthetic Quality of Hilton Head." April 12, 1979.

———. "A Program of Development Activities: Hilton Head Island, S.C., 1955–1957." Hilton Head Company, 1955.

———. "The Sea Pines Company: An Overview of Current Prospects and Summary of the Successful Recession Era Debt Elimination." July 1978.

———. "Sea Pines Plantation: The Shared Environment." Unpublished ms., 1981.

———. *This Other Eden: The Story of Hilton Head Island and Sea Pines Plantation.* Hilton Head Island, S.C.: Sea Pines Plantation Company, 1969.

———. "A Thoroughly Incomplete Chronology of Hilton Head Island, South Carolina from 12000 B.C. to 1986." Hilton Head Island, S.C., May 1986.

———. "Time for a Vote on the City of Hilton Head Island." *Islander,* December 1982.

Fraser, Joseph B. Jr. Interview by Michael N. Danielson. Hilton Head Island, S.C., July 9, 1990.

Gale, Bob. "Hilton Head: The Canopy View." *American Forests* 96 (November/December 1990), 61–64.

Galehouse, Richard F. "Land Planning for Large-Scale Residential Development." *Urban Land* 40 (October 1981), 12–18.

Gans, Herbert. *The Levittowners: Ways of Life and Politics in a New Suburban Community.* New York: Pantheon, 1967.

Gardo, Doughtie and Rose. "Hilton Head Business and Employment Survey." Hilton Head Island, S.C., 1985.

Gardo, Thomas. "Sea Pines Plantation Alumni." *Islander,* June 1982.

Garreau, Joel. *Edge City: Life on the Urban Frontier.* New York: Doubleday, 1990.

Goddard, C. R. Letter to the Editor. *Island Packet,* July 15, 1971.

Grafton, Patrick. "Exclusively Charles Fraser." *Islander,* June 1982.

Grant, Carolyn. "Island's Leaders Peer into Future." *Island Packet,* January 26, 1990.

Grant, Moses Alexander. *Looking Back: Reminiscences of a Black Family Heritage on Hilton Head Island.* Orangeburg, S.C.: Williams Associates, 1988.

Grass Roots Group. Advertisement. *Island Packet,* December 2, 1986.

Greer, Margaret. *The Sands of Time: A History of Hilton Head Island.* Hilton Head Island, S.C.: SouthArt, 1988.

———. "Time to Remember." *Islander,* June 1982.

———. "What Makes Bobby Run?" *Hilton Head Report,* March 1985.

Grush, Henry S. Letter to the Editor. *Island Packet,* October 28, 1987.

Hack, Billie. Interview by Michael N. Danielson and Patricia R. F. Danielson. Hilton Head Island, S.C., July 22, 1987.

Hack, Frederick C. Interview by Michael N. Danielson and Patricia R. F. Danielson. Hilton Head Island, S.C., July 31, 1987.

"Hack Leaving Hilton Head Presidency." *Island Packet,* August 17, 1972.

Hack, Orion D. Interview by Michael N. Danielson and Patricia R. F. Danielson. Hilton Head Island, S.C., July 17, 1987.

Hall, Arthur B. Interview by Michael N. Danielson and Patricia R. F. Danielson. Hilton Head Island, S.C., August 13, 1987.

Hamrick, Tom. "Plush Living Contrasts with Poverty at Hilton Head." *Columbia State,* February 21, 1972.

Harris, Ron. "Plantations Again." *Los Angeles Times,* August 28, 1988.

Haworth, Prentiss. Interview by Michael N. Danielson and Patricia R. F. Danielson. Hilton Head Island, S.C., August 17, 1987.

Herbers, John. *The New Heartland: America's Flight beyond the Suburbs and How It Is*

Changing Our Future. New York: TimesBooks, 1986.

"H.H. Co., Oxford 1st Biggest Developer." *Island Packet,* December 9, 1971.

Hill, Teresa. "Incorporation Controversial, but Islanders Say 'Yes.'" *Island Packet,* August 5, 1987.

———. "Island Issues Come to Full Boil in Summer of '82." *Island Packet,* August 4, 1987.

———. "Jerry Dunn Believes He Can Make a Difference." *Island Packet,* October 12, 1987.

———. "Judge Calls Grass Roots Repugnant, Incompatible, Orders Permit Granted." *Island Packet,* October 22, 1987.

———. "Melrose Plans Change in Name for Indigo Run." *Island Packet,* April 12, 1991.

———. "Russ Condit: Improve Communications First." *Island Packet,* October 19, 1987.

———. "A Town Was Born, but Instant Happiness Was Not." *Island Packet,* August 6, 1987.

Hilton Head Beach Club. Advertisement. *Islander,* January 1974.

Hilton Head Island Chamber of Commerce. "Media Facts." 1986. Hilton Head Island Chamber of Commerce and Town of Hilton Head Island. "Hilton Head Island Commercial Information Packet." Hilton Head Island, S.C., 1989.

"Hilton Head Islanders Split Racially over Incorporation Vote." *New York Times,* May 10, 1983.

Hilton Head Plantation. Advertisement. *Island Packet,* August 15, 1974.

"Hilton Head: Something Beautiful Being Created." *Miami Herald,* April 15, 1973.

Hilton, Mary Kendall. "Islander: Charles E. Fraser." *Islander,* December 1966.

———. "Islander: Emerson Mulford." *Islander,* August 1968.

———. "Islander: Frank Royce." *Islander,* December 1968.

———. "Islander: Fred C. Hack." *Newsletter,* Hilton Head Island Chamber of Commerce, November 1966.

———. "Islander: Gerald H. McBride." *Islander,* September 1967.

———. "Islander: Joseph B. Fraser, Sr." *Islander,* May 1967.

———. "Islander: Richard A. McGinty." *Islander,* April 1967.

———. "Islander: William H. Fries, M.D." *Islander,* August 1967.

———. "Islander: Wilton Graves." *Newsletter,* Hilton Head Island Chamber of Commerce, October 1965.

Hilton, Tracy. "Personality Profile: Martin Remembers and Welcomes Island Changes." *Hilton Head Report,* June 1985.

Hilton, William. *A Relation of a Discovery Lately Made on the Coast of Florida.* Lisbon: Simon Miller, 1664.

Holmgren, Virginia C. *Hilton Head: A Sea Island Chronicle,* Hilton Head Island, S.C.: Hilton Head Island Publishing Co., 1959.

Horn, Huston. "Nothing to Do—but Enjoy Yourself." *Sports Illustrated,* December 17, 1962.

Horton, Gerald. "The Hideaway and Community Tightwire." In *Charles E. Fraser in*

BIBLIOGRAPHY

Print. Hilton Head Island, S.C., 1983.

Hunter, Floyd. *Community Power Structure: A Study of Decision Makers.* Chapel Hill: University of North Carolina Press, 1953.

————. *Community Power Succession: Atlanta's Policy Makers Revisited.* Chapel Hill: University of North Carolina Press, 1980.

Hyatt, Wayne. *Condominium and Homeowner Association Practice: Community Association Law.* 2d ed. Philadelphia: American Law Institute–American Bar Association, 1988.

"Incorporation Election Results." *Island Packet,* May 17, 1983.

Indigo Run Plantation. Advertisement. *Wall Street Journal,* June 8, 1990.

"Indigo Run Rescue Welcome at Last." Editorial. *Island Packet,* December 11, 1990.

"Industry for Victoria Bluff." Editorial. *Island Packet,* March 23, 1972.

Inglesby, Edith. "Low Country Sketches—Honey Horn Plantation: The Old and the New." *Islander,* January 1974.

"Island Club's $15 Million Project Is Announced." *Island Packet,* March 2, 1972.

"The Island Packet in Its Own Home." Editorial. *Island Packet,* January 25, 1973.

"Islander Interview: Jack Barry." *Islander,* April 1989.

"Isolated." Editorial. *Island Packet,* August 16, 1973.

Jackson, Kenneth T. *Crabgrass Frontier.* New York: Oxford University Press, 1985.

Jenkins, Dan. "A Course with Rare Bite." *Sports Illustrated,* November 9, 1970.

————. "Jack's Course Is Arnie's Too." *Sports Illustrated,* December 8, 1969.

Jennings, M. Kent. *Community Influentials: The Elites of Atlanta.* New York: Free Press, 1964.

Jones-Jackson, Patricia. *When Roots Die: Endangered Traditions on the Sea Islands.* Athens: University of Georgia Press, 1987.

Jordan, Michael L. M. Interview by Michael N. Danielson. Hilton Head Island, S.C., July 10, 1990.

Jordan, Michael L. M., and Horace W. Fleming. "Organizing Local Government: The Hilton Head Island Experience." Unpublished ms., 1984.

Judge, Joseph. "Exploring Our Forgotten Century." *National Geographic,* March 1988.

Kenney, Harold D. Letter to the Editor. *Island Packet,* March 12, 1990.

Killingsworth, Robert. Interview by Michael N. Danielson. Hilton Head Island, S.C., June 26, 1990.

Kling, Rob, Spencer Olin, and Mark Poster, eds. *Postsuburban California: The Transformation of Orange County since World War II.* Berkeley: University of California Press, 1990.

Lader, Philip. "A Shared Responsibility." *Islander,* June 1982.

Lader, Philip. Interview by Michael N. Danielson and Patricia R. F. Danielson. Hilton Head Island, S.C., August 18, 1987.

"'Lifestyle' Set by Hilton Head Co." *Island Packet,* February 24. 1972.

Liston, Linda. "The Fraser/Sea Pines Concept: A Sound Investment in Environment." *Travel Investment,* 1969 Supplement.

"The Little Emperor of Hilton Head." *Atlanta Journal and Constitution Magazine,* June 24, 1979.

Littlejohn, Jim. "Businessman, NAACP Head Remembers Island's Past." *Hilton Head Report,* November 14, 1987.

―――. Interview by Michael N. Danielson and Patricia R. F. Danielson. Hilton Head Island, S.C., July 15,1987.

―――. "Islander of the Month: Charles Price." *Islander,* September 1973.

―――. "Islander of the Month: Donald O'Quinn." *Islander,* November 1972.

―――. "Islander of the Month: Frederick Hack." *Islander,* March 1972.

―――. "Neighborhoods Form Plantation's Backbone." *Hilton Head Report,* March 12, 1988.

―――. "Our Island's Greatest Dreamer—and Most Practical Man." *Island Events,* March 25, 1978.

"Local House Members Give Quick Response on Plant." *Beaufort Gazette,* October 2, 1969.

Logan, John R., and Harvey Molotch. *Urban Fortunes: The Political Economy of Place.* Berkeley: University of California Press, 1987.

Logan, John R., and Min Zhou. "Do Suburban Growth Controls Control Growth?" *American Sociological Review* 54 (June 1989), 461–71.

Lynd, Robert S., and Helen Merrell Lynd. *Middletown: A Study in Modern American Cultures.* New York: Harcourt, Brace, 1929.

―――. *Middletown in Transition: A Study in Cultural Contrasts.* New York: Harcourt, Brace, 1937.

Malanick, Michael J. Interview by Michael N. Danielson. Hilton Head Island, S.C., June 25, 1990.

Marscher, Bill. Interview by Michael N. Danielson and Patricia R. F. Danielson. Hilton Head Island, S.C., July 13, 1987.

Marscher, Bill. "Slavery in the Lowcountry? An Honest Look." *Island Packet,* October 9, 1990.

Martin, James A. "Hilton Head: Once-Isolated Island Now a Tourist's Utopia." *Charleston News and Courier,* August 8, 1982.

Massey, Brian L. "Poll: Most Voters Undecided on TSA Referendum." *Island Packet,* March 26, 1989.

Masters, Gordon. Letter to the Editor. *Island Packet,* August 2, 1990.

McCaskey, Glen. "Sea Pines Plantation Alumni." *Islander,* June 1982.

"McCrary Plans New Role." *Islander,* October 1972.

McGinty, Aileen. Interview by Patricia R. F. Danielson. Hilton Head Island, S.C., April 2, 1990.

McGinty, Richard A. Interview by Michael N. Danielson and Patricia R. F. Danielson. Hilton Head Island, S.C., August 27, 1987.

McGrath, John. "Sea Pines Plantation Alumni." *Islander,* June 1982.

McGregor, Pauli. "B-Ginn the B-ginner B-gins A-gin." *Islander,* August 1979.

McIntosh, John M. Interview by Michael N. Danielson and Patricia R. F. Danielson. Hilton Head Island, S.C., August 17, 1987.

"McNair Assures Pollution Control." *Columbia Record,* December 10, 1969.

McNeill, Julia. "Faith in Island 30 Years Ago Key to Richardson's Success." *Hilton*

Head Report, August 22, 1986.

McPhee, John. *Encounters with the Archdruid,* New York: Farrar, Straus and Giroux, 1971.

"Memories of Hilton Head Island." *Island Packet,* January 20, 1972.

"Milestone Reached by Island Developer; Hilton Head Company Now 20 Years Old." *Islander,* March 1970.

Millard, Hal. "Del Webb Project 'a Wonderful Thing' for Jasper County." *Island Packet,* December 19, 1993.

Miller, John M. "Hilton Head: Club or Community?" *Island Packet,* January 15, 1987.

"More Hotel Rooms." Editorial. *Island Packet,* August 17, 1972.

"Multi-Million Dollar Development Program Begins for Gun Club Lands." *Islander,* July 1967.

"NAACP Officials Tour Island Fri." *Island Packet,* October 12, 1972.

NAACP v. Town of Hilton Head Island, U.S. Court of Appeals for Fourth Circuit, No. 83–2029, March 7, 1984.

NAACP v. Town of Hilton Head Island, U.S. District Court, District of South Carolina, Charleston Division, Civil Action No. 83–1707–8, October 20, 1983.

NAACP v. Town of Hilton Head, 287 S.C. 254, 335 SE2d 808 (1985).

"Off-Island Plantation Comes Full Circle." *Island Packet,* December 10, 1989.

Old South Golf Links. Advertisement. *Island Packet,* November 5, 1991.

Olson, Robin. "BT Interview: Charles Fraser." *Business Today,* Spring 1977.

"On Becoming a Municipality." Editorial. *Island Packet,* July 13, 1972.

"100 Apartments, Shops, Small Plants for Buckingham." *Island Packet,* February 15, 1973.

Oneufer, Ruth. "Council Tables Plantation Zoning Controversy Again." *Hilton Head Sun,* April 23, 1988.

———. "Mayor at Odds with RHOC Position that Council Not Producing Solutions." *Hilton Head Sun,* February 18, 1989.

———. "Skull Creek Change OK'd by Town Council." *Hilton Head Sun,* May 7, 1988.

Onorato, Robert C. Interview by Michael N. Danielson and Patricia R. F. Danielson. Hilton Head Island, S.C., August 7, 1987.

O'Quinn, Donald. Interview by Michael N. Danielson. Bluffton, S.C., June 27, 1990.

Otis, Jonathan W. "Sea Pines: A Model for Planned Communities from Virginia to the Philippines." In *Charles E. Fraser in Print.* Hilton Head Island, S.C., 1983.

"Palmas Del Mar: The Doomed Gem of Puerto Rico." *Sports Illustrated,* January 28, 1974.

"Palmetto Dunes Moves into Heavy Construction Stage." *Islander,* August 1969.

"Palmetto Dunes Now under Phipps Control." *Island Packet,* January 13, 1972.

Palmetto Dunes Resort v. Brown, 287 S.C. 1, 336, S.E.2d 15, 19 (1985).

Palmetto Dunes. Advertisement. *Island Packet,* August 10, 1972.

Patrick, John. "Fraser's Edge: Innovation Is His Most Important Product." In *Charles E. Fraser in Print.* Hilton Head Island, S.C., 1983.

Peeples, Robert E. H. *Tales of Ante Bellum Hilton Head Island Families: Hilton Head*

Island and Our Family Circle. Hilton Head Island, S.C., 1970.

Peeples, Tom. Letter to the Editor. *Hilton Head Sun,* February 18, 1989.

Perry, David C., and Alfred J. Watkins, eds. *The Rise of the Sunbelt Cities.* Beverly Hills, Calif.: Sage, 1977.

Phillips, Cabell. "Let's Not Blow Up the Bridge—Yet." *Islander,* May 1973.

"Plantation Leaders Debate Call to Open the Gates." *Hilton Head Sun,* January 25, 1989.

"Please, Santa, Buyers Who'll Straighten It Out." Editorial. *Island Packet,* September 4, 1987.

Plumb, Terry. "Black Islanders Lambast Idea of a Municipality." *Island Packet,* February 17, 1983.

Polsby, Nelson W. *Community Power and Political Theory.* New Haven: Yale University Press, 1963.

Porter, Chris. "Bennett Ponders 'Potholes' on Road to Incorporation." *Island Packet,* November 9, 1982.

Price, Charles. "Slightly South of Heaven, S.C." *Signature,* January 1975.

"Public Service Official Blasts County Authorities." *Island Packet,* November 19, 1974.

Putnam, John J. "Savannah to Charleston: A Good Life in the Low Country." *National Geographic,* December 1983.

Racusin, Benjamin M. Interview by Michael N. Danielson and Patricia R. F. Danielson. Hilton Head Island, S.C., July 30, 1987.

Racusin, Benjamin, Michael Malanick, and Martha Baumberger. "Former Mayors: Cross-Island Route Is the Right Thing to Do." *Island Packet,* February 4, 1990.

Ramsey, Gretchen. "Islander of the Month: Thomas C. Barnwell, Jr." *Islander,* May 1973.

Reichley, A. James. "Charlie Fraser's Island Paradise." *Fortune,* October 1967.

"Residents Concerned about Timesharing Neighbors." *Hilton Head Report,* October 31, 1987.

"RHOC's Poll Sets Stage for 1987 Election Campaign." Editorial. *Island Packet,* August 20, 1987.

Richards, Gwen. "Building Industry Facing Referendums Nationwide." *Island Packet,* April 17, 1989.

———. "Developers Purchase Spring Island." *Island Packet,* March 4, 1990.

———. "Kiawah Partner to Buy Amenities from Fogelman." *Island Packet,* October 20, 1989.

———. "Native Landowners Dislike Transportation Impact Fee." *Island Packet,* July 20, 1989.

———. "Ralliers Decry Sea Pines Mini Golf." *Island Packet,* January 31, 1990.

———. "Shipyard Approaching 'Build-Out.'" *Island Packet,* August 20, 1989.

———. "Smith: Cross-Island Alternative to Restricting Development." *Island Packet,* January 18, 1988.

Roberts, Winston. Letter to the Editor. *Island Packet,* October 29, 1987.

Rosen, Robert W., and David R. Pender. "Economic Impact of the Proposed BASF Project and Satellite Plants." In *The BASF Controversy: Employment vs. Environment.* Essays in Economics, No. 25. Columbia, S.C.: Bureau of Business and Economic Research, College of Business Administration, University of South Carolina, 1971.

Rosenbaum, Walter A., and James W. Button. "Is There a Gray Peril?: Retirement Politics in Florida." *Gerontologist* 29:3 (1989), 300–306.

Rosengarten, Theodore. *Tombee: A Portrait of a Cotton Planter.* New York: William Morrow, 1986.

Rowan, Jan C. "Design of Exterior Spaces." *Progressive Architecture* 41 (July 1960), 108–26.

Rutter, Nancy. "Charles Fraser Played a Key Role." *Island Packet,* September 18, 1986.

———. "Dozens Get Fees in Transaction." *Island Packet,* September 22, 1986.

———. "Ginn, Fraser: Solution Is Close at Hand." *Island Packet,* March 26, 1986.

———. "Purchases Require Big 'Pool of Cash.'" *Island Packet,* September 17, 1986.

Sander, Brian. "Driving Force." *Island Packet,* February 12, 1988.

Scardino, Albert. "A Gust of Bankruptcy and Scandal Rattles Elegant Hilton Head Island." *New York Times,* March 15, 1987.

Schlecter, Arnold. "The Blossoming of the Barrier Islands." In *Charles E. Fraser in Print.* Hilton Head Island, S.C., 1983.

Schneider, Mark. *The Competitive City: The Political Economy of Suburbia.* Pittsburgh: University of Pittsburgh Press, 1989.

Schulte, Brigid. "Mayor Calls Traffic Safety Amendment 'Frivolous.'" *Island Packet,* August 17, 1988.

———. "Water System for North End on the Way." *Island Packet,* April 25, 1988.

Schwab, Valborg. Interview by Michael N. Danielson and Patricia R. F. Danielson. Hilton Head Island, S.C., August 13, 1987.

"Sea Pines: Bench Mark for Scores of New Resorts." In *Charles E. Fraser in Print.* Hilton Head Island, S.C., 1983.

Sea Pines Company. "1973 Sea Pines Plantation Owners Survey." 1973.

Sea Pines Company. "Notice of Special Meeting of Shareholders to be Held June 9, 1983." May 12, 1983.

———. "Ownership of Property within Sea Pines Plantation." Memorandum for Mr. E. F. Heizer, Allstate Insurance Company, August 26, 1964.

———. "Press Release." 1983.

———. "Special Meeting of Shareholders of Sea Pines Company Called for the Purpose of Approving the Merger of Sea Pines Company with Vacation Resorts Holdings." June 9, 1983.

"Sea Pines Golf Club, Inc. Enlargement Is Opposed." *Island Packet,* November 18, 1971.

Sea Pines Plantation Company. Advertisement. *Islander,* November 1970.

———. "Agreement." June 17, 1984.

———. "Introductory Price Lists—Beach Residential Areas of Sea Pines Plantation, Hilton Head Island, South Carolina." July 1, 1957.

———. "Jobs for the Future: A Proposal for Area Redevelopment, Hilton Head Island, Beaufort County, S.C." 1963.

————. "Land Use Restrictions, Protective Covenants, Building Standards." March 1, 1965.

————. "Political Subdivisions for Hilton Head Island." Memorandum from Joe Fraser to Charles Fraser and others, August 10, 1971.

————. "Sea Pines Plantation: Community Basic Data." June 1, 1964.

————. "Sea Pines Plantation Price List." January 1962.

Sea Pines Plantation Co. v. Wells, 294 S.C. 266, 363 SE2d 891 (1987).

"Sea Pines Property Owners Organizing Association." *Island Packet,* March 8, 1973.

"Sea Pines Property Owners Respond to Questionnaire." *Island Packet,* December 21, 1972.

"Sea Pines Resident Advocates Property Owners Association." *Island Packet,* January 4, 1973.

"Second-Home Communities." *Architectural Record* 15 (November 1965), 143–46.

Shipyard Plantation. Advertisement. *Island Packet,* March 30, 1972.

————. Advertisement. *Island Packet,* March 1, 1973.

Simmons, Fritz R. "Island Frontier off Georgia Coast." *New York Times,* April 29, 1956.

Simon, Arthur. "Battle of Beaufort: Conservation Collides with the Jobless." *New Republic,* May 23, 1970.

Simpson, Franny. "Analysis and Profile of the Sea Pines Market." Sea Pines Company, March 1974.

Singleton, Vernie. "We Are Endangered Species." *Southern Exposure* 10 (May/June 1982), 37–39.

Skidmore, Owings, and Merrill. *Master Plan for Hilton Head Island.* Prepared for the Hilton Head Company. Washington, D.C., June 1972.

Smith, Fran. "Craighead to Battle against Incorporation." *Island Packet,* March 1, 1983.

————. Interview by Michael N. Danielson. Hilton Head Island, S.C., July 2, 1987.

Smith, Janet. "Blatt Leaves Bankruptcy Case, Lashes Out at FSLIC Lawyer." *Island Packet,* February 3, 1988.

————. "Court Orders Blatt off Bankruptcy Case." *Island Packet,* July 13, 1988.

————. "Creditors OK $673,000 Loan; More Needed." *Island Packet,* January 7, 1987.

————. "Federal Judge Sets Oct. 1 Sale Deadline." *Island Packet,* May 5, 1987.

————. "Group of Sea Pines Residents Makes Offer to Purchase Company." *Island Packet,* March 10, 1987.

————. "Hilton Head Holdings: The Bankruptcy Saga." *Island Packet,* January 8, 1988.

————. "Judge Blatt Leaves Case after Ruling." *Island Packet,* December 3, 1987.

————. "Judge Had Key Role in Legal Saga." *Island Packet,* January 1, 1988.

————. "Legal Battles Keep Plans on Hold," *Island Packet,* June 12, 1988.

————. "New Offer Made for Sea Pines, Other Assets." *Island Packet,* June 18, 1987.

————. "Sea Pines Associates, Marathon Only Bidders." *Island Packet,* October 16, 1987.

Smith, John Gettys. Interview by Michael N. Danielson. Hilton Head Island, S.C., June 21, 1990.

————. "Sea Pines Plantation Alumni." *Islander,* June 1982.

BIBLIOGRAPHY

Stevens, William A. "Condominium Owners Grapple with Governing Themselves." *New York Times,* September 1, 1988.

Stone, Clarence. *Regime Politics: Governing Atlanta, 1946–1988.* Lawrence: University Press of Kansas, 1989.

Stuart, Reginald. "Hilton Head, Seen as Island Paradise, Is Straining under Big-City Problems." *New York Times,* December 14, 1982.

Taylor, Luke M. Letter to J. Prentiss Haworth. July 31, 1986.

Teaford, John C. *City and Suburb: The Political Fragmentation of Metropolitan America, 1850–1970.* Baltimore: Johns Hopkins University Press, 1979.

"$10 Million Island Club Rises above Shoreline." *Island Packet,* December 28, 1972.

Ternes, Alan. "An Introduction to the Setting and Characters of the Tragical Farce or Farcical Tragedy of Victoria Bluff, S.C." *Natural History,* April 1970.

Thomas, G. Scott. "Micropolitan America." *American Demographics,* May 1989.

———. *The Rating Guide to Life in America's Small Cities.* Buffalo, N.Y.: Prometheus Books, 1990.

"The Traffic Mess." Editorial. *Island Packet,* September 21, 1972.

Trinkley, Michael. "Archaeological Survey of Hilton Head Island, Beaufort, South Carolina." Research Series 9. Prepared for the Town of Hilton Head Island, S.C., and the South Carolina Department of Archives and History. Columbia, S.C.: Chicora Foundation, 1987.

———, ed. "Indian and Freedman Occupation at the Fish Haul Site (38BU805), Beaufort County, South Carolina." Research Series 7. Columbia, S.C.: Chicora Foundation, 1986.

Vacation Resorts Holdings. *Annual Report.* 1984.

Van Amberg, Norma. "'Budget-Priced' Island Lodging." *Island Packet,* September 2, 1988.

Vogel, Ronald K., and Bert Swanson. "The Growth Machine versus the Antigrowth Coalition: The Battle for Our Communities." *Urban Affairs Quarterly* 25 (1989), 63–85.

Wamsley, Thomas F. Interview by Michael N. Danielson and Patricia R. F. Danielson. Hilton Head Island, S.C., July 21, 1987.

Warner, Sam B. Jr. *The Private City: Philadelphia in Three Periods of Its Growth.* Philadelphia: University of Pennsylvania Press, 1968.

"We Must Learn from 1987, Both the Good and the Bad." Editorial. *Island Packet,* December 31, 1987.

Weiher, Gregory R. *The Fractured Metropolis: Political Fragmentation and Metropolitan Segregation.* Albany, N.Y.: State University of New York Press, 1991.

Weiss, Mark. *The Rise of the Community Builders.* New York: Columbia University Press, 1987.

"What Is Our Focus and Who's Promoting It in Columbia?" Editorial. *Hilton Head Sun,* September 21, 1988.

Wilbur Smith and Associates. *Traffic and Earnings: Hilton Head Short Route.* Prepared for Sea Pines Plantation Company, 1969.

BIBLIOGRAPHY

Williams, John C. "Fraser Sees Sale as Passing of Torch." *Savannah Morning News,* March 10, 1985.

Williams, John C., and Bob Bender. "Ginn Purchases Hilton Head Co. for $100 Million." *Savannah Morning News,* March 1, 1985.

Williams, Oliver P. *Suburban Differences and Metropolitan Policies: A Philadelphia Story.* Philadelphia: University of Pennsylvania Press, 1965.

Wirt, Frederick M., et al. *On the City's Rim: Politics and Policy in Suburbia.* Lexington, Mass.: Heath, 1972.

Wood, Cathy. "The Sea Pines Architectural Influence." *Islander,* June 1982.

Wood, James Playsted. *This Little Pig: The Story of Marketing.* New York: Thomas Nelson, 1971.

Wood, Oliver G. Jr. "Economic Profile of the Beaufort Economic Area." In *The BASF Controversy: Employment vs. Environment.* Essays in Economics, No. 25. Columbia, S.C.: Bureau of Business and Economic Research, College of Business Administration, University of South Carolina, November 1971.

Wood, Robert C. *1400 Governments.* Cambridge: Harvard University Press, 1961.

———. *Suburbia, Its People and Their Politics.* Boston: Houghton, Mifflin, 1959.

Younce, Scottie Davis. "Projections, Projects and Proposals." *Islander,* September 1985.

Young, James M. "Island Residents Seek to Purchase Assets of Hilton Head Holdings' Developments." *Columbia State,* April 13, 1987.

Index

316

development of Forest Beach, 69–71; formation and initial development activities, 13–16, 20, 24–26, 42, 46, 61; Hilton Head Holdings, 207–8; land holdings, 40, 61–62, 69, 81–82, 128, 240; land-use and architectural controls, 63, 68, 72, 81–82, 87–88, 98n.7, 288; Marathon Oil Corporation, 193, 196–99; marketing, 63, 86; ownership changes, 90–91, 189, 197, 199–200; planned community developments, 62–64, 87, 197–99; public services and facilities, 83–86; relations with other development companies, 86–90; relations with property owners, 108, 110, 112–13, 197
Hilton Head Cultural Council, 269–70
Hilton Head Fishing Cooperative, 153–54
Hilton Head Holdings, 205–8, 212–19, 222–30
Hilton Head Inn, 44, 46, 48, 192, 227, 233n.33
Hilton Head Island, S.C.: accessibility to mainland, 6, 13–16, 21; and Beaufort County, 146–49, 160, 169–72, 177–78, 180; and development of adjacent areas, 149–61; attractions, 14–16, 22–26, 29, 40, 100–103, 123–24, 213, 296–98; economic conditions, 68–77, 122–23, 190–91, 212–14, 230, 234–35, 242–48, 282; history before 1950, 7–12; incorporation as municipality, 3, 160, 164, 173–84; physical features, 6, 124–25, 135–38, 144, 296; population, 77, 100–4, 122, 140n.1, 230n.3, 238, 241–42, 258, 296
Hilton Head Island Chamber of Commerce: Cross-Island Expressway,

271–72; land-use controls, 166, 171, 264, 267, 269; local autonomy, 178–79; political influence, 243, 259–60; promotional activities, 245–47
Hilton Head Island Community Association, 116–17, 152, 264, 267, 271
Hilton Head Island Health Project, 85–86
Hilton Head Island Hospital, 132, 147
Hilton Head National, 159
Hilton Head Plantation: development, 67–68, 86, 91, 95, 191, 241; property owners, 248, 283, 289, 291–92
Hilton Head Rural Water Service District, 284, 299n.10
Hilton Head Toll Bridge Authority, 15
Hilton, Ralph, 133
Hilton, William, 7
Hinesville, Ga., 12, 14, 22, 26–27
Holiday Inn, 70
Home Builders Association, 269, 272
Honey Horn Plantation, 10–11, 21, 77n.3
Hook, Donald, 268–69
Hotels and motels: and resort development, 67–71, 190, 192, 235–37, 244–47; opposition to: 87–88, 194–95, 202, 250
Housing, 122, 129–31, 172, 190–91, 238–39, 253n.5, 257, 295, 300n.27
Hudson, Benny, 71
Hurricanes, 136

Indigo Run Plantation, 197–203, 220–23, 227–29, 238, 241
Intercapital Savings and Loan Association, 203–4, 210n.24, 223
International Paper Realty Company, 158, 160
Island Club, 72–73
Island Commission, 177–78
Island Packet, 133–35, 142n.26, 142n.32, 243, 260
Island West Golf Club, 159